More Advance Praise for *New York at War*

"Foreign foes have rarely attacked New York directly, but the city has been profoundly involved in the nation's many military conflicts. As Steven Jaffe shows in this novel and absorbing study, Gotham has been banker and arsenal, staging ground and recruiting post, cheerleader and critic, fortification and tempting target. Seen in a series, the wartime experiences are strikingly different, and Jaffe respects each war story's particularity. But he's also good at spotting commonalities, the most intriguing being the way wars abroad become wars at home, with New York's polyglot citizenry battling over a conflict's legitimacy, or which combatant to back. Highly recommended."

—Mike Wallace, co-author of the Pulitzer Prize–winning *Gotham*

"Anyone who's ever lived in New York, or visited it, or thought about visiting it will be fascinated by this book. Even historians will be surprised by some chapters. Steven Jaffe has dug deep and come up with literary gold, again and again."

—Thomas Fleming, author of *1776: Year of Illusions*

"*New York at War* provides a fascinating look at a forgotten aspect of the city's history—its central role in so many of America's military conflicts. Steven Jaffe brings this neglected aspect of New York's past back to life with impressive insight and a great eye for the telling details that make history come alive."

—Tyler Anbinder, author of *Five Points*

"Steven H. Jaffe's vividly written narrative restores a crucial thread to the way we understand the history of New York City. In a highly readable style, *New York at War* tells a story of tenacity and endurance, and of social conflict on a grand scale. With a story filled with drama and the drum-beat of violence, culminating with the destruction of the World Trade Center, Jaffe has much to tell us about the way a city responds to crisis."

—Eric Homberger, author of *The Historical Atlas of New York City*

"While most Americans probably see New York as America's capital of finance and fashion, Steven Jaffe shows how the city has also been the nation's epicenter during times of war. While New York may have profited from America's many wars, it also proved the nation's most vulnerable city, subject to attack both from without and from within. With an impressive span greater than that of the Brooklyn Bridge, *New York at War* reminds readers of Gotham's centrality in America's wartime experience from colonial times to 9/11. A great idea for a book, masterfully done."

    —Edward P. Kohn, author of *Hot Time in the Old Town*

NEW YORK AT WAR

NEW YORK AT WAR

FOUR CENTURIES *of* COMBAT, FEAR, *and* INTRIGUE *in* GOTHAM

STEVEN H. JAFFE

BASIC BOOKS

A Member of the Perseus Books Group
New York

Published by Basic Books,
A Member of the Perseus Books Group

Designed by Trish Wilkinson
Set in 11.5 point Goudy Old Style

Library of Congress Cataloging-in-Publication Data

Jaffe, Steven H.
    New York at war : four centuries of combat, fear, and intrigue in Gotham / Steven H. Jaffe.
        p.   cm.
    Includes bibliographical references.
    ISBN 978-0-465-03642-4 (hardcover : alk. paper)—ISBN 978-0-465-02970-9 (e-book) 1. New York (N.Y.)—History, Military. 2. War. I. Title.
F128.3.J34 2012
355.009747—dc23   2012000454

10 9 8 7 6 5 4 3 2 1

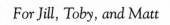

For Jill, Toby, and Matt

Contents

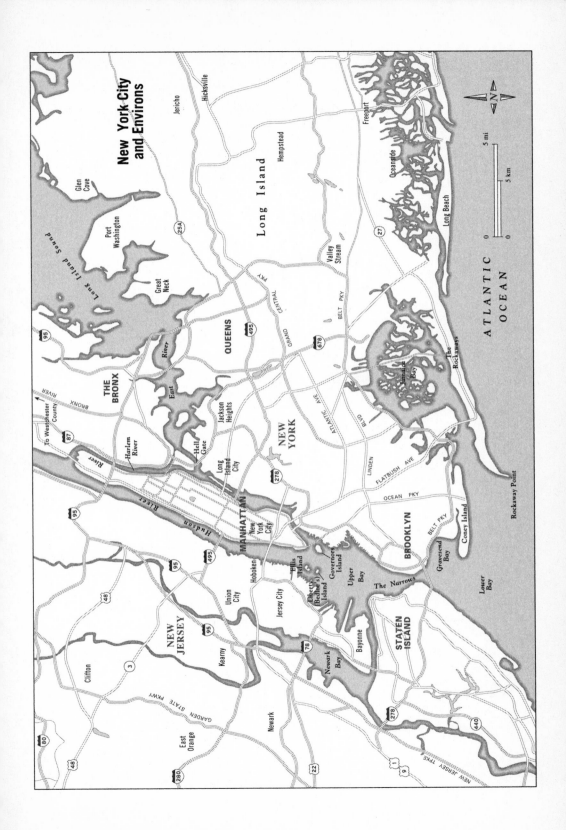

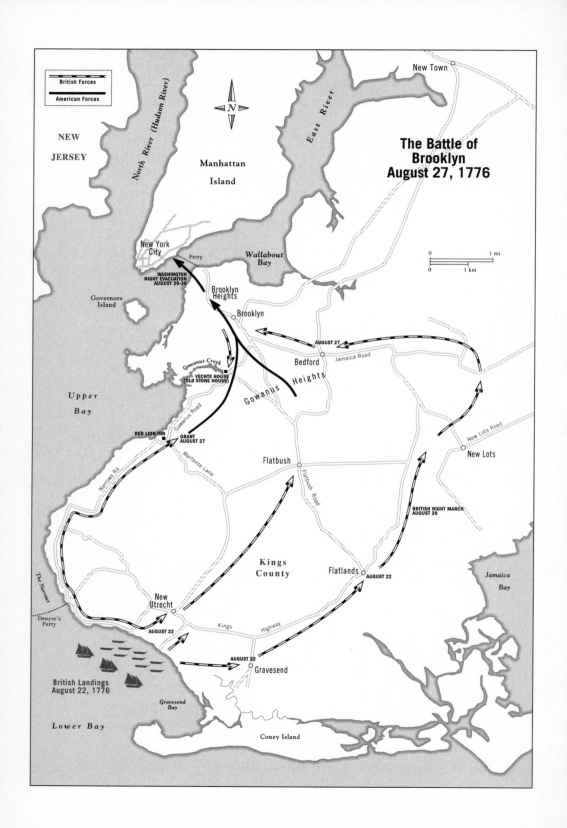

The Battle of
Brooklyn
August 27, 1776

NEW
JERSEY

Manhattan
Island

North River (Hudson River)

East River

New Town

Wallabout
Bay

New York
City

Ferry

WASHINGTON
NIGHT EVACUATION
AUGUST 29-30

Brooklyn
Heights

Brooklyn

Governors
Island

Gowanus Creek

VECHTE HOUSE
(OLD STONE HOUSE)

Bedford

Jamaica Road

AUGUST 27

Gowanus Heights

Upper
Bay

Gowanus Road

RED LION INN

GRANT
AUGUST 27

Martense Lane

Flatbush

Flatbush Road

New Lots Road

New Lots

BRITISH NIGHT MARCH
AUGUST 26

Narrows Rd

Kings
County

Flatlands

AUGUST 22

Jamaica
Bay

The Narrows

Denyse's
Ferry

New
Utrecht

AUGUST 22

Kings   Highway

AUGUST 22

Gravesend

British Landings
August 22, 1776

Gravesend
Bay

Coney Island

Lower Bay

British Forces
American Forces

N

0   1 mi
0   1 km

Introduction

This book evolved out of my experiences on September 11, 2001, and during the days and weeks that followed. On that sunny morning, I stood in a hillside park near my home, about fifteen miles west of lower Manhattan, watching the Twin Towers billowing black and gray smoke. "It's time to bomb some mosques," a distraught man standing on a nearby bench was yelling—this before al Qaeda was positively identified over the airwaves as the perpetrator of this act of war.

At the time I was working as a historian and curator at the South Street Seaport Museum on the East River waterfront of lower Manhattan, an institution dedicated to preserving and interpreting New York's four-hundred-year history as a place linked by sea to the rest of the world. When I finally returned to my office a week after the attacks, I encountered a traumatized landscape. The museum was located about seven blocks from the World Trade Center site, and the air at that distance was full of an acrid smell from the fires that continued to burn in the ruins of the complex. A light gray dust covered many façades, even this far from Ground Zero. "Rebuild," someone had scrawled with an index finger in the dust of a table outside a shuttered restaurant. On the street in front of my office door, usually a loading zone for retailers picking up seafood crates from the Fulton Fish Market, stood a khaki tent manned by gun-toting National Guardsmen in combat fatigues. My routine journey to and from work had also been transformed. Accustomed to riding a commuter train whose terminal was beneath the

Twin Towers, I now boarded a ferryboat each day; the train tunnel under the Hudson River had been flooded by the towers' collapse.

I was fortunate not to have lost anyone I knew on September 11. Yet, as with millions of other people living in or near the city, I did experience grief, anger, numbness, and a range of other emotions that I struggled to understand. Like my colleagues in the museum and history professions, I began to try to make sense of the events not only in personal and emotional ways (and, in my case, as a native New Yorker) but also in terms of my work as an urban historian and my knowledge of the city's past.

Over the ensuing months, it dawned on me that I was in the midst of an urban landscape whose historical affinities to the events of 9/11 were hard to avoid. Some of this history I already knew; other pieces fell into place as I began to look for them. A few blocks to the south, for instance, stood Wall Street—so named for the defensive rampart built there by Dutch colonists to keep English armies and Indian warriors at bay. A mile to the north, at Corlears Hook on the East River shore, those same Dutch colonists had launched a brutal surprise attack on Indian families during a bloody and protracted war. If I glanced out my office window, I saw Brooklyn Heights across the river—site of the American Revolution's most fateful evacuation and of frantic efforts to forestall an expected British attack during the War of 1812. When I took a walk out onto Pier 17 and looked north past the Brooklyn Bridge, I could make out the location of Wallabout Bay—once notorious as the site where thousands of American prisoners suffered and died during the Revolutionary War, later recast as the shoreline of the Brooklyn Navy Yard, a bustling city unto itself during the fight against Nazi Germany and imperial Japan. A stroll in another direction took me to the front door of a sister museum at Fraunces Tavern, another landmark of the American Revolution, where in 1975 four people lost their lives to a bomb planted by terrorists seeking independence for Puerto Rico.

Once I started looking for them, these sites of military significance—and of turmoil and violence—multiplied: Manhattan street corners where Civil War draft resisters, virtually in control of the city, lynched fellow New Yorkers because of the color of their skin; a strip of the Jersey City waterfront across the harbor, shattered by a massive explosion triggered by the kaiser's saboteurs during World War I; the waters off the beach at Coney Island, where generations of warships, privateers, and U-boats had laid in wait to prey on New York's cargo-laden merchant fleets. For each era of the city's history—from its origins as a Dutch outpost on the edge of the wilderness, to its role as a key garrison in the British Empire and as a crucible of revolution, then as the financial and industrial capital of Abraham Lincoln's Union, and finally as the great metropolis of a globally assertive United States—I found each of these venues distinctive to the events of its day but also part of a larger pattern spanning four centuries. In short, this cityscape was dotted with landmarks of a largely forgotten military history of attacks and attempts to defeat or prevent them.

I also found that no book-length attempt to narrate and assess the city's entire military past had ever been published. To be sure, numerous books and articles have analyzed particular wars and battles in New York's past, and, indeed, this book could not have been written without the splendid work of these historians. For the most part, however, these works have treated their topics in isolation, often leaving the impression that the issues and conflicts they recount have been anomalous or relatively short-term in the city's history. On the other hand, while the grand historical narratives of New York City have covered the wars and their implications for the city, they have, understandably, cast war as a minor theme against the larger sweep of the city's rise in economic, social, political, and cultural terms.

My purpose in this book is not to recast New York's history—inaccurately—as that of a perpetual armed camp. When compared to other world cities (London, Tokyo, Calcutta, and Moscow make only a partial list), New York has been lightly touched by war and its devastation. Closer to home, battle is far more conspicuous in the history and public memory of a host of North American cities, ranging from Quebec to Atlanta, New Orleans, San Antonio, and Mexico City. Looked at another way, New York's nineteenth-century emergence as the nation's commercial, industrial, and cultural capital, and its twentieth-century role as the world's largest and arguably most influential metropolis, dwarfs its military history. War is something largely extraneous to New

York's experience, most educated New Yorkers seem to think. And yet New York City occupies a distinctive place. Simply put, no other major American city has so repeatedly faced the risks and realities of wartime turmoil and attack as has New York.

The horror of 9/11 was unique in our urban and national life, and facile historical comparisons run the risk of trivializing events that remain raw, painful, and present for many people. Yet it seems to me that New York's long past as a military site does afford a context—a deep background—for reflecting on 9/11 and its place in the city's and nation's history. The landmarks of bygone conflicts, in fact, suggest a particular double narrative of New York's relationship to war.

On one hand, the city has repeatedly been a military stronghold. It has been a workshop, warehouse, and bank furnishing the tools of war; a mobilization center and embarkation point for armies and navies; and a vital hub protected by a ring of forts, batteries, and early-warning systems. With their urban economy tied to these imperatives, New Yorkers used war as an opportunity. Making money from war, or trying to, has been a recurring theme in the city's history, from colonial merchants and privateers to Civil War manufacturers and Depression-weary workers during World War II.

On the other hand, just as repeatedly, the city has proved vulnerable to attack, a target for a steady stream of enemies provoked and lured by New York's strategic location, wealth, and political importance and eventually by its role as a symbol of American might and values. Indeed, the city's evolving defenses—from earthen parapets and cannon to air raid wardens and Nike missiles—have represented four centuries of responses to this sense of vulnerability and to the changing nature of the threat.

These two aspects of the city's history are ironically intertwined, for New York's very importance—first as one of the major seaports on the colonial seaboard, then as the nation's largest and most influential metropolis—is precisely what has made it an attractive target and hence vulnerable to attack. New York's evolution from a marginal to an increasingly central place in American society has repeatedly reshaped the circumstances of its vulnerability and its defense. As the city grew in size, population, and influence, and as it became more complex and more porous, officials, soldiers, and its own people faced the ever-changing challenge of how to defend and safeguard it. In another irony, as New York's unrivaled size, sophistication, ethnic diversity, and extremes of wealth and poverty led many Americans (including many New Yorkers) to see it as a place standing apart from the rest of America, the city's very primacy ensured that enemies would target Gotham as the most effective and satisfying way of attacking the United States.

The tension between a sense of immunity and denial on the one hand, and of vulnerability on the other, runs as a deep current through New York's history. Urban life (and not just in New York) tends to breed two contrasting sensibilities. On one side, cities imply a sheltering anonymity, a safety in numbers, a calculation that the odds of survival favor the individual who can disappear into the crowd or find safety behind one of a million closed doors. On the other side, cities evoke disorder, claustrophobia, random misfortune, and the threat of becoming a prime target for dangerous and often devious enemies. These two sensibilities can pit city dwellers against each other and just as often unite them in ambivalence. At moments of crisis and war, New Yorkers have grappled with these two aspects of their city on a day-to-day basis, weighing the odds of safety against the risks of danger—sometimes consciously, sometimes below the surface of conscious intent.

Other tensions have also pulsed through the city's streets and neighborhoods in times of stress. The ocean that brought commerce to its shores also made New York the world's great landfall for immigrants, a role that shaped the city's identity from its earliest decades. The diversity of its communities, the ongoing invigoration and rejuvenation of New York by the peoples of the world seeking opportunity and freedom here, has always been one of the city's greatest strengths and glories. But the challenges of mutual toleration and accommodation between different religious, ethnic, and racial groups, many of whom brought deep animosities from their distant homelands and embraced new ones here, has also repeatedly shaped New York. So have tensions between natives and newcomers and between rich and poor. In times of international stress and war, New Yorkers have turned on each other, transforming the city's streets into battlegrounds and its public forums into arenas of mistrust and repression. Battles over ostensibly antagonistic or hidden loyalties, the legitimacy of dissent during wartime, and the extent to which "enemies within the gates" undermine unity and safety have all been fought here. New York has recurrently been a city at war with itself.

These tensions have been vented in both explosive and trivial ways. In late September 2001, I watched on lower Broadway as a turbaned Sikh driver tried, mistakenly, to enter the no-drive zone around Ground Zero. A burly New York City policeman brusquely waved him onto Chambers Street instead. "Bin Laden himself couldn't get through here," the officer half-smirked, half-sneered to a colleague. The anger, fear, and indiscriminate suspicion embodied in that casual remark has a long history in New York, although the specific wars and suspected groups have changed. This is not to deny that, over the course of the city's history, as we shall see, some New Yorkers have served as spies, saboteurs, and agents of belligerent powers, and hence as real threats to the city's and nation's security. Rather, it is to acknowledge that New York has been a place where the task of picking out real enemies from the communities whose innocent majorities provide them with unwitting cover has been a recurrent challenge.

During times of war, New Yorkers have grappled with the conundrum of how to ensure domestic security while maintaining a society defined by openness and inclusion. Too often, they have failed to temper their answers with wisdom or justice. The difficulty of distinguishing enemies from innocents in a place where different peoples converge but remain suspicious of each other is one of the more sobering legacies of New York's experiences. So is the difficulty of sustaining tolerance in times of great stress and fear, a truth borne out by the speed and eagerness with which generations of New Yorkers have been willing to accuse each other of disloyalty and treachery during wartime. New Yorkers have repeatedly had to confront the conflicting demands of toleration and "homeland security," and their struggles over these conflicts, as well as their failure to come up with perfect or, often, even viable solutions, can produce a shock of recognition.

My goal in this book is to restore a military dimension to New York's history—a dimension that has been largely erased from the city's historical narrative and public memory. New Yorkers have always been quick to forget yesterday's battles, and most Americans have no awareness of the city's role in the nation's wars. After September 11, as I stumbled on sites of military significance scattered across the city, I was struck by how thoroughly erased their history was, or at best how modestly they were distinguished by plaques and monuments largely ignored by natives and visitors alike. Founded not as a refuge for embattled religious groups but as a base for commercial exchange, New York has always been about pursuing the main chance today or tomorrow and has little time for the events of yesterday. "The present in New York is so powerful that the past is lost," John Jay Chapman recognized in 1909. Looking to the future and to appreciating land values, New Yorkers have consistently torn down the landmarks of their past (despite the lamentations, and intermittent victories, of the minority of preservationists in their midst). "The very bones of our ancestors are not permitted to lie quiet a quarter of a century," former mayor Philip Hone complained in 1845, "and one generation of men seems studious to remove all relics of those who preceded them." As New York became ever more spectacularly the "capital of capitalism," looking forward meant building the city anew, over and over again, while effacing its obstructive, irrelevant, and profitless past.[1]

By the same token, New York's role as the great immigrant city has played a part in reducing its consciousness of its own history. Wave after wave of immigrants brought their own deeply felt memories and allegiances to New York's shores, and they continue to do so. For these multitudes, New York has been the place to start afresh, to grapple with the pain and exhilaration of preserving cherished traditions while also reinventing oneself as something new and different. For these newcomers, the meaning of abandoned forts glimpsed out of a ferry or trolley window proved as immaterial as for the real estate developers bent on demolishing old sites and building anew. When new wars loomed in the daily lives of these New Yorkers, the conflicts often fostered segregated sets of meanings, rather than a unifying narrative that survived in the city's shared public memory, precisely because war pitted different groups, and their divergent agendas, against each other.

There is, of course, a simpler and more obvious reason why New Yorkers, like people in many other places, have forgotten so much of their city's past. Memories of communal conflict, loss, and fear are painful in much the same way as traumatic individual memories. Such memories nag at us with the reminder that we can be attacked again, that we can feel vulnerable again, that once more we can become prey to anxiety and suspicion. Putting such things behind us becomes a kind of psychic insurance policy against their future recurrence. Much of this amnesia is healthy and vitally necessary for urban existence. Cities, after all, are neither museums nor mausoleums but living, breathing places. Cities (and nations) survive because their populations are able to put sorrowful pasts behind them. "Rebuild," the finger scrawl in the dust commanded in late September 2001.

Rebuilding, however, poses the risk of so eradicating vestiges of our history that we are unprepared when unfolding events throw new challenges—new "history"—in our way. We can find no solace or perspective for present tragedies in a past that has been erased from memory and whose landmarks are no longer visible. As long as New York City remains one of the world's great urban centers, and as long as it persists as an open society worth living in, it will be vulnerable to attack. This is one lesson of its four centuries of survival and glory. It is a history we should face and seek to understand, rather than turn our backs on.

CHAPTER 1

Savages and Salty Men

The Dutch-Lenape Encounter, 1609–1664

Early on September 6, 1609, Henry Hudson, the English captain of the Dutch ship the *Halve Maen*, dispatched John Colman and four other sailors to reconnoiter an inlet to the north of their anchorage. Two days earlier, Hudson had nosed the eighty-ton vessel into what Robert Juet, one of his officers, described as "a very good harbour," sheltered by a long grassy sandbar. Steering a small boat northward, the five men passed through the Narrows separating Staten and Long Islands into the broader expanse of Upper New York Bay and possibly Newark Bay, observing a shoreline, in Juet's words, "pleasant with grass and flowers, and goodly trees, as ever they had seen, and very sweet smells came from them."[1]

As the boat headed back to its mother ship, Colman and his comrades saw something that must have quickened their pulses: two Indian canoes—one carrying twelve men, the other fourteen—bearing down on them. At some point, the five sailors decided that trying to outrun their pursuers would be fruitless. As the Indians closed in, the Europeans tried frantically to ignite the fuse of the matchlock gun they had brought along, but a sudden rainstorm extinguished their match. An arrow plunged into Colman's neck, killing him. Two of his boat mates were also wounded. Somehow, the four survivors managed to escape further pursuit, but spent an exhausting night rowing to regain the *Halve Maen*, which they could not find in the darkness.

Colman's death constitutes the first one documented in what is to-day the New York City region and the first recorded fatality of an act of war in the region's history. While the Lenape people of the river estuary may well have warred among themselves and against neighboring Indians before the arrival of Europeans, scant evidence of their military history survives. Early European accounts mention instances of belligerence between the Lenape and the Mahicans and Iroquois to their north and west, but the exact nature of these conflicts, and whether they predated European arrival, remains murky. The lack of a Lenape written language and written records has consigned their "prehistory" to an obscurity that archaeologists and historians have only recently begun to illuminate.[2]

John Colman was far from his home that day in 1609. In the five months since the *Halve Maen* had sailed from the island of Texel on the Netherlands coast under orders from the Dutch East India Company, he and his fellow seamen had first headed into the frigid arctic waters above Scandinavia in a failed search for a navigable passage to the riches of Asia, then west across the Atlantic to seek a similar channel through the New World of North America.

On September 4, after working his way along what we now know as the New Jersey coast, Hudson had anchored his vessel in the bay behind the sandbar later called Sandy Hook. As some of his twenty-odd crew members cast nets from the beach to catch edible fish, they were joined by curious visitors. Robert Juet noted in his log that "this day the people of the country came aboard of us, seeming very glad of our coming, and brought green tobacco, and gave us of it for knives and beads. They go in deer skins loose, well dressed . . . and are very civil."[3]

The next day more Lenape Indians, both men and women, came aboard the ship, some adorned with copper amulets and carrying tobacco pipes, many wearing feathers and "diverse sorts of good furs." Although the Indians brought hemp as gifts or items of barter, Juet recorded the crew's relief upon their guests' departure. "At night they went on land again," he noted, "so we rode very quiet, but durst not trust them."[4]

The Indians' friendly overtures did little to overcome the Europeans' engrained distrust. In the century and more since Columbus's first voyages of discovery, European mariners had told, heard, and embellished stories of encounters with New World natives—Indians who, in some accounts, remained docile and friendly but also sometimes proved treacherous and hostile. This early lore often demonized native peoples and justified their exploitation, and it probably shaped the crew's first encounter with Indians on the Maine coast six weeks before the Sandy Hook landfall. For reasons not fully clear, twelve of Hudson's men, armed with muskets, had descended on a village of "savages . . . and took the spoil of them, as they would have done of us." Hudson's mixed crew of Dutch and English sailors slept more easily the night of September 5 knowing that the *Halve Maen's* high deck and cannon stood between them and the natives who had disappeared back into the high grass and oak forests of the shore.[5]

After Colman's death and the return of his boat mates, Hudson's crew carried their comrade's corpse ashore and buried him at a place they named Colman's Point, probably amidst the dunes of Sandy Hook. That night, Hudson ordered a particularly vigilant watch. On September 8, Indians returned to the ship with tobacco and corn to trade for knives and beads, with the Europeans anxious to see if "they would make any show of the death of our man." The barterers seemed ignorant of the confrontation.[6]

We know nothing about John Colman's life except that he was one of the English seamen hired for Henry Hudson's voyage. For that matter, we know little about the events leading to his demise, since our only account of it appears in a few brief lines in Robert Juet's logbook. Only Europeans left written accounts justifying their interactions with Native Americans in the region Hudson claimed for the Dutch Republic—and all too often, these records offer only a brief glimpse into the area's tumultuous past.

Hudson would have two other violent confrontations with Indians before sailing back to Europe. On September 11 the *Halve Maen* began ascending the river that would one day bear the captain's name. Hudson had taken hostage two Lenape men to ensure his ship's safety (and probably as "gifts" to be presented to the East India Company back in Amsterdam), although they managed to escape from the ship further upriver. After determining on September 22 that the river was not the channel to Asia he had hoped it would be, Hudson sailed back downstream from the vicinity of what is now Albany toward the open Atlantic. He continued to greet and trade with Indians when he sensed it was safe to do so. But on October 1, an Indian climbed from a canoe through the cabin window at the *Halve Maen*'s stern and made off with Juet's pillow, two shirts, and two belts. A sailor shot and killed the thief. When crewmen manned their small boat to retrieve Juet's belongings, another Indian, seeking to overturn the boat from the water, had his hand severed by a sword wielded by the *Halve Maen*'s cook and drowned. The next day, incited by one of the escaped hostages, two canoes full of warriors pursued the ship, leading to an exchange of arrows and musket balls that left two or three of the Indians dead. A full-fledged skirmish ensued, with about one hundred Lenape on the shore and in canoes wielding their bows against the ship. Blasts from the ship's cannon and muskets killed six or seven more. Two days later, having passed the place "called Manna-hata," the *Halve Maen* was back out to sea, headed for the Netherlands.[7]

We remember that Henry Hudson explored the river and that the beaver and otter pelts he brought back with him sparked the ambition of merchants in Amsterdam and her sister city of Hoorn. We remember that his voyage led to the settlement of a Dutch colony and the genesis of the town that would one day become New York City. We don't always remember that the process of exploration, settlement, and trade came at a price—to be sure, a price paid sporadically and at unpredictable intervals—in human life. From its very inception, the European encounter with the New York region possessed a military dimension, marked by the corpses of ten or twelve Lenape men and by the bones of John Colman, left behind to settle beneath the New Jersey sands.

Fifteen years after Hudson's voyage, in the summer of 1624, thirty families of Protestants from what is today Belgium arrived in the river estuary under the auspices of a new commercial entity, the Dutch West India Company, or WIC. Inspired by visions of a wilderness teeming with fur-bearing animals and Indians who could be paid to trap them, the company deployed these settlers to small outposts on the Delaware, Connecticut, and Hudson rivers and to a tiny, presumably defensible speck of land (today Governors Island) at the mouth of the strait separating the tip of Manhattan Island (Juet's Manna-hata) from the Long Island shore. The Dutch had already christened the entire colony New Netherland.

In the spring of 1625, as more vessels arrived carrying settlers and livestock, the Dutch set about turning Manhattan's tip into their colonial capital. One passenger, an engineer and surveyor named Cryn Fredericks, landed with detailed instructions from the WIC, authorizing him to plan and build a proper settlement for the colonists. Working with the colony's on-site director, Willem Verhulst, Fredericks chose the southern tip of Manhattan Island as the optimal site for the principal town and administrative headquarters. Fredericks's choice made sense: the Hudson River estuary afforded a logical landfall for vessels completing or beginning the three-thousand-mile Atlantic crossing, and it was an equally logical port of call for vessels sailing to and from the navigable headwaters of the river 150 miles to the north, where Mohawks of the Iroquois League brought fur pelts from the northern and western wilderness to trade. New York Bay's secondary conduit to the Atlantic through the East River and Long Island Sound seemed to clinch WIC domination of the southern New England coast and Long Island's north shore.[8]

Fredericks also appreciated the natural blessings of the site. The land masses of Staten Island and Long Island sheltered the Upper Bay from the worst ocean storms and fogs, and the bay's navigable channels made it the best natural deepwater harbor on the East Coast. If the stiff westerly winds and winter ice floes of the lower Hudson River made Manhattan's western side less than ideal as a place to dock ships, no such problems hampered the East River shoreline. In time the lowermost reaches of that seashell-covered shore, stretching a mile and more east and north from the island's southern tip, would become North America's busiest seaport.[9]

In charging Fredericks and Verhulst with picking a site that would facilitate trade and communication, the West India Company's directors had an additional goal in mind. They wanted to create a military base of formidable proportions, the first in a network of such bases they anticipated for the Americas and one that would enable them to exert Dutch military might throughout the Western Atlantic. This goal was rooted in the mission of the company from the very start.

The Dutch colony in New Netherland, like the WIC itself, was born from the impetus of war. Dutch merchants had established the WIC in 1621 at the expiration of a twelve-year truce between Spain and the Dutch Republic. Since 1568, the Dutch had been in revolt against their overlords, the Catholic monarchs of Hapsburg Spain. In 1581 the northern Netherlands had declared its independence from Spain in the name of time-honored Dutch liberties, freedom of conscience, and the Reformed (Calvinist) Church. Spain, unwilling to grant the Dutch their independence, fought on; in turn, Dutch patriots—the founders of the WIC among them—extended the war to the high seas, where they intended to raid Spanish ships and overseas Spanish colonies.

The bitter and draining war between the Dutch and the Spanish coincided with a spectacular economic boom in the Netherlands. By the time they dispatched Henry Hudson to find a new, improved route to the Orient, the merchants of the Dutch seaport cities were well on their way to creating Europe's richest and most urban society. The traders of Amsterdam, Hoorn, Rotterdam, and Haarlem became the continent's middlemen par excellence, carrying the raw goods and manufactures of the North Sea, the Baltic, the Mediterranean, England, Russia, and France from one end of Europe to the other and earning hefty profits in the process. Dutch traders became the master capitalists of their day, sophisticated bankers and creditors as well as buyers and sellers, always with an eye to exploiting new markets and sources of supply wherever their ships might take them. As a Dutch saying put it, "any Amsterdam skipper would trade with the devil in hell if he could avoid burning his sails."[10]

While Dutch merchants consolidated their fortunes, the war had dragged on, exhausting treasuries and armies on both sides and resulting in the twelve-year truce due to expire in 1621. Many in the Netherlands craved peace, not the least because peace amplified opportunities for lucrative trade across borders and oceans. But a war party also existed, led by hard-line Calvinists blazing with anti-Catholic and anti-Spanish fervor. As they saw it, no contradiction existed between waging war and making money; in fact, resuming war meant that Spain's cargo ships and colonies were fair game as plunder. These merchants and civic officials had gained the political upper hand by 1621 and had resumed the military crusade against Spain. It was such men as these who envisioned, organized, and managed the Dutch West India Company.[11]

From its very inception, the WIC was a military as well as a commercial organization. Even though the WIC remained a private stock company that had to raise most of its capital from individual investors, the States General of the Netherlands authorized it to wage war, maintain a private army and navy, and negotiate treaties with "foreign princes and potentates," all in the name of *Patria* (the fatherland). Within the vast territory set aside for it in the Atlantic and eastern Pacific, the company was free to establish outposts and colonies and to monopolize trade. The States General encouraged the WIC to carry the musket and the firebrand to the Spanish Empire, especially to the string of colonial possessions that Spain and its vassal Portugal had claimed in the Americas and the Caribbean.[12]

The directors of the WIC, nineteen merchants based in Amsterdam and four other cities, needed little encouragement to wage war. While it sent Protestant families and organizers like Cryn Fredericks to the mouth of the Hudson, the company expended far more of its budget and energies dispatching armed fleets to raid prosperous Spanish settlements and ships throughout the Caribbean. It sent sailors and soldiers to seize the Spanish silver fleet off Havana and to elbow the enemy out of Curacao, Aruba, the Angola coast, and Portuguese Brazil, the last of which, with its rich resources in sugar and slave labor, ultimately engaged the attention and money-lust of the "Nineteen Gentlemen" far more than would their fur-collecting base on the Hudson.

It was no surprise, then, that the instructions the company sent to guide Fredericks emphasized the critical importance of building a fort on Manhattan. Such a fort could prove an invaluable stronghold from which to launch and resupply privateers bent on pillaging Spanish fleets and settlements to the south. Moreover, a well-constructed fortress at the mouth of the Hudson, equipped with cannon to sweep interlopers from the watery "roads" before its walls, would secure the gateway to the northern interior of the continent, from which a treasure in fur pelts was pouring down the river.

The WIC directors had every reason to be confident in Fredericks's success, for the Dutch had earned their reputation as Europe's leading military engineers. Centuries of expertise gained erecting dikes against the ravages of the North Sea and draining marshes to create farmland proved to be of great use in wartime. By the early seventeenth century, Dutch armies and their university-trained engineers were adept at building fortifications, a skill they put to use in the Dutch overseas commercial empire. From the East Indies to South Africa to Brazil, the Dutch guarded their colonial outposts against attack from the hinterland and the sea with extensive walls, fronted on the landward side by moats or canals. Almost always, these fortified bases were positioned at the meeting point of a major river with a coastal shore. The forts thus became crossroads and secure warehouses for inland river trade and the traffic it engendered to and from the fatherland.[13]

Such was the template handed by the WIC directors to Cryn Fredericks. Whoever drafted the drawings (now lost) that the engineer brought with him left little to the imagination. The company demanded a fortification with broad ramparts and five bastions to be located near the water, so "that its fire can sweep both sides of the river"; its outer walls were to be precisely laid out to enclose twenty-five house lots, a market square, a warehouse, and a school. Around the entire fort, Fredericks was supposed to dig a wide moat at a depth of at least eight feet, filled with water from the adjoining bay. This was to be done even on the seaward side, which was to be set back slightly from the shoreline. To accomplish all this, the company instructed Fredericks to enlist the "farm laborers, sailors, and colonists," women and able-bodied children included, all of whom would be paid for their labor. Even Indians could be hired, although the WIC was careful to underscore that they would be paid a fraction of the wages of white men.[14]

Fredericks improvised. The company's grandiose plans suited neither the narrow tip of Manhattan Island nor the resources at hand, so the engineer devised a more modest and practical schema, staking out a four-sided rampart covering a smaller area (today bounded roughly by Whitehall, State, and Bridge Streets and Bowling Green). He built no moat to surround it. Still, the fort's interior was ample enough to contain a warehouse, WIC offices, barracks, and space for additional public buildings as needed, if not for the multiple house lots the WIC directors had ordered. The fort's proximity to the small Noten (today Governors) Island, situated like a cork stopper at the mouth of the

East River, meant that Dutch artillery placed strategically in the fort and on the island could rake the approaches to the inner harbor with cannon fire, staving off attack by a hostile fleet.

The new fort was the most important structure in all New Netherland. Fort Orange (today's Albany), constructed 150 miles up the Hudson, might be the critical station for tapping the fur wealth of the interior, but Fredericks's fort served the entire colony stretching from the Delaware to the Connecticut as administrative headquarters, clearinghouse for contact with the fatherland, and symbol of the WIC's power. The open space just outside the fort's northwest gate became an official parade ground and a place to negotiate with Indian delegations. (Today, as Bowling Green, the spot remains a threshold to Manhattan's southern extremity.)

Although they did not build the fort exactly to specification, Fredericks and Verhulst followed one of the company's directives to the letter: they christened the stockade Fort Amsterdam, after the Dutch city whose WIC chamber had organized the new colony. Thereafter, the fort would give its name to the town that sprouted up around it: New Amsterdam.[15]

As more emigrants arrived, bringing materials and skills with them, a presentable village of thatch-roofed, wood-framed, and stone houses emerged outside the fort, punctuated here and there by mills, taverns, gardens, and storehouses. By 1629, some 270 Europeans occupied the town nestled in the shadow of the fort. Bakers, brewers, shopkeepers, and their families lived cheek by jowl with fur traders, mariners, servants, and company clerks. Over the next three decades, settlers spread out to plant grain and tobacco in the meadows and woods beyond the fort, buying land from Indians and clearing farms in the countryside of Manhattan, Staten Island, northern New Jersey, western Long Island, and the Bronx.[16]

The fort, however, enjoyed a strange fate as New Amsterdam and its satellites continued to grow. As colonists focused their energies on the fur trade, they neglected to complete the structure Fredericks had started before returning to the Netherlands in 1626. The four rampart walls built by WIC laborers were little more than extended mounds of earth that eroded easily. By 1643, a visitor noted that even those

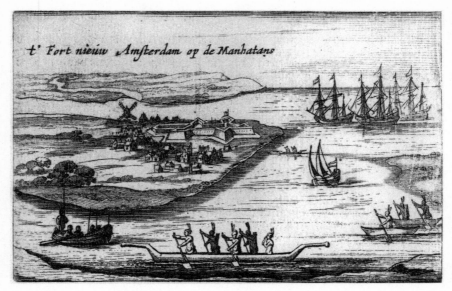

t' Fort nieuw Amsterdam op de Manhatans

Fort Amsterdam and the surrounding town of New Amsterdam about 1630, depicted in a seventeenth-century Dutch engraving. In reality, the fort was much smaller, and square in shape. Joost Hartgers, *t' Fort nieuw Amsterdam op de Manhatans* (Fort New Amsterdam on Manhattan), 1651. NEW YORK STATE ARCHIVES.

mounds had largely "crumbled away, so that one entered the fort on all sides." Most significantly, Fort Amsterdam was not even manned by a contingent of troops until 1633, when the company dispatched 104 soldiers to accompany a new director to Manhattan. The town's anticipated role as a privateering base would prove to be similarly modest. True, two of the town's settlers, the mariner Willem Blauvelt and a barber-surgeon named Harmen van den Bogaert, went on privateering voyages to the Caribbean, returning with plundered Spanish tobacco, wine, and sugar. But no crowd of their townsmen followed them out to sea, as the directors had hoped.[17]

Privateers did play one signal role in the town's early history. In 1625 or 1626, a privateering ship entered the harbor carrying an unprecedented human cargo: eleven African men seized from Spanish or Portuguese vessels. The names of some of the men—John Francisco, Antony Portugese, Simon Congo, Paul D'Angola—indicated their African origins and Latin ownership. They promptly became slaves of the Dutch West India Company, which put them to work in New Amsterdam. While regular traders would subsequently bring a far larger number of slaves from the Caribbean and Africa to the port on the East River for sale, privateers continued to do their share, since they regarded slaves as prize loot to be plundered from *Patria*'s New World enemies. The global war on Spain and Portugal thus helped to establish chattel slavery as one of New Netherland's native institutions.

For the next two centuries following the arrival of these first African slaves in New Amsterdam, slavery would be entwined with every aspect of the city's life, including its military affairs. In the short term, the WIC used its Africans to undertake the task no one else seemed to want. Under a Dutch overseer, the enslaved men toiled to rebuild the crumbling walls of Fort Amsterdam. Indeed, they may have been the first workers charged in 1626 with bringing Cryn Fredericks's ground plan to fruition.[18]

Given the West India Company's military vision for Manhattan, the end result was decidedly lackluster. Part of the reason for this shortfall lies in the priorities of the company itself. Because the colony's output in fur pelts never proved to be a reliable source of profit over and above expenditures, the Nineteen Gentlemen paid more attention to colonial adventures that seduced them with the lure of vast fortunes and the satisfaction of direct hits against the Spaniards and Portuguese. Thus, at a time when a few slaves were tending the walls of Fort Amsterdam, the WIC was devoting huge sums to employ thousands of sailors, soldiers, and civilians in a war to dominate Brazil that went on intermittently for a quarter of a century.

The company's neglect of New Amsterdam aggravated another factor that would play a role in the town's history: resentment of WIC authority. The absolute authority granted to WIC officials by the States General ran up against a stubborn Dutch tradition of self-rule stretching back to the Middle Ages. Dutch villagers and city dwellers alike were used to putting limits on the powers and pretensions of larger, overarching institutions. Nor was the company much loved by the rowdy, unbridled characters who came over from *Patria* on company ships in an era when most solid citizens preferred to prosper safely at home. "Lick my ass," jeered Paulus Heyman, overseer of the company slaves and sometime brothel keeper, in response to a taunt from a town sentry one night, helping to set off a brawl that left Hey-man's friend Piere Malenfant with stab wounds. Such unruly types may have been in the minority, but their presence colored a more general and abiding reluctance to follow WIC orders and requests.[19]

Further undermining the company's vision for the colony was the fact that many settlers in New Amsterdam (and New Netherland generally) were not Dutch. Some were transient adventurers. Others were displaced persons, refugees from Northern Europe's wars and religious persecutions who often had already settled for a time in the Dutch Republic before crossing the Atlantic. For the polyglot array of English, French, Danes, Norwegians, Germans, Bohemians, and others who ended up on Manhattan Island, any sense of patriotic obligation to the Dutch Republic or the WIC was tenuous at best. Rather than strengthening the town's military role, the pursuit of wealth by a trans-European array of traders, artisans, and farmers undermined it. The situation boded ill for any vision of New Amsterdam as a strategic citadel.

In the end, it would be the conflict foreshadowed by John Colman's death in 1609, rather than the global crusade against Catholic Iberia, that would turn New Amsterdam into a military base. The relationship forged by the Dutch and Indians in the wake of Hudson's voyage remained complex and volatile. While Cryn Fredericks busied himself planning Fort Amsterdam, a war had broken out between Mahican and Iroquois tribes up the Hudson River, partly motivated by rivalry over control of the fur trade with the Dutch. In order to keep New Netherland's settlers from getting caught in the crossfire, Peter Minuit, Verhulst's successor as the colony's director in 1626, had summoned most of the outlying colonists on the Connecticut and Delaware rivers and the upper Hudson to relocate to the tip of Manhattan, in reassuring proximity to the incipient fort. The town itself was partly the result of this ingathering. So was Minuit's legendary purchase of the entire island from a band of local Lenape, who probably misunderstood the transaction as a mutual sharing of land.[20]

Suspicion, concealed motives, and a jockeying for advantage underlay even cordial relations between Dutch and Indian. To the Dutch, Indians were *Wilden*, savages who migrated from one primitive bark-and-sapling longhouse and ragged forest village to another, rather than settling in permanent towns like civilized Christians. To the Lenape, the Dutch were *Swannekens*, "salty people," a reference to their coming from over the sea or perhaps a judgment on the European temperament.

Although Dutch-Lenape relations were fraught from the very beginning, acts of generosity, kindness, and mutual respect between the two parties were not unknown. Some European men and women were genuinely curious about the Lenape way of life, with its loosely affiliated bands of several dozen families who moved from campsite to campsite in a seasonal cycle of planting, harvesting, hunting, and fishing. These colonists endeavored to understand the larger tribal groupings into which these bands organized themselves and jotted down approximations for the Lenape names the Indians used for each tribe: Raritan, Canarsie, Hackensack, Rockaway, Navesink, and a dozen others. The company, like the colonists, exhibited a modicum of respect for the original inhabitants of New Netherland. Convinced that the Indians held legitimate sovereignty and ownership, WIC officials made sure that the settlers paid for Indian land and meticulously recorded their purchases, "lest we call down the wrath of God upon our unrighteous beginnings." In turn, the Lenape shared their maize and fish with the early settlers, helping to sustain the food supply of the fledgling colony.[21]

Respect between the two groups, however, was qualified. "I find them entirely savage and wild," Jonas Michaelius, New Amsterdam's first clergyman, declared of the *Wilden*, "strangers to all decency, yea, uncivil and stupid as garden poles. . . . They are as thievish and treacherous as they are tall." Disdain was a two-way street. When angered, Indians called the Dutch *materiotty* (cowards). Dutch fighters "might indeed be something on water," Lenape warriors taunted them, but they were "of no account on land."[22]

Both the colonists and the Lenape had good reason to feel uneasy. Like other European colonists in the seventeenth-century Americas, the Dutch faced what their Puritan neighbors to the north described as "a howling wilderness," a thick forest that began at their back doors and stretched interminably into the recesses of the continent. New Netherland was never much more than an expanse of woods and river valleys dotted here and there by a handful of trading posts, with farms cleared by settlers radiating out from them. Indians emerged from those woods, sometimes unpredictably, and melted back into them when their business with whites was done. The people of New Amsterdam, with its cluster of streets open on two sides to canoe-frequented waters and on the third to the woods of northern Manhattan, were not immune from this awareness of encroaching wilderness. The sense of vulnerability that Europeans carried with them in their fields and streets was inflamed by the knowledge—shared by both Dutch and Lenape—that the Indians greatly outnumbered the newcomers. While the European settlers of New Amsterdam may not have known about John Colman, some certainly knew that *Wilden* had killed the crew of a Dutch trading vessel off Noten Island in 1619. They all heard the news when Mohawks slaughtered four WIC employees (one was roasted over a fire) who meddled in an Indian conflict near Fort Orange in 1626 and when tribesmen massacred thirty-two Dutchmen in a small whaling outpost at the mouth of the Delaware in 1632. On their side, the Lenape harbored long memories of sporadic humiliations, threatened beheadings, and the occasional murder of their own people by ill-tempered or drunken whites.[23]

Despite the tensions, the social boundary between the two cultures remained open out of mutual necessity and desire. Indians wandered in and out of Dutch houses in New Amsterdam and Fort Orange, where colonists eager for furs overcame their own reservations about "admitting them to the table, laying napkins before them, presenting wine." The Lenape appreciated the axe blades, hoes, woolen cloth, and copper kettles the colonists traded for furs and land. They also prized the guns, lead, and gunpowder that traders sold them despite repeated prohibitions issued from Fort Amsterdam. Lenape sachems (chieftains) and traders were adroit bargainers who sought the highest prices for their furs from rival European traders, and they became discriminating purchasers of Dutch manufactures. For their part, whites embraced an array of Indian wares and ways: maize, venison, *sappan* (cornmeal porridge), canoes, and *sewant* or wampum, the whittled seashells that became the colony's currency. Most emblematic of the cultural exchange was the presence of half-Dutch, half-Indian boys and girls, the children of traders and burghers who cohabited with "well favoured and fascinating" Lenape and Mohawk women.[24]

This Indian man, very possibly a Lenape, was taken by Dutch soldiers to Europe and displayed as a curiosity to paying audiences at fairs. Engraving by Wenceslaus Hollar, *Unus Americanus ex Virginia. Aetat 23*, Antwerp, 1645. LIBRARY OF CONGRESS.

The interpenetration of the European and Lenape worlds, however, accelerated tensions to the breaking point. Outside of Manhattan—on Staten Island and Long Island, in the marshlands near Newark Bay, and at discrete landings along the Hudson Valley—Dutch settlers, hungry for land, purchased tracts from the Indians and cleared farmsteads, pressing deeper and deeper into traditional Lenape territory. These settlers' unfenced cattle trampled and ruined Lenape cornfields, while dogs belonging to the Lenape preyed on farmyard chickens. Homesteaders hired Indians as farmhands but sometimes cheated them out of their wages, or so the Indians claimed. Moreover, it was dawning on the tribes that the land whose use they thought they were sharing with Europeans in exchange for gifts or payments, the *Swannekens* viewed as exclusive property for their own purposes. On the trading front, the Lenape felt increasingly squeezed between the Dutch and the Iroquois to their north. As the Europeans relied more and more heavily on the Iroquoian Mohawks as primary suppliers of pelts, the Lenape accurately discerned that their bargaining position and their power to command respect were slipping away. Some bands had become almost completely dependent on European trade, producing wampum for the Dutch in exchange for the food, clothing, and tools they no longer made themselves. And out on the frontier, as well as in the homes and taverns of New Amsterdam, one ingredient always proved toxic. "They all drink here," reported a settler, "from the moment they are able to lick a spoon." The Lenape, who previously drank only water, took quickly to European liquors. Imported and locally produced alcohol was a prime lubricant in Dutch-Indian relations, but the aggression and lack of self-control unleashed in both whites and natives by brandy and beer defeated amity. An explosion awaited only the right trigger.[25]

The explosion came in 1640, after the colony's petulant and short-sighted director-general, Willem Kieft, imposed a tax on the local Lenape. A Dutch merchant who had gone bankrupt in France, Kieft managed to flee from his creditors into the good graces of the West India Company, which dispatched him in 1638 to run New Netherland from Fort Amsterdam. The stupidity of many of Kieft's actions seems glaringly obvious today. But the new governor was up against the perennial challenge faced by his predecessors: how to support the colony financially when the Nineteen Gentleman at home proved stingy and the colonists themselves resisted paying taxes for public expenses they argued were the company's responsibility. Desperate for revenues, Kieft sent sloops across the bay and up the Hudson to impose a tax payable in *sewant*, corn, or furs. The Dutch soldiers and fortifications this tax paid for, Kieft's agents proclaimed to the sachems, would protect them from their powerful enemies, the Mohawks. Extorting what amounted to protection money from villages and farms had become a customary way for armies back home to survive on the land; Kieft perhaps imagined himself merely doing what any self-respecting Dutch general would have done.[26]

The Lenape response was furious. They had not asked for Dutch protection from the Mohawks, and they viewed the tax as extortion. In the following months, panicked colonists came into Fort Amsterdam with news of isolated clashes flaring up like brushfires out in the countryside, where nothing shielded Dutch farms from the surrounding wilderness. In the spring of 1640, Raritan Indians attacked one of Kieft's boats, the *Vrede* (Peace), near Staten Island. Losing patience in the face of what he regarded as *Wilden* impudence, Kieft decided to nip their defiance in the bud by unleashing his soldiers against the Raritans.[27]

By 1640 the garrison at Fort Amsterdam was home to about one hundred WIC soldiers and officers. With their muskets, sabers, and gunpowder horns clinking and rattling as they drilled before the fort to the martial beat of their drummers, the soldiers must have been a reassuring sight to settlers fearful of Indian attack. Yet their presence in the town was not always a pacific one. Seventeenth-century soldiers were a callous and often brutal lot, exploited and exploiting. The wars tearing apart Europe in this era, including the Dutch war against Spain, the French religious wars, and the Thirty Years War in Central Europe, created a labor market for thousands of men whose job requirements boiled down to their willingness and ability to kill and destroy. A roving international pool of poor transients—the sons of peasants and laborers—flocked into mercenary armies raised by princes and entrepreneurs who sold their services to the highest bidder. In return for fighting, the soldiers received meager wages, often supplemented by whatever loot and pleasures they could extort or pillage from the populace around them. The Dutch Republic relied on thousands of such hirelings in its war against Spain, much to the harm of Dutch civilians, whose villages and farms ended up in the path of troops who robbed, raped, and put communities to the torch with little regard to the political loyalties of the victims. "In the figure of the soldier God has cursed us all," the Dutch poet Vondel wrote in 1625.[28]

WIC soldiers, Kieft's troops among them, tended to be as intractable as they were violent. In Amsterdam and other Dutch ports, tavern keepers known as *zielverkopers*, "sellers of souls," recruited men to fill the ranks of the WIC army and navy, but not before they made sure the recruits ran up a tab that entitled the recruiters to a big cut of their pay, which the company dutifully advanced to them. Most recruits had little choice as to where the WIC might send them: these boys and men, as often German, French, Swiss, or Czech as Dutch, could end up guarding a slave market in West Africa or a Brazilian plantation as easily as being dispatched to Manhattan. Drunken brawls and stabbings were not unknown within the walls of Fort Amsterdam or out on the streets, where soldiers and townsmen sometimes clashed. Most soldiers regarded the island only as the setting for a tour of duty and felt little loyalty to the community around them. As one of them explained, since neither "trades nor farming have we learned, the sword must provide our living, if not here, then we must seek our fortune elsewhere."[29] These were the men Willem Kieft expected to restore order, to exact from the Raritans the respect and obedience due him.

On July 16, 1640, fifty soldiers accompanied by several other WIC employees sailed across the bay from Fort Amsterdam, their destination a Raritan village in the New Jersey meadows west of Staten Island. The soldiers plundered and burned the village. After killing a number of Indians and losing one of their own, the Dutchmen marched back to their boat with a prisoner, the brother of the village's sachem. On the ride back across the bay to Manhattan, Govert Loockermans, a ship's cook who had risen to become a WIC clerk, "tortured the chief's brother in his private parts with a piece of split wood," or so a WIC official later told a confidante. When the troops reached Fort Amsterdam and reported to the director, Kieft seemed satisfied with the expedition's results.[30]

The Raritans bided their time immediately following the raid. They waited thirteen months and then, in September 1641, attacked in the Staten Island woods, burning the farmhouse and tobacco sheds of a Dutch plantation and killing four of its tenant farmers. Kieft offered a wampum reward for the head of any Raritan brought to him. Two months later, Pacham, a leader of the Tankiteke Indians north of Manhattan, walked into the fort bearing a grisly present for the director-general, a severed hand on a stick, which he claimed to belong to the Raritan sachem who had led the Staten Island attack. The Tankitekes had captured and executed the culprit because Pacham "loved the Swannekens . . . who were his best friends." Whether this was a genuine trophy of war, or an Indian ruse meant to fool Kieft, by the end of the year the Raritans had agreed to a formal peace treaty with the Dutch.[31]

Despite the best efforts of some local Indians to avert catastrophe, Pandora's box had been opened and now proved impossible to shut. In August 1641, a young brave of the Wecquaesgeek Indians dwelling north of Manhattan entered the home of Claes Swits, an elderly wheelwright living near Turtle Bay in the woods above New Amsterdam. As Swits bent over a chest to retrieve goods to trade with the Indian, the brave smashed in his skull with an axe. Outrage and fear seized the Dutch settlement anew, especially when a Wecquaesgeek sachem answered Kieft's demand for the perpetrator by refusing and jeering that "he was sorry that twenty Christians had not been murdered." The fact that the brave was avenging the robbing and slaying of his uncle by three Dutchmen sixteen years before, a senseless crime he had witnessed as a boy on the shore of Manhattan's Fresh Water Pond, did little to quell the anger and concern of the settlers, or Kieft's intention to exact retribution for Swits's death. Who was safe if an innocent wheelwright could be tricked and killed in cold blood?[32]

Bridling under the criticism of a faction of townspeople who blamed him for mishandling the Indians, Kieft now decided he needed some show of popular support before taking his next step. This, presumably, would silence his critics, as well as deflect blame if the Nineteen Gentlemen at home started asking hard questions. On August 28, he convened a meeting of New Amsterdam's male family heads to confer with him about the proper response to Swits's murder.

The council that Kieft had assembled immediately pushed for another confrontation with the local Indians but also took steps to curb the director's inept leadership. A majority agreed on the need to punish the Wecquaesgeeks if they did not hand over the killer, but they counseled that an attack should be delayed until after the fall maize harvest was in, perhaps during the winter when the natives would be hunting and easier to catch off guard. With Kieft's approval, the family heads chose a group of twelve leading citizens from among themselves to make preparations for such an attack. Overnight this new committee of twelve, appointed to prosecute war, became the first forerunner of representative government in New York's history.

The Twelve Men, as they came to be called, included some of New Amsterdam's most respected burghers and merchants. Particularly notable in their ranks was one David de Vries, a ship captain who owned land on Staten Island and on the Hudson River shore a few miles above the fort. He had been at sea since his teenage years, and early on he had stated his ambition "to travel and see the whole wide world in all its four quarters." By the time he took possession of land on Staten Island at age forty-five, he had traded with Russian fur hunters and (allegedly) battled a polar bear in the Arctic Ocean, fought and beat North African and Turkish pirates, and served as a commander in the French royal navy.[33]

De Vries's memoirs, published in the Netherlands in 1655, provide us with much of what we know of Kieft's Indian wars. That his account skews and exaggerates those events is obvious, painting most other New Netherlanders (including Kieft) as drunkards and cowards and himself as a paragon of wisdom and virtue. De Vries held a long-standing grudge against the WIC for its interference in some of his trading ventures and also seems to have coveted the post of director-general of New Netherland for himself. But David de Vries also had genuine grievances. Raritans had destroyed his Staten Island farm and killed his tenants in 1641 after Kieft provoked them. Now that he was one of the Twelve Men, de Vries intended to stand up to Kieft and check his reckless course.[34]

In January, the Twelve Men agreed with Kieft that it was time to teach the Wecquaesgeeks that they could not escape punishment for Swits's death. But de Vries and others cautioned against rash measures that would escalate the conflict as the attack on the Raritans had done. Several weeks later, an expedition of soldiers, civilian militia, and company slaves moved through the forests of what is now Westchester County in pursuit of the *Wilden*. While the mission turned into an embarrassment—the Indians merely moved deeper in the woods, leaving the Dutch to burn two palisaded native "castles" to the ground and return to Manhattan empty-handed—the sachems decided to make peace and agreed to a treaty.

Military action also offered de Vries and his eleven colleagues an opportunity to expand the purview of their job. Now that they had consented to Kieft's war, they wanted something in return. They peti-

David de Vries. No portrait survives of his adversary, Director Willem Kieft. Engraving by Cornelis Visscher, 1653.
COURTESY OF THE NEW YORK PUBLIC LIBRARY, WWW.NYPL.ORG.

tioned the director to create a full-fledged town government for New
Amsterdam complete with independently nominated magistrates to
consult with him, like villages and cities in *Patria*. In response, Kieft
abruptly disbanded the Twelve Men, reminding them that redress for
Swits's killing was their only authorized topic for discussion.

While de Vries was surely relieved by the return of peace, he could
not have been entirely comfortable with the means that were used to
achieve it. De Vries trusted the Indians no more than most of his countrymen did, and he described them as "savage heathens" in his memoirs. He warned one settler not to mistreat the Indians because "they
are a very revengeful people, and resembled the Italians that way." But

he also asserted that "there is not one-fourth part as much roguery and murder among them as there is among Christians." De Vries treated the Lenape with a modicum of empathy that earned their gratitude, and from time to time they enlisted him as an emissary who could talk sense to other Dutchmen for them. He understood a basic fact of colonial life that seems to have eluded Kieft and his supporters: violence against the Indians, especially in the form of attacks on noncombatants and acts of wanton sadism, led only to an escalating cycle of devastation deadly to vulnerable white settlers who had spread out into the hinterland far from Fort Amsterdam's sheltering walls. De Vries was himself one of those settlers, seeking to create a new farm on the New Jersey banks of the Hudson after the Raritans burned his Staten Island plantation.[35]

On February 22, 1643, de Vries's Staten Island nightmare seemed to spring to life again. On that day, groups of panicked Indian families, most of them Wecquaesgeeks and Tappans, suddenly overran his farm. They were fleeing before an onslaught of eighty or ninety Mahicans from the north, "each with a gun on his shoulder," bent on subordinating them. Having decided to ask Kieft to lend several soldiers to protect his homestead, de Vries paddled a canoe down the frigid river to Fort Amsterdam, where he found the director excitedly anticipating some impending event that he would not divulge. Kieft refused to lend the soldiers to de Vries, but the director's odd behavior sufficiently piqued de Vries's curiosity to keep him at the fort.

Kieft soon revealed to de Vries his plan for handling the Indians. On the twenty-fourth, while conversing with de Vries at table, Kieft revealed that he intended "to *wipe the mouths* of the savages" and justified the plan by declaring that he had been petitioned to do so by three of his cronies who had served among the Twelve Men. The "savages" they had in mind, however, were not the Mahican aggressors, but rather the families of defenseless Tappans and Wecquaesgeeks, many of whom now sought refuge under the very guns of Fort Amsterdam, some along the East River shore at Corlears Hook north of the town, others across the Hudson at the Dutch village of Pavonia (today Jersey City). Kieft had lost his patience with the local bands, whose sachems promised to hand over wrongdoers to face Dutch justice but never did. Kieft seemed incapable of recognizing that negotiation might better serve his purpose. Now, he surely thought, the Indians would learn a lesson.[36]

Flabbergasted, de Vries exploded at Kieft, but to no avail. "You wish to break the mouths of the Indians," he claimed to have warned the director, "but you will also murder our own nation. . . . My own dwelling, my people, cattle, corn, and tobacco will be lost." Waving de Vries off, Kieft readied his companies of soldiers and volunteers to launch two simultaneous nighttime attacks at Pavonia and Corlears Hook. Despondent and now powerless to sway the one man who could halt the attack, de Vries remained in Kieft's house inside the fort. "I went and sat by the kitchen fire, when about midnight I heard a great shrieking, and I ran to the ramparts of the fort, and looked over to Pavonia. Saw nothing but firing, and heard the shrieks of the savages murdered in their sleep." De Vries was able to accomplish one good deed that night: a terrified Indian couple, acquaintances of his, arrived at Fort Amsterdam, seeking refuge from what they assumed to be an attack by their Mahican enemies. De Vries warned them that the attackers were in fact Dutch and managed to help them escape back to the woods before any soldiers stopped them.[37]

De Vries's memoirs go on to describe the Pavonia attack: "When it was day the soldiers returned to the fort, having massacred or murdered eighty Indians. . . . Infants were torn from their mother's breasts, and hacked to pieces. . . . Some were thrown into the river, and when the fathers and mothers endeavored to save them, the soldiers would not let them come on land but made both parents and children drown. . . . After this exploit, the soldiers were rewarded for their services, and Director Kieft thanked them by taking them by the hand and congratulating them."[38] Some historians have suggested that de Vries may have exaggerated the horrors he described. Regardless of the level of wanton cruelty involved, there seems little doubt that Kieft's troops killed about eighty Indians at Pavonia for no good reason. Even more grimly, the dirty work at Corlears Hook was performed not by soldiers but by forty-nine civilian volunteers. Fear, resentment of Indian "insolence," perhaps even brutalizing past experiences with war in *Patria* may explain but not excuse their actions.

As de Vries had predicted, New Netherland now reaped the whirlwind. Through his unprovoked attack, Kieft managed to enrage every

band of Lenape dwelling in the expanses of forest and meadowland surrounding the town. Eleven local tribes now joined together to avenge
themselves on the *Swannekens*. Indians descended on isolated farmsteads, torching houses and haystacks, slaughtering livestock, murdering farmers, and taking their wives and children into captivity. The
patchwork frontier of settlements on Long Island, in New Jersey, and
up the Hudson dissolved as refugee families swarmed into the streets
of New Amsterdam and the smoke of their burning homes drifted over
the bay. Before boarding a London-bound ship on the East River in
March, Rhode Island's Roger Williams witnessed the stampede of terrified settlers. "Before we weighed anchor," he later remembered, "mine
eyes saw the flames at their towns, and the flight and hurry of men,
women and children and the present removal of all that could for
Holland."[39]

David de Vries had correctly foreseen the fate of his own farm,
where Indians destroyed his "cattle, corn, barn, tobacco-house, and all
the tobacco." His farmhands managed to survive by huddling in his
house and keeping the warriors at bay by shooting through the loopholes de Vries had built into its walls. Luckily, the Indian whose life
he had saved at Fort Amsterdam soon appeared and prevailed on the
attackers to move on. De Vries returned to Fort Amsterdam and confronted Kieft once more, asking him, "Who would now compensate us
for our losses? But he gave me no answer."[40]

In the first week of March 1643, Indians appeared on the Long Island shore opposite the fort, waving a white flag. De Vries and another Dutch emissary agreed to accompany them to Rockaway, far
across Long Island on its Atlantic coast. There, in the woods, the two
Dutchmen sat in the middle of a circle of sixteen sachems. The most
eloquent of the chiefs, possibly Penhawitz of the Canarsie, rose to re-
monstrate with the two agents from New Amsterdam. "He told how
we first came upon their coast; that we sometimes had no victuals. . . .
They helped us with oysters and fish to eat, and now for a reward we
had killed their people. . . . They had preserved these people [the
Dutch] like the apple of their eye; yea, they had given them their
daughters to sleep with, by whom they had begotten children . . . but
our people had become so villainous as to kill their own blood." With
the recriminations aired, de Vries escorted the sachems by canoe to

Manhattan, where Kieft agreed to negotiate a treaty with them. As a peace offering, Kieft gave them gifts, but some of the chiefs told de Vries privately that the gifts were paltry, considering the loss of Indian lives.[41]

The war flared up again repeatedly over the next two years, as embittered Indians continued to prey on remote farmsteads. Kieft responded with a sporadic series of hit-and-run ambushes on Lenape villages, much in the fashion of the "little war" in which Dutch and Spanish rovers ravaged the countryside of the Low Countries. A modern map of the Greater New York area bears mute testimony to the protracted bloodshed of Kieft's War. At an Indian village near Hempstead on Long Island, Kieft punished the Canarsie by sending Captain John Underhill, an English mercenary, to lead an attack that took 120 Indian lives. At Pound Ridge in Westchester County, Underhill's men surrounded a Lenape village and burned it to the ground, killing several hundred men, women, and children. On what is now the Hutchinson River in the Bronx, Indians killed the great religious dissenter Anne Hutchinson and seventeen others, sparing only her eight-year-old daughter, Susannah, whom, like many female and juvenile captives, they adopted into their band. From the woods, Indian braves yelled to the Dutch: "What scoundrels you Swannekens are! You war not against us, but against our innocent women and children, whom you murdered; while we do your women and children no harm, but give them to eat and drink, yea, treat them well and send them back to you." One of Kieft's critics confirmed the justice of the charge. During prisoner exchanges, he averred, "our children . . . on being returned to their parents would hang around the necks of the Indians, if they had been with them any length of time." Susannah Hutchinson, who was ten years old before she was returned to Europeans, had forgotten how to speak English and left her adoptive Lenape parents only with great reluctance.[42]

In the autumn of 1645, Kieft's War finally burned itself out. Both sides were exhausted, and the parade ground before the fort was busy with delegations of sachems arriving to make treaties. About a thousand Indians had lost their lives; untold scores of colonists had died, seen their homes ruined, or fled back to Europe. Following the massacres of early 1643, New Amsterdam's resources had declined perilously. The

fort's soldiers lacked ammunition and gunpowder, and surviving farmers hunkered down in the town, too fearful to plant their autumn corn
and grain crops: the specter of a famine loomed.

Kieft's position as director of the colony had shown signs of weak-
ening even before his war petered out. Once again in need of popular
support to raise taxes and pursue his war, Kieft had consented to the
election by forty-six family heads of a new committee, now consisting
of eight men. This time, however, Kieft's foray into providing the
townspeople with representation had backfired on him. While agreeing that the war, once started, had to be pursued against all hostile
tribes, the Eight Men also began covertly to send complaints and petitions back to WIC headquarters and the States General in *Patria*. All
that the settlers had spent two decades building, they told the authorities at home, had now been "through a thoughtless bellicosity laid in
ashes." One conscience-stricken writer claimed that on Judgment Day
the *Wilden* "will stand up against us for this injury." The critics demanded Kieft's recall and the creation of a full-fledged municipal government for New Amsterdam with independent magistrates, as in
Holland. When Kieft insisted that the Eight impose a tax in order to
pay the ongoing expenses of the war, a majority refused, at which
point he summarily dismissed them. But their complaints had reached
powerful men in the Netherlands, and Kieft's days were numbered.[43]

Well before the cessation of hostilities, David de Vries had had
enough. Impoverished by the destruction of his two farms, he took a
job as a pilot on board a trading ship bound for English Virginia.
De Vries left New Netherland in October 1643, never to return, just
as a new Indian raid left the village of Pavonia a corpse-strewn, smoking ruin. He could not go, of course, without offering his nemesis a
bitter parting shot. "In taking leave of Willem Kieft," de Vries noted
in his memoirs, "I told him that this murder which he had committed
on so much innocent blood would yet be avenged upon him, and thus
I left him."[44]

In 1655, nine years after the WIC divested Willem Kieft of his direc-
torship of New Netherland, and eight years after he drowned when
the ship carrying him back to *Patria* sank off the Welsh coast, the
Lenape made a final stand against the strangers who had so violently

upended their world. At dawn on September 15, the citizens of New Amsterdam awoke to shouts and the echoes of running feet in the streets outside their homes. Seemingly out of nowhere, hundreds of Lenape braves milled about the town, having landed on the Hudson River shore just above the fort, where they had beached some sixty-four war canoes.

As Dutch householders fumbled to get their clothes on and reached for the nearest saber or musket, Indians declared that they had come down the Hudson River to attack enemy tribes on Long Island and were stopping at Manhattan to ferret out their "northern" foes hiding in the town. Alarmed townspeople realized the explanation made no sense, since few if any Mohawks or Mahicans were present. Their anxiety grew as groups of Indians pounded on house doors, demanding entrance to check for their enemies. What made the bizarre behavior even more ominous was that the fort's contingent of soldiers was absent, having sailed under Kieft's successor, Peter Stuyvesant, to the Delaware River to vanquish Swedish interlopers there. In short, the town was virtually defenseless, a fact the Indians realized. It was as if the Lenape, in one last angry thrust to maintain their way of life and their dignity, were striking at the heart of everything that threatened them: the town that had sent forth the tax collectors and soldiers.

Tensions soon reached the breaking point. In the late afternoon, as braves continued to loiter about menacingly, an Indian woman picked some peaches from a tree in Hendrick van Dyck's orchard on the outskirts of New Amsterdam. Van Dyck, a veteran of Kieft's punitive expeditions, raised his pistol and killed the woman. Pandemonium ensued, as braves running for their canoes aimed their arrows at armed civilians, who came scrambling out of the fort's gate and over its walls to respond with gunfire. The year 1643 was replaying itself in all its misery. Over the course of the following days, Indians killed at least forty whites, captured a hundred more, and destroyed twenty-eight plantations, where they burned thousands of bushels of grain and slaughtered or drove away five hundred head of cattle.[45]

Upon his return from the Delaware, Stuyvesant, a far more astute leader than Kieft, ransomed most of the captives and managed to make peace. With a foresight that his predecessor never possessed, Stuyvesant ordered outlying farmers to consolidate themselves into fortified villages surrounded by palisades and guarded by log block-houses, to which he deployed small details of his soldiers. The village of New Haarlem (later Harlem) at the northern end of Manhattan was one byproduct of this policy.[46]

The "Peach War" would not be the final agony of the Dutch-Lenape confrontation. War would rage again a few years later on the Esopus Creek, one hundred miles north of the city. But apart from a number of such sporadic incidents, the tribes of western Long Island, northern New Jersey, and the lower Hudson Valley buried their war hatchets for good. No longer would they challenge Europeans for domination of the estuary surrounding Manhattan Island.

A tragic convergence of factors had blighted whatever chances the Dutch and Indians possessed for living in peace: Dutch anxiety at be-ing surrounded by a numerous and strange people, a fear that easily turned into panic and aggression; Lenape anger at the encroachment of settlers whose conceptions of land tenure and so much else were ut-terly alien; and a foolish tax imposed by a myopic administrator hard-pressed to find a way to finance his colony. Also in play were a clash of two military cultures whose members found retaliation easier than making a lasting and meaningful peace, the pervasive abuse of alcohol on both sides, and European presumptions of Indian savagery that, in turn, were used to justify European savagery against Indians. Where now stand the red-brick housing projects of Corlears Hook and the brownstones of Turtle Bay, 250 years of North American war between Europeans and Indians began, just as surely as they began in the woods of the Chesapeake and New England.

In the end, it was the decades-long decimation of their populations by contagious diseases contracted from the Europeans, more even than war, that spelled the downfall of Greater New York's native peoples. Their decline was most timely for Peter Stuyvesant, who found him-self obliged to turn and face other threats to New Netherland's very existence.[47]

CHAPTER 2

Trojan Horses

New Amsterdam and the English Threat, 1653–1674

Peter Stuyvesant probably viewed the scene with grim satisfaction, or at least some relief. Stretching almost half a mile from river to river at a height of nine feet, the new wooden wall cut clean across Manhattan Island, separating the bustling town to its south from the meadows and woods to the north, terrain where an enemy army might well gather to launch an attack. It was July 1653, two years before the outbreak of the Peach War, and the people of New Amsterdam nervously awaited the arrival of an English invasion force intent on besieging and conquering their town. When that enemy army materialized, it would now face a continuous wooden barrier, a rallying point from behind which the soldiers and citizens of New Amsterdam could defend their homes and the honor of the Dutch Republic.

The oak planks of the wall, while undoubtedly reassuring, were a far cry from the formidable stone bastions and earthworks Dutch cities built to encircle and protect their populations. When Stuyvesant and city officials had first proposed the wall, they had envisioned a palisade of stout vertical posts hewn from tree trunks. But when they solicited bids from the townspeople, none were willing to provide the posts at a cost the authorities felt the city could afford. Neither fear of attack nor a sense of public duty could persuade the bidders to accept fewer guilders than they asked for. So the wall, ultimately built out of thinner and cheaper plank wood, left something to be desired from the start.

The erection of the wall had been spurred by alarming rumors that had arrived to trouble the eight hundred inhabitants of the port that spring. Travelers reported "warlike preparations" in New England, which seemed linked to the recent outbreak of war between England and the Netherlands. While the English and Dutch nations shared a commitment to Protestantism, their mutual interest in trade produced bitter rivalry on the high seas and led to the outbreak of the Anglo-Dutch War in 1652. The conflict mobilized long-simmering resentments and suspicions on both sides. "The English are a villainous people, and would sell their own fathers for servants in the islands," New Netherland's David de Vries once complained. "I think the Devil shits Dutchmen," snorted a seventeenth-century English statesman. The people of New Amsterdam had long sustained amicable trade relations with the colonists of New England, and Stuyvesant himself behaved cordially toward selected English acquaintances and correspondents. But the Dutch settlers could hardly forget that the national loyalty and territorial ambitions of the New Englanders might override neighborliness, especially now that Puritans—many of whom had fled to the New World to free themselves from the critical scrutiny of the Crown and the Anglican Church—had overthrown the English monarchy and ruled on both sides of the Atlantic. By August 1652, WIC headquarters in Amsterdam was instructing Stuyvesant to "arm all freemen, soldiers and sailors and fit them for defense."[1]

Fearing a possible combined attack by fleets and armies raised in both Old and New England, the people of New Amsterdam tried to prepare for the worst—but they did so armed with new rights and privileges. In February 1653, the townsmen had gained something for which they had long been clamoring and which the WIC finally agreed to grant them: a full-fledged municipal government of two burgomasters (mayors) and five *schepens* (aldermen), authorized to govern "this new and growing city of New Amsterdam" independently. Stuyvesant and his own hand-picked provincial council of three advisors still ruled the entire colony of New Netherland in the company's name, and the four of them actually had final say as to who would be appointed to serve as burgomasters and *schepens*. But they now had to contend with a municipal government whose members expected certain privileges for the town and were willing to fight Stuyvesant for them.[2]

Faced with the English threat, negotiations between the new city magistrates and Stuyvesant—part tug-of-war, part horse trade—immediately focused on defense. Each side tried to get the other to bear the largest possible share of the expenses. But in the process of arguing over preparations for war, New York's first city government began to define its duties and forged a functioning if combative relationship with the overarching colonial administration.

Stuyvesant and the burgomasters found a way to cooperate to bolster the defenses of the town perched on the southern tip of Manhattan Island. In order to repair and strengthen the fort as a stronghold against English aggression, and to build the wall across the island to prevent an attack from the rear, the city magistrates agreed to raise 6,000 guilders by immediately borrowing the sum from New Amsterdam's forty-three most prosperous merchants, who would be repaid with interest out of the proceeds of a general tax to be imposed on the city population. In this way, the necessity for military defense inspired New York City's first experience with deficit spending as well as its first tax assessment. The city government and Stuyvesant also jointly imposed mandatory labor on all able-bodied townsmen, who were divided into four "divisions" that toiled for three-day shifts in rotation until defense work was completed. The town's carpenters prepared the wall's planks and rails, while soldiers, enslaved Africans, and free blacks erected a new parapet for the fort. Farmers hauled turf to build up earthworks, mariners fetched wood and stone from nearby forests and quarries in their sloops, and other townsmen sawed boards for gun carriages. However much they might begrudge such labors, the threat of invasion compelled occupants to cooperate in fortifying their city. [3]

Had the citizens of New Amsterdam been able to read Oliver Cromwell's mind, they would either have frantically redoubled their efforts or have dropped their shovels and saws in despair. For England's Lord Protector and dictator, immersed in his maritime war against the Dutch, had his eye on their island settlement. When he communicated his

The defensive wall of 1653 at the East River shore, as imagined by an early-twentieth-century artist. Engraving by Samuel Hollyer, 1904. COURTESY OF THE NEW YORK PUBLIC LIBRARY, WWW.NYPL.ORG.

desires to his colonial governors in February 1654, nearly a year after rumors of New England belligerence first reached New Netherland, his message was decisive. Given the "unneighbourly and unchristian" behavior that Cromwell ascribed to the Dutch settlers, he urged New Englanders to vanquish the Dutch once and for all. In order to accomplish this, Cromwell notified the governors that he was dispatching a fleet of naval vessels with troops and ammunition to Boston, where his officers would coordinate a campaign "for gaining the Manhattoes or other places under the power of the Dutch." Upon conquering Manhattan and the surrounding hinterland, Cromwell insisted, the Old and New English forces should "not use cruelty to the inhabitants, but encourage those that are willing to remain under the English government, and give liberty to others to transport themselves to Europe."[4]

Cromwell's vision came close to being fulfilled. Four warships carrying some eight hundred men (a force equivalent to New Amsterdam's total population) left England at the end of February, but a winter storm on the Atlantic drove them off course. In June the ships straggled into Boston harbor, where Cromwell's commissioned officers,

Robert Sedgwick and John Leveret, set about the task of organizing New England's military forces to augment the planned attack on New Amsterdam. The governors of Connecticut and New Haven Colony, long angered by Dutch claims to western Connecticut, offered to raise hundreds of additional troops. But now things started to unravel. Massachusetts and Plymouth Colony dragged their feet. Lacking a common border with the Dutch to inflame tensions, these two colonies had long enjoyed profitable trade connections with the ship captains and merchants of New Netherland, exchanging fish, salted meat, and lumber for the sugar, molasses, and tobacco carried by Dutch sloops and coast-hugging galliots. Indeed, two of Plymouth's most esteemed settlers, Thomas Willett and *Mayflower* passenger Isaac Allerton, had relocated to Manhattan Island.

In the end, Massachusetts officials concluded that "they had not a just call for such a work" as an attack on New Amsterdam. By the time it dawned on Sedgwick and Leveret that New England's Puritans could not be counted on to mount a united front against the Dutch, news arrived from Europe that the Anglo-Dutch War had ended with an English victory. With eight hundred armed men on his hands, Sedgwick decided to sail north rather than south. His troops captured Fort St. John and Fort Royal from the French, thereby creating an English foothold on the coast of Nova Scotia, rather than reducing the Dutch of Manhattan Island. Only in mid-July did a ship arrive from Amsterdam with "tidings of peace," as Stuyvesant put it, "to the joy of us all."[5]

New Amsterdam had escaped this time, but just barely. Had Leveret and Sedgwick decided to launch an amphibious assault on Manhattan, their sailors, troops, and cannon would easily have vanquished the small garrison of several dozen soldiers manning Fort Amsterdam, even without reinforcements from Massachusetts and Plymouth. The Dutch colony's new wooden wall would have been breached with little difficulty.

Peter Stuyvesant's awareness of a persistent English ambition to wipe the Dutch West India Company off the map of North America overshadowed his entire tenure as director-general of New Netherland. Indeed, the possibility of invasion colored the day-to-day life of most of the inhabitants of the bustling little port town that now called itself "the City of New Amsterdam." As with other elements in the city's military history, moreover, the wall he built would leave its mark on the world in a way its builders never anticipated. For the dirt path running along its base, where the soldiers and militiamen of New Amsterdam mustered to guard the outer perimeter of their settlement, would one day be known as Wall Street. In future, paper currency and securities would come to replace oak planks as its preferred instruments of defense.[6]

Peter Stuyvesant's preoccupation with defense was not merely a product of local and international circumstances, for the director-general considered himself a soldier above all else. Stuyvesant was a man made by war. His most distinctive physical trait—the wooden, silver-banded peg leg on which he hobbled around New Amsterdam—was a souvenir of the moment that had brought him front and center to the attention of his employers, the Dutch West India Company. As acting director for the WIC on the island of Curacao in 1644, Stuyvesant led troops in an assault aimed at conquering the nearby Spanish island of St. Martin. A Spanish cannonball shattered his right leg, which was amputated below the knee. Before the siege of St. Martin, which ultimately failed, Stuyvesant had been a restless but obscure company bureaucrat with some military training, the college-educated son of a Calvinist minister from the province of Friesland in the northern Netherlands. After the battle, he was known as a bold and decisive soldier.[7]

Sent to New Amsterdam to replace the hapless Willem Kieft following the disastrous war against the Lenape, Stuyvesant found the colony in disarray. Upon arriving at Fort Amsterdam in May 1647, the new director announced to the inhabitants that "I shall govern you as a father his children, for the advantage of the chartered West India Company, and these burghers, and this land." But if the director-general assumed that the freewheeling townspeople of New Amsterdam would obey him like youngsters complying with their father's orders, or troops following their general, they were happy to disabuse him of his illusions. Wearied by war and hungry for traditional Dutch political privileges the company denied them, settlers were soon engaged in angry confrontations with an autocratic governor whose short temper matched their own. Townspeople derided their new ruler as a "peacock," a "vulture," an "obstinate vagabond," a martinet who

Peter Stuyvesant wears a soldier's armor in this por-
trait painted in New Amsterdam. Attributed to
Hendrick Couturier, ca. 1660, oil on wood panel.
Negative #6071. COLLECTION OF THE NEW-YORK HISTOR-
ICAL SOCIETY.

stormed about like "the Grand Duke of Muscovy," and who raged so violently at his subjects "that the froth hung from his beard." Stuyvesant
in turn blasted his critics as "clowns," "bear-skinners," and "vile mon-
sters." If any misguided colonist dared to appeal his rulings to company
headquarters in Amsterdam, Stuyvesant warned, "I will make him a
foot shorter, and send the pieces to Holland, and let him appeal in that
way." But despite his vitriol, Stuyvesant was an able and intelligent administrator. On his watch the town began to acquire the trappings of a
true city, including a wharf on the East River that gave the port a sheltered harbor, fire wardens who inspected hearths and chimneys to prevent conflagrations, and a court to oversee the financial affairs of the
colony's orphans, including those who had lost parents to Indian attacks in Kieft's War.[8]

Never far below the surface of the bickering between Stuyvesant
and his critics was a nagging awareness of the colony's vulnerability to

attack. If the Lenape constituted the most immediate threat, European power politics made New Netherland a tempting prize for other predators, as well. Although Henry Hudson had scouted the region of New Netherland on behalf of the Dutch, England claimed the entire east coast and hinterland of North America on the basis of John Cabot's 1497 voyage of discovery. Well before Oliver Cromwell turned his eyes westward across the Atlantic, the English had come to view the Dutch in the Hudson Valley as "intruders upon his Majesty's most hopeful country of New England." And, indeed, it was the English settlers of Connecticut and New Haven who most resented the Dutch presence. As Puritan families poured westward into the Connecticut River Valley and crossed the Sound to establish towns on eastern Long Island, they ignored WIC claims to the territory. Meanwhile, farmers and merchants in Massachusetts pressed covetously toward the Hudson and its Indian fur trade.[9]

Given a choice, Peter Stuyvesant would have defied and challenged those he viewed as arrogant English interlopers on WIC lands. But from the start, a sobering demographic reality hindered the director-general. Simply put, the New Englanders grossly outnumbered the New Netherlanders. By the time he arrived in 1647, the total population of New England amounted to some 25,000 people, as opposed to a mere 1,500 in New Netherland. So Stuyvesant the soldier turned diplomat. In 1650 his emissaries journeyed to the Puritan outpost of Hartford and negotiated a treaty that conceded to Connecticut all land east of what is now Greenwich. The treaty also drew a line bisecting Long Island from north to south, with everything west of Oyster Bay remaining Dutch and everything east going to the English colonists.[10]

Operating from a position of weakness, Stuyvesant had bought peace—for the time being. But the terms of the Hartford Treaty underscored New Netherland's desperate need for reinforcements, both human and material. If, to many of his subjects, Stuyvesant was the very symbol of WIC arrogance and intransigence, he shared with them a deep frustration over the inability of the nearly bankrupt company to support its colony. The letters Stuyvesant periodically sent home to the WIC directors in Amsterdam became a continuous litany of pleas for settlers and soldiers. Neither the quantity nor the quality of arriving Europeans pleased the director-general. Rather than being populated by a steady flow of trustworthy colonists from the fatherland, he complained, New Netherland was being "gradually and slowly peopled by the scrapings of all sorts of nationalities," since the WIC was unwilling to recruit large numbers of Dutch emigrants for the transatlantic voyage.[11]

Amsterdam obliged Stuyvesant from time to time, dispatching small contingents of soldiers and boatloads of settlers to reinforce New Netherland. But the gap between need and reality was painful to Stuyvesant and others in the colony, especially given their awareness that their fatherland had become the envy of Europe for its military skill and prowess. While Dutch engineers had, in their decades-long war with Spain, perfected the stone fortress and the walled city, eroding sod parapets and wooden planks were supposed to shield New Amsterdam. While well-drilled Dutch armies had become the crack infantrymen and artillerymen of the continent, the few dozen WIC soldiers manning Fort Amsterdam took pot shots at hogs when not skewering each other and townsmen in drunken brawls. In the face of these inadequacies, Stuyvesant's pleas to *Patria* were, in reality, threats: strengthen us with soldiers, supplies, and settlers, he was saying, or face the fact that this territory will be seized by a strong and determined foe.

Other enemies also remained a concern. Indians were a continuous worry for the settlers, as were other European powers with colonial aspirations. In 1655, when Stuyvesant's pride and patience could no longer brook the encroachment of a Swedish colony on the Delaware, and the WIC endorsed aggression, he sailed forth with his soldiers to drive the Swedes out and won a victory made possible by the fact that the Swedes were even fewer in number than the Dutch. But by removing his small contingent of troops from Fort Amsterdam to attack the Swedes, he left Manhattan open to incursion by the Lenape, resulting in the destructive Peach War. Even his victory on the Delaware underscored nothing so much as New Amsterdam's extreme vulnerability.

Indians and Swedes were unmistakably outsiders, dwellers beyond the pale of New Amsterdam's wooden wall and the ambit of New Netherland's scattered farm villages. In the English presence, however, Stuyvesant faced a more perplexing problem. If the Hartford Treaty drew a clear line separating Dutch from English colonial territory, the social boundary distinguishing New Netherlanders from New Englanders was far more porous, sometimes threatening to evaporate altogether. English was a language spoken daily in the streets of New Amsterdam and its outlying settlements. English emigrants seeking commercial opportunity or adventure had joined the ethnic mix of New Amsterdam virtually from its inception, often marrying into the families of Dutch and other European settlers. English mercenaries in the employ of the West India Company were among the garrison manning Fort Amsterdam. The very dearth of population that weakened New Netherland in relation to its neighbors had led Kieft and Stuyvesant to accept the arrival of enclaves of English families on Long Island and in what is now Westchester. As frontier settlers, they provided New Amsterdam with a buffer and early warning system against possible Indian attacks. As farmers and consumers, they bolstered New Netherland's economy. So important was such migration to the colony that by the 1650s, of the ten Long Island villages on the Dutch side of the Oyster Bay boundary, the populations of five were largely English.[12]

The steady influx of English colonists into Dutch communities and territories was at the heart of the problem now facing Peter Stuyvesant. All English settlers were required to swear an oath of loyalty to the WIC and the Dutch Republic. But, Stuyvesant and his councilors asked themselves, what would such "loyalty" amount to in the face of an out-and-out confrontation with Old or New England?

For Stuyvesant, a hard-line Calvinist, fears about English obedience took on a vivid religious coloring as well. The Dutch Reformed Church was the only religious body authorized to conduct public worship in the colony. But many of New Netherland's English settlers were vigorous nonconformists—Baptists and "Independents" who had fled Puritan intolerance in New England with the expectation that the Dutch West India Company would accord them freedom of worship. To be sure, English "infidels" were not the only ones whose activities troubled Stuyvesant. By the mid-1650s, families of Dutch Mennonites, German Lutherans, a few Catholics, and a small group of Sephardic Jews had also found refuge in New Amsterdam. To the director-general and his clerical allies, the presence of all these "heretics and fanatics" constituted a source of social chaos and an affront to God. Their insistence on conducting their own worship services in Dutch territory was outright blasphemy. When Englishmen in what is now Queens conducted unauthorized baptisms in the East River, Stuyvesant had their leader banished. When English Quakers arrived in the port and started preaching in the streets, Stuyvesant promptly deported them to Rhode Island. The director-general sent soldiers to an English village at what is now Jamaica, Queens, to force the inhabitants to swear an anti-Quaker oath when he suspected that the contagion borne by this particular group of *dwaalgeesten* ("erring spirits") was spreading.[13]

Company directors in Amsterdam, worried about alienating settlers and investors, and exhibiting the religious toleration prevailing in many circles in Dutch society, ordered Stuyvesant to soften his stance and allow Jews, Lutherans, and even Quakers to worship inconspicuously in private. "You may therefore shut your eyes," they instructed him, "at least not force people's consciences, but allow everyone to have his own belief, as long as he behaves quietly and legally." Under WIC pressure, the director-general even had to allow Asser Levy, one of the Jewish settlers, to join the burgher guard in patrolling and defending the town. But Stuyvesant begrudged such compliance. He remained deeply upset by religious heterodoxy, not least when it was expressed by Englishmen whose dissent seemed to go hand in hand with a dubious political loyalty.[14]

The invasion threat of 1653 and 1654 only served to confirm the director's suspicions. For every English settler he could trust during that defense emergency, it seemed as if a whole army's worth of them were at or near the point of open rebellion, eagerly waiting for Connecticut's foot soldiers or Cromwell's fleet to descend on Manhattan Island. At Heemstede (Hempstead) in western Long Island, John Underhill, the English soldier who had once led Willem Kieft's troops against the Lenape, unfurled Cromwell's banner in defiance of the West India Company. Thomas Baxter, the very man who had sold wood to the city for the defensive wall, turned privateer and with other Englishmen raided Dutch farmsteads on Long Island's north shore. Rumors flew back and forth about Connecticut's and Parliament's secret agents, operating "under the color and guise of travelers," who were allegedly taking careful note of New Amsterdam's defenses in advance of the expected English assault. Lacking the troops he desired for policing and securing his borders, Stuyvesant nevertheless noted that he was exempting the English villagers of Long Island from labor on the city's fortifications, "that we may not ourselves drag the Trojan horse within our walls." The frontier settlements, the early warning system for Indian attacks, had themselves become the enemy's front line.[15]

It would take another decade to be fulfilled, but in the end Peter Stuyvesant's fear of the Trojan horse, of betrayal from within, would be confirmed dramatically by two long-time inhabitants of New Amsterdam, Samuel Maverick and George Baxter. Having left his native Devonshire for Massachusetts in the 1620s, Maverick was soon in conflict with the Puritan authorities there, even as he prospered in maritime trade. His home on Noddle's Island in Boston harbor became a bastion of support for the Church of England. By the early 1650s, Maverick had had his fill of the Puritans and relocated to the more congenial shores of Manhattan Island, where he nursed his abiding faith in Anglicanism and the cause of the English monarchy. A man like Maverick was precisely the kind of Englishman Peter Stuyvesant knew he had to fear—self-possessed, contentious, well connected with colonists up and down the North American coast—whether or not he advertised his royalist sentiments.[16]

The actions of George Baxter, on the other hand, probably struck Stuyvesant as a personal betrayal. Baxter had arrived in the entourage of Lady Deborah Moody, a religious dissenter expelled from Massachusetts in 1645, whose followers Willem Kieft had allowed to settle at Gravesend near the western end of Long Island. Baxter quickly made himself useful to the Dutch, leading militiamen against the Lenape in Kieft's War. On Stuyvesant's arrival, Baxter became the director-general's most reliable liaison with English speakers and was one of the key negotiators of the Hartford Treaty.

Yet, like Samuel Maverick, George Baxter came to harbor other loyalties. Baxter's disaffection, however, was played out in public, and in this case Stuyvesant had only himself to blame. In late 1653, at the height of the crisis over a possible English invasion, Baxter protested on behalf of the English villagers of Dutch Long Island, who believed it was high time that they be allowed to exercise political autonomy in the selection and appointment of village magistrates, rather than be forced to accept court officers imposed by New Amsterdam. Instead of seeing strategic wisdom in conceding some rights to his English subjects, Stuyvesant fired Baxter, who moved to Connecticut and then Rhode Island. Disgusted with the West India Company, Baxter made up his mind to throw in his lot with his homeland. On the accession of Charles II in 1660 following the death of Cromwell, both Maverick and Baxter realized that their intimate knowledge of New Amsterdam might well serve their new monarch.[17]

By 1661 Maverick, having traded the East River for the Thames, was ensconced at Whitehall as a principal advisor on colonial affairs to Edward Hyde, the Earl of Clarendon, Lord Chancellor to the king. Maverick lost no opportunity to remind Clarendon and other statesmen of "his Majesty's title to that great and most considerable tract of land usurped by the Dutch." By 1663 he was joined by Baxter, present in London as Rhode Island's official agent. Appearing before the king's Council for Foreign Plantations, the former Manhattan denizen and the former Long Islander underscored the weakness of New Amsterdam's defenses and the need for the king to assert his proper claim to the valleys of the Hudson and the Delaware.[18]

Baxter and Maverick were preaching to the converted. A militantly anti-Dutch coterie of courtiers and soldiers had formed around James Stuart, Duke of York, Lord High Admiral, and the king's younger brother—and the Earl of Clarendon's son-in-law. James reserved his special hatred for the WIC, which had found a compelling source of profit in the African slave trade—the very traffic that James's own Royal Company of Adventurers was bent on monopolizing. The duke's animus against the Dutch was further fueled by Sir George Downing, president of the Council of Trade, and by Downing's cousin John Winthrop Jr., who happened to be governor of Connecticut. In 1661 Winthrop had arrived in London with a meticulous description of Fort Amsterdam's defenses. Ironically, Stuyvesant and Winthrop had sustained a courteous correspondence for years, and when political complications made it awkward for the Connecticut governor to sail to England from the neighboring colony of New Haven, Stuyvesant obliged him by letting him embark from Manhattan. Winthrop took advantage of the sight-seeing opportunity on behalf of his king.[19]

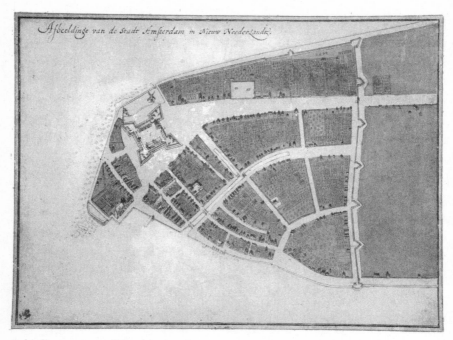

A bird's eye view of New Amsterdam about 1660, showing Fort Amsterdam (upper left) and the wall along the city's northern boundary, today's Wall Street (right). Jacques Cortelyou, *Afbeeldinge van de Stadt Amsterdam in Nieuw Neederlandt* (the Castello Plan), c. 1660. COURTESY OF THE NEW YORK PUBLIC LIBRARY, WWW.NYPL.ORG.

Like Cromwell before them, royal bureaucrats pored over maps showing a North American coast that appeared solidly English from the borderlands of Spanish Florida to the frontier of French Canada—solidly English, that is, except for the irritant called New Netherland. On March 22, 1664, Charles II bestowed on his brother James a gift consisting of the territory stretching between the Delaware and Connecticut Rivers—in essence, New Netherland. The king also lent James four warships, 150 sailors, and 300 soldiers in order to secure his gift. By May, the Duke of York's expedition was ready to embark from Portsmouth.[20]

Joining the English attack force were Samuel Maverick and James's hand-picked commander, Richard Nicolls. The duke couldn't have chosen a better leader for the mission. Forty-year-old Colonel Nicolls came with impeccable royalist credentials. A close friend of the duke's, Nicolls had commanded cavalry during the English Civil War and then followed the royal family into exile on the continent during the years of the Commonwealth. In an age when soldiers routinely viewed arson, pillage, rape, and murder as first rather than last resorts, Nicolls possessed something extra—patience, a taste for diplomacy, perhaps even empathy for the predicament of his adversaries. He grasped the weakness of the Dutch position in North America, but also the folly of overkill, of needlessly bludgeoning the enemy into submission if persuasion might work just as well.

To storm the port of New Amsterdam, battering it with cannon fire or burning it to the ground, would serve nobody, Nicolls reasoned—certainly not the duke, nor the merchants and Westminster dignitaries dreaming of fur-laden ships sailing up the Thames. And by harming and humiliating the Dutch colonists, it might buy years of trouble. Annihilation as a threat, as a lever to compel negotiation, only to be unleashed as a last resort: this was the card Nicolls intended to play once he reached Manhattan Island. The one variable he didn't include in his reasonable equation was Peter Stuyvesant.

On August 26, 1664, "four great men-of-war, or frigates, well manned with sailors and soldiers" and bristling with a total of ninety-three cannon, arrived in New Netherland. The vessels anchored off Gravesend, just beyond the Narrows separating Long Island and Staten Island. Nicolls's soldiers disembarked and marched through Long Island farmland to occupy the ferry landing at the small village of Breuckelen (Brooklyn), which hugged the East River shore opposite New Amsterdam (at the modern site of the Brooklyn Bridge ramp and anchorage). "In his Majesty's name I do demand the town, situate upon the Island commonly known by the name of Manhatoes with all the forts thereunto belonging," Nicolls told the delegation sent by Stuyvesant to demand an explanation.

The arrival of the vessels, and the presence of hundreds of English soldiers brandishing muskets and pikes on the Breuckelen shore, sent the citizens of New Amsterdam into a panic. Anxiety had been building since early July, when rumors of an impending invasion had arrived. The English were bent on seizing the colony, reported the Reverend Samuel Drisius, one of the town's leading Dutch clergymen: "if this could not be done in an amicable way, they were to attack the place, and everything was to be thrown open for the English soldiers to plunder, rob and pillage."[21]

Nicolls, Maverick, and their comrades in arms had been busy setting their plan in motion. Arriving first in Boston in late July, Nicolls had demanded that Massachusetts march its troops overland to participate in the assault on New Amsterdam, but he found the Puritan leaders as loath to move as they had been when importuned by Cromwell's agents a decade earlier. Instead, Nicolls turned to Governor Winthrop of Connecticut, who agreed to "beat the drum" to rouse the English settlers of Long Island for the attack on Manhattan. When New Amsterdam's townspeople peered across the East River at the enemy force on the opposite shore, they saw Long Island farmers (from both sides of the Hartford Treaty line) whose eagerness to end Dutch dominion equaled that of the English soldiers with whom they were rubbing shoulders.[22]

Peter Stuyvesant and the city burgomasters had tried to prepare New Amsterdam, now a town of 1,500 inhabitants, for eventual English attack. They had hired masons to line the fort's earthen outer walls with stone and to build two imposing, cannon-lined defensive bastions along the ramparts of the wooden wall that guarded the northern approaches to the city. Even more ambitiously, they had finally agreed to collaborate on a project that, when finished, promised to protect New Amsterdam in a familiarly Dutch way: a wall of unbroken wooden palisades completely encircling and enclosing the town. Stuyvesant, paying careful heed to rumors that the Lenape, with English encouragement, were planning to rise once more, had also insisted that the outlying villages of New Haarlem, New Amersfoort, Midwout, and New Utrecht be fortified with palisades and blockhouses. He sent company slaves to help build them.[23]

But the perennial problems had surfaced. The loans that Stuyvesant exacted from city merchants—again, after hard bargaining over rights and privileges with the city fathers—never met the financial needs of defense expenditure. The grandiose plan for a wooden wall sealing off the city of New Amsterdam from its foes was never completed; in fact, it was barely begun. Once more Stuyvesant was reduced to futile pleas to Amsterdam for help, signing one of them, "your faithful, forsaken and almost hopeless servant." The town magistrates added their own request, naively writing to Amsterdam for three or four thousand "good soldiers, one-half with matchlock, the other half with flintlocks." In response, the company had sent fifty.[24]

The condition of the town's fortifications remained feeble in the days before Nicolls and his men appeared on the Breuckelen shore. Stuyvesant lamented the flimsy state of the wooden wall, periodically weakened by townspeople who tore off planks for firewood. Fort Amsterdam, its walls now braced with stone, was in somewhat better shape. Throughout the summer of 1664, slaves, soldiers, and burghers toiled with "shovels, spade or wheelbarrow" to repair its ramparts and gun carriages. But gunpowder was low, and a mere 180 soldiers, augmented by some 300 civilian militiamen and other townsmen, would face the challenge of defending the wall, the fort, and two riverfronts. Food would be scarce; the autumn grain had been harvested but not yet threshed. Aggravating the food shortage, in mid-August the Dutch vessel *Gideon* had arrived in the East River from the Guinea Coast, carrying 290 slaves ready for sale—each with a desperately hungry mouth to feed. Even in the face of invasion, Stuyvesant was unwilling to starve a human cargo worth so many guilders, whether or not his conscience might have permitted it.[25]

But despite the holes in the city's defenses, Stuyvesant was defiant. On September 1, Nicolls, now ensconced in a Staten Island blockhouse the Dutch had built as a defense against the Lenape, sent a delegation over to Fort Amsterdam bearing a letter advising Stuyvesant that Charles II, "being tender of the effusion of Christian blood," would guarantee "Estate, Life and Liberty" to every New Netherlander "who shall readily submit to his Government." Those who did not surrender unconditionally "must expect all the miseries of War." Lacking other resources, Stuyvesant played for time, insisting that he could not resolve the confrontation before receiving direct orders from the Netherlands. Nicolls's reply was curt. Stuyvesant had forty-eight hours to surrender New Amsterdam, or his people would face the consequences.[26]

Nicolls was calling Stuyvesant's bluff. Maverick and others in his entourage assured him New Amsterdam should fall like a house of cards when faced with the prospect of assault. The presence of his warships, along with the sight and sound of hundreds of English soldiers clamoring on the Breukelen shore, must have convinced any reasonable man that the only course was to accept generous terms and surrender honorably. But *was* Stuyvesant bluffing?

Nicolls decided to try negotiating one last time. On September 4, as the forty-eight-hour deadline expired, a small boat approached Fort Amsterdam from across the bay. Six emissaries disembarked, among them Governor Winthrop of Connecticut. They brought a letter, once more spelling out peace terms that included freedom of domicile, property, trade, and religion for any Dutchman who laid down his arms. That was the carrot; the stick soon materialized. Two of Nicolls's warships moved ominously up the bay under full sail and soon faced the fort broadside at the entrance to the East River. So close were the vessels to the populous tip of Manhattan that their cannon muzzles were clearly visible from the shore. Nicolls's clock was ticking.

Stuyvesant read out the surrender terms to a hastily assembled group of his councilors and city magistrates inside the fort. When the city's two burgomasters later returned to request a copy of the letter so they could share it with their fellow townsmen, Stuyvesant vehemently refused and ended the scene by ripping Nicolls's missive to shreds and throwing the pieces to the floor. As angry burghers snatched up the fragments in order to piece the document back together, Stuyvesant knew what the result would be once his townsmen learned its terms. Outgunned, weary of the West India Company's indifference to their fate, valuing their lives and property above loyalty to a distant homeland, and already acquainted with English ways through contact with their neighbors, New Amsterdam's people would make an easy choice.[27]

With or without the support of his townsmen, Stuyvesant was determined to put up a fight. As Nicolls's warships loomed at the island's tip, Stuyvesant mounted the rampart of Fort Amsterdam and instructed a gunner to prepare an artillery barrage against the vessels. As the soldier readied his match to ignite the cannon's fuse, Johannes Megapolensis and his son Samuel, two of the town's Calvinist clergymen, clambered up and sought frantically to talk Stuyvesant out of it. The fort had only twenty-four cannon, the two clerics argued, arrayed against the combined fire power of four well-armed warships. The gesture of defiance would be a suicidal one, possibly leading to the deaths of hundreds of helpless townspeople. Stuyvesant listened, told his gunner to stand down, and resignedly descended the parapet in the company of the two relieved ministers.[28]

Peter Stuyvesant had toiled hard to prepare his city for war. But his people would not fight. Even worse, New Amsterdam was coming apart at the seams. The wife of a prominent merchant warned her neighbors against trusting the company's soldiers, for "those lousy dogs want to fight because they have nothing to lose, whereas we have our property here, which we should have to give up." With English soldiers on the Long Island shore itching for the opportunity to ransack the town, some of the WIC's resentful, impoverished mercenaries inside Fort Amsterdam decided to beat them to it. One soldier was overheard to gloat that "we know well where booty is to be got and where the young ladies reside who wear chains of gold." A group of townsmen had to beat back their own soldiers trying to pillage merchant Nicolaes Meyer's house.[29]

On September 5, the day after Stuyvesant had readied his gunner to fire on the invaders, a group of ninety-three townsmen signed a petition pleading with the director to avoid "misery, sorrow, conflagration, the dishonor of women, murder of children in their cradles, and, in a word, the absolute ruin and destruction of about fifteen hundred innocent souls," lest they be obliged to "call down on your Honor the vengeance of Heaven for all the innocent blood which shall be shed." One of the signers was Stuyvesant's seventeen-year-old son, Balthasar. Stuyvesant sent word to Nicolls and had the white flag hoisted over the fort. He was ready to negotiate.[30]

On or about September 8, 1664, the soldiers of the Dutch West India Company marched out of the gates of Fort Amsterdam and boarded the *Gideon*—the vessel that had recently carried African slaves—for the voyage back to the Netherlands. In marched Colonel Richard Nicolls and his English troops. Forty years of Dutch rule over New Netherland ended that day. Nicolls proudly wrote to his friend and master the duke from what he had renamed Fort James in "New Yorke upon the Island of the Manhatoes"—the "best of all his Majesty's towns in America." As for Peter Stuyvesant, the former director-general sailed to Amsterdam to face a West India Company inquest, defending himself spiritedly before returning to New York and retiring to play the role of family patriarch and slave master on his farm in the Manhattan countryside north of the old defensive wall. When Richard Nicolls handed over his governorship to his replacement, Francis Lovelace, and returned home to England in 1668, he could look back on four peaceful years during which he had adroitly eased 1,500 Europeans and Africans on Manhattan, as well as their countrymen living throughout the region, into accepting English rule.[31]

In leaving New York, Nicolls could not have predicted that the Dutch would make one last, brief stand on Manhattan Island. In 1672—the same year Peter Stuyvesant passed away peacefully on his farm—the English Empire and the Dutch Republic went to war again. This time, New Yorkers looked seaward one afternoon to find Dutch warships sailing through the Narrows and into the Upper Bay. On August 8, 1673, Commander Cornelis Evertsen the Younger brought eight frigates, with the Dutch tricolor flag fluttering on their masts, in off Fort James. September 1664 was suddenly played in reverse. Dutch New Yorkers who rowed out to the invading fleet dutifully reported that the fort's defenses remained weak and undermanned. In the absence of Governor Lovelace, who was off visiting Winthrop in Connecticut, the fort's commander, Captain John Manning, stalled for time while he prepared his ninety soldiers for a confrontation. When a party of English emissaries from Fort James querulously asked to see Evertsen's official commission, the commander pointed impatiently at his ship's guns and told them that his commission "was stuck in the mouth of the cannon, as they would soon become aware if they did not surrender the fort."

When Evertsen gave the English half an hour to surrender, Manning decided to fight. As the cannon of the fort and the ships exchanged fire, six hundred Dutch marines landed on the Hudson River shore, just below the wooden wall. Within an hour or two, Manning surrendered, having lost one soldier; two or three Dutchmen were wounded. Jubilant Dutch townspeople, aware that the conquest was organized by the admiralties of Amsterdam and Zeeland, and that they would thus be spared the vagaries of WIC control, cheered Evertsen's soldiers and sailors through the streets. In the days that followed, Evertsen's men rechristened the town as New Orange and seized the rest of the Hudson Valley towns back from the English. Echoing but reversing Stuyvesant's old fears of the English "Trojan horse within our walls," a sullen John Manning groused about the Dutch "enemy in our Bowels." [32]

But the Dutch reconquest would be short-lived. At peace talks, Dutch diplomats willingly traded Manhattan and the Hudson Valley back to Charles II and his brother James for confirmation of their claim to Surinam. In November 1674, a new English governor, Edmund Andros, arrived on the banks of the East River, and to the disappointment of many townspeople, the Dutch troops boarded a frigate for the journey home. The conclusion of this final Anglo-Dutch War also ended Dutch attempts to regain their North American colony. (War news also brought word of the death of Richard Nicolls, killed by a Dutch cannonball while standing next to the Duke of York aboard an English warship in the North Sea.) Men, women, and children continued to speak Dutch in the streets and houses of Manhattan, but they did so under flags bearing the Cross of Saint George.[33]

The Dutch had left their mark. Out of Henry Hudson's initial encounters with the Lenape and Cryn Fredericks's efforts to fortify an outpost had arisen a bustling, polyglot seaport. The imperatives of trade and moneymaking had given it a reason for being and shaped the ambitions and expectations of its people. Yet hand in hand with commercial necessities had gone military ones. The need to protect the town's trade, and the people who conducted it, had dictated the very form of the place, from the fort at its southern tip to the wooden wall at its northern boundary. The exigencies of defense had given the town its first semblance of a representative government, its first debates over the proper sharing of power between city and province, its first tugs of war over deficit spending and taxation, even its first hospital. War had also given dwellers on Manhattan their first apprehensions and misgivings about what it meant to harbor strangers of different tongues, faiths, and nationalities within the city gates.

All of these issues would persist, under new guises. The Dutch had come to Manhattan singing a discordant medley of Calvinist hymns and lusty tavern ballads. Often, in their years of building homes and trading goods, they had found that they were singing those songs to the martial beat of a soldier's drum. That drumbeat would continue sounding, keeping time now to English rather than Dutch melodies.

CHAPTER 3

Key and Bulwark

New York in the
English Empire, 1664–1774

With cannon thundering, the *Adventure Galley* neared its prey. William Kidd's crewmen readied themselves to board the targeted vessel. The date was August 15, 1697; the place was the Babs-al-Mandab, the narrow strait separating the Red Sea from the Gulf of Aden off the coast of Yemen. Kidd's vessel, almost a year out of New York, was closing in on a large Indian merchant ship, heavy with its cargo of coffee, ivory, spices, and gold, and its Muslim merchants returning home from their pilgrimage to Mecca.[1]

The 150-man crew aboard the *Galley* preparing for hand-to-hand combat was a mixed group. About half were English and European sailors Kidd had hired in London. The other half were mostly New Yorkers, men like shoemakers John Burton and William Wakeman, carpenter Edward Grayham, and seaman and tavern keeper Edward Buckmaster. They were a mix of young tradesmen and mariners bent on profit and adventure and, perhaps, fleeing the hardships of a recession-plagued economy in New York. Some of them were neighbors of Kidd's from Manhattan streets fronting the East River wharves.

Kidd sailed from New York with the blessings of some of the city's (as well as some of London's) most powerful men and with two government commissions. One was a letter of marque, a certificate issued with admiralty approval legally permitting and encouraging Kidd to attack and seize any French vessels he might encounter. England had been at war with France now for eight years, and such privateering licenses were viewed by English officials and colonists alike as useful weapons in the imperial arsenal, as well as potential sources of great profit to the ship owners, captains, and crew lucky enough to capture a well-laden French cargo vessel. The other document, arranged by Whig parliamentary leaders with the approval of King William III, directed Kidd to apprehend four pirate vessels believed to be operating in the Red Sea.[2]

Ironically, three of the four pirate captains named and targeted in Kidd's commission had themselves sailed from New York as privateers authorized to attack French shipping. Their letters of marque had been issued by New York's increasingly disgraced royal governor Benjamin Fletcher. Fletcher had become notorious for the friendly reception he accorded pirates—a mutually beneficial reception, since the governor pocketed a share of pirate loot in exchange for providing safe haven. Although Fletcher justified his public coach rides through Manhattan streets with one pirate captain by explaining that he was endeavoring to cure the man of his "vile habit of swearing," London was not amused. Nor was it amused by evidence that a sizeable number of Manhattan merchants (including Frederick Philipse, one of the richest and most politically influential men in the colony) were doing a brisk trade in the looted silks, calicoes, spices, ivory, sugar, and slaves brought for sale by Indian Ocean pirates, or the fact that that these same New Yorkers welcomed the hard currency in the form of gold and silver coins the outlaws spent in town.[3]

Despite such local enthusiasm for his friendly stance toward pirates, Fletcher had been recalled to face inquiry at Whitehall. The man who would soon replace him as New York's appointed royal governor, Richard Coote, Earl of Bellomont, was one of the clique of English politicians and Manhattan dignitaries who had secured Kidd's commissions. In sending the *Adventure Galley* forth from its East River anchorage in the early autumn of 1696 to pursue Fletcher's old friends, these men sought simultaneously to clean up New York, rid the seas of some of the king's enemies (Frenchmen and pirates), and turn a profit by sharing in whatever riches Kidd might legally seize.

But now, eleven months later, on this day in the Babs-al-Mandab, something had gone wrong. The vessel Kidd was attacking was neither French nor a pirate. Far worse, the vessel was officially under English protection. An impatience for prize loot and restiveness among some of his more hardened and potentially mutinous crewmen had overridden Kidd's sworn commitment to do the king's bidding. But by turning pirate, Kidd and his men would also incur the wrath of the East India Company, a London-based trading firm under great pressure to do something about piracy. As luck would have it, an armed company vessel hove into view just as Kidd prepared to take his Indian prey. The *Adventure Galley* veered off and fled, its crew free to attack other ships on better days—which they did, ultimately boarding and plundering at least seven cargo vessels belonging to Indian, Dutch, and Portuguese merchants.[4]

When, in June 1699, Kidd sailed into an anchorage off Long Island (after having off-loaded much of his loot in the West Indies), he evidently believed he could talk his way out of trouble. After all, New York was his town. Although a Scotsman by birth, Kidd had become a New Yorker through and through. He had married a wealthy Manhattan widow and settled down in a comfortable waterfront townhouse. He had even helped to build Trinity Church, the center of Anglican worship in the town, and on Sundays occupied a pew there. Like other New Yorkers before and since, Kidd possessed an abundant confidence in his ability to talk his way out of sticky situations: he was, in fact, well-known for his verbal "rhodomontadoe and vain glory" (one old Dutch New Yorker derided him as *de Blaas*, a "windbag"). Additionally, he counted on the colony's lax reputation as an enforcer of English regulations. Crown customs officials had previously looked the other way when confronted by smuggling or piracy, especially when their palms were well-greased, and Kidd may have believed bribery—and loot delivered to his backers—might silence critics. His trump card was a set of documents seized from one of the ships he had plundered, French passes that ostensibly proved he had been preying on enemy vessels as his privateering commission directed him to do.[5]

What Kidd did not realize was that the haven of New York could not shelter him from the aroused fury of the English Empire. Royal

Navy officers, East India Company lobbyists, and Tory members of
Parliament out to discredit the Whig "Junto" to which Bellomont belonged had all made Kidd's name anathema in London. It was only a
matter of time before the net tightened around him. Desperate to sal-
vage his own reputation and political career, Bellomont lured Kidd
from Long Island to Boston (where the busy earl also filled the office
of royal governor of Massachusetts and New Hampshire). There, Bellomont sprang his trap, dispatching a marshal to drag the flabbergasted Kidd off to jail just as he was knocking at the front door of
Bellomont's townhouse. Kidd was shipped to London, where he was
tried, convicted of piracy and murder, and, alongside one of his crew,
fellow New Yorker Darby Mullins, hanged until dead from the gallows
on Execution Dock overlooking the Thames on May 23, 1701.[6]

Amid the complexities and multiple betrayals of Captain Kidd's story are
two lessons about New York City in its new guise as an English colonial
port. The first is that New Yorkers had come to understand organized
violence and predation, whether defined as privateering or piracy, as a
source of profit for themselves and their city. (To be sure, the line between the two was decidedly blurry: one New Yorker defined "privateers"
as "a soft name given to pirates.") This connection between waging war
and making money would characterize life and business in Manhattan
throughout its decades as an English town and beyond. From 1689 to
1763, England and its colonies would fight five wars against France
and/or Spain (King William's War, 1689–1697; Queen Anne's War,
1702–1713; a brief maritime war against Spain, 1719–1720; King
George's War, 1739–1748; and the Seven Years War, 1756–1763, known
in its North American campaigns as the French and Indian War). As
seaport, market town, military garrison, and imperial outpost, New York
would play a key role in each of these conflicts. The cycle of war and
peace shaped the daily lives of the city's people, putting bread in their
mouths (and sometimes withdrawing it) and filling them with a succession of emotions—pride, exultation, anger, and fear—as the fortunes of
war revolved. Above all other impulses, however, the eagerness to make
money from war (as well as from every other endeavor they engaged in)
became a hallmark of New York's identity, recognized by New Yorkers
themselves and by English subjects elsewhere.[7]

The second lesson—that New York was now a relatively prominent outpost in a worldwide empire—had more complex ramifications. As New Amsterdam, the city had been like a lonely and neglected child, its needs largely ignored or denied by the Dutch trading company that had founded it. As New York City, it found itself with an at least sporadically attentive mother in the London-based imperial government, a mother who provided numerous siblings, places with names like Bristol and Glasgow, Dublin and Boston, Port Royal and Charles Town, Tangier and Calcutta. As the fur trade declined in relative importance, New Yorkers prospered and built their city through trade with their fellow imperial subjects in the British West Indies, shipping them lumber, horses, pork, whale oil, and, most importantly, Hudson Valley grain and flour, in exchange for sugar, molasses, dye woods, and slaves. London and the other British ports became the emporia from which New Yorkers imported the manufactures and refinements that put the finishing touches on their new identity as Englishmen.[8]

Royal Navy warships fill the East River before the "flourishing city of New York" in 1717. Engraving by John Harris, *A South Prospect of ye Flourishing City of New York in the Province of New York in America,* ca. 1719. COURTESY OF THE NEW YORK PUBLIC LIBRARY, WWW.NYPL.ORG.

Membership in the empire could be empowering and liberating, a source of profit and pride through commerce and war. But it could also prove confining. New Yorkers faced the obligations as well as the benefits of empire—taxes, requisitions, and trade restrictions, especially during wartime. At the same time, city dwellers usually sidestepped, ignored, or bribed their way out of enough of these burdens to keep them satisfied with their place in the imperial firmament and make any notion of serious disloyalty to the empire unthinkable. Still, being obliged to fight the empire's wars also reminded New Yorkers of their constant vulnerability to attack by the empire's enemies, which might literally make war profits—and much more—go up in smoke. The city's economy and the daily experiences of its people were tied as never before to a boom-and-bust cycle of international war. And that cycle would infest the dreams of New Yorkers with visions of new kinds of enemies within the gates, enemies even Peter Stuyvesant had never imagined.

In June 1697, a few weeks before Captain Kidd turned pirate in the Babs-al-Mandab, a visiting doctor from Boston named Benjamin Bullivant received a tour of Fort William at the tip of Manhattan Island from its master, the soon-to-be-replaced royal governor, Benjamin Fletcher. Like all royal governors appointed by the Crown to serve in the colonies, Fletcher's official commission included the title "captain general and vice admiral" of New York. This signified that he was the commander of a garrison devoted to the defense of the English Empire, which in this instance meant ensuring that the city and colony of New York would not fall if invaded by the French foe.

Fletcher showed Bullivant around his residence within the fort, its walls lined with "about 300 choice fire arms . . . 8 or 10 large and well cleaned blunderbusses . . . some scimitars very pretty to behold and set in good order." Moving outside, the Bostonian beheld forty cannon lining the fort's walls at a height of twenty feet above the surrounding city streets, "well disposed to make a gallant defense, if an enemy should come before it." Bullivant also noted that the governor stored 1,500 guns, bayonets, swords, drums, and "other furniture for the war" in a nearby magazine, and that Fletcher was building "a low battery of 8 or 10 guns" in front of the fort at the island's tip, facing the mouth of the Hudson River—an emplacement that would one day give its name to the public promenade Battery Park, which today stands on its shoreline. Bullivant was duly impressed.[9]

Indeed, Fort William (the former Fort Amsterdam, to be known later as Fort Anne and Fort George, its name changing with the accession of each new English monarch) now constituted a crucial link in a chain of defenses stretching the length of the colonial coast and down into the West Indies. The garrison of redcoats on Manhattan played a special role in imperial strategy, a role dictated by the geographical significance of the colony. Situated roughly at the midpoint of the British North American seaboard, New York could play an equally useful role in operations against French Canada, Spanish Florida, and the islands of the French and Spanish Caribbean. Poised on the edge of the Atlantic, Manhattan provided an excellent base for incoming or outgoing navy fleets or troop convoys, an asset not shared by Philadelphia, located one hundred miles up the sometimes ice-bound Delaware River.

Of equal importance for its military role, New York was an unambiguously royal colony, secured for the Crown by James Stuart, Duke of York, who had become King James II in 1685. The same could not be said for such colonies as Massachusetts, Connecticut, Rhode Island, Pennsylvania, or Maryland, which continued to belong to private proprietors or chartered bodies, or resented the imposition of royal dominion. Garrison commanders in those colonies sometimes looked over their shoulders, wondering whether the most hostile force they might confront would be the local populace. New York, in fact, which Bellomont hailed as "the key and bulwark of all His Majesty's colonies," would be the only North American province to have troops stationed in it over the entire period of British rule, an emblem of its centrality and fealty within the empire.[10]

To be sure, New York had its own prolonged moment of turmoil. In 1689, a German-born merchant and former WIC soldier named Jacob Leisler became the leader of a faction of the city's middling and poorer Dutch residents, who resented the second-class status they felt they were being handed by newly arrived English officials and by the dominant clique of wealthy Dutch merchants who cozied up to them. Leisler and other staunch Calvinists were also outraged that the English king James II had openly embraced Roman Catholicism; they feared an international Catholic conspiracy whose agents might be found among new English colonists and other Manhattan residents. Leisler seized Fort James (as it was then named) at the head of a band of militia and made himself dictator of the colony. When a new (and Protestant) English king, William III, dispatched an army and a new governor to New York to restore stability in 1691, Leisler refused to relinquish authority, forcing a stand-off and an exchange of gunfire in which several men were killed. Upon Leisler's surrender, his local enemies made sure that he was convicted of treason, hanged until dead, and then decapitated (supporters sewed his head back on before burial). The lasting legacy of Leisler's Rebellion was the rise of partisan politics in Manhattan: for twenty years, embittered factions of his supporters and detractors fought their battles in acrimonious campaigns for election to the representative assembly King William sanctioned for the colony in 1691. But while legislators denounced each other in debates and pamphlets, Crown control of the colony was secured. New Yorkers would not threaten royal authority so drastically again for another seven decades.[11]

Another factor besides its loyalty and its coastal primacy made New York a strategically critical province of English America: the city's location at the mouth of the Hudson, the great highway into the northern interior. No other river played so important a role, for the Hudson led directly from the open ocean and the shores of Manhattan to the heartland of two critically powerful entities: the Iroquois Confederation and, beyond it, French Canada. Both proved to be troublesome to British strategists, albeit in different ways. By the time the Earl of Bellomont replaced Benjamin Fletcher in Fort William, the Iroquois of the northern frontier had become adept at playing the French and English against each other, squeezing gifts and trade concessions out of both sides, deigning to ally with one side or the other momentarily, while preserving their long-term independence.[12]

But it was the French in Canada, able to muster the support of various frontier Indian allies, who posed the most ominous threat. Unbeknownst to New Yorkers, in 1689, at the start of King William's War between England and France, the French king Louis XIV approved a plan to send 1,600 Canadians and French regulars from what is now Quebec Province down Lake Champlain, Lake George, and the Hudson to seize Albany and New York City, where they would be aided by two warships sailing in off the Atlantic to secure Manhattan. Most Protestants would be expelled, and New York would become part of Catholic New France. Poor coordination and a raid on Montreal by hostile Iroquois kept the plan from getting off the ground, but the following year, a force of French Canadians with Algonquin, Sault, and pro-French Iroquois warriors did descend on English settlements, destroying the town of Schenectady and sparking fear of a combined French and Indian assault down the Hudson.[13]

The proximity of the French scared New Yorkers. At the onset of the French and Indian War in 1755, no less a personage than the Reverend Samuel Johnson, president of King's College (later to become Columbia University), noted that "things look somewhat terrifying. . . . How God will deal with us he only knows." After news arrived of the defeat of General Braddock's redcoats (including detachments from Fort George) by French and Indians in Pennsylvania, Johnson commented that "this put us yesterday in a great panic." Until 1760, when Britain wrested Canada from the French, Manhattan residents remained painfully aware that the Hudson River, their prized artery of commerce, might also prove an effective road for an onslaught of Frenchmen and Indians bent on spreading havoc and terror to the very shores of their Upper Bay. A chill perhaps ran up the backs of spectators when, in June 1753, they watched a delegation of seventeen Mohawk sachems march from their encampment on the city's outskirts (near what is now the exit ramp from the Holland Tunnel) down Broadway to confer with Governor Clinton at the fort, carrying, as one spectator later recalled, "a number of human scalps, suspended on poles, by way of streamers, which scalps they had taken from the French and Indians, their enemies."[14]

Just as frightening was the idea that the French or Spanish—or worse yet, a combined force of French *and* Spanish—could sail a fleet in off the Atlantic to blockade or besiege the port. On a modest scale, New Yorkers got repeated and unpleasant tastes of what this might mean for the city. At least sixteen times between 1690 and 1760, enemy privateers from the French or Spanish Caribbean prowled between Sandy Hook and the waters off eastern Long Island. In 1704, a French privateer with fourteen guns stopped an incoming ship off Sandy Hook, intercepting letters from the Lords of Trade in London to New York's Governor Cornbury. In 1758 another French predator seized the supply ship bringing in the baggage and clothing of the Forty-seventh Royal Regiment. More tempting to enemy privateers were the vessels carrying commercial cargoes into or out of New York port, a number of which they captured during the successive colonial wars.[15]

New York sent out naval vessels, hastily commissioned "coast guard" sloops, and its own privateers to defend the city's ocean gateway. On some occasions this produced spectacular outcomes. In 1748, Captain John Burges sailed the *Royal Catharine* out past Sandy Hook and engaged the French privateer *Mars* in a running battle that resulted in the enemy's surrender; when Burges escorted the defeated *Mars* into New York harbor, the city's relieved merchants subscribed 100 pounds as a reward to the victorious captain. But coastal defenses were porous, and the enemy was unpredictable. In 1704, a French raiding party came ashore at Navesink on the New Jersey shore, a mere twenty miles from the city, where they burned several houses before rejoining their privateer. Such a raid seemed a foretaste of what the city might expect should a French fleet ever arrive in force.[16]

The sense of vulnerability felt by many in the city was compounded by a virulent and anxious anti-Catholicism that Protestant New Yorkers imbibed almost with their mother's milk. Like the Dutch colonists before them (and from whom many were descended), New Yorkers saw the battle against Spain and France not merely as a global clash of dynasties and empires but as a Protestant crusade against the forces of the Vatican. While few overt Roman Catholics actually lived in New York (and no Catholic church would be allowed to open in the city until after the American Revolution), many Protestants saw themselves living in a besieged world, one where French and Spanish Papists would gleefully massacre defenseless Protestants and where Canadian priests might unleash cannibal Indians to collect Protestant scalps and feast on Protestant flesh.

The fear and hatred of Catholicism—a presence that continued to loom in English politics, with Catholic Stuart "pretenders to the throne" launching rebellions against the Protestant monarchy in 1715 and 1745—shaped popular consciousness at every turn in eighteenth-century New York. The monarch's orders to royal governors extended "freedom of conscience" to Protestants and Jews but not to Catholics, who could be expelled from New York without question, while "Jesuits and Popish missionaries" could be jailed for life. Manhattan crowds celebrated Guy Fawkes Day, which marked the triumph of English Protestants over a Catholic plot to blow up the Houses of Parliament in 1605, by burning effigies of the pope and his companion, the Devil. When, in 1753, plans were underway for King's College, lawyer William Livingston argued that the school should be a bastion for the "equal toleration of conscience" but should, "for political reasons, exclude Papists from the common and equal benefits of society." Such hatred and fear only reinforced the expectations of New Yorkers that their port city, a bulwark in the line of defense against Catholic France and Spain, needed to be fortified by and for the English Empire.[17]

Yet despite New Yorkers' hopes for security against foreign foes, the truth was that New York's defenses were a house of cards. Governor Fletcher could put on a good show for the sight-seeing Dr. Bullivant, and Englishmen on both sides of the Atlantic might talk themselves into believing that Manhattan was the bulwark against the French and Indians for all the colonies west and south of the Hudson. But anyone taking the time to make a careful inspection would have found the port's defenses beset with problems, just as they had been under the Dutch. For all the majesty of the fort's walls and cannons, its sod ramparts were endlessly crumbling, its gun carriages decaying, and its barracks in a perpetual state of disrepair. Outside the fort, defenses remained minimal: the battery of guns at the island's tip, the "half moon" (a semicircular artillery emplacement) on the East River waterfront, and a few other clusters of cannon placed here and there. The weakness of the city's defenses surprised visitors. Viewing the unfortified Governors Island in 1744, Alexander Hamilton, a Maryland doctor (and no relation to the later New York statesman of the same name), thought that "an enemy might land on the back of this island

British New York in the 1730s. The shoreline in front of Fort George holds the artillery battery that later provided the name for Battery Park. Engraving by John Car-
witham, *A View of Fort George with the City of New York from the SW.*, 1736. LIBRARY
OF CONGRESS.

out of reach of the town battery and plant cannon . . . or even throw
bombs from behind the island."[18]

As in Dutch days, money—or more precisely, the lack of it—
remained at the root of most of New York's defense difficulties. For all
of Parliament's high-sounding phrases about safeguarding the empire,
funding for defense was often meager and slow in coming. Many in
Parliament opposed the notion of a standing army and especially in
peacetime found ways to skimp on the military budget. Moreover,
when royal councilors thought about the defense of America, they focused on protecting the Newfoundland fishing banks (seen as a training ground for seamen and hence the "nursery of the navy") and the
lucrative sugar-producing Caribbean islands, and less on funding
troops to guard the fur and cereal trade of the Hudson or the city that
channeled those goods to the rest of the empire.

While the troops defending New York were better behaved than
their Dutch predecessors, moreover, they were no better treated. The
fort at Manhattan's tip was the headquarters for four independent
companies of fusiliers and grenadiers raised in Britain and accountable

to the governor. Their total number fluctuated between about two and four hundred men as successive governors dispatched contingents to outposts at Albany, Schenectady, Oswego on Lake Ontario, and Fort Hunter on the Mohawk River. Service as a foot soldier in the king's army was the lot of poor men, recruited or forcibly enlisted in Britain's cities and countryside, where the alternatives were often hunger and joblessness. Pay was low and sometimes literally took years to arrive from London. Basic supplies were often nonexistent; one observer in New York described soldiers "lying in their red coats and other clothes on the bare boards or a little straw." Common soldiers may also have been at least partly aware that everyone from the governor on down to their own officers were skimming off as much of their pay as they could get away with. Governor Bellomont boasted to London in 1699 that he could feed and clothe a soldier for 12 pence sterling a day— only 3 pence more than it cost him to similarly accommodate a slave imported from the Guinea Coast of West Africa.[19]

Exploiting armed men is always a risky proposition, and tensions exploded in October 1700, when a newly arrived contingent of 129 redcoats from Dublin—"a parcel of the vilest fellows that ever wore the King's livery," Bellomont claimed—mutinied on the parade ground in front of the fort, demanding their pay and clothing. "Damn me! Don't stir a man," the soldiers shouted when ordered to march. Their cry was answered by a sentry on the fort's ramparts: "Gentlemen, don't march till you have your pay for now is the time to get it. O! God! . . . I can't be with you but my heart is with you." Bellomont promptly called out the city militia—in effect, the adult male population of the city, who were required by law to arm themselves and drill in preparation for any emergency. Two hundred militiamen obeyed, outnumbered the mutineers, and faced them down. The only shots fired were those of Bellomont's firing squad after his court-martial reached its verdict. Two men were executed, and two others were "severely whipped," while four were kept for a month in an isolation tank in the fort known as "the hole."[20]

In the future, desperate soldiers learned to mutiny by using their feet rather than their muskets; their desertion rate was steady and high, not surprising given the wages such men could make as artisans or common laborers in the colonial economy. Other redcoats, as well as sailors from the Royal Navy "station ship" in New York harbor, gained permission to live in rented quarters in the town, where they could find part-time work and sustain families.[21]

While a succession of royal governors repeatedly implored London for more soldiers and more funding, they also wrangled over defense matters with the elected colonial assembly. The tug-of-war over appropriations that had beset Stuyvesant's relationship with his burghers now took on a distinctly English cast. Governors and their appointed councils demanded or cajoled military funds from assemblymen who, as "free-born Englishmen," insisted on their right to determine whether defense expenditures were the responsibility of the colonists or the Crown. The city government, now consisting of an appointed mayor and an elected common council of aldermen and assistants, also entered the fray, turning debates over military spending into three-way struggles.

Resisting a governor's insistence on raising war monies proved to be good politics, combining as it did appeals to English freedom and sheer opportunism. No New Yorker wanted to pay higher taxes, and most had also imbibed English political ideas, sincerely believing that the duty of the colonial legislature was to manifest its fealty to the Crown while opposing anything that smacked of royal encroachment on popular liberties, including the right of the assembly to determine how the people's money would be spent. As for the governors, their conviction that the crown was doing its share by providing sheer manpower—soldiers and sailors whose duty, after all, was to defend the colonists' homes, property, and lives—often spurred them to fury toward what they viewed as "a selfish niggardly people."[22]

Typical were the disputes over protecting the Narrows, the mile-wide channel between Staten Island and Long Island that served as the main passage from the ocean to the city and the Hudson. In April 1703, during Queen Anne's War and in the face of rumors of an impending French naval attack, Governor Cornbury and the assembly agreed to erect batteries of guns on both sides of the Narrows. Next came wrangling over who should pay for the batteries. Assemblymen asked Cornbury to press Queen Anne or neighboring colonies for the money, which the governor refused to do. In June the assembly agreed to impose a special defense levy on New Yorkers. Three years later, however, the batteries remained unbuilt. Charging that the assembly had never collected the tax, a seething Cornbury reminded New Yorkers that the city "yet lies very open, naked and defenceless." In 1756, during the French and Indian War, Governor Charles Hardy advised that heavy guns be placed at the Narrows. After half a century and three wars, the batteries did not yet exist.[23]

Legislators were not always so evasive. Many recognized the need for defense and voted to provide funds for protection, as well as to underwrite the provisioning and quartering of royal troops and enlistment of local volunteers for wartime campaigns. During Queen Anne's War, King George's War, and the French and Indian War, the legislature sponsored an early-warning system of shoreline "beacons"—tall poles topped by barrels filled with pitch, to be lit by militiamen or local residents to alert the city at the first sighting of an enemy fleet. In 1745, when the city again feared a French invasion from the sea, officials built a protective wall of cedar logs from river to river on the city's outskirts at what is now Chambers Street to stave off an attack from the north. The colonists, however, sought to subsidize these works on their own terms, doing their best to hold out for the maximum funding from London before committing themselves to the full expense.[24]

This frugal strategy seemed shrewd when English monies arrived. Manhattan pedestrians could only gape in wonder when, in August 1756, they watched as twenty-four cartloads of gold and silver coins worth 115,000 pounds sterling, the English government's "reimbursement" to the northern colonial legislatures for monies spent against the French and Indians, trundled up their streets from the wharfs. Ultimately, however, such subsidies, most of which were earmarked to feed, clothe, and arm troops on the frontier, could not pay the bill for city defense. As New Yorkers worried about preventing invasion while safeguarding their liberties and purses, legislative frugality impeded preparedness just as surely as royal and parliamentary parsimony did. Pitch-filled barrels might be cheaper than cannon at the Narrows, but they were no substitute.[25]

New Yorkers spent their own money on defenses with great reluctance, but it was another story entirely when it came to profiting from war. In each of the colonial wars, New York City became the marshaling yard, supply depot, and jumping-off point for British expeditions aiming to wreak havoc in the French and Spanish Caribbean and French Canada. The first two wars, King William's and Queen Anne's, brought mixed results at best to the city's economy: Manhattan-based privateers gleefully plundered cargo ships belonging to the Catholic foe, but war also disrupted New York's markets in the Caribbean, slowing trade in a period when mounting rivalry with Philadelphia was already hurting profits in the city's all-important grain and flour trade.

It was King George's War and the French and Indian War that brought prosperity with them, as Westminster and Whitehall sought to strike ever more decisive blows in the Americas. The city and its harbor, stuck in economic doldrums before the outbreak of each war, became a crossroads and a staging ground for military missions whose size dwarfed anything colonists had ever seen before. Fleets of men-of-war and transports came and went, filling the skies of the port with sails and disgorging hundreds of redcoats from Gibraltar and Cork sent to Manhattan in preparation for attacks on Cartagena, Louisbourg, or Martinique, or buckskin-clad militiamen from Virginia and Maryland on their way up the Hudson by sloop for assaults against Canada. Officers, troops, and sailors brought money to spend, to the profit of the city's tavern keepers, artisans, and clothiers, as well as the prostitutes who cruised the Battery after dark.[26]

Big money was to be made during wartime by those with the right connections. Leading gentlemen like Oliver De Lancey and John Watts, already enriched by large landholdings or by trade links to England, got richer by providing war loans of hundreds or even thousands of pounds at 5 and 6 percent interest to the provincial government, or contracted on a grand scale to provide the troops and militias with food, clothing, and supplies. Others, less established, found war a stepping stone into the ranks of well-heeled traders. Except for the two groups—African slaves and Roman Catholics—who were banished from equitable treatment in New York society, war proved an equal opportunity employer, bringing profit to enterprising Englishmen, Scotsmen, Irishmen, Dutchmen, Huguenots, Germans, Jews, and others in Manhattan's increasingly diverse population. Complaining of the way pious and puritanical New Englanders viewed New York during wartime, a city newspaper, the *Mercury*, carped in 1756 that "they constantly speak of us . . . as a province whose whole politics consists in forming schemes to enrich ourselves, at the expense of every thing, that ought to be held sacred amongst men." But neither self-consciousness nor the sincere patriotism of most New Yorkers impeded the moneymaking.[27]

The most controversial and covert financial opportunity war offered was that of trading with the enemy. From the inception of their commerce with the West Indies, New York merchants had recognized that Jamaica, Barbados, and other English islands were not the only markets beckoning to them. New Yorkers exchanged their flour, grain, and lumber for sugar, molasses, and slaves on Spanish and French islands, often for better prices than they could get in the English colonies and in flagrant disregard of English measures that sought to regulate or prohibit such trade. War turned such smuggling into a form of aiding the enemy, of outright treason in the eyes of English admirals and parliamentarians, but skyrocketing prices on the enemy's islands proved too tempting to Manhattan businessmen like Thomas Lynch, James de Peyster, Waddell Cunningham, and dozens of others. To the north, supplying the French at Louisbourg on the Canadian coast with food, canvas, and gunpowder also proved profitable. But by doing so, a writer in the *New-York Mercury* complained in 1756, Manhattan merchants were providing the French "with everything necessary for our destruction."[28]

Some also found a useful cover for trade in the prisoner exchanges fostered by both mid-century wars. Each conflict brought a stream of prisoners of war to Manhattan: French and Spanish sailors, French troops captured in Canada, Catholic families expelled from Nova Scotia. Each enemy prisoner was poised to collect information about the city's defenses, and local officials were eager to rid themselves of potential spies who, moreover, had to be fed and housed. But in authorizing New York shipowners to carry prisoners to Saint Domingue and to bring back British prisoners of war, royal governors sparked a lucrative trade in which captains filled their holds with valuable trade goods. A small group of French merchants, who managed to stay in the city despite fears of wartime subversion and espionage, covertly provided ship captains with passports and licenses facilitating this trade with the enemy.[29]

The fortunes of war did not lift everyone equally. Higher wartime insurance rates on shipping cut into profits from overseas trade, hurting some merchants (including smaller traders) while benefiting those who sold insurance. Wartime inflation burdened the city's poorest people— widowed, orphaned, ill, disabled, or aged laborers, servants, seamen, soldiers, lesser tradesmen, and their families. "What must our poor suffer!" the New York *Post Boy* lamented during the winter of 1747, after noting steeply rising prices for poultry, butter, and firewood. Carpenters and shipwrights, meanwhile, hated being "impressed" by the army to build bateaux (small boats used in the Canadian campaigns) at fixed prices. The threat of actual impressment, however, was very real: most despised and feared in both war and peace was the press gang, the detachment of Royal Navy sailors who rounded up seamen, waterfront workers, and even landsmen for forced labor on His Majesty's warships at low pay under miserable conditions for what might become a lifetime of service.[30]

War drained off some of the city's poorer or transient men, like nineteen-year-old German-born tailor Jacob Murweis, twenty-year-old stonecutter and native New Yorker Mathew Sindown, forty-seven-year-old laborer Walter Murphy from Dublin, and forty-year-old Scotsman John Ramsey, who wryly described himself to a recruiter as "an old smuggler." In 1759 these men enlisted in newly formed colonial regiments that the legislature raised for one of the repeated assaults on Canada. High bounties and wages attracted enlistees. So did patriotism, which motivated at least some of the seven hundred men who enlisted for frontier duty after news arrived in town of the disastrous loss to the French at Fort William Henry on Lake George in 1757. But the prospect of risking one's life to French bullets, Indian tomahawks, or disease in a remote wilderness clearly deterred many men who had something to live for in New York City.[31]

For rich and poor, privateering was one of the most attractive opportunities the wartime city offered. As the scale of each successive imperial conflict grew, so did the number of privateering vessels sailing from East River docks: from seventeen during Queen Anne's War to seventy-three during the French and Indian War, the latter number unrivaled by any other port. In a given year, a thousand men might be on board New York privateers. "The country is drained of many able bodied men," Lieutenant Governor James De Lancey explained to

William Pitt in 1758, "by almost a kind of madness to go a privateering." Members of some mercantile families, like the Beekmans and
Van Hornes, got into the habit of launching privateers from war to war
and generation to generation. They recruited crewmen through word
of mouth on the waterfront or through advertisements in that new urban vehicle of information, the newspaper (New York's first weekly,
the *Gazette*, had begun publication in 1725). For seasoned seamen,
accustomed to low pay, hard labor, and the hazards of life at sea, privateering made obvious economic sense. The only group kept from privateering was that half of the population consisting of women: when,
in 1743, a woman trying to pass as a man was discovered shipping out
on the *Castor and Pollux*, the crew ducked her in the water from the
yard arm and then tarred her "from head to foot."[32]

Once furnished with an official letter of marque from the royal governor, New York sloops and brigs, well-armed with cannon and men,
usually headed south for the cruising grounds north of Hispaniola and
Puerto Rico, where they had the maximum chance of catching rich
French and Spanish prizes. But privateering could be dangerous. Out of
108 New York privateering vessels in the two mid-century wars, 25
never returned home; hundreds of crewmen died, were wounded, or
ended up languishing in French and Spanish prisons.[33]

In the face of the many risks that accompanied privateering, crew
members focused on the rewards. Privateers returned to New York harbor with captured cargo ships loaded with European textiles, wine, and
hardware. Even more lucrative were the ships seized while carrying
sugar, molasses, rum, coffee, cocoa, or indigo from the West Indies to
Europe. Enslaved Africans were another valuable commodity ripe for
pillaging. The return of privateers with their prizes was a stirring event
that brought thousands of New Yorkers out to the wharves along Dock
Street to look and cheer. Merchants now learned whether their invest-
ments had paid off (indeed, the speculative trading of shares in privateers, driven by news of the shifting fortunes of given vessels still
plying the Caribbean, became one of New York's earliest securities
markets). Sometimes the results were spectacular, as in the Great Capture of August 1744, when the privateers *Royal Hester*, *Polly*, *Clinton*,
and *Mary Anne* entered the harbor with six captured French vessels

and their freight valued at 24,000 pounds sterling. The vessels "saluted the town with near 50 guns to the rejoicing of the inhabitants."[34]

Once anchored off Manhattan, prize vessels and their cargoes had to be "condemned" in the city's Vice Admiralty Court, where Justice Lewis Morris Jr., a friend of the merchants through thick and thin, ensured that most prizes quickly became the legal property of the New Yorkers who had captured them—an outcome that also guaranteed hefty fees to Morris and a small army of attorneys, registrars, and appraisers, as well as to the auctioneers who offered the looted merchandise for sale. Most privateering contracts stipulated that, after costs, the vessels' owners would receive one-third of prize revenues, with the remaining two-thirds divided among officers and crew.[35]

As in Captain Kidd's day, a thin line separated privateering from its unsavory half-brother, piracy. Like pirates of old, some privateers raided neutral ships or beat and tortured captured crew and passengers, especially when they thought rough treatment would force captives to reveal where treasure was hidden aboard ship. One New York privateer captain, John Lush, gained a special reputation for his piratical behavior. Lush's sloop *Stephen and Elizabeth*, manned by one hundred men, prowled the Caribbean in 1739–1740 for Spanish prizes, which he towed into Charleston and Manhattan, where the proceeds from the looted cocoa, indigo, slaves, and pieces of eight were distributed among the captain and crew. Lush took part of his largesse in human cargo; nineteen "negroes and mulattoes" seized by him were condemned as prizes by Judge Morris. Rumors soon surfaced that Lush had tortured a Spanish crewman in order to get him to divulge the location of gold on his ship; when confronted with the allegation, Lush dryly responded that he "had not realized that you could use a Spaniard too cruel." Other charges would soon circulate as well: allegations that the seized "slaves" had in fact been free sailors before their capture. Regardless of the stories passing from mouth to mouth on the East River docks, the captain played his role to the hilt. "When Lush landed," the New York *Weekly Journal* reported in April 1740, "he was rowed to shore by his men in rich laced and embroidered clothes taken from the Spaniards." As successful businessmen who embodied wartime prosperity, Lush and other privateers found their alleged breaches of honor and humanity were quickly forgotten by most townspeople in the streets and auction rooms of Manhattan.[36]

In the late winter and spring of 1741, as privateering sloops came and went in the waters of the Upper Bay, and at a moment when hundreds of redcoats and militia volunteers were off fighting the Spaniards in a major Caribbean offensive, a strange and disturbing series of events began to unfold in New York City. Ten fires, at first seemingly random and accidental, broke out over the course of three weeks in March and April. While no lives were lost, several homes and warehouses were badly burned. Hardest hit was Fort George, where on March 18 the barracks, chapel, and governor's house burned to the ground despite the efforts of a bucket brigade and the city's two water-pumping fire engines. Next to the little-understood smallpox and yellow fever epidemics that periodically swept the city, nothing struck fear in the hearts of New Yorkers like fire: with hundreds of buildings and roofs at least partly constructed of wood, the town could become an inferno in a matter of minutes.

By April 5, uneasiness was turning into panic. While looking out her window onto Broadway that day, Abigail Earle overheard Quack, the slave of butcher John Walter, laughingly exclaim to a fellow slave, "fire, fire, scorch, scorch, A LITTLE, damn it, by-and-by." When four blazes broke out the following day, furious mobs ran through the streets yelling, "The Negroes are rising!" Then, on April 21, Mary Burton, a white teenage servant in a waterfront tavern popular among slaves and soldiers from Fort George, offered authorities a remarkable confession: her employer, John Hughson, was the head of a slave conspiracy "to burn the whole town . . . the Negroes were to cut their masters' and mistresses' throats; and when all this was done, Hughson was to be king, and Caesar [a local slave] governor."[37]

New York had been a slave-owning city from its inception, but New Yorkers had never resolved the complications of owning other human beings. Enslaved African men and women toiled in households and workshops for their white masters; most lived in their owners' homes, sleeping in kitchens or garrets. Some wed slaves of other owners and created families that were spread between different neighborhoods. As they served their owners, African New Yorkers concealed their own customs, ethnic traditions, and resentments. In 1712, the resentments exploded: a group of about thirty slaves, many of them belonging to the Coromantee (Akan) people of Ghana, who were known for their military tradition, rebelled, killing nine whites and wounding six before they were captured and executed. The rebellion brought harsher laws, designed to keep blacks under constant scrutiny by whites. But the need to move around the city, often beyond the purview of watching eyes, was essential to the daily labor that masters expected their enslaved servants, laborers, and assistants to perform, thus defeating the intent of the laws. In 1741, one in every five New Yorkers—a total of two thousand men, women, and children—was enslaved. Present in about half the city's white households, dwelling in every part of town, slaves made up almost one-third of New York's workforce. In short, slaves were everywhere.[38]

Armed with Burton's allegations against the tavern owner and his cohorts, the city's judicial authorities swung into action, commencing a roundup of slave suspects that continued through the spring and summer months. As New Yorkers erected shoreline beacon poles at Rockaway and the Narrows to warn of possible Spanish invasion that spring, eleven slaves convicted of arson were burned at the stake; five other prisoners, including the white "king" Hughson and his wife, were hanged after being convicted of conspiracy.

As the jail in City Hall filled with dozens of suspects, however, it became clear that those slaves who confessed to complicity in the plot, and named other coconspirators, often had their lives spared. Suspects quickly learned the advisability of cooperating with their interrogators. By midsummer, details of an "unparalleled and hellish conspiracy" were emerging from the testimony of numerous slaves. Some prisoners testified that the plotters had calculated that a Spanish and French invasion was imminent and, arming themselves with stolen swords and guns, had planned to turn over the city to the invaders; when no invasion fleet materialized, they had decided to "kill all the white men, and have their wives for themselves." Prosecutors and judges focused on the alleged treachery of the "Spanish Negroes," who stubbornly insisted in court that they had been free Spanish seamen before being captured by Lush and other privateers. Witnesses reported that Hughson had promised "to tie Lush to a beam and roast him like a piece of beef."

For many frightened New Yorkers, the pieces were all falling into place. The New York plot—"one of the most horrid and detestable pieces of villainy that ever Satan instilled into the heart of human creatures," Judge Daniel Horsmanden called it—was no doubt part of a global Catholic conspiracy to incite these "latent enemies amongst us," "these enemies of their own household," to literally stab their masters in the back.[39]

Horsmanden, one of three Supreme Court Justices, refused to believe that black slaves—"these silly unthinking creatures"—or a mere tavern keeper like Hughson was capable of launching such a shrewd plot. "There is scarce a plot but a priest is at the bottom of it," Horsmanden concluded, and the city authorities began a roundup of suspected secret Catholics. Four Irish-born soldiers from Fort George were arrested; to save himself, one of them "confessed" that a plot was afoot to burn down Trinity Church, the city's bastion of English Protestantism. John Ury, an eccentric teacher of Latin and Greek recently arrived in the city, was arrested and accused of being a secret priest and the true ringleader of a diabolical Spanish or French plot, launched with Vatican approval, to burn New York. Horsmanden, for one, persuaded himself that a joint Catholic-slave uprising, originally planned for St. Patrick's Day, had been coordinated by "our foreign and domestic enemies" to destroy the seaport and prevent the city's ships from bringing food and supplies to British armies and navies fighting Spain in the West Indies. Ury's protests of innocence could not save him from conviction or the gallows. By the time he was hanged on August 29, he joined thirty black men, two white women, and one white man (Hughson) who had already met their end; eighty-four other slaves, including many who had confessed, were ultimately banished by being sold outside the colony.[40]

We will never know fully the true nature and extent of the "Negro Plot" of 1741. Some scholars have argued that militant slaves probably did plan an uprising, to coincide with a hoped-for Spanish or French invasion. More likely is the possibility that a small number of

"Latent enemies amongst us." An enslaved African is hanged on the eighteenth-century city's outskirts. Lithograph by George Hayward, *Ye Execution of Goff ye Neger of Mr Hochins on ye Commons,* 1860. AUTHOR'S COLLECTION.

slaves set some of the fires as limited acts of resistance, rather than hatching the murderous plot imagined by panicking whites and sworn to by coerced suspects. Engaged in an imperial, global, and ultimately religious war, protected by flimsy local defenses, ever mindful of enemy privateers and the attacking fleets they might lead into the harbor, propertied white New Yorkers found it easy to detect enemies all around them: plebeian Irish soldiers in the fort, lowly tavern keepers on the waterfront, hidden priests, their own duplicitous slaves. An unrelenting Daniel Horsmanden continued to insist that the lesson of 1741 was "to awaken us from that supine security . . . lest the enemy should be yet within our doors."[41]

Over the two decades following the events of 1741, New Yorkers would enjoy only seven full years of peace, as the British Empire fought and concluded one war against the Spanish and French, and then in 1756 commenced another one. By late 1760, however, British victories had settled the fate of Canada, vanquishing the looming French presence to the north. As redcoats and sailors left New York City by the hundreds in 1761 and 1762, off to conquer the French islands of Martinique and Dominica and to besiege Havana, New Yorkers could congratulate themselves on having survived five colonial wars without ever setting eyes on an enemy armada sailing up the bay or down the Hudson.[42]

Yet for all New Yorkers' relief, the end of the cycle of imperial wars left the city an abruptly poorer place. The removal of troops and fleets was one key factor in an economic slump that now hit New York and the other colonial ports hard. To make matters worse, Parliament decided to reorganize and increase its taxation and commercial regulation of the colonies in order to recoup some of the war's expenses and to fund the continued British military presence on the frontier.[43]

Like other American colonists, New Yorkers now brought a range of escalating grievances to their concerns about their place in the empire. Merchants and lawyers championed "smuggling" as free trade, arguing that freedom of the seas was a social good Parliament dare not strangle. Militiamen who had felt the disdain of British regulars on the Canadian front returned home to view redcoats with new eyes. Men who had learned how to fight on privateers—New Yorkers Alexander Mc-Dougall, Isaac Sears, and George Clinton among them—had taken the measure of British allies as well as French foes. McDougall and Sears would soon be leading a group called the Sons of Liberty. And young Clinton would go on to serve as New York's revolutionary governor and under Thomas Jefferson and James Madison as vice president of a nation no New Yorker could yet imagine at the conclusion of five wars for the empire.[44]

CHAPTER 4

Demons of Discord
The Revolutionary War, 1775–1783

Accompanied by officers and sentries, George Washington inspected his army's handiwork in lower Manhattan's narrow
streets. It was mid-April 1776, and New York was swarming with thousands of soldiers pledged to fight king and Parliament. Log barricades
now extended across Wall Street, Crown Street, and a dozen other
waterfront thoroughfares, while redoubts of freshly turned earth sheltered artillery batteries along the wharves and on the crests of hills beyond the city's outskirts. Washington's second in command, General
Charles Lee, had followed his orders conscientiously, arriving in Manhattan with a thousand Continental soldiers and militiamen in order to
turn the city into "a disputable field of battle against any force." Lee,
known for his political radicalism and his hatred of British loyalists, had
ordered New York City's male population to help in the effort. Mustered every morning by a fife and drum corps, one thousand civilians—
leather-aproned artisans, merchants and shopkeepers, slaves delivered
up by their masters—took their turn at the shovel and the axe. One of
Washington's generals noted approvingly that the wealthiest men
"worked so long, to set an example, that the blood rushed out of their
fingers."[1]

If Washington feared that these defenses might prove flimsy
against the full brunt of the British Empire's might, he most likely
kept those fears to himself. The general was still learning to command

an army whose ranks were filled with amateur soldiers. One year earlier, in April 1775, war had broken out when British troops had faced
minutemen at Lexington and Concord. Two months later, Washington assumed command of the American troops surrounding Boston's
peninsula, where the British commander, General William Howe, had
entrenched his army after the Battle of Bunker Hill. When Howe put
his troops on transport ships and sailed away in March 1776, Washington strongly suspected that Howe's next landfall would be Manhattan Island. By that time, Washington had already sent Lee south to
prepare New York City for invasion. In fact, Howe's destination was
Halifax, Nova Scotia, but Washington's foreboding was correct: Halifax was merely a provisioning station and rendezvous for the grand expeditionary force Howe was mobilizing for an assault on Manhattan.

Washington had consulted with the Continental Congress before
marching and shipping his entire army two hundred miles south from
Massachusetts. Washington believed strongly that New York City was
crucial to American victory in the war. Congress agreed. Writing to
the general from Philadelphia, John Adams concurred that New York
was "a kind of key to the whole continent." In believing this, Washington and Adams were merely echoing what had been obvious in North
American and European strategic thinking for a century. Whoever
controlled the Hudson River between its southern terminus at New
York City and its northern borderland in Canada not only possessed
one of the continent's great water highways but also held the natural
boundary separating New England from the Middle and Southern colonies. For Howe to seize New York City would raise the specter of an
impregnable British line stretching from Manhattan to Montreal and
Quebec, geographically cutting the revolution in two and making it
that much easier to quash.[2]

With congressional consent secured, Washington made New York
his new base of operations. By his own arrival there on April 13, over
fourteen thousand American troops—most of them veterans of the
Boston campaign—had already filled makeshift camps in and around
the city, while thousands more were making their way on foot or by
boat from Delaware, Maryland, Pennsylvania, Connecticut, Rhode Island, New Jersey, Long Island, and the Hudson Valley. The city awed

Washington's soldiers, most of them farm boys who had never encountered a place so large or so cosmopolitan. Ensign Caleb Clap from Massachusetts was intrigued by the services he attended in the city's synagogue and Lutheran church. Clap's commanding officer, Colonel Loammi Baldwin, a young land surveyor from Woburn, wrote to his wife of another of the city's attractions: the "bitchfoxly jades, jills, hags, strums, prostitutes" he encountered while on duty in the city's brothel district west of Trinity Church. The soldiers commandeered houses, many of them abandoned by fleeing civilians, and hunkered down in barns and tents from Paulus Hook on the New Jersey shore to Red Hook on the Long Island shore. "Our tent living is not very pleasant," wrote Philip Fithian, a young army chaplain with a New Jersey regiment stationed at Red Hook. "Every shower wets us. . . . But we must grow inured to these necessary hardships."[3]

By the 1770s, New York was a city of over twenty thousand, home to a jostling array of peoples and interest groups; its rural environs across the harbor and in northern Manhattan consisted of tidy farms and small hamlets linked to the city by roads and waterways. The town had continued to grow through the mid-century cycle of war and peace, extending north beyond Stuyvesant's old defensive wall, which had fallen into disrepair by 1699 and soon disappeared as New Yorkers used its wood and stone for new buildings. On some blocks, elegant brick townhouses had replaced wooden Dutch cottages; church steeples and the masts of cargo ships now towered over wharves and winding thoroughfares. "Here is found Dutch neatness, combined with English taste and architecture," an admiring immigrant observed. In Manhattan's streets one saw Germans and Jews and heard English spoken with a Scottish burr or Irish brogue; newcomers mingled with the native sons and daughters of intermarried Dutch, English, and French Protestant families.[4]

But the city Washington and his troops entered had become a deeply divided community. For a decade, while the city continued to grow, New Yorkers had grappled with a succession of parliamentary enactments many viewed as economically burdensome, as affronts to their tradition of self-determination within the British Empire, and ultimately as proof of an English plot to force Americans "to wear the yoke of slavery, and suffer it to be riveted about their necks," as John Holt's weekly *New York Journal* put it. In response, New Yorkers had taken to the streets in a series of demonstrations, besieging Fort George in protest against the Stamp Act in November 1765, trading blows with angry redcoats at Golden Hill near the East River in January 1770, and dumping tea into the harbor in emulation of Boston's patriots in April 1774. "What demon of discord blows the coals in that devoted province I know not," an exasperated William Pitt commented in 1768 after reading a petition denouncing Parliament's trade policies signed by 240 Manhattan merchants.[5]

The Sons of Liberty—the semisecret society of patriots who, from 1765 onwards, organized the street rallies in New York and elsewhere—drew most of their numbers from the craftsmen, seamen, and laborers of the city's workshops and wharves. The leaders of these "Liberty Boys" were Isaac Sears and Alexander McDougall, privateer captains during the French and Indian War. Sears and McDougall were men on the make, individuals aspiring to wealth and influence. But they were also heirs to a vernacular tradition that posited the common laboring people, the "hewers of wood and drawers of water," as the true source and ultimate repository of virtue. While artisans and seamen were well aware that men of their station were expected to leave decision making to their "betters," some Liberty Boys brought to the patriotic movement a willingness to confront men who sported powdered wigs and knee breeches.[6]

For their part, patrician merchants and lawyers—"men of sense, coolness and property," as one of them put it—looked on uneasily. Also angered by British policy, such men sought to channel and contain the boisterous energies of the Liberty Boys. Temporary boycotts, formal petitions, newspaper essays and pamphlets, letters to lobbyists in London: these were the weapons wielded in New York's elite circles, not tar and feathers or hurled stones. The lingering perception that class interest might split the patriot movement in which they themselves were invested, and even threaten the established social order, troubled patricians in New York. The wealthy young lawyer and landholder Gouverneur Morris, a devoted patriot but also a social conservative, noted privately in 1774 that "the mob begin to think and reason. . . . They bask in the sunshine, and ere noon they will bite, depend on it. The gentry begin to fear this."[7]

But the most urgently troubling social division in New York by mid-decade was that separating those who contemplated war from those who recoiled from the prospect of breaking the empire. Despite its demons of discord, New York was the most loyal of the colonial seaports. Fort George at Manhattan's tip remained the headquarters for the British Army and "the grand Arsenal of America"—the closest thing the Crown enjoyed to an administrative center for the colonies, and a source of patronage and employment for hundreds of New Yorkers. For many, a final breach with the mother country was unthinkable, a catastrophe that would turn the world upside down. But by September 1774, William Smith Jr., lawyer and member of the royal governor's council, a man who loved American liberty and the British crown equally, noted that respect for the king was waning in the streets of Manhattan. "You now hear the very lowest orders call him a knave or a fool," he observed. "The first act of indiscretion on the part of the army or the people . . . would light up a civil war."[8]

By the time Washington arrived in April 1776, New Yorkers had already gotten their first tastes of such a war. The previous summer, a popularly elected Provincial Congress and a new revolutionary city government had wrested power from the old colonial authorities and raised militia regiments loyal to the Continental Congress. To avoid ambush, the hundred redcoats in Fort George evacuated to new quarters aboard the sixty-four-gun man-of-war *Asia* out on the Upper Bay. In August, when patriot militiamen (including a young King's College student, Alexander Hamilton) confiscated artillery from the royal Battery at the island's tip, the *Asia* fired some retaliatory cannonballs and grapeshot into lower Manhattan, damaging several buildings and spurring a mass panic in which eight thousand people—a third of the population—fled the city for safer environs elsewhere.[9]

As the situation grew tenser, revolutionaries decided that the intimidation of suspected loyalists should be a central tactic in the port's defense. Militia officer Isaac Sears gladly assisted in rounding up, disarming, and interrogating Tories in Queens, where his men demanded that they take an oath of loyalty to the Continental cause, which, as he put it, "they swallowed as hard as if it was a four pound shot that they were trying to get down." Unrepentant loyalists faced rougher treatment. A friend watched in horror as architect Theophilus Hardenbrook "was taken from his house by a desperate mob, who tore all his clothes from his body, rode him round the city in a cart, pelted and beat him with sticks" until he was almost dead. Patriot authorities made sure that some of the more recalcitrant Tories were sent to the dreaded Simsbury mines, a warren of subterranean tunnels in Connecticut once mined for copper and now converted into a prison for loyalists.[10]

While the patriots' harsh measures intimidated some loyalists, they also had a potent opposite effect, pushing many New Yorkers to throw in their lot with the king. Some of the city's ablest and most influential men had already removed themselves and their families to country houses beyond the easy reach of city radicals. Much of the farmland across the water in Queens, Kings County, and Staten Island, moreover, remained home to loyalists and neutrals—Anglican congregations devoted to the king, conservative Dutch farmers wanting no part of changes promoted by city hotheads, "skulkers" in the coastal marshes waiting to make quick money supplying goods or information to the king's troops. Washington realized that his army would "have internal as well as external enemies to contend with."[11]

In late June, a group of over a dozen Tories and two of Washington's own soldiers were detected in a plot to kidnap or possibly assassinate the general. New York's mayor David Mathews, an alleged plotter, was arrested and sent to Connecticut, but never tried; Thomas Hickey, one of Washington's bodyguards, was quickly court-martialed and hanged. To be sure, beyond the perimeter of Washington's own quarters as well as within it, sincere patriots populated the city and its hinterland. But so did spies, saboteurs, and eager recruits waiting to participate in an English invasion. Civil war might indeed be the outcome of these deepening fault lines.[12]

George Washington did not know New York City or its surrounding terrain; neither did most of his officers. By the summer of 1776, his ragtag army supposedly numbered over 30,000 men, but it was seriously weakened by continual desertions, the withdrawal of soldiers returning home after fulfilling their enlistment terms, a dearth of experienced and competent officers, a woeful lack of supplies and armaments, and diseases the soldiers had carried with them from Massachusetts, plus new ones (including syphilis) they contracted in New York. The discipline and training of the average soldier left much to be desired; most, their commander noted, "regarded an officer as no more than a broomstick." The army's strength in men fit to fight fluctuated between about 13,500 and 23,000. Washington seriously questioned the ability of this underdisciplined citizen soldiery to withstand fire from the world's finest professional army.[13]

Sure that Howe was coming, but uncertain where and when the British would attempt a landfall, Washington spread his troops out across Manhattan and its adjoining territories, placing some of them in the array of outlying fortifications begun by Lee and completed by generals Israel Putnam and Lord Stirling. (Stirling, a New Jersey patriot whose given name was William Alexander, sported the noble title in support of his dubious claim that the Crown owed his family vast tracts of colonial land.) American troops now occupied trenches, earthworks, redoubts, and batteries on Governors Island, at Red Hook on the nearby Long Island shore, at King's Bridge overlooking the Harlem River, and at the fortresses (soon named Fort Washington and Fort Lee) placed high above each bank of the Hudson to prevent the British from sailing up the river. Washington also made sure that Fort Stirling, the wood and earth stockade his troops built on the plateau known as Brooklyn Heights, was well equipped with artillery. The Heights commanded lower Manhattan across the mouth of the East River, as well as the entire expanse of the port's harbor.[14]

At the beginning of July, a Maryland private named Daniel McCurtin happened to be peering out from the upper story of a Manhattan townhouse when he saw a sight that astounded him: "The whole Bay was full of shipping as ever it could be. I declare that I thought all London was afloat." General Howe's force was finally arriving; no longer would the king be represented in New York only by the handful of redcoats cooped up on ships in the harbor. By August, 32,000 soldiers—British redcoats and German mercenaries hired by George III from the principality of Hesse-Cassel—plus about 8,000 sailors and

2,000 royal marines would be on Staten Island and aboard the armada of thirty warships and four hundred transports crowding the bay, preparing for battle. It was the largest expeditionary force ever mounted by a European nation up to that time, larger than the Spanish Armada. Loyalists flocked to their standard. Staten Island's militia pledged fealty to the king en masse; five hundred men, well versed in the local terrain and roads, switched sides in an instant by raising their right hands.[15]

As New Yorkers chose sides, a rider galloped into the city on July 6, bearing momentous news from Philadelphia. The Continental Congress had declared the colonies to be independent states, a move Washington had been pressing for some time. In compliance with Congress's instructions and his own elation, the commander in chief had all regiments drawn up, and on July 9, 1776, the Declaration of Independence was read aloud to the army. The troops responded "with loud huzzas." That night, a crowd of soldiers and civilians gathered at Bowling Green outside the northern wall of Fort George and toppled the gilded lead equestrian statue of George III that New Yorkers had erected in 1766 in gratitude for the repeal of the Stamp Act. Most of the lead was carted off to Connecticut to be turned into musket balls; one patriot quipped that the king's troops "will probably have melted majesty fired at them."[16]

A moment of rebirth was at hand; soldiers would now be fighting for their own country. But no rebirth strengthened the ailing, ramshackle American army. "The time is now near at hand which must probably determine whether Americans are to be slaves or freemen," General Washington told his soldiers in a written address. "The fate of unborn millions will now depend (under God) on the courage and conduct of this army. . . . We have therefore resolved to conquer or die." Only one thing was certain as Washington and his men watched and waited: the next battle would be fought, for the first time in history, by the army of the United States of America. Whether the new nation would survive that battle was an open question.[17]

On the pleasant, sunny morning of August 22, 1776, fifteen thousand British and German soldiers boarded flatboats along the Staten Island shore for the short passage across the Narrows to the beach at Gravesend in Kings County. Here the troops lined up in formation, awaiting

New Yorkers topple the statue of George III at Bowling Green, July 9, 1776. Engraving by John C. McRae, *Pulling Down the Statue of George III by the "Sons of Freedom," at the Bowling Green, City of New York, July 1776*, ca. 1875. LIBRARY OF CONGRESS.

further orders. One after the other, the regiments peeled off and marched briskly up the farmer's path called the King's Highway, each unit distinguished by its insignia, flag standards, and brightly colored uniforms: English regiments of foot in their red wool jackets and white leggings, Black Watch Highlanders with their blue wool bonnets (officers sporting black ostrich feathers in theirs), Hessian Jaegers (riflemen) in their smart green jackets faced with red. Bringing up the rear was a baggage train of wagons carrying the army's supplies: ammunition, food, rum, tents, cooking equipment, bedding, and furniture for a mobile fighting force superior in numbers to all but the largest American towns. A few lines of American skirmishers took shots at the advancing enemy, then melted away into the countryside. "They climb trees, they crawl forward on their bellies for one hundred and fifty paces, shoot, and go as quickly back again," a Hessian officer complained, but this morning the resisters did little damage. Conducted with exemplary discipline and textbook precision, General Howe's invasion of Long Island was underway.[18]

Five miles to the north, on the long brush-and-forest-covered ridge known as Gowanus Heights (stretching from what is today Sunset Park east to Bushwick), several hundred American soldiers waited nervously. Here the uniforms were even more varied, to the point of confusion: some companies of a single Massachusetts regiment wore blue jackets, other companies green or gray. Many wore no uniform at all, but a medley of ragged and threadbare civilian garments. These men, spread along five miles of the ridge's crest and the three principal roads that cut through it, constituted a first line of defense.

Behind Gowanus Heights lay the inner line of American fortifications on Long Island: a three-mile network of trenches, earthworks, and stockades manned by another five thousand soldiers, stretching from Fort Defiance at Red Hook to Fort Greene near Gowanus Creek and on to Fort Putnam overlooking Wallabout Bay on the East River, all of them protecting Fort Stirling on the summit of Brooklyn Heights above the shoreline village of Brooklyn, facing Manhattan. While the outer line of troops would hope to keep any attacking British forces well away from this interior line of fortifications, the string of forts was Washington's last true defense for the heights that commanded Manhattan. Now Howe's army was on the march toward them all, across the fields and farms of Kings County.

By that evening, British and Hessian regiments under Charles Lord Cornwallis had taken the village of Flatbush, where Dutch farm families welcomed them with open arms and the Dutch Reformed pastor invited them to raid the wine collection of David Clarkson, one of the few local "rebels." Over the next three days, Pennsylvania riflemen sent out from the American lines skirmished inconclusively with the enemy around Flatbush.

Washington remained wary. Convinced that the Long Island assault might well be a feint to divert him from an impending main attack on northern Manhattan, he redeployed some regiments from Manhattan to Kings County but continued to spend most of his time at his command center in a townhouse at No. 1 Broadway, in the shadow of Fort George. On August 25 he replaced his Long Island field commander, General John Sullivan, with his own second-in-command, Israel Putnam. All three generals were convinced that defending Gowanus

Heights and three of the roads that passed through its center was the key to holding Long Island and preventing Howe from approaching Manhattan from the east. If held back here, the redcoats would never threaten the interior line of fortifications that stood precariously close to the city itself. "At all hazards prevent the enemy's passing the wood and approaching your works," Washington ordered.[19]

But Sullivan, Putnam, and Washington had committed a fatal blunder, one that exposed their near-total inexperience as battlefield commanders. They had posted troops on three roads—the Martense Lane Pass, the Flatbush Pass, and the Bedford Pass—that ran through Gowanus Heights toward the villages of Brooklyn, Bedford, and the inner defensive line. But somehow they had neglected to position more than a light patrol on a fourth road, the Jamaica Pass, "a deep winding cut" that also ran through Gowanus Heights, further to the east.[20]

One officer did perceive how the Jamaica Pass utterly jeopardized the American hold on Gowanus Heights and the inner line behind it. Unfortunately for the Continental army, that officer was General Sir Henry Clinton, Lord Howe's second in command. Moody and petulant, Clinton quarreled often with Howe and other staff officers over campaign strategy. As the son of a former royal governor of New York Colony, Clinton had spent part of his youth in the city, and he felt that his superior knowledge of the city's terrain and surroundings entitled him to direct the New York campaign. Clinton argued doggedly for a main assault against northern Manhattan to cut the rebels off from the mainland—the assault Washington feared—but he failed to convince the cautious Howe, who preferred an offensive through Kings County to secure Brooklyn Heights and the commanding artillery positions that could sweep the city.

Now, with the Long Island campaign in motion, Clinton was the first to see an opportunity for a brilliant victory—one that might even end the war in a single sharp blow. Clinton grasped that the unguarded Jamaica Pass exposed Washington's army to a classic textbook maneuver. If Howe's troops could get through the pass undetected and then move west behind the backs of the Americans on Gowanus Heights, they would flank the Continental regiments there, cut them off from their inner line of defenses, and subject them to a total rout.

Taking the wooden stockades at Fort Putnam and Fort Greene would then be a mere mopping-up operation, leaving the door wide open for an assault on the vulnerable Fort Stirling. Clinton lobbied hard for his plan, this time finally managing to sway the skeptical Howe. The assault was set for the night of August 26. Sir Henry himself would have the honor of leading an advance guard of four thousand through the Jamaica Pass.[21]

By 9 that evening, under a full moon, Clinton's force, followed by corps commanded by Howe, Hugh Earl Percy, and Cornwallis, started moving up the King's Highway from the hamlet of Flatlands toward the Jamaica Pass. Fourteen thousand men were on the march; their column, complete with baggage wagons and horse-drawn field pieces, stretched along the road for two miles. Behind them they left campfires burning to deceive the distant Americans. Tory scouts from the nearby village of New Utrecht guided the army off the road through adjoining fields so as to minimize the risk of being discovered by American pickets or patrols.

Moving slowly and quietly, with frequent stops so paths could be cleared through underbrush using saws rather than noisy axes, the column reached Jamaica Pass by 3 AM, when the redcoats easily surprised and captured the only American force posted to defend the crucial passage—five mounted officers. The cold night march exhausted and irritated its participants, who could hardly believe that the Americans would not discover the maneuver and ambush them. Captain James Murray of the King's Fifty-seventh Regiment of Foot complained of "halting every minute just long enough to drop asleep and to be disturbed again in order to proceed twenty yards in the same manner." But as the sun rose at 5:30, the army, having covered eight miles, reached its destination: the village of Bedford, directly in the rear of the still-oblivious front line of Continental regiments spread along the crest of Gowanus Heights.[22]

By then, as the sound of distant cannon and musket fire told the tired British regiments, the battle had already begun. Howe and Clinton had decided on a three-pronged assault. As Clinton's main assault force flanked Gowanus Heights, five thousand troops under Major General James Grant would divert the Americans by attacking the right (western) end of their forward line near the Martense Lane Pass, while General Philip von Heister would launch a similar feint by leading Hessian and Highlands regiments in a frontal assault on the American center ranged along the Heights. The gunfire must have initially puzzled Howe and Clinton, for the three attacks were supposed to commence simultaneously, in response to signal cannons to be fired at 9 AM. But Grant's troops had literally jumped the gun. During the night, hungry scouts from one of his regiments had been spotted by American pickets as they hoisted watermelons from a field next to the Red Lion Tavern, just west of the Martense Pass. By dawn, Grant's men had been exchanging fire with Pennsylvanians in the woods on the American right flank for several hours.[23]

In the townhouse at the foot of Broadway, George Washington awoke that morning to the "deep thunder of distant cannon" drifting over the East River from Long Island. Continuing British troop movements from Staten Island to Long Island had finally convinced him that Howe's invasion of Kings County was the main event. He had already begun to redeploy regiments from Manhattan to Brooklyn, and now, on the morning of the twenty-seventh, he ordered over more troops as he prepared to cross the river himself. One of the soldiers making the passage was a sixteen-year-old Connecticut private named Joseph Plumb Martin, who later recalled stuffing his knapsack with hardtack from casks standing by the Maiden Lane Ferry, just north of Wall Street, as he boarded a small boat bound for the Brooklyn shore. "As each boat started, three cheers were given by those on board, which was returned by the numerous spectators who thronged the wharves," Martin remembered. Unbeknownst to Washington or Martin, the reinforcements from Manhattan were stepping into the trap Clinton and Howe were ready to spring on them.[24]

At 9 AM on August 27, with the firing of the British signal guns, the Battle of Brooklyn (also known as the Battle of Long Island) began in earnest. As Grant's troops intensified their musket and cannon fire against the right flank of the American forward line, and as von Heister's Hessians and Scotsmen marched with fixed bayonets on the American center, Clinton's grenadiers and light infantry surged west and south from Bedford, firing into the American rear along the Heights. As musket balls shattered tree branches and cracked into stone walls, clusters of British and American soldiers intermingled in a murderous free-for-all. William Dancey, a British infantry captain, found himself and his men running across a field, "exposed to the fire of 300 men. . . . I stopped twice to look behind me and saw the riflemen so thick and not one of them of my own men. I made for the wall as hard as I could drive, and they peppering at me. . . . At last I gained the wall and threw myself headlong."[25]

The Continental line on Gowanus Heights soon collapsed, as Clinton's redcoats drove most of the fleeing Americans before them back toward the inner line of fortifications or toward the right flank of the American front line, where Grant was still pressing forward. On the south slope of Gowanus Heights, a similar rout was taking place, as von Heister's men rounded up bloodied and surrendering rebels. The plain remained a killing field after the Americans laid down their arms, for some of the Germans and Highlanders vented their fatigue, rage, fear, and contempt by butchering prisoners. "It was a fine sight to see," bragged one English officer, "with what alacrity they dispatched the rebels with their bayonets after we had surrounded them so they could not resist." Another British officer was appalled to witness "the massacres made by the Hessians and Highlanders after victory was decided."[26]

As panicking Americans ran west toward their own right flank, Washington and his field commanders sought desperately to regroup the army and make a stand there. With Cornwallis's corps hammering down from the northeast, von Heister pouring through the Flatbush Pass from the southeast, and Grant pressing from the southwest, Lord Stirling rallied several regiments in the marshy fields near a farmhouse and a millpond that ran into Gowanus Creek. Recalling that Grant had boasted in Parliament that he could easily march from one end of the American continent to the other with five thousand British regulars, Stirling tried to calm his shaken troops. "We are not so many," he declared, "but I think we are enough to prevent his advancing farther over the continent than this millpond."[27]

But the onslaught of enemy musket fire and cannon volleys was relentless; the noose around the American front line grew ever tighter.

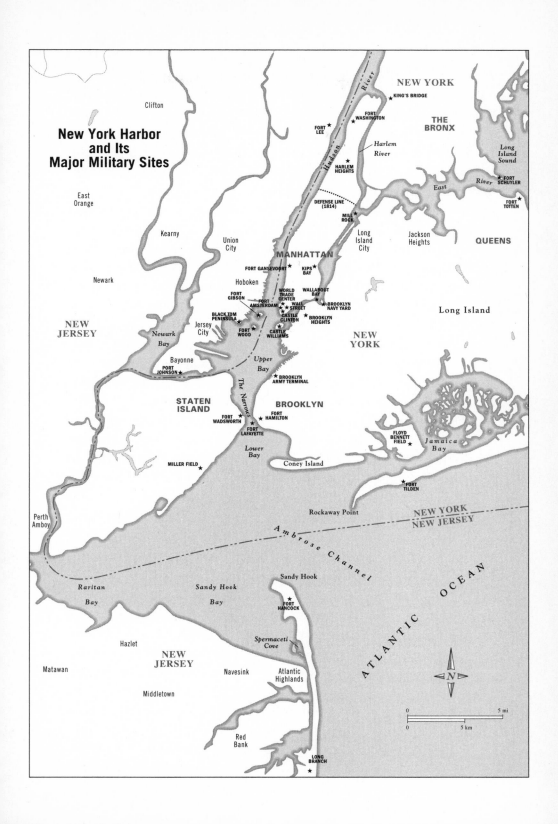

New York Harbor and Its Major Military Sites

Clifton

NEW YORK

KING'S BRIDGE ★

FORT WASHINGTON ★

FORT LEE ★

THE BRONX

Harlem River

HARLEM HEIGHTS ★

Long Island Sound

★ FORT SCHUYLER

FORT TOTTEN ★

DEFENSE LINE (1814)

MILL ROCK ★

East

River

East Orange

Hudson

Long Island City

Jackson Heights

QUEENS

Kearny

Union City

MANHATTAN

Newark

Hoboken

FORT GANSEVOORT ★

KIPS BAY ★

WORLD TRADE CENTER ★

WALLABOUT BAY

FORT GIBSON ★

FORT AMSTERDAM ★

WALL STREET ★

★ BROOKLYN NAVY YARD

NEW JERSEY

BLACK TOM PENINSULA ★

CASTLE CLINTON ★

BROOKLYN HEIGHTS ★

Jersey City

FORT WOOD ★

CASTLE WILLIAMS ★

Long Island

NEW YORK

Newark Bay

Upper Bay

★ BROOKLYN ARMY TERMINAL

Bayonne

PORT JOHNSON ★

The Narrows

BROOKLYN

STATEN ISLAND

FORT WADSWORTH ★

FORT HAMILTON ★

FORT LAFAYETTE ★

FLOYD BENNETT FIELD ★

Jamaica Bay

MILLER FIELD ★

Lower Bay

Coney Island

Perth Amboy

FORT TILDEN ★

Rockaway Point

NEW YORK
NEW JERSEY

Ambrose Channel

Raritan Bay

Sandy Hook Bay

Sandy Hook

ATLANTIC OCEAN

Hazlet

NEW JERSEY

Navesink

Atlantic Highlands

FORT HANCOCK ★

Spermaceti Cove

N

Matawan

Middletown

Red Bank

LONG BRANCH ★

0   5 mi

0   5 km

New Yorker fought New Yorker, as the British threw Tory militia against local Continental units. Stirling came to see that the stand was hopeless and resolved on a holding action that would, he hoped, permit the bulk of the army to escape back to the inner line of defense. Leading four hundred of his best-trained troops, the Fifth Maryland Regiment (the "Dandy Fifth," for its elegant scarlet and buff uniforms and the tidewater aristocrats who peopled its ranks), Stirling charged Cornwallis's front six times, each time enduring a withering fire of canister and grapeshot "like a shower of hail." One American participant remembered how the British cannon fire wreaked havoc, "now and then taking off a head." Behind them, other Americans tried to make their escape, many of them plunging west and north across Gowanus Creek and the eighty yards of the marshy millpond. Arriving with his regiment too late to be thrown into the fray, Joseph Plumb Martin watched from the far bank: "such as could swim got across; those that could not swim, and could not procure any thing to buoy them up, sunk. . . . When [the survivors] came out of the water and mud to us, looking like water rats, it was truly a pitiful sight." Watching the Marylanders' last-ditch effort from a temporary command post on the rise called Cobble Hill behind the inner line of fortifications, Washington allegedly exclaimed, "Good God, what brave fellows I must this day lose!"[28]

All the survivors of the American forward line now retreated to the inner fortifications, running or limping into the trenches and stockades of forts Greene and Putnam and the line of redoubts connecting them. By early afternoon, it was over. "Long Island is made a field of blood," a Manhattan minister wrote to his wife. Only gradually did the full horror of the disaster become clear to Washington and his battered army. The commander concluded that he had lost over a thousand men (modern estimates place American losses at about three hundred dead, several hundred more wounded or missing, and over one thousand taken prisoner). Howe reported total British and Hessian casualties as fewer than four hundred. Among Howe's prisoners were generals Stirling and Sullivan; a third general, Nathaniel Woodhull, had been mortally wounded by his captors, allegedly after he refused their demand that he say, "God save the King." And now

Howe's army stood poised at the gates of forts Putnam and Greene. In many instances the Americans had fought bravely, but they had been outgeneraled, outmaneuvered, and outfought. The Continental army's first full-fledged field engagement was over. The question now was whether it could survive another one.[29]

But General Howe hesitated, to the disbelief of the spent Americans and the consternation of his own officers. Rather than following up his triumph with a decisive blow, Howe ordered his sappers to begin digging trenches toward the American lines, a sign that he intended to besiege the enemy in his lair rather than breach his walls with a frontal assault. Howe's caution remains puzzling more than two centuries later. Why not follow through with another charge and defeat Washington's army once and for all? The answer, however, is not hard to find. Howe was by nature deliberate and careful, traits that served him poorly during the New York campaign. Just as inhibiting, perhaps, was his long-standing hope that he and his brother, Admiral Richard Lord Howe, could serve as peace commissioners, persuading the American leaders to see the wisdom of ending the rebellion and resuming their proper place in the empire. Even the brief respite that siege preparations required, following the drubbing the Americans had received on Gowanus Heights, might give Congress the time it needed to come round. But the general had miscalculated—gravely. Washington had blundered at the Jamaica Pass; now it was Howe's turn.

By the evening of the twenty-ninth, Washington had made up his mind. As a driving rain soaked his troops and as Howe's trenches snaked slowly forward, the American commander had conferred with his generals, most of whom argued that Brooklyn was a trap whose jaws would spring shut once the British coordinated their land attack with a cannonade from Admiral Howe's warships sailing up from their Staten Island anchorage.

One by one, the American regiments manning the line from Wallabout Bay to Red Hook on the night of the twenty-ninth were ordered to stand down and began an orderly but hasty march to the ferry landing at the foot of Brooklyn Heights, opposite the Manhattan shore. "We were strictly enjoined not to speak, or even cough, while on the march,"

Joseph Plumb Martin recalled. "What such secrecy could mean we could not divine." At water's edge, the soldiers encountered a surprising sight: a flotilla of small craft—rowboats, flatboats, sailboats, sloops—that had been hastily gathered from around New York harbor and piloted to the Brooklyn shore by two Massachusetts regiments.[30]

The Massachusetts men—almost all of them seamen and fishermen from Marblehead, Lynn, and Salem, including several dozen black mariners—began a methodical evacuation, rowing boatfuls of soldiers half a mile to the Manhattan shore near Peck Slip, then shuttling back across for more. One rower later remembered making eleven round trips through the night. General Alexander McDougall, the old Son of Liberty and seasoned mariner, directed the embarkations from the Brooklyn ferry steps. Washington had gambled that prevailing winds would keep Admiral Howe's ships from entering the mouth of the East River. American luck held when a southwesterly breeze, favorable to the Royal Navy, did not produce the feared onslaught of grapeshot-spewing frigates from the Upper Bay. So far, the British seemed completely oblivious to the evacuation.[31]

But as dawn broke on the morning of the thirtieth, thousands of troops still waited on the Brooklyn beach, and nerves began to fray. Soldiers started a disorderly stampede into the boats. Washington, a man who had spent a lifetime learning to master his formidable temper, now displayed it to good effect. Hoisting a large rock from the shore and balancing it above his head with both hands, he loomed over an overcrowded boat and threatened to "sink it to hell" unless the men cleared it. Order was restored, and the embarkations, aided by a morning fog that concealed them from potential British observers, continued. By 7 AM, as the fog lifted, the last of some nine thousand American soldiers climbed out of boats onto the Manhattan shore. At 8:30, looking across the East River, they saw the red jackets of British soldiers on the ramparts of Fort Stirling. Tory informers and British scouting parties had detected the retreat in progress by 4 AM, too late to alert and move Howe's forces with sufficient speed to surround Washington's regiments. A mere hour or two kept Howe from ambushing the Continental army and, arguably, ending the American Revolution on the bank of the East River.[32]

Almost miraculously, George Washington had saved his army. It had been his turn to execute a flawless maneuver. The Americans also recognized that they had been phenomenally lucky. "General Howe is either our friend or no general," snorted Israel Putnam. But in lower Manhattan, Ewald Shewkirk, pastor of the Moravian Church, peered into the faces of weary and demoralized soldiers. "The merry tones of drums and fifes had ceased," he wrote. "Many looked sickly, emaciated, cast down."

Savoring good fortune was a luxury the Continental army could not afford. Washington redeployed his battered army up and down the length of Manhattan to await Howe's next move. But Howe continued to hold back. On September 11, his brother the admiral hosted a secret conference on Staten Island at which he tried to persuade congressional envoys Edward Rutledge, John Adams, and Benjamin Franklin to negotiate toward peace. When it became clear that Congress would not revoke the Declaration of Independence, the Howe brothers gave up further talks as futile. Warfare would resume. Once more, Washington's men were forced to watch and wait.[33]

This time the Continental army did not have to wait long. In the early afternoon of September 15, the British launched an amphibious assault at Kip's Bay, a sandy cove on the Manhattan shore of the East River some three miles north of the city. The previous night, as American sentries along the shore called "all is well" to each other, sailors on one of His Majesty's frigates plying the river had called back, "We will alter your tune before tomorrow night." In the morning they made good on their promise. Two forty-gun ships and three frigates opened up with a deafening broadside barrage aimed at American positions inland from the cove. The "peal of thunder" stunned Joseph Plumb Martin: "I made a frog's leap for the ditch, and lay as still as I possibly could, and began to consider which part of my carcass was to go first." By the time the British forces—4,000 redcoats and Hessians—landed from flatboats, Martin and his 1,500 comrades had fled.[34]

Hearing the artillery fire from his new command post on Harlem Heights four miles further north, Washington galloped south to find the regiments he had posted to the middle of the island retreating in disarray. Officers and enlisted men ran together, leaving guns, ammunition, coats, and knapsacks strewn across the fields and dirt roads. Stories of Hessian atrocities at Gowanus Heights had played on many minds. "'Take the walls!' 'Take the cornfield!'" Washington bellowed from his steed, to no avail. When he failed to rally his fleeing troops to fire at pursuing Hessians, the general grew so enraged that he nearly allowed himself to be captured before an alert aide guided his horse to safety. "Are these the men with which I am to defend America?" he muttered in despair as his army retreated north toward Harlem Heights.[35]

Once again, luck and Howe's leisurely pace favored the Americans. The king's army moved west across what is today midtown Manhattan, seeking to bisect the island and cut off the remaining Americans who were now retreating northward from the city. But they moved too slowly, allowing Israel Putnam's troops (guided along back roads by Major Aaron Burr) to slip through their fingers and join Washington on Harlem Heights. Nevertheless, the day had brought another near-catastrophic humiliation for the Americans. At one point during the retreat, Adjutant General Joseph Reed recalled, "the enemy appeared in open view, and in the most insulting manner sounded their bugle horns as is usual after a fox chase. I never felt such a sensation before. It seemed to crown our disgrace." Looking ahead, Washington could see only misery. "In short, it is not in the power of words to describe the task I have to perform," he wrote to his brother John. "Fifty thousand pounds would not induce me again to undergo what I have done."[36]

By nightfall on the following day, Washington's men could finally enjoy a flash of pride. On the sixteenth, about four hundred Americans managed to beat back several British detachments in a wooded gulley in northern Manhattan. This so-called Battle of Harlem Heights was not much more than a prolonged skirmish, but its positive outcome bolstered the morale of Washington's badly dispirited force. "You can hardly conceive the change it has made in our army," the general's aide, Joseph Reed, wrote to his wife. "The men have recovered their spirits, and feel a confidence which before they had quite lost." The victory also restored some of their commander's badly shaken faith in his men. "They find," Washington wrote, "that it only requires resolution and good officers to make an enemy (that they stood in too much dread of) give way." Morale, Washington and his officers knew, was an

Harlem Heights, September 16, 1776. Engraving by A. R. Waud, *The Battle of Harlem Heights, September 16, 1776*, 1876. AUTHOR'S COLLECTION.

all but exhausted commodity in the Continental army, one that had to be sustained at all costs, by small successes if not by large ones, in order for the army to continue to exist.[37]

On the night of September 21, John Joseph Henry, an American prisoner of war aboard HMS *Pearl* some four miles distant from the city, noticed "a most beautiful and luminous, but baleful sight," seemingly "the size of the flame of a candle . . . to the east of the battery and near the wharf." The conflagration New Yorkers feared was finally upon them. Fanned by a stiff southeasterly wind coming off the harbor, the flames quickly jumped from house to house, sparked by embers that floated from one cedar-shingled roof to the next. The wooden steeple of Trinity Church soon "resembled a vast pyramid of fire." The British, who had been in control of the city since their offensive of the fifteenth, threw soldiers and sailors into fighting the blaze. But their bucket brigades proved largely ineffectual, and the city's hand-pumped fire engines malfunctioned. By daylight the next morning, nearly five hundred buildings stretching through the heart of the city's west side— a quarter or more of New York's housing stock—had been reduced to ash.[38]

Thanks to prompt fire alarms and the diminished size of the city's population, few lives were lost. Most of the handful of people who did perish during the fire were, in fact, summarily executed. The redcoats fighting the flames strongly suspected American sabotage, and they caught several men and one woman acting suspiciously during the fire—carrying matches dipped in "rosin and brimstone," cutting the handles of water buckets, darting out of houses that soon were ablaze. One suspect was grabbed, bayoneted, and then hung by his feet from a tavern signpost. English soldier Lee Ashton later remembered helping to push another man, allegedly caught red-handed with matches, "into the flames."[39]

Whether or not patriotic free agents decided to help amplify the destruction, the fire probably started accidentally in a tavern or outbuilding near Whitehall Slip on the East River waterfront. To be sure, Washington had pondered carefully the question of burning New York, once the city had fallen to Howe. Among his own staff and in Congress, some, including General Nathanael Greene and John Jay, himself a lifelong New Yorker, had strongly advocated torching the city in order to deprive the British of winter quarters and a "general market." But Congress, reasoning optimistically that the Continental army might recapture the city, forbade it. "Providence, or some good honest fellow," Washington confided in a letter to a cousin after the fire, "has done more for us than we were disposed to do for ourselves."[40]

American soldiers encamped in the woods of northern Manhattan may have smirked grimly at news of the partial destruction of Howe's city, but the autumn only brought them more defeats. In mid-October, the Americans did manage to repel redcoats and Hessians who came up the East River in flatboats and landed at Throg's Neck and Pell's Neck in the Bronx in an attempt to cut Washington off from his escape route into Westchester County. The attacks convinced Washington of the folly of keeping the main body of his army on Manhattan, and in late October he evacuated most of his men over the Harlem

New York's great fire of September 21, 1776, as imagined by a Parisian artist. Red-coats bayonet and beat suspected American arsonists. Engraving published by Chez Basset, *Representation du feu terrible a Nouvelle Yorck*, ca. 1778. LIBRARY OF CONGRESS.

River to the hills at White Plains. There, on October 28, Howe administered another defeat, driving the Americans from the hills, but again without gaining a decisive victory. Washington retreated further north to a more defensible position on hills near the village of North Castle.

Howe's control of Manhattan now sealed the fate of the nearly three thousand soldiers the American commander had unwisely left at Fort Washington, overlooking the Hudson near the island's northern tip. On November 16, English, Scottish, and German regiments scaled the ridges (today's Washington Heights) on which the fort perched and, after a prolonged musket and artillery barrage, secured its surrender; 2,800 hungry men and boys, many clad in rags, marched out into captivity. This time, although many of the prisoners were beaten and looted, there were no bayonetings. The Hessians instead found themselves laughing in disbelief at the forlorn appearance of their prisoners. "A great many of them were lads under fifteen and old men," reported an English officer, "and few had the appearance of soldiers." Four days earlier, Washington had led his Westchester survivors across the Hudson. Soon they were heading toward the Delaware River, at a healthy

distance from Howe's victorious main army, but with a confident Cornwallis hard on their heels.[41]

It was an inglorious and dismal end to the New York campaign for
the Americans. Despite the smoldering ruins of the city's west side and
Howe's failure to corner Washington once and for all, the British army
could find satisfaction in its successes, and assurance that the war was
nearly won. Major General James Grant judged the campaign "a cheap
and complete victory." In private, the Continental leaders did not
disagree with Grant's assessment. "We all think our cause is nearly
ruined," Israel Putnam confided to a correspondent. Tories embraced
Howe's arriving troops with open arms; a neighborhood woman had
been the first to enter Fort George in September to grind the American flag underfoot in the mud. As fall turned into winter, the presence
of thousands of American prisoners of war—ill, filthy, depressed,
crowded into makeshift prisons scattered throughout the city and floating on its waterways—was a daily reminder of imperial triumph and
rebel ineptitude.[42]

One of the luckier prisoners was John Adlum, a seventeen-year-old
Pennsylvanian who had been captured at Fort Washington. Confined
to a private house in the city, Adlum was permitted to run errands, a
privilege that allowed him to move through the streets and make
covert contact with patriot civilians who now found themselves having to conceal their true allegiance. Late on Christmas day, a grocer
pulled Adlum into a back room and, while trying to say something to
him, stood speechless, overcome with emotion. "I looked at him and
thought him crazy or mad," Adlum wrote, "but as soon as he could
give utterance to his word he says to me, 'General Washington has defeated the Hessians at Trenton this morning and has taken 900 prisoners and six pieces of artillery!'" As news of Washington's victories at
Trenton and Princeton was spread through town by riders crossing the
Hudson, British expectations of a quick victory abruptly evaporated,
and Adlum's fellow prisoners took heart. Only one thing now seemed
sure: the war that George Washington had nearly lost in Brooklyn,
and William Howe had nearly won, would go on.[43]

By the end of 1776, then, New York was, once again, an outpost of the
British Empire—indeed, it was *the* outpost, the command center for all

of the king's military operations in North America. Each tide seemed to mark the arrival or departure of another fleet of warships or troop transports, carrying the war to the rebel enemy wherever he lurked—in Connecticut, the Delaware Valley, Rhode Island, the Chesapeake, Martha's Vineyard, northern New Jersey, the Carolinas. The Sons of Liberty and their allies were gone, having fled to safer quarters or joined the rebel army. Taking their place was a continuous influx of loyalist refugees from Boston, Newport, Philadelphia, Norfolk, and Savannah, cities held by the insurgents. They settled into houses formerly owned by rebel families—dwellings confiscated by British authorities who, as in some Old Testament chastisement, marked their front doors or lintels with the initials "G.R." (George Rex) before distributing them to refugees.[44]

Once again, civilian New Yorkers got into the martial spirit, especially when lured by the prospect of profit. "Seldom a day passes without a prize by the privateers," boasted William Tryon, New York's wartime royal governor, in March 1779. Over 180 vessels sailed forth to prey on rebel maritime traffic, returning with fortunes in flour, sugar, tobacco, and gunpowder, all of which flowed through the city's shops and auction rooms. Perhaps six thousand men and boys, including deserters from Washington's army, crowded onto the privateers in order to strike a blow for the empire while filling their pockets. Even loyalist ladies got into the act. In 1779, several well-heeled Manhattan women agreed to fit out a "fast privateer" christened *The Fair American* (later renamed *The Royal Charlotte*, after the queen) to "aid in chastising the rebels."[45]

Other forays against the rebel enemy were fueled more by hatred than by profit taking. As displaced Tories flooded into the city, they joined New York loyalists in military units raised to wreak vengeance on their persecutors. They did not have to travel far, for a sporadic but deeply bitter guerilla war persisted just beyond the city's outskirts. The Continental Congress continued to control much of the territory surrounding the city, including parts of northern New Jersey, the Hudson Valley, eastern Long Island, and coastal Connecticut. As a result, the so-called neutral ground of farmland lying between the British and American lines became a zone of recurrent skirmishes, pillaging, kidnapping, and terrorist raids conducted by partisans of both sides, as well as by apolitical marauders who used the war as a cover for plundering. Tory dragoons and irregulars known as "cowboys" rode at night through southern Westchester and northeastern New Jersey, punishing alleged pro-rebel farmers by stealing their livestock and burning their homes. Patriot "skinners" responded in kind. In their boldest retaliation, a band of New Jersey rebels crossed the Hudson in dead of night and ransacked the suburban mansion of Brigadier General Oliver De Lancey, one of the city's leading Tories, a few miles above the city.[46]

One community of loyalists had an added incentive for crushing the revolution. In November 1775, Lord Dunmore, the royal governor of Virginia, had issued a proclamation offering freedom to any slave who ran away from a rebel owner in order to aid His Majesty's forces in putting down the rebellion. Nine months later, Dunmore was on Staten Island, recruiting additional runaways to join the "Ethiopian Regiment" he had brought north to take part in Howe's New York campaign. Sir Henry Clinton, who replaced the unsuccessful Howe as British commander in North America in 1778, repeated Dunmore's promise, making New York City a mecca for hundreds of slaves who fled patriot masters in order to gain their liberty by serving the king. Patriot families who had fled the city for refuge in New Jersey or the Hudson Valley learned to their consternation that their bondsmen preferred to slip back into Manhattan in order to become black Tories.[47]

But the influx into New York also included refugees from farther afield, men with names like Ralph Henry (lately the property of the patriot who had declared, "Give me liberty or give me death!") and Harry Washington (who viewed British Manhattan with emotions different from those of his recent master, the rebel commander in chief). British warships raiding the Chesapeake and the Carolinas brought back whole extended families of runaways from rebel plantations. In Manhattan, the men enlisted as foragers, teamsters, woodcutters, seamen, and soldiers, while their wives found employment as laundresses, seamstresses, and hospital orderlies. Fugitive slaves and free blacks understood that the British offer of emancipation was opportunistic and one-sided; loyalist masters were permitted to keep their human property, and slave auctions continued on the wharves of British Manhattan. But they also recognized that serving the British was their best hope for freedom. A revolution led by Virginia planters was most decidedly not going to provide their ticket to emancipation.[48]

For all their determination to sustain the empire, loyal civilians faced another, bleaker side of wartime New York, one that threatened to overwhelm them. With the British army in residence consuming enormous quantities of local foodstuffs, hay, and firewood, supplies plummeted and retail prices skyrocketed, staggering even well-to-do civilian families. Overcrowding and homelessness also became endemic. Hundreds of poor squatters—workers and seamen, British enlisted men, refugee families, prostitutes—hunkered down in the charred ruins of the city's burned district, where they scavenged fragments of ship's sails and spars to raise roofs over their heads. To respectable New Yorkers, "Canvasstown" stood as an open sore, but it was also a vivid proof of the war's lingering disorder.[49]

Tories grew increasingly unhappy with the way the British military was managing the city's affairs. The refusal by Clinton and royal governor William Tryon to reinstate civil courts and a representative assembly was an affront to some of the Crown's most ardent local allies. So were the bribes, kickbacks, and padded contracts that made a mockery of honest dealing in the army's local provisioning system. New Yorkers inundated the army's courts-martial with charges of theft, assault, and rape against marauding redcoats; officers often let their accused men off lightly. Those New Yorkers with open eyes and open consciences were, perhaps, also appalled by the condition of the thousands of rebel prisoners of war—sick, hungry, "mere walking skeletons . . . overrun with lice from head to foot," as one captive put it—who were crammed into poorly adapted warehouses, confiscated churches, and decrepit "prison hulks" that the British kept anchored in Wallabout Bay and the harbor. (As many as 18,000 of these prisoners may have died in and around Manhattan from diseases aggravated by hunger, cold, and abuse, dwarfing the war's 6,800 American battlefield deaths and making them the largest group of human beings to perish during the city's entire military history.) So disenchanted had the king's loyal New Yorkers become by March 1782, one of them claimed, that if George Washington attacked with his army, half the city's populace "would receive him with open arms."[50]

The failure of the British military to bag the fox, to bring Washington to ground and end the rebellion, was the single most aggravating topic of conversation in Manhattan's taverns and drawing rooms. The fox himself had New York on his mind more or less constantly. He had learned on the ridges and farms of Brooklyn that he would lose the war if he tried to fight the king's army in conventional open-field battles with inferior numbers, armaments, and supplies. "The war should be defensive," Washington wrote nine days after the East River evacuation. "We should, on all occasions, avoid a general action . . . unless compelled by a necessity into which we ought never to be drawn." Let the British get frustrated and weary, Washington argued, by avoiding battle when it offered the enemy the prospect of a decisive victory. Let the war drag on until Parliament and the English people got tired of it. The lesson Washington learned from the near disaster in Kings County was the lesson he would hew to through the seven years of war that followed.[51]

Washington also recognized the city as a prize to be retaken. "New York is the first and capital object upon which every other is dependent," he wrote. "The loss of the army and fleet there would be one of the severest blows the English nation could experience." The question was how to do it while avoiding a "general action" in which his forces would be hopelessly outnumbered and crushed. The answer was to enlist the revolution's French allies in a coordinated attack on Manhattan. Three times between the summer of 1778 and the summer of 1780, Washington sought to enlist the French navy for a joint assault on New York. Twice, Admiral Charles-Hector, Comte d'Estaing, drew near the port with a fleet of warships and transports carrying troops, as Washington prepared his main army, encamped in the hills around White Plains, for an attack on Manhattan. But each time, d'Estaing sailed away, evidently daunted by the prospect of facing Admiral Howe in the city's Upper Bay. A third time, in 1780, the Marquis de Lafayette attempted to convince General Rochambeau that New York, "the pivot on which turn the operations of the enemy," warranted conquest. But Rochambeau concluded that a vast fleet and thirty thousand fit men would be required to win a siege of Manhattan, a number even the combined Franco-American forces could not muster, and Washington had to acquiesce—for the time being.[52]

The persistent threat of an American or French attack rattled many in New York, both in and out of uniform. Howe and Clinton had already turned Manhattan and its environs into an armed camp, a place girdled by fences made of intertwined tree trunks and branches, earth embankments bristling with sharpened stakes, and hilltop artillery batteries. Despite the fortifications, many expected Washington to make a bold move sooner or later. It was now the loyalists' turn to fear enemies within the gates—covert rebels and spies who watched everything and reported it to the rebel foe.

Indeed, these hidden enemies did exist within the city, and George Washington used every opportunity to employ as many as he could secure. The commander took a personal hand in creating a network of spies inside New York City, men who could report on troop and ship movements, regimental strength and location, and the state of provisions and morale. Washington, who relished playing the role of spy master, corresponded directly with several key agents. One network ran from a Peck Slip store from which shopkeepers Amos Underhill and Robert Townsend wrote coded letters (some in an invisible ink) carried by courier to agent Abraham Woodhull at Setauket, Long Island. Woodhull sent the letters across Long Island Sound to a command post in Connecticut, from which riders carried them to wherever Washington's headquarters happened to be.[53]

His preoccupation with the city also led Washington to grasp a useful truth: so long as New York remained the British center of power, it could also be made a burden on the British war effort. Clinton's need to protect the city forced him to keep troops there who might more effectively be used in aggressive campaigns against the rebels elsewhere. Washington wanted to keep it that way, so repeatedly during the war his army launched raids into British-held territory daringly close to the city—at Paulus Hook (today Jersey City) in 1779, Staten Island in 1780, and Washington Heights in 1781. These hit-and-run attacks accomplished their goal of keeping numerous regiments of redcoats, Hessians, and Tory militia tied down in defensive positions, as well as reminding Manhattan's loyalist populace that their enemy remained cunning and close.[54]

Even more critically, the prospect of an American attack on New York City repeatedly led the British to deplete their forces in the field to reinforce Manhattan, thereby seriously hampering the king's military effort throughout the colonies. "The most powerful diversion that can be made in favor of the Southern states will be a respectable force in the neighborhood of New York," Washington wrote in March 1781, and he now kept the bulk of his army in a ring of encampments around the city's periphery, from Morristown in New Jersey and West Point on the Hudson to King's Bridge on the Bronx side of the Harlem River and Danbury in Connecticut.[55]

For the fourth time, the prospect of a concerted Franco-American assault on New York surfaced in the spring of 1781, when, in a conference in Connecticut, Washington and Rochambeau agreed that the attack should be attempted, provided that an expected French fleet commanded by Admiral de Grasse made its landfall near the port. Once again, Washington believed that, at the very least, a French naval blockade of the harbor might frighten Clinton into recalling thousands of troops from Virginia, where they were enjoying success against Continental forces. Not until mid-August did dispatches arrive from de Grasse, explaining that he would make his landfall with twenty-eight ships and three thousand men in the Chesapeake rather than near the mouth of the Hudson. Washington and Rochambeau abandoned the plan to attack New York, agreeing instead that six thousand Continental and French soldiers encamped in Westchester would march south to cooperate with Lafayette's southern army and de Grasse in bottling up British troops on the Virginia coast.[56]

Once more indulging his taste for covert operations, Washington planned an elaborate ruse to conceal his true intentions from Clinton. Continental regiments attacked British outposts near the city, as if in preparation for a major assault; in reality, Washington left a mere 2,500 men near the city to keep Clinton's 14,500 soldiers pinned down. The Americans and French left fires burning in largely empty camps in the New Jersey meadows, much as Clinton's men themselves had done during the Battle of Brooklyn; army bread ovens were set up to convince Clinton's spies that a siege was in the offing. Meanwhile, by crossing the Hudson from Westchester and marching to the west and south of the city, the Continental and French armies slipped away. Not until the last week of August did New Yorkers learn that they had been spared—and that Washington's true target was the 7,000-man army operating in coastal Virginia under the command of General Charles Lord Cornwallis.[57]

As Washington's army and de Grasse's fleet closed in on Cornwallis at Yorktown, the British field commander sent tense dispatches to Clinton, pleading for reinforcements to withstand the enemy siege; if they did not arrive, he warned, he would leave the field to the enemy and retreat toward New York. Leading Tories in the city were beside themselves with anxiety. "A week will decide perhaps the ruin or salvation of the British Empire!" William Smith Jr. wrote upon hearing of the situation at Yorktown. On September 5, de Grasse fended off a British fleet sent from New York in the waters off the Virginia Capes. Cornwallis, however, sat tight, persuaded not to evacuate by letters from Clinton promising that additional troops were making their way to him.[58]

But Cornwallis's situation on the Yorktown Peninsula was getting desperate; the relief force of five thousand men that Clinton now organized seemed to be taking an agonizingly long time to leave the East River and Upper Bay. Finally, on October 19, the fleet set sail. Four days later, New Yorkers were stunned by news carried into the city by a group of redcoats arriving from New Jersey as part of a prisoner exchange: Cornwallis had surrendered on the very day the relief force had sailed forth. Many refused to believe it; Smith felt it was probably another rebel ruse. But as other travelers arrived with confirmation, hearts sank throughout loyalist New York.[59]

On the afternoon of November 25, 1783, General George Washington, mounted on a white steed and accompanied by General Henry Knox and New York State's revolutionary governor, George Clinton (no relation to Sir Henry), led a triumphal procession down Broadway to mark the conclusion of the British evacuation from the city and

thus the end of the War for Independence. For the thousands of
"rebels"—now confirmed citizens of the United States of America—
who had flocked back to their old homes in New York City, Washington's entry represented the victorious end of an eight-year struggle
that had repeatedly brought chaos to the island of Manhattan. On the
whole, only minimal friction attended Washington's reentry. The reason for the generally tranquil mood was starkly clear: not only had the
bulk of the British army and navy already withdrawn, but thousands of
Tories had also left the city to begin new lives as refugees from their
homeland.[60]

In early 1782, when a majority in Parliament had supported resolu-
tions to end "a fruitless war" and concede American independence,
the dark hour that loyalists had been dreading descended upon them.
"Never was despair and distraction stronger painted than in the coun-
tenances I momentarily see," noted an Englishman in Manhattan.
Writing in his diary, William Smith Jr. was more succinct: "We are
slighted and cast off as beggars." While some loyalist New Yorkers received pensions and honors from the British government, many never
fully made peace with their sense of abandonment and betrayal or the
bitterness of exile.[61]

By March 1782, wealthy loyalists had begun putting their suburban
estates on the auction block and making arrangements to immigrate to
England or the British West Indies. By autumn the British government
had offered to transport loyalists, free of charge, to land set aside for
them in Nova Scotia. By the spring of 1783, flotillas of brigs, sloops,
and schooners were beginning to shuttle back and forth between the
East River and the Bay of Fundy. New York became the designated embarkation point for this mass migration, and loyalist families flooded
into Manhattan from all points in the colonies. The city became host
to one of the greatest out-migrations in American history. In sum,
twenty-nine thousand civilians left, as did twenty thousand redcoats
and German mercenaries. Some nine thousand loyalists settled at Port
Roseway, almost overnight turning that Nova Scotian outpost into a
frontier replica of Tory Manhattan. Three thousand black loyalists left
New York to take up the king's offer of land in Nova Scotia, although
the racism and poverty many experienced there eventually led some to

the abolitionist colony of Sierra Leone. Other black Tories accompanied the king's army back to England; Bill Richmond, born a slave on Staten Island, became one of the British Isles' most renowned bareknuckle boxing champions.[62]

The patriots who flooded into New York City in the wake of the British evacuation by and large wanted to put the war and its miseries behind them. New Yorkers of all political views heeded the toast that returning patriots offered at a banquet at Cape's Tavern honoring Washington: "May an uninterrupted commerce soon repair the ravages of war." True to form, Isaac Sears and Alexander McDougall, once leaders of the leather aprons, embraced the city's revived spirit of commerce: Sears as a merchant in the incipient China trade, McDougall as first president of the Bank of New York. Manhattan was back in business; indeed, thanks to its many wartime industries, it had never really been out of business, even at the war's most critical moments.[63]

Yet despite the rebounding of the city's economy, the war's handiwork lingered, as did an awareness of how the city's vulnerability to attack had opened the door to occupation, chaos, and devastation. In the incised letters "G.R." adorning doorposts, in the weed-sprouting earth embankments surrounding the city, in the charred shambles of Canvasstown, in the unmarked graves of countless war prisoners, and in memories of neighbors, friends, and enemies gone forever, the Revolutionary War, the single most destructive sequence of events in the city's history, remained omnipresent. Little did New Yorkers suspect that another revolution would soon slow the healing of their own wounds and open new ones.

CHAPTER 5

Hot Shot and Heavy Metal
France, England, and War at Sea, 1793–1815

The spectators had come to see a duel, and they were not disappointed. This duel, however, differed from those fought on land by two gentlemen armed with pistols. It was being fought by six hundred men and boys at the muzzles of sixty-four cannon on the waters of the Atlantic, six miles southeast of Sandy Hook. It was the morning of August 1, 1793, and excited New Yorkers lined the decks of nine chartered excursion boats to watch Jean-Baptiste Bompard, captain of the French Republic's frigate *Embuscade* ("Ambush"), take up the gauntlet thrown down by Captain William Augustus Courtney of His Majesty's frigate *Boston*. Four days earlier, Courtney, cruising off the Narrows near New York harbor, had asked an American go-between to carry a challenge to Wall Street's Tontine Coffee House, crossroads of Manhattan's maritime traffic: "Tell Captain Bompard that I have come all the way from Halifax, on purpose to take the *Embuscade*, and I shall be very happy to see her out this way." By July 31, Bompard had posted his reply in the Coffee House, for all to see: "Citizen Bompard will wait on Captain Courtney tomorrow, agreeably to invitation; he hopes to find him at the Hook."[1]

The *Embuscade* sailed forth from its anchorage on the lower Manhattan waterfront to defend the honor of the French Republic and the Revolution that had given it birth, and to defy the English foe the Republic had been fighting on the high seas for six months. At 5:30 in the

morning, the *Embuscade* found the *Boston*, and the battle began. For
two hours, the two frigates hammered at each other, while the boats full
of city spectators (many with bets riding on the outcome) bobbed on
the waters nearby. According to a French prisoner on board the *Boston*,
Bompard could be seen calmly striding the quarterdeck of his ship
"with his hands behind his back, now and then . . . taking a pinch of
snuff," seemingly impervious to the efforts of English musketeers to gun
him down. The *Embuscade*'s artillery shattered the *Boston*'s main top-
mast and hurled it into the sea. By around 7:30, when the *Boston* dis-
engaged and limped southward toward Delaware Bay, Courtney and at
least eleven of his crew were dead; between twenty and thirty others
were wounded. Bompard was unscathed, but he, too, had ten men
killed and fifteen wounded. After pursuing the *Boston* for a while, the
Frenchmen pounced on the *Two Brothers*, a "richly laden" cargo brig
flying the Portuguese flag (despite Portugal's claim of neutrality, the
French Republic viewed it as an English ally). The *Embuscade* sailed
triumphantly back into New York harbor with its prize in tow.[2]

In New York as elsewhere throughout the nation, the gallantry of
the *Embuscade*, and the presence along the coast of at least fourteen
French privateers (some of which had recruited sailors in Manhattan
and other US ports), triggered an outpouring of pro-French fervor.
When the *Embuscade* returned to port after battle, New Yorkers hoisted
Bompard on their shoulders as a hero. When his wounded sailors were
carried off the vessel, one witness noted, "the ladies tore their chemises
to bind up their wounds. . . . Surgeons and nurses in numbers repaired
to the sick ward." In gratitude to New Yorkers, Bompard's crew formally
presented their tattered battle flag to the city's Tammany Society "as a
token of that respect which those virtuous patriots merit, in our opinion, from their Republican Brethren of France."[3]

The gesture was significant. Originally an apolitical patriotic club,
the Tammany Society was rapidly becoming a nerve center for the New
York allies of Secretary of State Thomas Jefferson and Congressman
James Madison, men who believed that the brave new world ushered in
by the French Revolution—a world wiped clean of kings, aristocrats,
and priestly superstition—represented the best and brightest legacy of
America's own revolution. Tammany Hall would soon become an orga-

nizing base for the Democratic-Republicans (or Republicans for short), the incipient national political party through which Jefferson and Madison sought to bind the fortunes of the United States to those of revolutionary France, while maintaining a cautious neutrality in the maritime shooting war.

Not everyone, however, was cheering the *Embuscade*'s valor. Some New Yorkers remained unconvinced that the rights of humankind required sympathy for the radicals who had overthrown the French monarchy a year earlier, beheaded their king in January, and declared war on Britain in February. Americans had responded with near-unanimous enthusiasm to the Paris uprising in 1789. But as news of massacres, mass executions, and plans to export revolution throughout Europe reached New York, enthusiasm evaporated in some quarters. The ties of language, culture, and Protestantism continued to predispose numerous New Yorkers toward England rather than France, despite vivid memories of the hardships of the War for Independence. The city's economy also remained predominantly tied to the transatlantic trade with London and Bristol, not Le Havre or Bordeaux. Many wealthy merchants and lawyers, fearing the French Revolution as a contagion fatal to order and hierarchy on both sides of the Atlantic, soon were flocking into the emerging Federalist Party to quash the anarchic delusions of "the gaping infatuated mob" and to vanquish Jefferson's Republicans.[4]

No wonder, then, that angry words and deeds repeatedly disrupted the chorus of huzzas for Bompard. Politically, the summer of 1793 had been a long and hot one in New York City. By June, the "vast throng" that filled the Tontine Coffee House every evening had divided into "two parties," and one night a brawl erupted between "Whig & Tory, or, to modernize it, Democrat & Aristocrat"—labels that linked the fracas to two revolutions. On the afternoon of the *Embuscade*'s triumphal return to the city, a Tontine crowd roughed up a British naval lieutenant, who escaped only by jumping over an iron railing to the street below. Charles William Janson, an English businessman, believed that a similarly pro-French "mob" at the Tontine "would have torn me piece-meal had I been pointed at as a stranger just arrived from England." In mid-August, two melees broke out between roaming bands of French and English sailors.[5]

The passions of the French Revolution, and the global war it had sparked, were boiling over into the streets of New York. Yet even the most agitated Republicans and Federalists recognized that the United States had no navy, that its small army might subdue frontier Indians but was good for little else, and that local militia units would be no match for a European enemy sailing in through the Narrows. In their cooler moments, New Yorkers could hope that the Atlantic would be vast enough to keep the conflicts of the Old World at bay. But they would learn over the next twenty years that the agents of conflict would not stay away.

The truth was that New Yorkers could not easily disentangle their domestic concerns from international affairs. For one thing, Manhattan remained a global crossroads, attracting a dissonant array of émigrés: French refugees, some from the mother country and others fleeing a bloody slave rebellion in Saint Domingue (Haiti), who brought their own antagonistic royalist and revolutionary loyalties with them; Irish emigrants, many aflame with the French Revolution's challenge to English domination; radical English workingmen and intellectuals, alienated from their king; loyal Britons like Janson, appalled by the French assault on the very idea of monarchy itself. These adversaries sharpened the animosities of native Republicans and Federalists, already busy hurling the epithets "monarchist" and "Jacobin" at each other.

More crucially, the city's economy was also enmeshing its inhabitants in the European conflict. New York was riding the wave of a new commercial prosperity that depended on the ability of its merchants to exploit the global shortage in shipping caused by the Anglo-French war. As the French and British navies blockaded each other's ports and seized each other's ships, American shippers—New Yorkers prominent among them—stepped into the breach. New York–based brigs and schooners, their holds bulging with English manufactures, French West Indian sugar and molasses, and Hudson Valley flour, grain, and lumber, were soon conveying highly profitable cargoes across the Atlantic, the Caribbean, and the Indian Ocean. This trade positioned New York to surpass Philadelphia as the nation's busiest seaport by the mid-1790s. "Every thought, word, look, and action of the multitude seemed to be absorbed by commerce," noted an English visitor a few years later as he walked through streets "jammed up with carts, drays, and wheel-barrows" near the East River docks.[6]

As the maritime war dragged on, and neither Britain nor France proved able to score a knockout blow, the belligerents began to cast hostile glances at America's merchant fleets, the "neutral carriers" whose cargoes provided aid and comfort to the enemy. By January 1794, Governor Clinton was warning the state legislature of "the naked and exposed condition of our principal seaport" and its vulnerability to "insult and invasion." The war-driven trade that was enriching them, New Yorkers understood, might end up imperiling their city; taking advantage of Europe's disorder might draw them into Europe's conflicts. If London or Paris felt sufficiently provoked, either the British or French navy might descend on New York to blockade it, attack it, or even occupy it.[7]

Over the next decade, the issue of whether Britain or France posed a greater threat seesawed back and forth. In 1794, as the Royal Navy seized 150 American vessels suspected of trade with the French West Indies, contingents of civilian volunteers worked to fortify the Upper Bay, restoring the trenches and redoubts built on Governors Island by American troops in 1776. In 1796, when the French Revolutionary government authorized French vessels to prey on American merchantmen, the New York state and city governments used volunteers and paid laborers to tear up the Battery promenade, "the finest walk in the world" in the view of one observer, to make room for new gun carriages and breastworks. Eager enlistees in the Patriotic Blues, Washington Troop of Horse, and other volunteer "uniform companies" drilled on the Battery and readied themselves to "march at a minute's notice" if the French dared to land.[8]

Meanwhile, partisan bands continued to taunt each other on the streets, as Samuel Malcolm, President John Adams's young secretary, learned during a visit to New York in July 1798. While singing "Hail, Columbia," a Federalist anthem, during an evening stroll to the Battery with friends, Malcolm was recognized. In the words of a Federalist Philadelphia paper, a crowd "of boatmen and low fellows, from the wharves and docks, immediately collected . . . instigated by the deluding demon of French Jacobinism," and retaliated with the French

Revolutionary song "Ca Ira." A brawl erupted, with the "low fellows" outnumbering and beating Malcolm and his comrades. Even more sinister was the spiking, or disabling, of one of the Battery cannon by persons unknown, evidence to Federalists that pro-French extremism was becoming outright treason. A Europe at war seemed to guarantee that Manhattan would remain a battleground in microcosm.[9]

On March 4, 1801, New York's Republicans greeted the presidential inauguration of their hero, Thomas Jefferson, with cannon fusillades at the Battery, the ringing of church bells, and the hoisting of colors on vessels in the harbor. By voting for the "Sage of Monticello," New York's Jeffersonian coalition of artisans and liberal merchants had played a pivotal role in what the new president himself called the "Revolution of 1800," the nation's first peaceful transition of power from one party to another.

Gaining power, however, did not cool the hostility of Republicans toward England, especially as the Royal Navy replaced the French as primary predator on American merchant vessels. Perpetually shorthanded during the wars of the Napoleonic era, British commanders resorted to impressment, seizing any able-bodied mariner or landsman they deemed to be a British subject. Seamen aboard American cargo ships were considered fair game; indeed, many were native Britons who had never obtained US citizenship. But by the late 1790s, the taverns and coffeehouses of waterfront Manhattan were also alive with stories of Royal Navy captains seizing naturalized American citizens and even native-born Yankees. The Royal Navy justified its indiscriminate roundups by arguing that thousands of British sailors were working on vessels out of New York, Philadelphia, Baltimore, and Boston under the cover of fraudulently obtained citizenship certificates (known as "Protections") that were issued by federal customs officials and circulated freely in waterfront boardinghouses.[10]

But for New Yorkers who now feared British confiscation of men as well as of "contraband" goods and vessels, the cry of "Free Trade and Sailors' Rights" drowned out arguments over legal niceties. In new neighborhoods of modest two-story clapboard houses that replaced meadows and swamps north and east of the old city limits, families of working seamen and artisans felt the full impact of impressment in the void left by a missing husband and father or the fear that one's brother or friend might be the next sailor to disappear into the ranks of the Royal Navy. An unknown number of New Yorkers shared the experience that befell John Bateman in early 1807. A mariner who lived near the East River waterfront, Bateman was taken off the brig *Ulysses* at sea by the press gang of HMS *Demerara*. Nine months later, Bateman managed to get a letter to the US Customs office in New York: "I have got a wife & children in Bedlow Street. . . . [I have] suffered much in my mind in consequence of my helpless family. . . . They may be in much want of all necessaries. . . . I am all they have to look to for that." Bateman added that, for alleged "neglect of duty," he had suffered a dozen lashes applied to his back.[11]

It was bad enough when New Yorkers went to work at sea, only to disappear into British servitude; worse yet when the Royal Navy dared to harass merchantmen in the city's own waters. British warships, which periodically dropped anchor in the Upper Bay to exchange dispatches and take on provisions, also stopped, seized, and sent to Halifax any vessel they deemed to be trading with the French. On April 24, 1806, the moment New Yorkers of both political parties had long feared finally arrived. On that day, half a mile off Sandy Hook, the sixty-gun *Leander* signaled the New York–based sloop *Richard* to stop for inspection. The *Richard's* crew either misunderstood the signal or decided to make a run into port. In response, the *Leander* fired a warning shot across the *Richard's* bow, decapitating crewman John Pearce. Crowds of New Yorkers calling for revenge poured into the streets. Pearce was buried at public expense amid protest meetings condemning the "repeated outrages committed by foreign ships of war at the mouths of our harbors."[12]

Royal Navy forays into the city's streets stirred similar emotions. In early September 1807, the frigate HMS *Jason* sent a boat into the harbor with dispatches for New York's British consulate. Upon docking, six of her crew immediately scattered. Drawing his pistols, the boat's furious lieutenant threatened to shoot the deserters if they didn't return to their posts. But New Yorkers were in no mood to cooperate. A crowd closed around the refuge-seeking deserters and handled the lieutenant "very roughly." New Yorkers had the added pleasure of learning that John Bateman, now a crewman on the *Jason*, had been returned to his family on Bedlow Street after US Customs officials persuaded the *Jason*'s commander that Bateman was a bona fide American citizen. But small victories like these did not answer the question that increasingly dominated the conversation of the coffee houses as tensions escalated between the United States and Great Britain: if the Royal Navy unleashed the fullness of its fury, how could New York withstand it?[13]

One man thought he knew how to safeguard New York from an enemy fleet. At age fifty-five, Lieutenant Colonel Jonathan Williams of the US Army Corps of Engineers had enjoyed a varied career by the time he arrived in New York in 1805. Born in Boston, Williams had studied at Harvard and had joined his great-uncle, Benjamin Franklin, in London in 1770, becoming his private secretary. Settling in Philadelphia after the revolution, Williams became a successful merchant, an associate justice in the city's courts, and the author and translator of treatises on navigation, botany, mathematics, and military engineering. The latter helped secure for him a major's commission in the army from President Adams. His work also brought him to the attention of Thomas Jefferson. Despite Williams's Federalist loyalties, the new president persuaded him to accept an appointment as first superintendent of the new national military academy at West Point in 1802. In 1805, Williams accepted a subsidiary assignment, the kind of job to which his role as the army's ranking engineer entitled him: the task of planning the fortification of New York City. Williams plunged into the work. From a base camp on Governors Island, he sent forth boatloads of engineers and soldiers equipped with plumb lines, cables, and surveying equipment to gauge the distance between shores and the depths of navigable channels.[14]

By the summer of 1807, Williams had drafted a sweeping plan for recasting the port of New York as a defensive zone. He believed that the main danger to the city was the prospect of a British fleet arriving off the tip of Manhattan to bottle up the East River and effectively throttle its commerce; the Royal Navy could then "put the city under contribution," demanding a large ransom in return for not bombarding it or burning it to the ground. The inner harbor, moreover, now

Jonathan Williams, mastermind of New York's harbor
fortifications. Engraving by Charles Balthazar Julien
Fevret de Saint-Mémin, *Jonathan Williams, Head-and-
Shoulders Portrait, Right Profile,* 1798. LIBRARY OF CONGRESS.

lacked some of its traditional safeguards. In 1790, New Yorkers had
torn down the fort Cryn Fredericks had designed to protect the foot of
Manhattan, to make way for an executive mansion—one that President Washington never occupied, since the capital moved from New
York to Philadelphia that year.[15]

To counter the threat of an enemy fleet holding Manhattan hostage,
Williams proposed a network of new fortifications placed strategically
around the Upper Bay. The latest European treatises advocated the
erection of multitiered stone batteries, two or three stories in height,
encasing parallel lines of cannon. Williams agreed and called for six
new stone and mortar citadels: two on Governors Island, one each for
Bedloe's and Ellis islands, one on a rock platform just off the tip of Manhattan (Castle Clinton), and another at the foot of Duane Street a mile
up the Hudson. With the outer walls of the main installations hewn of
red sandstone blocks up to seven feet thick, these forts would stand

ready with their tiers of guns—"heavy metal," in Williams's words—to saturate an approaching naval foe with salvos of iron cannonballs, grapeshot, canister, mortar fire, and "hot shot," prepared in furnaces "for heating balls red hot." This chain of forts would be able to lay down overlapping fields of artillery fire, deterring the Royal Navy from trying to approach the mouth of the East River or sailing up the Hudson. For the Narrows, the city's outer portal, Williams called for a line of massive stone blocks to be sunk into the harbor bed, with their tops protruding over the surface of the water. A massive barrier chain would stretch from shore to shore, with artillery at both ends. While one channel would be left free for the passage of friendly vessels, ship hulls would be sunk between the other blocks to prevent enemy entry.[16]

It was a bold, visionary plan, and many New Yorkers responded enthusiastically. But critics pounced mercilessly. Thomas Paine, for instance, argued that filling the port's channels with stone blocks might actually dam the tide, leaving the city's wharves and those of the Hudson Valley high and dry. More crucial was the opposition of Jefferson's Treasury secretary, Albert Gallatin, who warned the president that Williams's "extravagant and inefficient" plan for the Narrows would be too expensive. Gallatin's scorn scuttled Williams's Narrows plan. But

Castle Williams, one of two forts designed by Jonathan Williams on Governors Island, photographed in the early twentieth century. Postcard, Hugh C. Leighton Co., c. 1908. AUTHOR'S COLLECTION.

city and state politicians improvised a funding scheme to pay for the other forts. Williams would get to impose his new, man-made military geography on the rocks and shifting sands of the shorelines of the Upper Bay. Five years of building, during which nothing seemed to quell John Bull's aggression on the high seas, brought the island and shoreline batteries to completion in the early months of 1812. By that time, James Madison had succeeded Jefferson as president, keeping political control of the country in the hands of the Republicans, who continued to bridle at English chauvinism. By the summer of that fateful year, New Yorkers would be thankful for the fortifications' presence—and praying that their thick walls and guns would keep an aroused and powerful foe at bay.[17]

On the morning of June 21, 1812, a squadron of three frigates, a brig, and a sloop of war commanded by Commodore John Rodgers sailed from New York bound for the open Atlantic. The war with Britain that many in New York had long expected had finally been declared by President Madison and Congress. The sailing of the squadron, bent on seizing English merchant ships and thus forcing the Royal Navy to defend British commerce and abandon its strategy of aggression, was the first official act of the War of 1812.[18]

British seizures and attacks on the high seas had accelerated in the years leading up to the war. Royal Navy cruisers "harass our entering and departing commerce," Madison had asserted in his war message to Congress; "to the most insulting pretensions they have added the most lawless proceedings in our very harbors." New Yorkers knew this all too well; during 1811, the frigate *Guerriere* and other Royal Navy vessels had plied the waters off Sandy Hook, looking for Napoleonic privateers, who were raiding British cargo ships, but also taking seamen and passengers off American vessels entering and exiting New York. For some New Yorkers, like those who gathered in City Hall Park to hear patriotic speeches by Revolutionary War veterans, the coming of war was thrilling. The economic embargo imposed by President Jefferson and the Non-Intercourse Act sustained by Madison had avoided war, but they had backfired, bringing economic woe to New York and other ports. War would redeem American honor; restore free trade on the seas to the relief and profit of the nation's merchants, craftsmen, and farmers; and humble the British foe.[19]

But many watching the warships sail out to sea frowned rather than cheered. New York's numerous Federalists—including those who had been elected to a majority on the Common Council, the city's legislature—largely opposed the war on principle, deriding it as a Jeffersonian adventure to satisfy western and southern "war hawks" lusting for the conquest of British Canada. Many Federalists also feared that the conflict would bring dire consequences to New York City; partners in most of the city's "large mercantile houses," for instance, had petitioned the Senate not to declare war. In their South Street counting rooms, worried merchants might admire the courage and bravado of Rodgers's little fleet, but they also knew that the commodore's five vessels and 1,500 seamen represented the US Navy's major concentration of force, while the Royal Navy, the most formidable maritime power on earth, possessed over one thousand ships manned by 146,000 sailors and marines. Indeed, the city's mayor, De Witt Clinton, sought to ride such fears into the White House. As the Federalist presidential candidate in 1812, this nephew of former New York governor and vice president George Clinton appeared to promise some mixture of firmness and mediation in response to British aggression. He narrowly lost the election to Madison that November, the first New York mayor to harbor presidential ambitions.[20]

The disparity between the American and British fleets, however, did not daunt New Yorkers who sought employment or profit from the war. By mid-October, twenty-six vessels "fitted out on private speculation" by waterfront merchants, bristling with over two hundred cannon and crowded with over two thousand eager men, had slipped out to sea to prey on British merchantmen. Privateers with jaunty, provocative names—the *Yorktown*, the *Retaliation*, the *Spitfire*—ranged from the coast of Surinam to the Azores and the Orkneys, capturing scores of British merchant vessels. Along with the fledgling Brooklyn Navy Yard established by the federal government in 1802, private shipyards lining the East River built, equipped, and repaired naval vessels. Hundreds of New York shipwrights also journeyed to the shores of lakes Ontario, Erie, and Champlain, where they built flotillas of brigs and gunboats to challenge British supremacy on fresh water.[21]

Meanwhile, a select group of New Yorkers inaugurated a new role for Manhattan as banker and underwriter to the government's wartime financial needs. In 1812, the government raised $3 million of its total $13 million in war debt from Manhattan merchants and banks. Shuttling between East River counting houses and Potomac offices, New Yorker Jacob Barker became de facto ambassador between Washington and a Wall Street beginning to flex its financial muscle. (The east end of that thoroughfare was becoming the city's enclave of banks, insurance offices, and brokerages, the place where waterfront merchants now gathered to invest the profits earned from overseas commerce in bonds and bank shares.) Barker received a fractional commission on every dollar he convinced a fellow creditor to subscribe, not to mention interest on the $100,000 or more of his own money he loaned directly. Other, bigger names in New York's financial community also jumped in. John Jacob Astor, soon to be America's first millionaire, played a crucial role in underwriting government paper, selling it to the public and collecting healthy commissions in the process. The success of privateers, shipwrights, and financiers affirmed a time-tested tradition: New Yorkers had a knack for finding the common ground between war and moneymaking.[22]

Out on the Atlantic, British naval commanders looked westward as they read orders from the admiralty in London and contemplated how best to put them into effect. Curtailing American overseas commerce was a key British strategy for ruining the enemy's economy and bringing him to terms, and from the onset of war, England brought its vastly superior navy to bear against American shipping, as Manhattan's merchants had feared. By early July 1812, a squadron of six British warships—HMS *Guerriere, Africa, Shannon, Sparta, Belvidera,* and *Aeolus*—sailed with impunity off Sandy Hook and the south shore of Long Island. Within three weeks they had seized fifteen American cargo vessels, among them four schooners and ships that called New York their home port.[23]

The Royal Navy turned up the heat further the following spring. In May, Admiral Sir John Borlase Warren, commander in chief of British forces in North American waters, proclaimed from his Bermuda headquarters a "most strict and rigorous blockade" on New York, Charleston, Savannah, and the mouth of the Mississippi (the Chesapeake and Delaware were already blockaded). By then, the forty-gun *Acasta*, the seventy-four-gun *Valiant*, and four other warships were already in place off the Hook to cut New York's lifeline of trade. When British commanders did not send "contraband" ships and cargoes to their prize courts in Halifax or Bermuda, they often ransomed them back to New Yorkers. Captain Lloyd of HMS *Plantagenet* made a specialty of this, picking up fishing smacks and small boats off Sandy Hook and selling them back to their owners for $100 or $200. In December 1813, Lloyd hit the jackpot when he stopped a coasting vessel from Philadelphia trying to head into New York. In its hold, Lloyd found a custom-made organ, ordered by vestrymen for Manhattan's Episcopalian St. John's Chapel, the place of worship for some of the city's wealthiest families. Lloyd exacted $2,000 from the church officers in return for delivering the instrument. Such depredations were sufficient to keep many of the city's oceangoing vessels at home. By September 1813, at least 140 brigs, ships, sloops, and schooners lay idle at their anchorages.[24]

American naval officers cooped up in the Brooklyn Navy Yard viewed the situation with impatience. True, the few seaworthy vessels at their disposal could not risk a direct confrontation with the concentrated fire power of the British squadron hovering nearby, but an opportunity to raid British merchant ships and thus dampen English enthusiasm for the war was being squandered. At the end of May 1813, Stephen Decatur, already a hero of the naval war against Tripoli in 1804, decided to make a run for it. As commander of a squadron that included the forty-four-gun *United States*, the thirty-eight-gun *Macedonian*, and the eighteen-gun *Hornet*, Decatur gambled that he could slip the ships through New York's maritime back door—the East River outlet to Long Island Sound, a passage unguarded by the British. To do so, however, he would need to maneuver the ships through the daunting waters of Hell Gate, a strait of treacherously shifting currents that had plagued mariners since Dutch days. The risks of running aground, or of shattering the bottoms of such large ships on Hell Gate's unforgiving rocks, were real. The unlikelihood of pulling off such a feat was a key reason for the laxness of Royal Navy patrols in western Long Island Sound.

On the night of May 18, the vessels in Decatur's squadron left their berths and headed up the East River. With luck and seamanship, Decatur got his ships through the gauntlet and out into safer waters. Soon, however, they faced a more formidable obstacle: a Royal Navy squadron of four ships carrying 230 cannon. Outgunned, Decatur sought safe haven at New London, Connecticut, where his flotilla remained bottled up for the rest of the war. To keep the American ships there, and to better police New York's back door, the British now blockaded the eastern end of Long Island Sound. Sir Thomas Masterman Hardy, captain of the seventy-four-gun *Ramillies*, assisted by the *Valiant*, the *Acasta*, and the thirty-eight-gun *Orpheus*, made Gardiner's Island, off the eastern tip of Long Island, a base from which to patrol the waters between Montauk and Block Island. Over the next year, British sailors freely ranged along the north shore of Long Island, buying provisions from friendly farmers and stealing sheep from unfriendly ones. British naval superiority at New York's two doorsteps seemed complete.[25]

Yet the British navy's show of force was more ambiguous than appearances suggested. London wanted to cripple American trade to end the war. But the pressing British imperative was to defeat Napoleon in Europe, an effort that required tons of foodstuffs and supplies for the redcoats slogging through a tough ground war against the French in Spain—matériel that America could offer in abundance. In short, the blockade of America worked at cross purposes with the war effort on the continent, and the pragmatic attraction of using American wheat, flour, pork, and beef to feed redcoats in Spain produced a highly porous blockade. British consuls routinely signed licenses that allowed American ship captains to sail without molestation to ports where their trade would aid the English war effort. While the British repeatedly changed the rules, at times tightening the blockade and disallowing licenses, a well-informed shipper looking out to sea from South Street had a fighting chance of remaining in business—although doing so might well entail trading with the enemy.[26]

Thus, during the summer of 1812, when the *Guerriere* and other frigates were seizing American vessels off Sandy Hook, dozens of others were arriving safely at their Manhattan berths. To be sure, some were

light, swift coasters that had slipped through Hell Gate or beat the
British to the Narrows. But many, sailing in flagrant violation of the
federal Non-Intercourse Act prohibiting trade with Britain, carried
British licenses. If they could endure the sneers of patriotic onlookers,
merchants and seamen could still make money, and safely, by keeping
the overseas British war machine well oiled. And even patriots had to
admit that such loopholes kept the city from feeling the full economic
brunt of John Bull's wrath. When Madison tried to crack down on such
commerce as a brazen betrayal of the war effort, he faced significant resistance in Congress before American vessels sailing under enemy licenses were made illegal.[27]

With British warships plying the waters off Sandy Hook and Long Island, New Yorkers took the threat of attack very seriously. They faced
it with Jonathan Williams's chain of harbor forts and with several new
batteries that were rushed to completion on the Greenwich Village
shore, at Corlears Hook facing the Navy Yard, and on Staten Island
overlooking the Narrows. But the protection of New York would also
take soldiers, and before long the city was playing host to a motley array of militia units. The city itself mustered ten regiments of infantrymen, three artillery regiments, and a cavalry squadron. There was the
Old Butcher Troop, consisting exclusively of men of that vocation,
dressed in buckskin breeches and blue coats trimmed with silver lace.
The Brooklyn Fusiliers were popularly known as the Katydids for the
green and yellow of their uniforms. By early 1813, 3,500 New York
and New Jersey militiamen and US Army troops guarded the city,
most of them posted to the harbor forts.[28]

Yet officials and officers warned that more men were needed. With
a frugal Congress refusing to expand the ranks of the regular army,
states tried to rely on their own militias. Able-bodied men ages eighteen to forty-five were legally obliged to serve in the state militia, but
New Yorkers both upstate and down resented duty as a burden that
took them away from their workshops or farms. Once the war began,
bad news from Canada, where American forces initially stumbled
from one humiliating disaster to another, hindered militia enlistments. Instead, many New Yorkers eligible for militia duty evaded it.

Rich men paid substitutes to serve in their place, as they were legally entitled to do; poorer men did not show up for musters or disappeared. The need for men produced the inevitable abuses; some made a wartime career of repeatedly enlisting for bounty money and deserting. One bounty jumper, caught and jailed on Governors Island, was put in front of a firing squad, blindfolded—and pardoned at the last second.[29]

While Daniel Tompkins, New York governor and commander of the Third US Military District, worried about inadequate numbers, he also fretted about the caliber of the men who *had* shown up. Whether from the far reaches of the Catskills or the Manhattan streets, the average militiaman was unruly and insufficiently trained. Moreover, arms and ammunition were in short supply. Few militiamen reenlisted after their ninety-day terms expired; green troops, ignorant of the rudiments of harbor defense, took their place. Major General Morgan Lewis complained that militia officers "permit their men to stray from their camp at all hours." One militiaman caught in larceny was led through the streets to the doleful melody of "The Rogue's March" with a sign reading "Thief" hanging around his neck; worse still, he was deprived of his whiskey ration for one month.[30]

One group of volunteers did render heroic service. Mobilized in the fall of 1812, the Sea Fencibles were meant to serve both on land and at sea as a "marine militia." Their mission was to guard the port's outer fringe, where the lonely sandbars and bluffs facing the Atlantic offered the British potential landings for invasion. The five hundred men of the Fencibles were recruited largely from the ranks of the city's seamen, boatmen, and fishermen, men liable to Royal Navy impressment and thus with a score to settle. Their commander, Jacob Lewis, had captained a privateer, the *Bunker Hill*, at the start of the war. While his surviving letters suggest a man of some education and literary polish, he was also at home in the East River's boatyards and sail lofts, and he shared the egalitarian republicanism of his men.

The weapons of the Sea Fencibles were the musket, the boarding pike, and, most importantly, the forty-five-foot gunboat armed with one or two cannon. Essentially a long rowboat, propelled by oars or by sail, it could carry about three dozen armed men. From its base at Spermaceti

Cove within the arm of Sandy Hook, Lewis's flotilla of thirty-one gunboats moved swiftly through the port's waters. The Federalist gentlemen who populated the navy's officer corps might smirk at this seaborne rabble, but New York City's government—thankful for any help it could get in protecting the coast—didn't. As for Commodore Lewis, he had full confidence in his men. "They shall be amphibious soldiers," he wrote to Secretary of State James Monroe. "I am perfectly satisfied to command what has been always despised by the Navy."[31]

For two years, Lewis and his men played cat and mouse with the British. In late March 1813, Admiral Warren announced to the admiralty his intention of seizing Sandy Hook and making it a base for British depredations on American shipping into and out of New York. Such a move would effectively make the British blockade of the Narrows airtight, and afford a launching point for further operations. Lewis, and other New Yorkers, sensed what was coming. "The enemy are at the Hook" was "the universal cry of the city," he wrote to Navy Secretary William Jones in May. A week later, seven boatloads of British sailors from the blockading warships tried to land on the Hook, relying on the dead of night and muffled oars to surprise the Fencibles stationed there; they were scared off when the aroused sentries started firing on them. The raid may have been less a concerted invasion than a ploy by the timorous Warren to appease an impatient admiralty. Nonetheless, the presence of the Fencibles had deterred a British assault on the city's threshold.[32]

Next, Lewis took the war to the British. On the Fourth of July, his men disguised a pilot boat, the *Yankee*, as a fishing smack. Three men posed as fishermen on deck; forty-three others, armed with muskets, hid on the foredeck and in the cabin. Sailing off the Hook, the *Yankee* soon lured its target, the British sloop of war *Eagle*, which had been seizing fishing boats and burning vessels at will. As the British sloop drew alongside, the Fencibles jumped from their cover and opened fire, killing a master's mate and a midshipman and capturing eleven Royal Marines. Jubilant spectators lined the Whitehall Dock at Manhattan's tip as the Sea Fencibles delivered the *Eagle* and its crew to the people of New York City as an Independence Day gift. Two months later, Lewis took twenty-six gunboats up the East River and through Hell Gate to harass a British frigate and schooner that were seizing vessels and landing sailors near Rye to steal sheep. After an artillery exchange in which neither side hit the other, the confrontation ended inconclusively. But the British ships withdrew toward the east end of Long Island Sound, and the Sea Fencibles could claim the skirmish as a victory.[33]

Lewis's Fencibles proved their mettle on land as well as at sea. One British tactic for taking American prizes was to drive them aground on New Jersey's Atlantic shore as they tried to make a run into New York, and Lewis kept his men on the lookout for vessels in distress. In November 1813, the schooner *John and Mary*, bound from New Orleans to New York with a lucrative cargo of cotton, sugar, and lead, lurched to a stop on the beach near the village of Long Branch, twelve miles south of Spermaceti Cove. Trapped by the predatory Captain Lloyd's seventy-four-gun *Plantagenet*, the hapless crew stood by as British sailors looted their schooner. Suddenly, one hundred Sea Fencibles materialized out of the dunes, having marched south from Sandy Hook. The Britons scattered to their boats and headed back to their mother ship. Captain Lloyd sent another boat ashore under a flag of truce. Lloyd insisted indignantly that the *John and Mary* was a legitimate prize of war. But he was also a reasonable man, and he offered to ransom the schooner and its cargo for $1,000. If the Americans refused, the *Plantagenet* would use its cannon to pummel Long Branch village, as well as the *John and Mary*, to pieces.

The Fencibles vowed to defend the grounded vessel. Under a cannonade from the British ship offshore, the Americans managed to offload much of the *John and Mary*'s cargo and cart it away; only one man was wounded. Losing interest, Lloyd sailed off in search of new prey, without leveling Long Branch. In January, the scene repeated itself, when the "flotilla men" marched down the beach again, this time dragging field artillery with them, to drive the British away from another grounded schooner, this one loaded with coal. The Fencibles safely and triumphantly brought the vessel into New York harbor. The boatmen of New York were proving to be their city's first and most pugnacious line of defense.[34]

Serving under arms was not the only way New Yorkers could defend their homes. War inflamed the imaginations of the city's mechanical tinkerers. Among them was Robert Fulton, an engineer who, while busy building the world's first truly viable steamboat in New York harbor, was convinced that his true place in history was as an inventor of weapons. Fulton had spent a decade in Europe trying to interest the British and French governments in sponsoring his two pet projects: a "plunging machine," or submarine for military use, and a "torpedo"—really a floating mine for blowing up enemy warships.[35]

Fulton's submarine was inspired by the Turtle, a contraption launched in New York harbor during the summer of 1776 by a Continental army soldier named David Bushnell. A pod-shaped wooden shell operated by a single passenger, the Turtle was supposed to get alongside the hull of Admiral Howe's flagship and attach a time bomb to it. The attempt proved abortive—as did Fulton's later efforts to interest the British and Napoleon in his refinements of Bushnell's design. Fulton arrived in New York in 1806, at the right moment to interest the city fathers and Jonathan Williams in his torpedoes—floating wooden boxes containing gunpowder and detonators that exploded on impact or when set off by a clockwork timer. Once more, glory eluded him; before a crowd of thousands gathered at the Battery, Fulton floated torpedoes toward an abandoned brig anchored offshore, but as a spectator reported, "the brig most obstinately refused to be decomposed."[36]

More successful was the scheme hatched by one John Scudder Jr. and two Manhattan merchants. In June 1813 Scudder fitted out a schooner, the Eagle, with a cargo to tantalize His Majesty's navy—barrels of flour, provisions, and naval stores. Below decks, however, he imbedded a deadly booby trap: ten kegs of gunpowder and a cask of sulphur, concealed next to gunlocks that would fire when a cord tied to two flour barrels was jerked. Scudder and a small crew sailed the Eagle through Hell Gate into the waters off New London, where Sir Thomas Hardy, commander of HMS Ramillies, took the bait. After Scudder's crew fled for shore, Hardy's men seized the schooner, anchored it near the British frigate, and began unloading cargo. Scudder watched anxiously from the shore for over three hours. Then, suddenly, "a column of fire" shot up several hundred feet, raining pitch and tar down on the Ramillies's deck. The Eagle, a British lieutenant, and ten of his sailors were instantly "blown to atoms." The only disappointment was that the explosion spared the *Ramillies* and its six hundred crewmen.[37]

For a moment Scudder and his comrades were the toast of the South Street taverns, but Robert Fulton was not to be outshone. By early 1814 he was planning his pièce de résistance of port defense: a massive behemoth of a ship designed to make New York harbor unassailable. Called both *Fulton I* and *Demologos* ("The People Speak"), it would be the world's first steam-powered warship, the culmination of the inventor's career as a visionary of steam propulsion and mechanized weaponry. Paid for by Congress, which spent close to a quarter of a million dollars in expectation that it would become a prototype for coastal defense, its gargantuan wooden hull gradually took form in a shipyard at Corlears Hook on the East River. A workforce of 260 men built its hull and machinery. Its foundry-cast engine cylinder, weighing over three tons and "said to be equal to 120 horses," was ready in July. Measuring 167 feet long, 56 feet in the beam, with vast paddle wheels and a hull 5 feet thick, *Demologos* would be a floating battery, carrying thirty-two guns firing "red hot shot," some of it weighing a hundred pounds—a mobile version of the forts with which Jonathan Williams had lined the city's approaches. Unlike every other military vessel afloat, it would not be at the mercy of wind or tide but would move under its own steam power at up to five miles an hour. At a height of twenty feet above the water line, *Demologos* towered over other vessels. No British flotilla brazen enough to brave the Narrows, Fulton believed, would dare face it.[38]

When Fulton's *Demologos* was launched on October 29, it slid into the East River, according to the *Evening Post*, "amidst the roar of cannon and the shouts and acclamations of upwards of twenty thousand people, who had assembled to witness the event" along the Manhattan and Long Island shores. But the ship never gained the glory Fulton wished for it. By the time it was fitted out with the engine and tested in the harbor's waters, the war was over. Naval officers judged it too cumbersome to be of use in the open sea, and *Demologos* ultimately languished in the Brooklyn Navy Yard as a floating infirmary, without ever firing a shot at an enemy.[39]

The launching of *Fulton I*, also known as *Demologos*, October 29, 1814. THE GRANGER COLLECTION, NEW YORK.

While the *Demologos* was unsuccessful as an instrument of war, it arguably played a part in taking one life. Ill and exhausted, Fulton toiled obsessively on the ship during the winter of 1814–1815 at his workshop on the Jersey City shore. After returning to his Manhattan lodgings one night, he took to bed with severe pneumonia. He died on February 23, at age fifty, to be remembered for his steamboat—and the ferry landings (and, eventually, streets) that bore his name on either side of the East River—rather than for his weapons of mass destruction. But recognized or not, Fulton had inaugurated New York's career as an incubator and cradle of mechanized warships that would help transform the nature of marine warfare.[40]

The full measure of that industrial revolution, however, would not be gauged for several decades. In the moment, the war's economic impact made daily life hard for many. The British blockade was effective enough to create shortages; this, combined with the government's requisition of foodstuffs and fuel for its fighting forces, brought a sharp inflation that outstripped the earnings of many working families. "The times are very hard . . . ," a New York lady wrote to her sister in October 1813. "It is high time this cruel war was at an end."

The economic stress of war intensified the sense of New York as a city under siege not only from the British warships hovering offshore, but also from foes much closer to home. Once more, New York appeared to be harboring enemies within its gates. The Royal Navy pounced so swiftly on vessels trying to sneak out of New York that it seemed obvious that local agents were providing the British with information about embarkations. Friendly fishermen and merchants covertly sailed out to the blockading fleets and sold them food. Republicans were primed to blast Manhattan's Federalists as pro-British traitors, but it was hard to single out individuals when that party dominated much of the city's public life. Instead, a more convenient scapegoat was found.[41]

At the start of the war, Charles Holt's Republican paper, the *Columbian*, had called on the authorities "to put the laws immediately in force against alien enemies, and to rid the city of spies." Such sentiment, aimed at the city's community of British émigrés, harmonized with the policy of the Madison administration. On July 7, 1812, the State Department issued an order requiring all British subjects living in the United States to go to the nearest US marshal's office to register their names and those of their family members, as well as their ages and places of residence. By April 1813, the names of 2,300 English citizens were on the books of Manhattan's federal marshal. Any resident British alien traveling into or out of the city needed to carry a passport and check himself into the local marshal's office on arrival.[42]

While British New Yorkers were neither prosecuted en masse nor deported, the registry system would linger as a humiliating memory of the war years. Such measures gratified the anger of native-born New Yorkers and offered a fleeting reassurance of security. But passports could not protect the city against the Royal Navy, should London adopt a more aggressive strategy. The key question remained unanswered: if New Yorkers peered seaward one day to see "all London afloat," as many still living had done once before, could they rest assured that their defenses would hold?

This was the question of the hour during the spring and summer of 1814. Napoleon's defeat in Europe freed up thousands of redcoats for redeployment to Britain's American theater. In June, reports arrived confirming an ominous buildup of British reinforcements at Halifax and Bermuda. Governor Tompkins and Mayor DeWitt Clinton used city money to hire spies who posed as friendly vendors, boarded Sir John Warren's and Sir Thomas Hardy's ships off Sandy Hook, and reported back that the British intended to attack the East Coast somewhere between Rhode Island and the Chesapeake. By mid-July, a special defense committee of the Common Council concluded that "the immense prize which this city affords to his cupidity" made New York a logical goal for the enemy's invasion. An English lady living on Broadway even claimed she had received word from her relative, Admiral Sir George Cockburn, who hoped very soon to "have the honor to dine with her at her house, as he expected to be in command of the city of New York."[43]

In response to the renewed threat of invasion, workmen were busy during the late spring and summer of 1814 on a new set of fortifications designed to fill gaps in the existing network. To the relief of New Yorkers, the port's new military engineer, Colonel Joseph Swift—the first man to graduate from West Point—proved as capable as his mentor, Jonathan Williams. Ranging across the city's shores and hinterland, Swift plotted out a ring of new outposts. Gun batteries were placed on the Long Island shore and an offshore reef facing the Staten Island forts, thereby strengthening the Narrows. A two-story wooden blockhouse, with cannon above and loopholes for muskets below, was built and garrisoned at Rockaway to deter the foe from landing on the barrier beaches of Jamaica Bay. Remembering well the lessons of 1776, Swift pressed for a series of defenses across Brooklyn and rural northern Manhattan to prevent a flanking British assault. Large blockhouses were built on Mill Rock in the East River and at Hallets Point on the Queens shore to guard the Hell Gate passage. Swift counted on the 44 guns of the frigate *President*, which had run the blockade into the harbor in February, to be a "floating battery" augmenting the 570 cannon and mortars of the harbor and shoreline forts.[44]

New forts would be useless if they lacked garrisons, and Tompkins worked tirelessly to expand the city's defensive army. The governor mustered upstate militia and volunteer regiments and ordered them to the city. Throughout August, New Yorkers watched as the Montgomery Rangers, the Albany Riflemen, West Point cadets, and New Jersey regiments took up positions in the harbor forts and in mass encampments staked out on Harlem Heights and Brooklyn Heights. By September 11, when the last troops arrived, Tompkins had assembled an active force of about six thousand men, with another ten thousand in reserve.[45]

The arrival of new troops was reassuring; slow progress in completing Swift's defenses was not. By late summer, city authorities concluded that civilians would have to volunteer their time, sweat, and muscle, as they had in previous crises. As the sun rose over the East River waterfront each morning in August and September 1814, an unusual scene repeated itself: hundreds of men, often accompanied by fifers, drummers, and flag bearers, marched onto Fulton's new steam ferryboat at Beekman Slip to perform a day's unpaid labor on Brooklyn's fortifications. The Tammany Society, the Washington Benevolent Society, law students, journeymen printers, "Patriotic Sons of Erin," the Common Council itself—all took up the spade and the wheelbarrow to complete a line of trenches and wooden stockades that stretched across the farmland of Brooklyn from Gowanus Creek to Wallabout Bay, often incorporating the moldering remains of the last war's redoubts. Other civilians finished a similar line of blockhouses and entrenchments across the fields of Harlem from river to river (remnants can still be seen today in Central Park). By mid-August, 1,000 or more were toiling daily and nightly; because many volunteered for only a day or two, the rotation of workers meant that a significant portion of Manhattan's population of 95,000 created the breastworks and ramparts at Brooklyn and Harlem.[46]

The volunteers represented a cross-section of the city's populace, but the effort also underscored the era's rigid social boundaries. Rather than being pressured to labor with their hands, wealthy gentlemen were permitted to provide money for "substitutes," just as they could when facing military mobilization. When over two hundred of the city's women journeyed to Fort Greene to perform "an hour's work," the Columbian thanked them and applauded "a lady of 72 years of age" who "wheeled a barrow of earth with great activity." But the paper quickly added that "more permanent and appropriate employment for the sex will be found in the associations for needle work for the soldiery forming throughout the city."[47]

VIEW FROM FORT FISH AT M^c GOWANS PASS
looking towards Harlem

Fort Fish, one of several fortifications built in 1814 in what is now the northern end of Central Park. Lithograph by George Hayward, *View from Fort Fish at McGowan's Pass Looking Towards Harlem*, 1856. COURTESY OF THE NEW YORK PUBLIC LIBRARY, WWW.NYPL.ORG.

Most poignant were the exertions of the city's free black men. By 1814, New York City was home to about nine thousand free African Americans and about a thousand slaves. Under a state law passed in 1799, all boys born into slavery after July 4, 1800, would be freed at age twenty-eight, and all girls at age twenty-five; thus an entire generation of enslaved New Yorkers could look forward to obtaining their freedom in the mid-1820s. Older slaves enjoyed no guarantee that they would ever be free, although some dared hope that a revision of the law might liberate them as well. The free black community sustained itself through the resilience of its evangelical church congregations and the leadership of a small cadre of clergymen and tradesmen. But they inhabited their own city, one of limited job and educational opportunities, poverty, segregated institutions, and property qualifications that kept black men from voting.

Thus it was noteworthy when, on August 20, an anonymous "Citizen of Color" used the newspapers to urge his brethren to shoulder the pick and shovel and head for Brooklyn. "There is a fair prospect of a period not far distant," he noted, "when this state will not contain a slave. Our country is now in danger. . . . We have now an opportunity of showing . . . that we are not traitors or enemies to our country." Two days later, about one thousand free black men, accompanied by a band and flags, answered the call and did their share on Brooklyn Heights. The *Evening Post* lauded "the hardy and patriotic sons of Africa" who, "knowing the value of freedom, are anxious to defend it." As sincerely patriotic as the gesture was, it was also politically astute. The war emergency let New York's African Americans remind white leaders of black loyalty and of the promises of freedom whites had yet to fulfill.[48]

On August 27, as work on the fortifications around the city continued, the bleakest news of the war reached New York. The British had seized and burned Washington, DC; President Madison had fled. "Let every man capable of bearing arms provide himself with a musket and the necessary accoutrements," the Common Council, fearing a similar fate for New York, implored the public. But the crisis passed. In mid-September, news arrived of the British failure to capture Baltimore, followed by reports of a decisive American victory on Lake Champlain. Gradually it dawned on New Yorkers that the momentum of the British summer offensive was ebbing away and that the immediate danger had passed. In November, Governor Tompkins started sending the upstate militia regiments home.[49]

It remains an open question whether the British intended to attack New York City. Admiral Warren's successor in Bermuda as Royal Navy commander, Sir Alexander Cochrane, proved to be as irresolute as Warren when it came to aggressive action against American coastal targets. Pressed by the War Office and admiralty in the summer of 1814 to select an objective for a joint navy and army attack, Cochrane hedged, weighing the pros and cons of a list of cities that included New York, Boston, Philadelphia, Baltimore, and Washington. If twelve thousand men were provided, he wrote in July, New York might well be destroyed or "put under contribution." If troops landed on Long Island, they could easily bombard the city across the East River with rockets and artillery.[50]

Cochrane had left the final choice of which American city to attack to the more decisive Admiral Cockburn, who picked Washington. But it is fair to speculate that the final decision was, in part,

shaped by a healthy British respect for the defenses Jonathan Williams
and Joseph Swift had fashioned for New York. By making New York
conspicuously less vulnerable than other targets, the forts and batteries served as valuable deterrents. The daily newspapers that city dignitaries ensured got through to the blockading squadrons further
underscored the determination of troops and civilians to fight for the
city. The British failure to take a similarly fortified Baltimore harbor
in September 1814 may have driven the lesson home. After all, easier,
more vulnerable targets beckoned—like New Orleans.[51]

On the frigid evening of February 11, 1815, a harbor pilot named
David Mitchell burst into the office of the New York *Gazette* in
Hanover Square, near the South Street docks. Gasping for breath,
Mitchell managed to whisper, "*Peace! Peace!* . . . An English sloop-of-
war is below with news of a treaty of peace." As the assembled men
tumbled out into the square shouting with joy, lit candles began appearing in windows, street by street. "The cry of 'Peace! *Peace!*
PEACE!' spread through the city at the top of all voices," a participant later recalled. "No one stopped to inquire about 'free trade and
sailors' rights.' No one inquired whether even the national honor had
been preserved. . . . It was enough that the ruinous war was over."[52]

New Yorkers had already learned of Andrew Jackson's stunning
victory on January 8 over the redcoats at New Orleans, a crushing
blow to the British offensive. Now their joy and relief were complete.
While the Treaty of Ghent left key American grievances unresolved,
the war's conclusion almost magically removed sources of tension that
had stirred New Yorkers for two decades: seizures of ships and seamen,
and antagonisms between Republicans and Federalists over foreign
policy. New Yorkers could share in a sense of having won, or at any
rate survived, what Alexander McLeod, one of the city's Presbyterian
ministers, labeled "this second war of independence."[53]

A new New York emerged out of the shadow of the War of 1812—
an assertively nineteenth-century city, a place of confidence and unleashed energies. South Street merchants, frustrated by the war's
capricious blockade, now quickly took advantage of revived trade
with Britain; soon they would be able to tout their city as "the great
emporium of North America." The city's population boomed as ves-

sels, no longer in fear of prowling warships, poured European emigrants across the East River piers. Interrupted by the war in their planning for a man-made waterway carrying the commerce of the Great Lakes to Manhattan's shores, merchants now helped to elevate their mayor to the governor's mansion in Albany, where DeWitt Clinton shaped American history by overseeing the construction of the Erie Canal.[54]

The war had bestowed on the city a new set of identities: a role for Wall Street as a financial underwriter of war, a role for foundries and shipyards to mass-produce the tools of war imagined by men like Robert Fulton. These new identities remained rooted in New York's oldest motive, the pursuit of profit, as well as in the imperatives of patriotism and self-defense. But New York's growing might also suggested a new paradox, easily forgotten in times of peace. As the city became the nation's marketplace, workshop, bank, and symbol of power and wealth, it also became that much more provocative a target for foes. As the batteries of heavy metal standing on its shores mutely testified, New York City remained at the edge of the Atlantic, warning off potential aggressors while simultaneously tempting them.

CHAPTER 6

The Front Door

The Civil War, 1861–1865

The massive crowd overflowed the bounds of Union Square and filled Broadway and Fourth Avenue, bringing horse-drawn drays and streetcars to a standstill. Thousands more men, women, and children lined the windows and roofs of the fashionable townhouses and hotels that surrounded the Square. It was the afternoon of April 20, 1861, and New York City had turned out to support the Union in its moment of crisis. Mounted on an open-air dais, Major Robert Anderson raised the splintered flagstaff and flag that his men had taken with them when they had surrendered Fort Sumter to Confederate troops a week earlier. The crowd of at least a hundred thousand roared and erupted into a resounding impromptu chorus of "The Star-Spangled Banner."

Like most of the participants, Wall Street lawyer George Templeton Strong found himself thrilled by an outpouring of patriotic fervor he would remember for the rest of his life. "Large companies of recruits in citizen's dress parading up and down, cheered and cheering," he recorded in his diary that night. "Flags from almost every building. The city seems to have gone suddenly wild and crazy." Two days earlier, Strong had watched as the men of the Sixth Massachusetts Infantry from Boston had marched down Broadway to the docks, on their way to Washington to answer President Lincoln's call for seventy-five thousand volunteers to put down the Southern rebellion. "Immense crowd;

immense cheering. My eyes filled with tears. . . . God be praised for the
unity of feeling here! It is beyond, very far beyond, anything I hoped
for. If it only last, we are safe."[1]

Horace Greeley's *New York Tribune*, the nation's most widely read
newspaper, claimed that the Union Square rally was "the greatest popular demonstration ever known in America." New Yorkers had much
to be proud of, and confident about, as the North mustered against the
Southern Confederacy that spring of 1861. Washington might be the
nation's political capital, but in the decades since the War of 1812,
New York had become the capital of virtually all else. The largest city
in the New World, its built-up area now extended well into the Forties,
with a checkerboard of constructed blocks and empty lots spreading
further up Manhattan. Wall Street was now acknowledged to be the
Western Hemisphere's headquarters for banking, insurance, and securities investment. In 1860, over two-thirds of all merchandise imported
into the United States arrived at New York docks, and over one-third
of all exports left from them. Manhattan held more industrial workers,
and a greater number and diversity of manufacturing businesses, than
any other single place outside Europe. Broadway had become the pre-
miere retail shopping street and promenade of the Americas, the place
where, in the words of the newspaperman and poet Walt Whitman,
one could enjoy watching "the beautiful ladies, the bustle, the show,
the glitter, and even the gaudiness." Fueled by immigration, New
York's dizzying growth had made it one of the world's most populous
cities—with over eight hundred thousand inhabitants—within a single lifetime; its satellite communities of Brooklyn, Jersey City, and
Hoboken held several hundred thousand more. The men of such a city
would surely beat the effete sons of the Southern aristocracy, the foe
Strong disparaged as "the slave-breeding woman-floggers of Charleston
and New Orleans and Richmond."[2]

Like most Northerners, New Yorkers believed that the South would
be defeated in a matter of weeks. With its thousands of footloose
young men, the city had repeatedly served as a recruiting ground during Latin America's wars of liberation against Spain, the Texas War
for Independence in 1836, the Mexican War, abortive "filibustering"
expeditions to seize Cuba and Nicaragua, even covertly for the British
during the Crimean War of 1854–1855. Now New Yorkers rushed to

volunteer, forming or joining regiments whose names—Corcoran's "Irish" Sixty-Ninth, the First German Rifles, the Garibaldi Guard—reflected the city's immigrant diversity. Thomas Southwick, a young workman for the Third Avenue Railroad Company, joined Duryee's Zouaves, known for their exotic uniform based on that of troops in French Algeria—baggy red pants, white leggings, blue jacket, and red fez with blue tassel. "Already in my imagination we were mounting the breastworks as they do in novels and scattering haughty Southerners like sheep," Southwick later recalled. "I'd be a hero, of course, if there were any Confederate flags to tear down or great generals to rescue. I'd be just the boy to do it."[3]

Would-be soldiers seemed to fill every promenade, parade ground, and saloon. At age forty-one, George Templeton Strong found himself with other professional men drilling in Washington Square, although his nearsightedness and his desire to support his wife and three young sons ultimately persuaded him to stay at home. Tent camps and make-shift wooden barracks sprouted in City Hall Park, in the new Central Park, at the Battery, on Staten Island and Rikers Island, and at Willets Point in rural Queens, wherever space could be found. One by one, regiments of enthusiastic volunteers boarded boats and trains for the nation's capital. By early May, New Yorkers could exult proudly in the fact that nearly half of the sixteen thousand troops guarding Washington hailed from Manhattan and Brooklyn.[4]

Then, on June 22, 1861, news arrived by telegraph that struck New Yorkers like a cold slap in the face. "We are utterly and disgracefully routed, beaten, whipped by secessionists," Strong wrote in his diary. Facing Confederate forces at Bull Run, the Union army—Manhattan regiments included—had evidently panicked and fled back to their trenches around Washington, "as rabbits to their burrows." Over-night, the humiliating disaster transformed expectations. Brooding in her townhouse on Eighth Street, another diarist, Maria Lydig Daly, descendant of one of the city's oldest patrician families, resigned herself to the meaning of Bull Run: "Now the war must be a thing of time. Our prestige is gone and must be reconquered."[5]

Although they did not yet realize it, New Yorkers faced a protracted war that would fracture the momentary unity for which Strong had thanked God in April. The city's inhabitants had already been in conflict with each other; the shooting war inflamed rather than quelled their tensions.

The truth was that New York was a deeply divided city. The emerging sectional conflict between North and South had been shaping political divisions, class tensions, and race relations in the city for three decades. Underlying all was a dominant reality: the heavy reliance of Manhattan's economy on Southern trade. New York City was immersed in the enormously profitable cotton economy of the South just as surely as were Charleston, Mobile, and New Orleans. New York bankers, brokers, and exporters provided planters with the credit and insurance they needed to harvest "white gold" and buy black slaves. In 1860, New York shippers exported over $12 million in cotton, most of it destined for the textile mills of Manchester, England. New York's merchants had made themselves the middlemen linking the American slave system to Britain's industrial revolution (earning further profits by cramming the holds of their ships with Irish emigrants on the return voyages).[6]

The link between New York and the South pervaded all aspects of the city's life. Southern whites, welcomed with open arms by retailers and wholesalers, came to Manhattan to do their spending. Merchants and planters from below the Mason-Dixon Line were familiar customers in the dry goods stores of Pearl Street and the showrooms of fashionable jewelers and carriage makers, and they made Hiram Cranston's New York Hotel on Broadway a home away from home for traveling slaveholders. Some Southerners became permanent New Yorkers, like the beautiful Martha Bulloch, who left her Georgia plantation to marry Manhattan merchant and financier Theodore Roosevelt Sr. According to her son, a future president of the United States, "Mittie" Roosevelt remained an "unreconstructed" Confederate; family lore has it that during the war she defiantly unfurled the rebel stars and bars from the window of her townhouse near Gramercy Park. Even Manhattan's entertainment industry contributed to the city's pro-Southern climate, as Thomas Rice and other white performers used the stage of the Bowery Theatre to create blackface minstrelsy, whose comic caricatures of happy-go-lucky plantation "darkies" challenged the far bleaker portrayals of slavery issuing from abolitionist printing presses a few blocks away. Some New Yorkers even broke federal law by sending covert expeditions to West Africa to buy slaves for sale in the Cuban, Brazilian, and Southern markets. "Down-town merchants of wealth and respectability are extensively engaged in buying and selling African Negroes," the *Journal of Commerce* charged in 1857. "The City of New York belongs almost as much to the South as to the North," the *New York Times* noted on the eve of the war.[7]

The Democratic Party leaders and voters who dominated the city's political life accepted and endorsed New York's links to slavery. Emboldened by the national party's strong base among slaveholders, the New York "Democracy" was an avowed bastion of white supremacy and of resistance to any effort by antislavery activists to sever the salutary bond between North and South. This ideology united Wall Street patricians like the banker August Belmont and the attorney Samuel Barlow, who bankrolled the national party, with the masses of working-class European emigrants, most of them Irish and German, who gave the local party its electoral majorities.

Although New York State went for Lincoln in 1860, the city delivered a resounding twenty-four-thousand vote majority to his Democratic opponent, Stephen Douglas. As the Southern states seceded from the Union over the winter of 1860–1861 in outrage at Lincoln's election, Democratic Mayor Fernando Wood proposed that the city declare itself an independent free port in order to sustain friendly trade with the Confederacy. ("I reckon that it will be some time before the front door sets up housekeeping on its own terms," Lincoln responded.) When the president-elect passed through town on his way to Washington in February, ship riggers on the East River welcomed him by hanging him in effigy from a mast, alongside a banner reading "Abe Lincoln, the Union Breaker." As Lincoln greeted well-wishers outside the Astor House on lower Broadway, Walt Whitman feared for the Rail Splitter's life: "Many an assassin's knife and pistol lurked in hip or breast-pocket there, ready as soon as break and riot came."[8]

The firing on Sumter had—momentarily—quelled the enmity toward the president, bringing New York's Southern-oriented businessmen and Democrats into patriotic alignment with Lincoln Republicans.

Merchants who had previously argued for appeasement to keep the South from seceding now pressed for a swift war to restore the Union. A short war would reestablish the status quo without disrupting slavery in the Southern states, pleasing Democrats. But bipartisan harmony remained superficial, for it compelled the city's Republican minority to work with a Democratic majority whose values and many of whose leaders they despised. For decades, men who disliked the Democratic Party's pro-Southern policies, embrace of workers and Catholic immigrants, and local reputation for corruption—usually native-born Protestant merchants, professionals, and artisans of middling or elite status—had flocked into opposition parties, the latest version of which was the Republicans.

Lincoln's party was opposed to the expansion of slavery, but only a minority of Republicans in New York were radicals bent on abolishing the South's "peculiar institution." A typical Republican was George Templeton Strong, who joined the local party organization in 1856. Proud scion of a family with deep roots in colonial New York and New England, owner of an elegant Gramercy Park townhouse, Strong embodied the conservatism of New York's Protestant elite. He joined the Republicans in outrage at what he perceived as "the reckless, insolent brutality of our Southern aristocrats." Of far less concern to Strong were the rights of black people, whom he persistently described as "niggers" in his diary, or the arguments of abolitionists, "who would sacrifice the union to their own one idea." By 1859, however, disgusted by what he viewed as Southern domination of the federal government, Strong was convinced that "the growing, vigorous North must sooner or later assert its right to equality with the stagnant, semi-barbarous South. . . . It must come."[9]

The only group who disgusted Strong as much as did Southern aristocrats was the city's mass of poor Irish Catholics, "those infatuated, pig-headed Celts." Disdain and fear of the Irish were shared by many native-born Republicans. "The most miserable and ignorant of other countries are shot into New York like rubbish," the Republican *Harper's Weekly* editorialized during the war. " . . . They are led by the demagogues who depend upon their votes for success." These tensions, pitting the Republican elite against the Democratic masses, em-

George Templeton Strong, patrician lawyer, di-
arist, and participant in many of New York's key
Civil War events. Illustration from *The Diary of
George Templeton Strong*, 71367. COLLECTION OF
THE NEW-YORK HISTORICAL SOCIETY.

bodied fissures of class, ethnicity, and religion that had permeated the
city's political and social life by the onset of war.[10]

The majority of New York's Irish emigrants lived in a very different
city from that inhabited by Strong. New York had an Irish Catholic
community by the 1820s; tens of thousands more, driven across the Atlantic by the potato famine of the 1840s and 1850s, landed in New York
without money to take them farther. By 1855, one-quarter of the city's
population—two hundred thousand people—had been born in Ireland.
Most were crammed into festering slums on the east side of lower Manhattan and into shanties and tenements on the city's northern outskirts,
often only a stone's throw from blocks of new row houses built for affluent families. The Irish performed the city's lowest-paying wage work,
toiling as day laborers, longshoremen, drivers, laundresses, seamstresses,

and servants. By the 1840s, bloody riots between gangs of Irish Catholics and native Protestants—and by both groups against constables and state militia—were commonplace. In the worst slums, a reform group would report in 1865, tens of thousands of immigrants were "literally submerged in filth and half stifled in an atmosphere charged with all the elements of death." The mortality rate in slum areas was more than twice that in the townhouses of the upper-middle-class Murray Hill district.[11]

While other Europeans were often welcomed into the social fabric of New York (German emigrants, for instance, the era's other large group of newcomers, gained a reputation for being "respectable" and steady), the Irish were stereotyped as primitive and brutish for their boisterous drinking culture, the crime and violence that beset some of their neighborhoods, and the Catholicism that led them to defy the anglophile Protestant elite. They embraced the Democratic Party, the only powerful institution in the city (apart from the growing Catholic Church) that welcomed them with open arms. They also shared in a brotherhood that exalted them for their white skin and made them equals at the ballot box with New York's richest bankers and merchants. Republicans, thundered Democratic journalist James Brooks, were bent on "the negation of the white race and the elevation of the negro." Such rhetoric posited the Irish as far superior to the African Americans with whom they competed for the city's worst jobs and housing, even superior to the Republicans who lived in mansions. Thousands of New York Irishmen enlisted and marched off to war in 1861, passionate in their patriotism and proud to affirm their American citizenship. But the war they entered was emphatically one to restore the Union, not to free slaves.[12]

While New York's Irish population was growing, the city's black community was a small but visible presence, its members numbering under 13,000 in 1860. New York State had only fully abolished slavery in 1827, and a rigid racial hierarchy continued to dictate the terms of daily life in the city. A small middle class of clergymen and tradesmen provided leadership, but the majority toiled in poverty as laborers, petty vendors, waiters, servants, and laundresses. Increasingly they had been displaced from many jobs by the influx of poor Irish. Al-

though not isolated in a distinct ghetto, and in some districts inter-
mingling and even intermarrying with their Irish neighbors, most
lived in scattered, segregated pockets—an all-black tenement here, a
row of shanties there.

While some elite white New Yorkers sympathized with the plight of
their black fellow Protestants, most shunned meaningful contact. "I
have an antipathy to Negroes physically and don't like them near me,"
Maria Lydig Daly confided to her diary a few days after Bull Run.
Streetcars and steamboat lines were racially segregated, and any number of businesses were off limits to black consumers. New York's state
constitution placed prohibitively high property qualifications on black
voters; the electorate rejected the elimination of this racist disenfran-
chisement in 1860, nowhere more decisively than at the Manhattan
polls. Wherever they looked, New York's blacks encountered a city that
denied them anything resembling equal rights and opportunities. The
physician James McCune Smith, one of the city's most distinguished
black residents, characterized such racism as the "damning thralldom
that grinds to dust the colored inhabitants."[13]

In the face of such discouragement, New York's black men and
women fought back, plunging ardently into the antislavery movement
and into efforts to improve their own lot. The city was home to black
congregations like Reverend H. H. Garnet's Shiloh Presbyterian Church
on Prince Street, a bastion of militant abolitionism and race pride. Black
abolitionists Albro and Mary Lyons turned their waterfront boarding-
house into a station for hundreds of fugitives fleeing the South along the
Underground Railroad. When James Hamlet, a fugitive slave, was seized
on the street and spirited back to Maryland under the terms of the Fugitive Slave Act in 1850, abolitionists raised $800 to buy his freedom, and
a triumphant, largely African American crowd welcomed him home to a
reception in City Hall Park.[14]

Black New Yorkers were aided in their struggle for equality by a
small group of white abolitionists. John Street in lower Manhattan was
the headquarters of the American and Foreign Anti-Slavery Society,
funded by the brothers and wealthy dry goods importers Lewis and
Arthur Tappan. So enraged were Southerners by the antislavery propaganda issuing from New York that Louisianans put a $50,000 price tag

on Arthur Tappan's head. Radicals also had to stand the storm aroused in New York by their message of immediate abolition. In 1834, a white mob had rampaged to prevent an interracial meeting of abolitionists in a downtown chapel, and the violence escalated into several days of attacks on blacks and the homes and stores of white antislavery activists.[15]

The emancipationists, black and white, persevered. With war now upon the nation, they persisted in viewing New York as a center for something more sweeping, more transcendent than a mere conflict to restore the Union. At the same time, they were as aware as anyone that the tensions dividing their city—separating Republicans from Democrats, rich from poor, natives from immigrants, Protestants from Catholics, blacks from whites—represented a tinderbox the war might ignite.

While the war's outbreak did little to quell the city's underlying frictions, it invigorated the city's economy. New York rapidly became the money city of the Northern war effort. After the Bull Run defeat, Treasury Secretary Salmon P. Chase borrowed $150 million from Wall Street bankers to pay the war's mounting bills. Over the next four years, New York financiers underwrote a dizzying expansion of the federal government's budget, enriching themselves in the process. A healthy portion of the funds loaned to the government, moreover, came back to the city in the form of military contracts. New York's merchants and manufacturers were able to think and deal on a scale that suited an institution like the US Army, which expanded almost overnight from 16,000 to over half a million men. The army's Department of the East, headquartered on Bleecker Street, became the point from which federal funds were dispensed into Manhattan pockets and bank accounts. Thousands of workers toiled in foundries and shipyards lining the Hudson and East River waterfronts, churning out huge engines and boilers for the navy. Raw materials and finished goods—bread, pork, medicines, uniforms, shoes, blankets, gun carriages—continually flowed out the Union's "front door" to the troops in the field. New York was awash in war money. "Look at her seated between two noble rivers forested with masts," the *Journal of Commerce* boasted after half a year of war. "She has learned how to prosper without the South."[16]

War prosperity, however, quickly revealed another side, one that inflamed rather than reduced the city's social tensions. Wages for workers rose, but not as fast as prices did. The cost of coal, flour, potatoes, beef, and milk doubled in the face of shortages and an inflationary paper currency, eroding family budgets. Skilled machinists could at least negotiate, and sometimes strike successfully, for wage hikes. Less skilled workers were not so fortunate. Thousands of the city's women and girls, a *New York Times* reporter charged in 1864, "whose husbands, fathers, and brothers have fallen on the battle field, are making army shirts at six cents apiece." To load military transports, employers replaced striking Irish longshoremen with prisoners of war (mostly Union army deserters), German immigrants, and, to the bitter fury of strikers in the spring of 1863, free blacks.[17]

In truth, the war increasingly came home to the families of poorer enlistees in the form of calamity: a husband killed, a father disabled—a wage earner who would never again help to support his family. The city government provided benefits to the families of soldiers away at the front and to war widows and orphans, but the funds did not reach everyone, and the money often arrived late, prompting public protests by working wives and mothers. "You have got me men into the soldiers, and now you have to keep us from starving," a woman implored officials during a rally in Tompkins Square late in 1862.[18]

Hardship at the bottom seemed unmatched by any pervasive suffering at the top. War contractors stood to make "killings" if they played their cards right. Some sought quick and easy profits by selling inferior or spoiled merchandise—"shoddy," as it was called—to a government too distracted to inspect every lot of goods or to purchasing agents who might get a kickback if they looked the other way. Honorable or not, war contracting sustained the city's lopsided distribution of wealth, as well as the widely held conviction that a small class of profiteers was enjoying luxuries beyond the reach of the urban masses. "Our importers of silk goods and our leading jewelers are selling their finest goods at the highest prices," the *Herald* noted in October 1862. War-generated ostentation pleased members of the established elite as little as it did the working poor. Complaining of a saddler's wife seen buying pearls and diamonds at Tiffany's, Maria Lydig Daly sniffed at magnificent carriages filled with "the commonest kind of humanity.

Old women who might be apple-sellers or fruit-carriers are dressed in velvet and satins."[19]

Late May 1862 found Corporal Thomas Southwick far from New York, trying to climb a Virginia hill "thick with glutinous blood, causing me to slip and almost tread upon one whose life had gushed out of an ugly wound behind his ear." Long gone were the fantasies of seizing rebel flags or rescuing generals. So were the illusions of most New Yorkers, whether at the front or at home. The newspaper casualty lists with their grisly shorthand ("Thomas McGuire, Co. A., leg amp; . . . H. Mcilainy, Co. I, forehead, severe") arrived now with a numbing regularity—numbing except to the families who learned from them of a brother wounded, a husband killed. With one son dead and another missing an arm, Columbia College law professor Francis Lieber and his wife, Matilda, came to scan the daily papers with "drained and feverish eyes" for news of their third son (who survived the war physically unscathed).[20]

Many of the surviving volunteers, like Thomas Southwick, had had enough. "Will this war ever cease? I cannot find a satisfactory answer," he wrote in his diary. Rather than stay in the army at the end of his two-year enlistment, he returned to work as a car painter at the Third Avenue Railway in May 1863, bearing memories of Gaines's Mill, Malvern Hill, and Fredericksburg that would last him a lifetime. If bullets and camp fever took the lives of rich boys as well as poor ones, it was in Thomas Southwick's New York—a city of working-class neighborhoods, workshops, and saloons—that a bitter phrase increasingly fell from the lips of veterans and noncombatants alike: "A rich man's war and a poor man's fight."[21]

Several hundred miles to the south, Confederates had their own understanding of New York City's role in the conflict engulfing them. Dependent for decades on New York's resources to finance the cotton economy, resentful of the profits New Yorkers made from the cotton trade, secessionists concocted vengeful fantasies. Edmund Ruffin, a Virginian honored by being allowed to fire one of the first cannonballs against Fort Sumter, brooded frequently about Manhattan. Ruffin filled his diary with dark musings on the apocalyptic strife he predicted would befall the city once its Southern sources of wealth disappeared and its underlying decadence surfaced. In 1860 the Charleston *Mercury* had serialized Ruffin's novel, *Anticipations of the Future*, written as a retrospective "history" of the coming struggle between North and South. Faced with the loss of Southern trade, spiraling food prices, and an unruly mass of unemployed workers, "the city of New York broke into open rebellion. Thousands of rioters raided the gun stores and plundered the liquor shops. The police were helpless. . . . Banks were broken open and their vaults robbed. Churches were looted. . . . Drunk and gorged with plunder, the mob set the city on fire. A high wind whipped the flames into a hurricane of fire, and when morning came New York was a blackened, charred ruin."[22]

Ruffin's vision represented more than merely a fantasy of Southern triumph. It was the start of a tradition in which its enemies would perceive New York not just as a narrowly defined military objective, but also as an encompassing symbol of moral and cultural evil. The city became a target for attack in sweeping and emotionally urgent terms. In previous wars, belligerents had targeted New York as the administrative center of a colonial hinterland, as the key to the Hudson River, and as one of several major coastal ports. Now, as the North's capital of commerce, finance, industry, and intellectual opinion, New York represented something larger to Southerners. Boston might be the citadel of abolitionism, and Philadelphia might be filled with meddlesome antislavery Quakers. But New York was the true Sodom, the place that exemplified and reveled in everything that was rotten about the North: the disorder of "free labor," capitalist greed and arrogance, social chaos and conflict. Of course, it was precisely because so many Southerners were familiar with New York, tied into its web of cotton financing and enticed by the charms of its goods and services, that the wartime renunciation had to be so vehement. The seductions of the place, as well as its power and conceit, needed to be checked. As large as it was, New York in the eyes of its enemies became even larger, the embodiment of everything the Confederacy was fighting against.

One man carried the preoccupation with New York into the inner sanctum of the Confederate cabinet. Stephen Mallory, Jefferson Davis's navy secretary, envisioned an ironclad steamer that could win the war, its metal armor impervious to shellfire as it sank wooden-hulled Union ships at will. In March 1862, after his prototype, the *Merrimack*, wreaked havoc on Union shipping in Virginia waters, Mallory wrote excitedly to its commander, Franklin Buchanan, of what would follow. The ironclad would be ordered north to New York harbor to "shell and burn the city and the shipping. . . . Peace would inevitably follow. Bankers would withdraw their capital from the city. The Brooklyn Navy Yard and its magazines and all the lower part of the city would be destroyed." Such an attack, Mallory concluded, "would do more to achieve our immediate independence than would the results of many campaigns."[23]

In the end, the *Merrimack* would not lob shells into New York. By the time Mallory wrote his letter, the ship had already been checked in battle by the ironclad *Monitor*, dispatched from New York harbor. Buchanan himself pointed out to Mallory the obstacles to a successful foray: the unlikelihood of finding Sandy Hook pilots to guide the *Merrimack* through the Lower Bay's treacherous sandbars and the possibility that New York's outer forts would open fire on it. Buchanan did concede, however, that if it reached the inner harbor, it could batter the city's houses and ships.[24]

Through the early months of 1862, New Yorkers feared just such an onslaught as the one that Mallory envisioned. More precisely, after the Union navy caused a diplomatic crisis by removing two Confederate envoys from the English-bound vessel *Trent* on the high seas, they feared two possible onslaughts: one from the much-discussed *Merrimack*, the other from the Royal Navy. George Templeton Strong worriedly questioned "whether we can stop iron-plated steamers from coming up the Narrows and throwing shells into Union Square." Lincoln's willingness to appease the English to avoid a transatlantic war, and the blowing up of the *Merrimack* in May, allowed New Yorkers to breathe a sigh of relief, but their anxieties resurfaced throughout the war. In September 1862, Union navy secretary Gideon Welles scoffed in his diary that "men in New York, men who are sensible in most things, are the most easily terrified and panic-stricken of any community. They are just now alarmed lest one iron-clad steamer may rush in upon them one fine morning while they're asleep and destroy their city."[25]

A few weeks later, however, such alarm seemed less ludicrous. On November 2, forty-four survivors from vessels sunk by the eight-gun Confederate navy steamer *Alabama* arrived in Boston harbor. The survivors carried a message for the New York Chamber of Commerce from Raphael Semmes, the *Alabama's* captain, informing the chamber "that by the time this message reached them, he would be off" the port of New York. After burning nine New England whaling ships in the Azores, Semmes had turned to the Atlantic coast, where over the course of October he captured ten Northern vessels, most of them bound from New York to Europe with grain and flour. Some of the ship captains showed Semmes papers indicating that their cargoes belonged to English owners, but the Confederate commander was not impressed. "The New York merchant is a pretty sharp fellow," he later wrote, "in the matter of shaving paper, getting up false invoices, and 'doing' the custom-house; but the laws of nations . . . rather muddled his brain." Declaring the documents invalid, Semmes sank eight of the cargo-laden ships.[26]

Next, Semmes planned to bring the war to New York's doorstep. Recent copies of the *Herald* and other New York papers found on board his prizes reassured Semmes that the harbor was lightly defended by the navy, which had dispatched gunboats that he managed to bypass on his way toward the city. Aware of the large number of cargo vessels riding in the Lower Bay, Semmes determined, in the words of one of his officers, "to enter Sandy Hook anchorage and set fire to the shipping in that vast harbor." But on October 30, with the *Alabama* still two hundred miles east of Sandy Hook, Semmes decided that the move was too risky because his coal supply was running low. The *Alabama* pulled off toward the Caribbean, to the disappointment of the crew. "To astonish the enemy in New York harbor," Master's Mate George Fullam noted in his log, "to destroy their vessels in their own waters, had been the darling wish of all on board."

As Semmes predicted, the city went "agog" as news spread of his audacious message to the Chamber of Commerce. Although Union navy commander Henry Wise argued that "any of the armed ferry boats now at the Navy Yard would make toothpicks of her [the *Alabama*] in five minutes," New Yorkers were not so sure. "It seems strange that the

Captain Raphael Semmes (center right) poses next to one of the Confederate raider *Alabama's* guns, 1863. NAVAL HISTORY & HERITAGE COMMAND PHOTOGRAPHIC COLLECTION.

energy and resources of the country cannot result in ridding the ocean of a pestering pirate," Horace Greeley's *Tribune* complained.[27]

In August 1864, Confederate "pirates" would return to New York waters. The three-gun cruiser *Tallahassee*, at seventeen knots one of the fastest steamers in the world, slipped out of Wilmington, North Carolina, past a Union blockade, under orders from Stephen Mallory to wreak havoc on Union shipping along the East Coast. Four days later, cruising off Long Island's south shore and Sandy Hook, the *Tallahassee's* captain, John Taylor Wood, commenced a two-day looting and burning spree. Soon the waters off New York were littered with the wrecks of twelve brigs, barks, schooners, and ships, scuttled or burnt to the waterline. Wood loaded the scores of crewmen and passengers he captured onto other vessels and sent them into Fire Island and the city with the news of his presence. Captain Reed of the captured brig *Billow* told a reporter that Wood "appeared to be a very affable man, and said he was doing what it was not pleasant for him to do." Wood told Reed that his mission was to "slacken up the coasting trade so that 'Uncle Abe' would be glad to make peace." But the commander also warned several of the prisoners he released that "he was coming into New-York harbor."[28]

Given Wood's audacious temperament, his vessel's unmatchable speed, and the dearth of Union warships in the vicinity of New York (almost all were on Southern blockade duty or Atlantic patrol), he probably intended to make good on his threat. But Wood could not persuade or pressure any of the Sandy Hook pilots he captured to aid him in his plan, which was to maneuver his steamer through the bay's shoals into the East River, shell anchored ships and the Brooklyn Navy Yard, and then slip through Hell Gate out into Long Island Sound. Instead, Wood decided to turn east and hunt in New England's shipping lanes. Although he was pursued by Union gunboats, August 26 found the rebel raider safely back in Wilmington, having sunk a total of twenty-eight Northern vessels. New Yorkers, especially ship owners and sailors, breathed a sigh of relief, but they also remembered Wood's warning that the Confederacy had other cruisers it would unleash against Northern shipping.[29]

Well before Semmes's or Wood's attacks, New Yorkers had worried about the vulnerability of the port's defenses. In 1821, a federal board had recommended that six new forts be built to seal off New York's outer approaches from possible attack. These works would protect the inner line of forts and guns that Jonathan Williams had placed on Ellis, Bedloe's, and Governors Islands. By 1861, granite-walled Fort Schuyler on the Bronx shore of Long Island Sound was complete; so was Fort Lafayette, built on an offshore reef in the Narrows channel, and Fort Hamilton, overlooking it from the Brooklyn shore (where an up-and-coming army engineer, Robert E. Lee, had served capably during the 1840s). But much was left undone. Construction continued on forts Richmond and Tompkins on the Staten Island side of the Narrows, and little had been done at Sandy Hook or on the Queens side of the Sound. Nervous New Yorkers shared George Templeton Strong's antebellum perception that "our fortifications at the Narrows, though quite picturesque of a summer afternoon, are still, considered strictly as defenses, about as much as a line of squirtgun batteries."[30]

One army officer who understood New Yorkers' fears threw himself into the work of making the port impregnable. Sixty-three-year-old Colonel Richard Delafield of the US Army Corps of Engineers was a native New Yorker, reared in his merchant father's Wall Street townhouse. A former superintendent of West Point like Williams before him, Delafield was an acknowledged expert on port defense who had toured Europe's great forts. Appointed engineer to the New York State Commission of Harbor and Frontier Defence, Delafield dedicated himself to keeping the Confederate foe at bay. With some 1,100 cannon already lining the ramparts and casemates of the port's defenses, Delafield promised New Yorkers that he would add another 242 heavy guns, "a greater number . . . than exists in most of the fortified harbors of Europe." Armed with a congressional appropriation, Delafield extended rudimentary defenses at Fort Lincoln (later renamed Fort Hancock) on Sandy Hook and began building what became known as Fort Totten on the Queens shore opposite Fort Schuyler.[31]

Delafield also solicited ideas from the city's inventors and scientists, professional and amateur, who were happy to oblige. One suggested a railway running along the Upper Bay with mobile guns to fire on invading ships. The magazine *Scientific American* argued that a pool of petroleum dumped into the harbor and ignited on the enemy's approach would prove an effective deterrent. Delafield himself advocated a system of chains and pontoons across the Narrows to let in friendly vessels and keep out hostile ones, and a string of electrically triggered "torpedoes" ("the fruits of American science and genius") across the riverbed between the Bronx and Queens, but expense and practical obstacles prevented these from being implemented.[32]

Although he fretted privately about insufficient funds and the slow pace of the work, Delafield tried to calm New Yorkers. Many of them believed that the Confederacy was acquiring fearsome new technologies from England or France, fast ironclad steamers and powerful riflebarreled artillery that might turn brick and granite forts into rubble. "No hostile force can ever reduce it," he wrote confidently of Fort Schuyler, provided it were properly supplied and garrisoned. New fifteen-inch guns he installed at Fort Hamilton in 1864, mounted on rotating carriages, promised to rain death and destruction on any enemy warship trying to enter the Narrows or Upper Bay.[33]

In the summer of 1863, however, it was Delafield's turn to vent his alarm. As Robert E. Lee's army surged north into Pennsylvania, Delafield realized that the city faced a threat that rendered its seaward-facing forts irrelevant. In an urgent letter to New York governor Horatio Seymour on July 3, Delafield sketched the probable result if Lee proved to be "a successful conqueror" in his northward march: Confederate occupation of Philadelphia, followed by the taking of Jersey City, from which the rebels could easily bombard Manhattan with their artillery and throw an army of fifty thousand across the Hudson. Delafield beseeched the governor to mobilize the state militia and reserves to expand New York City's home guard, as well as an army to strike Lee's rear from the Susquehanna Valley. "Now shall we stand with our arms folded," he asked, "and allow the resources within the limits of the State of New York in this eventful and momentous crisis to be 'not ready'?"[34]

Delafield's fears were unwarranted. As he wrote his letter, Meade's Army of the Potomac was turning Lee back at Gettysburg. Yet the war *was* soon to come to the city. Edmund Ruffin's nightmare vision—of civil war erupting in Manhattan's streets—was about to become a reality.

On the hot summer morning of Monday, July 13, 1863, crowds of men and boys swarmed through the streets of Manhattan, inviting and bullying others to join them from foundries near the East River docks and workshops scattered among the new blocks that had sprouted uptown in the Twenties, Thirties, and Forties. Some carried homemade placards and banners reading "No Draft."

The previous Saturday, federal provost marshals had begun to implement the first compulsory military conscription in the Union's history. Bounty money offered by government recruiters was failing to turn out the full complement of volunteers Lincoln had counted on to win the war. With veterans like Thomas Southwick retiring from the army and other young men thinking twice about risking their lives and limbs in a seemingly endless bloodbath, the administration and a Republican-controlled Congress had resolved on a drastic measure. The War Department set quotas for a national draft to begin in mid-July 1863, applying to all able-bodied single men ages twenty to forty-five and all married men ages twenty to thirty-five. New York City alone was to supply twenty-four thousand men to the Union army.[35]

The Conscription Act of 1863, however, was deeply unpopular with many New Yorkers, for two reasons. First, by signing the Emancipation Proclamation the previous January, President Lincoln had pledged the Union to the liberation of the Confederacy's slaves—a measure anathema to local Democrats who had long warned that such was the ultimate goal of "black Republicans." Since before Lincoln's election, newspapers like the *Herald* had been warning working-class readers that, should the abolitionists get what they wanted, "you will have to compete with the labor of four million emancipated Negroes." The specter of a mass influx of freedmen into New York's job market angered and frightened immigrant workers. The fear compounded a widespread belief in the Irish community that, as Maria Lydig Daly put it, "the abolitionists hate both Irish and Catholic and want to kill them off."[36]

Second, the Conscription Act contained a clause that gave a new and bitter meaning to the motto "rich man's war and poor man's fight": an exemption for any man who paid a $300 fee that would be used to hire a volunteer substitute. In a city where many laborers earned about $1 a day, this was class legislation with a vengeance, and, indeed, propertied men like J. Pierpont Morgan, Theodore Roosevelt Sr., and George Templeton Strong paid the fee and stayed clear of the battlefield. Over the spring and summer of 1863, *Frank Leslie's Illustrated Newspaper* warned that the draft law "converts the Republic into one grand military dictatorship," while John McMaster's vehement *Freeman's Journal* blasted that "deluded and almost delirious fanatic," Lincoln. Another Democratic paper ran a parody of a popular Union Army recruiting song:

> *Since poverty has been our crime, we bow to the decree;*
> *We are the poor who have no wealth to purchase liberty.*[37]

For thousands of working-class New Yorkers alienated from the war, the government's determination to enforce the draft was an intolerable challenge, one that momentarily focused their anger on the federal draft offices established in neighborhoods throughout the city.

In the morning hours on Monday, as crowds of machinists, iron-workers, longshoremen, and others listened to impromptu speakers in an empty lot above Fifty-Ninth Street just east of the new Central Park, they remained peaceful. But at 10 AM, when the drawing of names from a rotating drum—the "wheel of misfortune," the *Daily News* called it—commenced in the Ninth District draft office at Third Avenue and Forty-Sixth Street, the situation deteriorated. The throng of hundreds pressing around the office's door grew angrier and more boisterous until, finally, members of the Black Joke Engine Company, volunteer firemen with strong ties to local Democratic politicians, hurled paving stones through the windows. Shouting "Down with the rich men!" the crowd poured into the office, demolishing it and clubbing several draft officers. Armed with stones and sticks, the crowd beat back a company of fifty soldiers of the army's Invalid Corps who appeared on the scene. The draft office was soon consumed in flames.[38]

A block away, at Lexington Avenue and Forty-Fifth Street, George Templeton Strong watched as several hundred "of the lowest Irish day laborers" attacked two row houses because of a rumor that a draft officer lived there. After the mob (including "stalwart young vixens and withered old hags") shattered the windows with stones and forced several women and children to flee, "men and small boys appeared at rear windows and began smashing the sashes . . . and dropped chairs and mirrors into the back yard. . . . Loafers were seen marching off with portable articles of furniture." As smoke billowed out of the buildings, Strong turned away. "I could endure the disgraceful, sickening sight no longer, and what could I *do?*" The New York Draft Riot, the bloodiest mob action in American history, was beginning.[39]

By Monday afternoon, the pent up fury of Manhattan's white immigrant working class was exploding throughout the city. On Third Avenue alone, a crowd estimated at fifty thousand surged back and forth. Although many were spectators like Strong, a hard core of rioters numbering in the thousands ranged through the city. Breaking into stores, the mob armed itself with "revolvers, old muskets, stones, clubs, [and] barrel-staves," as well as with alcohol from saloons and liquor shops. Rioters and policemen battled for possession of a gun factory at Twenty-First Street and Second Avenue, partly owned by Republican

Mayor George Opdyke. By night, the building was a charred ruin littered with thirteen corpses. Another draft office at Broadway and Twenty-Ninth Street went up in flames. The many New Yorkers who frantically boarded ferryboats to escape, and especially the African Americans who sought refuge on the city's outskirts or tried to hide in Central Park, were well advised to take flight. Monday proved to be only the beginning of a rampage that continued for four days and nights.[40]

Although luck largely determined who escaped the mob and who fell victim to it, the rioters chose a predictable range of targets. The households of wealthier families who could be identified as Republicans or emancipationists were attacked, looted, and sometimes burned to the ground. On Tuesday, for example, some two hundred rioters converged on the West Twenty-Ninth Street townhouse of white abolitionist James Gibbons. Through the shutters of her aunt's house two doors down, Gibbons's daughter Lucy watched as men with pickaxes shattered the parlor windows of her home. She saw "sheets of music . . . flying in every direction" and observed "women, laden with spoils . . . leaning against the courtyard railing; one had a pot and was fanning herself with the lid." The Gibbons home barely escaped conflagration; neighbors, fearing for their own townhouses, climbed to the roof and lowered buckets of water into the house to douse the flames ignited by the looters.[41]

Isolated members of the Metropolitan Police Force—controlled by the Republican state legislature in Albany, rather than by local Democrats—also came in for rough treatment. Near the Ninth District draft office on Monday, a crowd recognized police superintendent John Kennedy, known for his success in arresting Union army deserters. They beat and kicked him savagely and left him for dead (miraculously, the sixty-year-old Kennedy survived). Patrick Dolan, an eighteen-year-old blacksmith, led a group to destroy Mayor Opdyke's Fifth Avenue mansion, but they were driven off by police. When, on West Twenty-Eighth Street, a drunken John Fitzherbert shredded the stars and stripes while shouting "Damn the flag!" and others offered "Three cheers for Jeff Davis!" they made clear their revulsion at a war they now saw as serving the rich man and the abolitionist.[42]

The most hated prey were black New Yorkers—men, women, and children. For four days, "Down with the bloody nigger!" and "Kill all niggers!" echoed through the streets. On Monday afternoon, a mob surrounded the Colored Orphan Asylum on Fifth Avenue at Forty-Third Street, a philanthropy funded by wealthy Quakers and hence a symbol of the link between the city's white abolitionists and its black population. As members of the crowd shouted "Burn the niggers' nest!" and split the front door with axes, superintendent William Davis led the asylum's residents—237 black children—out the rear. With looting under way and the edifice going up in flames, an Irishman in the crowd beseeched those around him: "If there's a man among you, with a heart within him, come and help these poor children." Their answer was to beat him. But elsewhere in the crowd, Paddy M'Caffrey with several fellow stage drivers and volunteer firemen protected twenty children who had become separated from the main group. Davis managed to get his charges, unharmed, to the sanctuary of the Twentieth Police Precinct House at Thirty-Fourth Street off Ninth Avenue.[43]

The assault on the asylum was only the beginning of the pogrom. Mobs looted and set fire to blocks of shanties occupied by black families. "Don't never show your face in this street again," laborer James Cassidy, who lived nearby, warned Mary Alexander as he expelled her and other African Americans from their homes on West Twenty-Eighth Street. By Monday night, lynching had also come to the streets of New York. William Jones made the mistake of walking down Clarkson Street, returning home with a loaf of bread bought at a neighborhood store. A group of white men caught him, hanged him from a tree, and then ignited a bonfire under his suspended corpse. On Wednesday in broad daylight, Abraham Franklin, a disabled coachman, was hanged from a lamppost at West Twenty-Eighth Street and Seventh Avenue; a Jewish emigrant tailor from England, Mark Silva, helped hoist Franklin to his death. After the body was cut down, a white sixteen-year-old butcher's apprentice, Patrick Butler, dragged Franklin's corpse by the genitals through the street, to the cheers of the mob. Before the week was out, one more black man, James Costello, was hanged; at least two others were beaten to death. Eighteen sustained injuries from beatings; four other African American men and women were hurt jumping from

African American New Yorkers being attacked during the Draft Riot, as pictured in the Republican periodical *Harper's Weekly*. Engraving by unidentified artist, *How to Escape the Draft*, in *Harper's Weekly*, August 1, 1863. AUTHOR'S COLLECTION.

the windows of their homes to escape the mob. Peter Heuston, a Mohawk Indian mistaken for a black man, died from his wounds after the riot ended. These numbers may reflect only a fraction of total African American casualties; others probably went unreported as black families fled for their lives.[44]

Some sought to defend their homes. At the height of the riots the black abolitionist William Wells Brown entered a tenement on Thompson Street to find eight black women, an "octet of Amazons," concocting a simmering mixture of water, soap, and ashes they called "the King of Pain." Brown inquired how they intended to fend off the mob if it materialized. "We'll fling hot water on them, and scald their very hearts out." "Can you all throw water without injuring each other?" he asked. "O yes, Honey," they replied, "we've been practicing all day." Downtown on Dover Street, Brown's fellow activist, William Powell, vowed not to leave his Colored Sailors' Home "until driven from the premises." By Monday afternoon, however, "king mob" had surrounded it, and the evening found Powell with his wife, children, and eight other men on the roof of the five-story building next door as rioters ransacked his house. How to escape? With the help of a Jewish neighbor—"a little, deformed, despised Israelite," as Powell put it— Powell, an experienced sailor, rigged a rope and pulley that allowed them all to descend, roof to roof, and land safely in a nearby yard. A few blocks away, Albro and Mary Lyons stood guard in the vestibule of their own hostel for black seamen. When a mob approached the doorway after midnight, Albro Lyons fired a gun into the crowd, scattering them. At dawn on Tuesday, the couple heard a voice outside crying, "Don't shoot, Al. It's only me." Officer Kelly, an Irish policeman from the local precinct, greeted with relief the news that they had survived the night. "This kind hearted man," their daughter Maritcha would remember, "sat on our steps and sobbed like a child."[45]

"The beastly ruffians were masters of the situation and of the city," George Templeton Strong wrote grimly after returning home to Gramercy Park from "the seat of war" in the East Forties. By Monday afternoon, the city's authorities were scrambling to meet the onslaught many of them had half-expected, but whose magnitude they had never fully anticipated. The rooms of Major General John Wool, commander of the army's Department of the East, in the elegant St. Nicholas Hotel on Broadway at Spring Street, became an impromptu command center for riot control. But the official response was alarmingly decentralized. While Wool's deputy, Brevet Brigadier General Harvey Brown, corralled about four hundred soldiers from the Invalid Corps and the harbor forts and prepared them for deployment, Major General Charles Sandford, head of the state militia, unaccountably kept some six hundred militiamen "in reserve" within the state arsenal at Seventh Avenue and Thirty-Fifth Street.[46]

All involved in the attempts to stop the rioters longed for the presence of the city's active regiments, but they were in Pennsylvania with the Army of the Potomac. New York City had been left with a skeletal home guard in the face of Lee's invasion. But by working together, Brown and Thomas Acton, energetic president of the Metropolitan Police Commission, emerged as capable commanders while Wool and Sandford dithered. With a combined force of 700 federal soldiers and 800 policemen, and with several hundred armed and deputized civilians, the two men dispatched squadrons. Telegrams and scrawled messages poured in and out of their joint base at police headquarters on Mulberry Street. "Quail on toast for every man of you, as soon as the mob is put down. Quail on toast, boys," Acton promised his policemen as they set off into the streets. Armed with hardwood clubs, over one hundred patrolmen under Sergeant Daniel Carpenter beat back a large group of rioters surging down Broadway at Bleecker Street on Monday afternoon. When a belligerent crowd of several hundred filled City Hall Park and threatened the *New York Tribune* Building that night, a contingent of 150 police, in the words of one of the riot's early historians, "fell in one solid mass on the mob, knocking men over right and left, and laying heads open at every blow." New York's civil war generated its own fratricide: if many of the rioters were Irish immigrants and their sons, so were the police who challenged them in hand-to-hand combat.[47]

It was Brown's soldiers—along with regiments that started arriving from the front by Wednesday evening—who brought the full thrust of the Civil War to Manhattan's streets: gleaming bayonets, loaded muskets, and field howitzers. In close formation, troops repeatedly fired down avenues to clear them of angry New Yorkers, much as some had recently swept Confederates from Pennsylvania cornfields. "I halted the company, and fired by sections, allowing each section to fall to the rear to load as fast as it had fired," Captain Walter Franklin of the Twelfth US Infantry later recalled of his unit's action against the mob in Second Avenue on Tuesday afternoon. The New York *World* reported the result: "The dead bodies of the killed were to be seen being borne away by their friends. . . . Pools of blood would be met at frequent intervals, and in a large number of houses lay the wounded writhing in pain." But in many cases rioters were firing too, from behind makeshift barricades and from tenement roofs. On Thursday evening, in the riot's last major engagement, 160 federal infantrymen marched up Second Avenue in the Twenties and low Thirties, only to be barraged by stones and bullets aimed at them from streets and buildings. While Union sharpshooters picked snipers off rooftops, artillerymen aimed cannon down the avenue, firing canister shot—cylinders that spewed forth metal balls with devastating force—to clear it of the enemy.[48]

By Friday, with over 5,000 Union troops brought up from Pennsylvania now occupying Manhattan, the riot had burned out. Dazed New Yorkers surveyed the results: over one hundred homes, businesses, and public buildings burned down, including two draft offices, the Colored Orphan Asylum, and the Eighteenth Police Precinct House on East Twenty-Third Street; two hundred other buildings looted or vandalized; property damage amounting to between $3 million and $5 million (about $60 to $100 million in today's dollars); 73 soldiers, 105 policemen, and 128 civilians reported injured; 105 reported dead, including 6 soldiers and 3 policemen. The actual number of wounded and killed was almost certainly higher, as rioters hid their wounded and covertly disposed of corpses; 500 dead is probably a more accurate estimate. Antidraft riots had simultaneously broken out throughout the North—in Boston, Detroit, Troy, and across the river in Brooklyn—but none remotely approached the magnitude of New York City's.[49]

For all the destruction they had wrought, the rioters failed to halt the draft: it resumed in August, with ten thousand federal troops patrolling Manhattan's streets. And yet the rioters had scored some victories for themselves. For one thing, the city's Democratic grand juries and courts proved loath to punish the 443 New Yorkers (including 38 women) arrested during the riot. Only 49 appear to have served any significant time in prison; most of the rest were acquitted or released without being charged. Patrick Butler, who had dragged Abraham Franklin's corpse through the street, was found guilty of "an offense against public decency" and was sent to the House of Refuge, a juvenile reformatory.[50]

Though the draft proceeded, key Democrats deflected its impact. The war had divided the city's Democratic Party into two factions—the "War Democrats" of Tammany Hall, critical of emancipation and the draft but committed to Union military victory, and Fernando

Wood's "Peace Democrats" (or "Copperheads"), known for their willingness to consider a negotiated peace and their barely concealed pro-Confederate sentiments. Their rivalry had split the usual Democratic majority and allowed the Republican Opdyke to be elected mayor in 1861. But now Tammany, in the guise of County Supervisor William Tweed, hit upon a scheme to ensure no further draft riots would trouble the city. As the driving force of a County Special Committee on Volunteering, Tweed oversaw a program whereby the city paid the $300 exemption fee for any drafted New Yorker who did not want to serve. Over the last twenty months of the war, the committee spent some $10 million, raised through a municipal bond issue, to pay the bounties of volunteer substitutes so 116,000 drafted New Yorkers could stay at home. The program provided the soldiers to fill President Lincoln's quotas, and it clinched Tammany's reputation as friend to the working man. The county supervisor's deft handling of the situation helped make him "Boss" Tweed, postwar master of the local Democratic Party and of the city itself.[51]

Republicans glowered at such pandering to voters who so recently had brandished the torch and the noose, but many in the party, including Lincoln himself, recognized what a fine line they had to walk. If they acquiesced in these Tammany machinations, enlistments would proceed peacefully, and "War Democrats" would continue to support the war effort. If, instead, they imposed a draconian draft, another maelstrom might be unleashed. Lincoln cut the city's draft quota in half. Pressed by some Manhattan Republicans to launch a federal inquest into the riots, the president held back, intimating that further antagonizing the North's Democrats would backfire: "One rebellion at a time is about as much as we can conveniently handle."[52]

The rioters scored one additional victory. The mass influx of freed slaves from the South never materialized. As word of New York's lynchings spread, migrating African Americans got the message about the reception that would greet them in the nation's largest city. In the years following the riots, Manhattan's black population declined rather than increased, as numerous survivors sought to leave behind the traumas of July 1863 and New York's persistent racism. Albro and Mary Lyons, whose home was finally wrecked by a mob on

Wednesday night, relocated their family to Providence, Rhode Island. Maritcha Lyons understood the situation precisely: she and her parents were living "in exile" from New York City.[53]

On the chilly afternoon of March 5, 1864, an interracial crowd lined the northern perimeter of Union Square to watch a committee of prominent Republicans bestow an honorary flag upon the men of the Twentieth US Colored Troops, the city's first African American regiment. Few if any recalled that black New Yorkers had been fighting in the city's wars since Dutch colonial days. Instead, for many present, like George Templeton Strong, the event marked a more pressing set of imperatives: the need to arm blacks to aid in defeating the South and the need to offer a resolute gesture to the Democrats who had risen in bloody insurrection eight months earlier.

The war had driven Strong, like other New York Republicans, steadily leftward in his thinking. Although he never fully shed his suspicion that blacks were biologically inferior to whites, he had come to understand abolition as a war strategy and as something due to four million enslaved Americans. The Union League Club, the organization of elite Republicans Strong cofounded to sustain the city's commitment to victory, had sponsored the Twentieth Regiment in defiance of state and city Democrats. Two other black regiments, the Twenty-Sixth and the Thirty-First, would follow. As the regiment marched down Broadway to board a ship for the Louisiana war zone, Strong was moved by their appearance—"armed, drilled, truculent, elate." Even Maria Lydig Daly, a racist and wife of a War Democrat, confessed that she was stirred: "They were a fine body of men and had a look of satisfaction in their faces, as though they felt they had gained a right to be more respected."[54]

The sense of helplessness that the Draft Riot induced in many affluent New Yorkers gave way to a redoubled commitment. The US Sanitary Commission, a quasi-public body founded by a handful of Manhattan businessmen, professionals, and doctors, worked with the federal government to improve health conditions for Union troops in the field and in military hospitals. From its executive headquarters at 823 Broadway, the commission controlled fleets of steamers, barges, and wagons; dispatched tons of medicine and supplies; hired doctors, orderlies, and nurses to supplement those of the army's overburdened Medical Bureau; and by early 1865, supervised over five hundred agents in the field who sought to monitor and remedy dismal conditions in the hospitals. New York society women, deprived of careers by prevailing gender roles, seized the opportunity to toil actively in a public cause. Some trained as volunteer nurses or doctor's assistants and were even paid for their work. Although often resented by male professionals, many served unflinchingly under daunting conditions. Maria Lydig Daly's unmarried friend Harriet Whetten nursed sick and wounded soldiers in Virginia. "She looked very happy," Daly observed when Whetten returned to New York in May 1862. "She has been longing for some active employment and would like to have gone soldiering, I think, long ago."[55]

While the wounds inflicted by the Draft Riot lingered, on the surface New York resumed its daily round of getting and spending, of feverish bustle and lavish consumption, especially in its upper social echelons. In early 1864, as Sherman had prepared his troops for the drive toward Atlanta, and Grant had primed his for a campaign against Richmond, New York still seemed able to insulate itself from the war's destruction, a fact that infuriated Southerners who learned of continued Northern tranquility through newspaper accounts and correspondence. Disappointed in their expectation that the Draft Riot would be followed by escalating Northern turmoil, Confederates decided to bring the war to New York themselves.

The prospect of a combined attack from inside and outside the city played on the minds of many New Yorkers. Republicans in particular refused to believe that the Draft Riot had not represented some deep-laid conspiracy between Confederate agents and local Copperheads. The *New York Times* went so far as to label the draft rioters "the left wing of Lee's army." In truth, the city had become a sanctuary for refugees from Southern war zones, estimated as numbering from ten thousand to fifty thousand. Some had come north to be near husbands or relatives who were among the hundreds of prisoners of war being held in Fort Lafayette in the Narrows and elsewhere around the harbor. "The city is literally swarming with rebel adventurers of an irresponsible and dangerous class," the *Times* warned. Many assumed that spies were conveying news of local troop and ship movements to Richmond. Major General John Dix, commander of the Department of the East, ordered all Southerners in the city to register with the army or else be considered "spies or emissaries of the insurgent authorities in Richmond," but only a few hundred bothered to show up at the Department's Bleecker Street headquarters to give their names, residences, and vital statistics. While Republicans remained enraged at Northern Peace Democrats, no evidence ever proved that Southern agents or New York Copperheads premeditated the Draft Riot (although local Democratic politicians clearly had tried to spark a more focused resistance to the draft itself). Such allegations nevertheless allowed Strong and others to overlook the grinding poverty, anti-Irish prejudice, and class discrimination that had helped fuel the riot.[56]

When it did come, in the fall of 1864, the Confederate plot against New York would mainly be the work of outsiders. During the last year of the war, a cadre of Southern agents led by a Mississippian, Jacob Thompson, used Toronto, Canada, as a base for a series of audacious assaults against the North. Most of their schemes, such as an attempt to get Midwestern Copperheads to rise in armed insurrection, failed miserably. But in September, when Union general Philip Sheridan's troops ravaged the farms of the Shenandoah Valley, Thompson's operatives meditated revenge. One of them, Dr. Luke Blackburn, proposed poisoning New York City's water supply in the Croton Reservoir on Fifth Avenue. Instead, Thompson's group settled on an idea broached in the Richmond *Whig*, which in October declared, "New York is worth twenty Richmonds. . . . They chose to substitute the torch for the sword. We may so use their own weapon as to make them repent, literally in sackcloth and ashes, that they ever adopted it."[57]

Under the Confederate plan, a group of saboteurs would infiltrate New York from Toronto, and on Election Day, November 8, they would set fires and foment an uprising by Copperheads, who would turn the city against the Union war effort. On October 26, eight men, including two Kentuckians, Colonel Robert Martin and Lieutenant John Headley, and a Louisianan, Captain Robert Cobb Kennedy, boarded a train in Toronto bound for New York. Fearing trouble on

Election Day, however, Secretary of War Stanton made sure that General Benjamin Butler and 3,500 Union troops were present. With Butler's troops circling Manhattan on ferries and gunboats, New Yorkers registered their protest with ballots rather than weapons, giving Lincoln's Democratic challenger, George McClellan, a thirty-seven-thousand-vote lead in the city. The presence of troops daunted the Confederate agents. They bided their time, meeting in boarding-houses and hotel rooms, until Butler's soldiers left on November 15.[58]

On the evening of November 25, New Yorkers who ordinarily ignored the tolling of the bell in the City Hall cupola took heed as the doleful sound echoed from fire towers and church steeples throughout the city. Dark smoke poured forth from one and then another of the city's hotels—from the St. James at Broadway and Twenty-Sixth Street, the Fifth Avenue, the Astor House, and nine others. As word spread through the Winter Garden Theatre that the Lafarge House next door was on fire, one theatergoer noted that "the wildest confusion, amounting to a panic, pervaded the vast audience." During the night, blazes also erupted on a barge along the Hudson River, in a West Side lumberyard, and in P. T. Barnum's famous museum on lower Broadway.[59]

Pedestrians, hotel guests, and streetcar riders quickly realized the fires were not accidents. As firemen and police converged on the various hotels and put out the flames, they congratulated themselves on their luck: the arsonists had saturated furniture and drapery in "greek fire"—a spontaneously combustible mixture of phosphorus in a bi-sulfide of carbon—but had closed room windows and doors when they fled, depriving the flames of oxygen. Most of the fires merely smoldered and were easily quenched. No one was killed or seriously hurt in the fires, although the St. Nicholas Hotel sustained $10,000 in damage. But the newspapers warned of what might have been: Manhattan would be "in flames at this moment," the *Tribune* averred, had the plotters properly ignited the fires. Meanwhile, the arsonists eluded a police dragnet around the Hudson River Railroad terminal at Thirtieth Street and Tenth Avenue, boarded a train for Albany, and were back in Toronto on November 28.[60]

City and federal officials looked northward, well aware from the reports of informers and Union spies that Toronto had become a Confederate base. The Metropolitan Police dispatched six detectives to Detroit and Toronto, where leads paid off. When Robert Cobb Kennedy tried to slip into Detroit on his way back to the Confederacy in late December, two detectives were waiting for him. "These are badges of honor!" Kennedy shouted to fellow passengers on a New York–bound train as he brandished his handcuffs at them. "I am a Southern gentleman!"[61]

A military commission appointed by Major General Dix convicted Kennedy as an enemy spy. At the last moment, as he faced the hangman's noose, Kennedy penned a confession: "We wanted to let the people of the North understand . . . that they can't be rolling in wealth & comfort, while we at the South are bearing all the hardship & privations. . . . We desired to destroy property, not the lives of women & children although that would of course have followed in its train." On the afternoon of March 25, 1865, Robert Cobb Kennedy was hanged in the courtyard of Fort Lafayette, the only man ever convicted in the arson plot and the last Confederate soldier executed by the Union during the Civil War. "Think of me as if I had fallen in battle," he wrote in his last letter to his mother.[62]

The question of Copperhead complicity in the plot remained a murky one. The police arrested and then released a number of Confederate sympathizers, including Gus McDonald, a Broadway piano dealer who had stored the arsonists' luggage. A mysterious Washington Place chemist who allegedly provided the agents with "greek fire" was never apprehended. Decades later, Kennedy's fellow conspirator John Headley, who had become Kentucky's secretary of state, charged that John McMaster, one of the city's bitterest anti-Lincoln newspaper editors, had promised the plotters an uprising by twenty thousand Manhattan sympathizers to coincide with the fires. Although impossible to disprove (McMaster was long dead), Headley's allegations against him and other New York Democrats seem implausible, and not only because Headley had various ulterior motives for making his claims. Why, after all, would New Yorkers—even ardent friends of the South—want their homes and businesses to burn down?

In the end, the plot had served to "give the people a scare," in Kennedy's words, but it smacked more of Ruffin's and Mallory's fantasies than of any realistic strategy for Southern independence. True,

A diabolical Confederate agent prepares to torch a Manhattan hotel room, as pictured in *Harper's Weekly*. Detail from engraving by unidentified artist, *Adjoining Rooms in a Hotel in New York*, in *Harper's Weekly*, December 17, 1864. AUTHOR'S COLLECTION.

if the fires had ignited and spread, New Yorkers might have had a formidable act of terrorism to contend with. But the fires merely sputtered, and for a city that sixteen months earlier had endured what the *Times* called "the Reign of the Rabble," the arson plot seemed paltry, the last gasp of a dying cause.[63]

"Never before did I hear cheering that came straight from the heart," George Templeton Strong wrote of the scene in Wall Street on April 3, 1865, as news of the Union army's entry into Richmond spread through the city. "Men embraced and hugged each other, *kissed* each other, retreated into doorways to dry their eyes and came out again to flourish their hats and hurrah. There will be many sore throats in New York tomorrow." Seven days later, the joyous news of Lee's surrender to Grant arrived; only a rainstorm kept the city from an uproarious celebration outdoors. But then, on the morning of April 15, New Yorkers awoke to the news of Lincoln's assassination. Throughout the war years, few New Yorkers had responded to the president with unbridled enthusiasm. War Democrats like Maria Lydig Daly had derided him as "Uncle Ape . . . a clever hypocrite," and even Strong had considered Lincoln "far below the first grade." Now, in the wake of the assassination, Strong changed his view. "I am stunned, as by a fearsome personal calamity . . . ," he wrote. "We shall appreciate him at last."[64]

In many ways, New Yorkers put the war behind them quickly, finding new ways to make money after the war contracts dried up. Never again would cotton loom so large in the city's economy; businessmen and investors looked elsewhere for profit, to railroad securities, industrial expansion, and maritime trade. Workmen largely eschewed rioting for a growing trade union movement—albeit one that sustained the spirit of the Draft Riot by rigidly excluding African Americans. The city's battles were now fought in newspaper columns, courtrooms, and polling places as reformers sought to dethrone "Boss" Tweed and to limit the power of the Tammany voters Strong called "ignorant emigrant *gorillas*." New Yorkers felt themselves to be living in a new and different era. Looking over a scrapbook of five-year-old newspaper clippings in May 1865, Strong observed that "it seemed like reading the records of some remote age and of a people wholly unlike our own."[65]

Yet the war's legacies—and its wounds—lingered. Racism remained the common currency of the New York Democrats, and the war was hardly over before the city's Democratic leaders resumed their overtly cordial ties with the South's former slaveholders. Both upstate and downstate, New York's electorate voted down a state measure that would have given black men equal suffrage rights in 1869; that right was only obtained through the federal Fifteenth Amendment in 1870. In the presidential election that spelled the end to Reconstruction in 1877, Manhattan lawyer Samuel Tilden, the Democratic nominee, repeatedly avowed the cause of white supremacy and black subservience. Many of the city's Republicans also turned their backs on African Americans,

weary of the issues that had torn the nation and city apart. By 1874,
George Templeton Strong, who a decade earlier had stood in Union
Square stirred by the sight of black soldiers, found little to choose be-
tween New York's Democratic "Celtocracy" and those reconstructed
Southern states allegedly dominated by a "Niggerocracy."[66]

The fissures of class, ethnicity, and politics never fully subsided in
postwar New York but continued as immigration brought hundreds of
thousands of newcomers to the city's slums and sweatshops. Reformers
who launched postwar inquests into housing and health conditions
pointed over their shoulders to the Draft Riot, warning that the city's
poverty could again incubate violence, perhaps even revolution. Their
efforts to improve daily life for what some were coming to call the urban "proletaire" could not put to rest fears about potential enemies
within the gate—enemies who might speak not with an Irish brogue or
a Southern twang, but in other, guttural accents.[67]

CHAPTER 7

Huns Within Our Gates
World War I, 1914–1918

On the evening of March 8, 1902, Prince Heinrich of Prussia, brother of the German kaiser, Wilhelm II, rose to address 1,300 American dignitaries who had gathered to fete him in the Grand Ballroom of the Waldorf-Astoria Hotel on Fifth Avenue. "The measure of confidence placed by two great nations in each other has grown and expanded," the prince, speaking in his native tongue, told his hosts. Enthusiastic applause greeted his comments from the men at the banquet tables and from the jewel-bedecked ladies seated in the ballroom's balcony boxes. Among the most conspicuous guests were New Yorkers of German birth or ancestry who had worked their way to success and distinction in the city, men like publisher Hermann Ridder, brewer Jacob Ruppert, real estate tycoon Henry Morgenthau, and banker Jacob Schiff.[1]

The prince had arrived two weeks earlier to take formal possession of the schooner *Meteor*, commissioned as a royal yacht by the kaiser from a shipyard on Shooter's Island in New York harbor. On February 25, President Theodore Roosevelt chatted affably with the prince at the yacht's ceremonial launching there. But the prince's goodwill tour had a larger diplomatic purpose. At the end of the brief American war with Spain in 1898 (a war in which Roosevelt and other New Yorkers figured prominently), the American and German Pacific fleets had almost come to blows in the waters off the Philippines. The episode seemed to presage further clashes between two industrial nations aspiring to world power, and German-American relations had been tense ever since. The prince, a polite man who also happened to be an admiral in the German navy, managed to defuse the tension. In New York he received the "Freedom of the City" from Mayor Low and stated how "inspiring" he found New Yorkers. In their faces, he told reporters, he saw "activity and ambition not dulled by too much contentment, yet not marred by discontent. Is not this the balance," he asked, "that makes your people so happy and so powerful?"[2]

No one was happier with all this than New York's vast German American enclave of 750,000, more than a fifth of the city's total population. The *New York Times* described a "spectacular" torchlight parade honoring the prince, in which over 8,000 members of 320 local German societies marched down Park Avenue. New York was, after all, the world's third largest German-speaking city after Berlin and Vienna. Decades of immigration had created an entire city within a city, proud of its own newspapers, churches, orchestras, choral groups, beer halls, and clubs, even as many German newcomers and their American-born children entered the city's English-speaking mainstream. Most of them cherished American freedoms while simultaneously expressing an exuberant pride in their German roots. Few people suggested that their dual affections should lay German New Yorkers open to the charge of disloyalty. Most observers, including those who viewed the rising tide of migrants from Eastern and Southern Europe with dismay, regarded German Americans as the ideal immigrant group: staid, responsible, upwardly mobile.[3]

What Prince Heinrich knew at the time, and Americans (including German Americans) did not, was that the kaiser and his naval high command nursed an abiding hostility toward the United States, which had come to shape imperial planning. In the German race to overtake Britain as the world's foremost power, Wilhelm II perceived a threat in the increasingly global ambitions of the United States, especially in American encroachment on territories, markets, and potential naval bases in the Pacific and Caribbean. "A war to the death" between the two powers was inevitable, the kaiser told his advisors.[4]

Accordingly, between 1897 and 1903, German admiralty staff officers and army strategists developed secret plans for the invasion of the American East Coast as the decisive blow that would knock America out of world competition. Naval officers proposed the seizure of Puerto Rico or Haiti as a staging area for attacking New York and New England, which they judged to be America's industrial and commercial heart. The planners foresaw one hundred thousand troops landing at Provincetown on Cape Cod and using it as a base for an attack on Boston and the New England coast. The invasion fleet would also prepare for "a joint advance by land and sea against Brooklyn and New York." After defeating the American navy off the coast, a quick, decisive thrust against New York City and Boston was imperative and far more crucial than the conquest of the mere political capital of Washington, DC.

By 1899 the German military attaché in Washington, Count von Gotzen, had provided the admiralty staff with detailed information on the forts guarding New York harbor. While some officers argued that the harbor's forts might foil the attack, Lieutenant (later Admiral) Eberhard von Mantey, the plan's mastermind, predicted that "in New York large-scale panic will result from just the mention of a possible bombardment," impeding defensive preparations and leading to American capitulation in the face of Germany's lightning-swift attack.[5]

It remains unclear whether Germany's plans for seizing New York represented a serious contingency or a mere academic exercise. At the very least, the plans reveal a vision in which New York and the entire Northeast, sources and symbols of American impudence, would be vanquished by German might. Resentment of the growing power of New York City and its business titans was widely shared. A popular German magazine warned in 1899 that in the new century, "much of Europe will go into the private ownership of the Rockefellers and Vanderbilts." In any event, by 1906 the admiralty had shelved its plans, to be forgotten as the army general staff persuaded Wilhelm that a swift land war against France and Russia could bestow the continental domination that Germany deserved. Revenge against American insolence would have to wait. By the time that occurred, some fifteen years after Heinrich's visit, fears and doubts about the loyalty of German Americans—and of other

New Yorkers, as well—would shape how the nation's largest city experienced a world war. That war's battlefields remained three thousand miles away, but its passions and allegiances would be urgently local.[6]

The outbreak of the Great War in August 1914 caught New York and the rest of the country off guard. A month after the assassination of Austria-Hungary's Archduke Franz Ferdinand by Bosnian Serb nationalists, the major European powers put into motion the grand offensives they had been planning for years. The armies of Germany, Austria-Hungary, and the Ottoman Empire (the Central Powers) and of France, Britain, and Russia (the Allies) battled each other in Europe and soon also in Africa and the Middle East. As Wall Street's markets slumped in response to the turmoil, and the New York Stock Exchange suspended trading for four months, President Woodrow Wilson counseled Americans to remain calm and to avoid taking sides in a deplorable conflict that was none of their business. "We must be impartial in thought as well as in action," he told his countrymen.[7]

As never before, New York in 1914 was the national capital in every sense but the political, and its international influence led people to call it an "imperial" city. Wall Street, Broadway, Fifth Avenue, and the Statue of Liberty had become catchphrases around the world. But to many Americans in 1914, New York City was also a kind of national litmus test, the most vivid case study of the policy of unrestricted immigration that had filled the metropolis and the country with the peoples of Europe. Almost one third of the nation, and 40 percent of New York City's five million people, were foreign-born. For many Americans, New York seemed the crucial laboratory for gauging whether immigration was forging a unified people in whose hands democracy was safe or instead a patchwork of ethnic neighborhoods blighted by conflict and degeneration. For many, especially among the native-born, the line between optimism and alarm was often perilously thin. Even liberals bent on preserving a tolerant society feared that national unity was a fragile affair, only preserved by keeping European conflicts at bay. To the German ambassador, Count Johann von Bernstorff, Wilson explained that the nation must stay neutral, or otherwise "our mixed populations would wage war on each other."[8]

But Europe wouldn't let New York alone. The belligerents, recognizing the city's pivotal role in American finance, industry, and opinion making, immediately sought to enlist hearts and minds on the Atlantic's western shore. From his headquarters in London's Wellington House, Sir Gilbert Parker, head of the American division of the newly formed, top-secret War Propaganda Bureau, wrote letters and sent pamphlets across the Atlantic to thousands of "influential and eminent people of every profession" to build "a backing for the British cause." Parker's men also fed their version of the war to the principal correspondents of the New York papers and press services, most of whom used London as their base for covering European news, thereby guaranteeing that the British perspective would be read throughout the United States. Such efforts intensified as the summer's illusions of quick victory gave way to the deadlock of trench warfare along a Western Front occupied by three million soldiers and stretching from the Swiss border to the English Channel. Exaggerated reports of German atrocities against Belgian civilians, disseminated from Wellington House, filled the headlines of New York's dailies. By May 1915, when a German U-boat sank the English liner *Lusitania*, six days out from New York, with the loss of 1,198 lives, including 128 Americans, the phrase "Remember Belgium" was already imbedded in millions of American minds as a token of German brutality.[9]

Many New Yorkers needed little prodding to side with the Allies, despite Wilson's plea for neutrality. This was especially true within the city's business and professional elite, dominated by Protestants of British descent who viewed the British Empire's constitutional monarchy and the French Republic as politically kindred to the United States. In their eyes, London and Paris, not Berlin and Vienna, were the cities whose standards of civilization New York had rightfully inherited. That the Allies, just like the Germans, might be concerned with maintaining their empires and seizing new territories and markets was rarely acknowledged. Endorsing American neutrality while supporting the Allies in spirit, the *New York Times* voiced the dominant position of the city's establishment: the war was one between "autocracy and democracy . . . between the slowly reached ideals of liberty toward which Europe has been struggling for a century and the old system of

absolutism." In short, the *Times* argued, the Allies stood for enlighten-
ment and progress; Germany and the other Central Powers embodied
tyranny and reaction.[10]

Among the new immigrants arriving at Ellis Island and settling into
the city's tenement districts, ardent Allied sympathizers could be found
as well. The city's Czechs and Slovaks, for instance, supported an Allied
victory as their best hope for freeing their homelands from the thrall
of the Austro-Hungarian Empire. After Italy joined the Allies in May
1915, the half million inhabitants of Little Italy, East Harlem, and other
Italian neighborhoods in Brooklyn and the Bronx festooned their shops
with flags and banners urging the Italian army to seize Trieste and
Trento from the Austrians. "Women and girls sat on the stoops" in Little Italy, a *Times* reporter noted, chatting "about the war and what Italy
was going to do to Austria and Germany. . . . In the streets little children played war and talked war." Thousands of young emigrants, reservists in the Italian army and navy, lined up outside the Italian
consulate on Spring Street; some boarded steamships for Genoa and
Naples. But older women on Mulberry and Mott streets looked somber:
many "had sons, grandsons, or relatives in the army of Italy, and it was
easy to see that they were thinking of what the war might mean to their
far-away kindred."[11]

Other groups in America, however, were averse to the Allied cause, a
fact appreciated by Sir Gilbert Parker's German rivals. Like the English
propagandists of Wellington House, dignitaries in Berlin covertly tried
to shape American opinion. In this they had the cooperation of the German ambassador to Washington, Count Johann von Bernstorff, who
feared that American links to Britain and France might eventually lure
the "great neutral" into the war on the Allied side. To help prevent this,
von Bernstorff relied on a slush fund of millions of dollars in German
Treasury notes, much of which he deposited in the Chase National Bank
on lower Broadway in July 1914. His emissaries enlisted a flamboyant
young German-born poet, George Sylvester Viereck, who began publishing a pro-German weekly magazine, *The Fatherland*, from an office on
Broadway. With undisclosed subsidies from von Bernstorff's fund, he
printed a steady stream of lively, provocative articles under the motto
"Fair play for Germany and Austria-Hungary." Viereck vowed to "break
the power of England upon our government" and exploited every oppor-

Vol. III, No. 25—January 26th, 1916 Price 5 Cents

THE

Fatherland

A Weekly (Title Reg. U. S. Pat. Off.)

THE GERMAN EMPEROR ON HIS FIFTY-SEVENTH BIRTHDAY

THE PROFESSIONAL "PATRIOTS" EXPOSED
By GEORGE SYLVESTER VIERECK

Celebrating the kaiser's birthday: the cover of *The Fatherland*, January 26, 1916. JOSEPH McGARRITY COLLECTION. DIGITAL LIBRARY, VILLANOVA UNIVERSITY, DIGITAL.LIBRARY.VILLANOVA.EDU.

tunity to undermine support for the Allies. Americans, he suggested, should prefer the "German imperial cross" to the "well-known double-cross of Great Britain"—a point he underscored by reminding readers of British "tyranny" during the American Revolution and War of 1812.[12]

Among the hundred thousand readers claimed by *The Fatherland* were, unsurprisingly, many New Yorkers of German birth or ancestry. A remarkably diverse group, German Americans abruptly found themselves having to sort out where they stood in relation to their homeland's war effort. After the *Lusitania* sinking, the number of German aliens applying for American citizenship in New York quadrupled. But others struggled with mixed feelings. A young writer named Hermann Hagedorn, raised in Brooklyn and educated at Göttingen and Harvard, spoke for many of his fellow German Americans in 1914: "Soberly gratified though I might be at every German setback, every German victory set my Teutonic heart beating faster." He would eventually become an ardent supporter of the Allied cause, convinced that only the defeat of Germany could lead to a new world of "Free Peoples Triumphant." Arguing with his pro-German brother Addie, he warned that "this country would be split into fragments as our family is now split, the members torn from each other and each member torn within himself," unless all Americans embraced the Allies. But such convictions came, as Hagedorn admitted, at the price of a painful inner struggle with his German identity.[13]

Most vocal among New York's German population were those who expressed pride in Germany's war aims. On August 4, 1914, thousands of young men, reservists in the German army, marched up Broadway singing "Die Wacht am Rhein," making sure to sing louder as they passed the British consulate. When some brawled with English and French reservists who tried to seize their banner, Mayor John P. Mitchel banned all foreign flags from public display. Facing the Royal Navy's blockade of the German ports, most of these German sympathizers ultimately stayed in New York. But the fervor and pride they felt ran deep in Yorkville, Williamsburg, Astoria, and the city's other German enclaves. When the *Brooklyner Freie Presse* solicited funds from its readers "to help the widows and orphans of their suffering countrymen in Germany and Austria," the paper distributed thousands of souvenir Iron Crosses so subscribers could remember "the heroic deeds of the German soldiers for which it is bestowed." Manhattan's German-language dailies, like the *Staats-Zeitung* and the *New Yorker Herold*, called for an embargo on American aid to the Allies. While the papers deplored the loss of life on the *Lusitania*, they also argued that the munitions the English liner was carrying made it a legitimate target.[14]

German immigrants and their children who had long recited the credo "Germania our mother; Columbia our bride" saw no reason to quell their voices simply because so many of their fellow Americans favored the Allies. Were they not also Americans and entitled to speak freely? Why should they not buy German war bonds and applaud their fatherland's military ambitions just as other New Yorkers backed England and France? "Organize, Organize!" Viereck exhorted his readers. Though many "ridiculed the hyphen" that distinguished German Americans from their fellow citizens, he insisted, "we shall make it a virtue."[15]

Other New Yorkers also leaned away from the Allies. The city's Irish population, still large, included numerous friends of the insurgency that would culminate in the Easter 1916 uprising in Dublin against British rule. John Devoy, editor of the *Gaelic American*, and his comrades in the city's Clan na Gael made New York the most important place outside Ireland for raising funds and smuggling supplies to Sinn Fein and the Irish Republican Brotherhood as they prepared their rebellion. To be sure, New York's Irish community also included nationalists who believed Irish home rule would follow an Allied victory. "I say not down with England but up with Ireland," lawyer William Bourke Cockran told a Carnegie Hall audience. But Devoy and many others found little to admire in the British war effort and believed that a victorious Germany would press a defeated England to grant Irish independence. Indeed, by 1915, Jeremiah O'Leary, a militant well-known on both sides of the Atlantic, was publishing his scathingly anti-British satire magazine, *Bull*, out of a Park Row office, using secret funds from von Bernstorff's bank account.[16]

Eastern European Jews also scrutinized the Allied cause skeptically. By the war years, Jewish emigrants from the Russian and Austro-Hungarian Empires had made New York the largest Jewish city in the world. On one hand, New York Zionists hoped that British victories against the Ottomans would lead to the recognition of a Jewish homeland in Palestine. On the other hand, the socialism that many Jews brought with them from Europe dictated that the war be rejected as a capitalist bloodbath. Above all, most Jews simply could not stomach the fact that the bitterly anti-Semitic czarist regime was one of the principal Allies. Many of the 1.5 million Jews on the Lower East Side and in Harlem, Brooklyn, and the Bronx had fled Russia and Russian Poland to escape pogroms, an oppressive draft, and the reactionary policies of Czar Nicholas II's government.

In 1915, bloody attacks by czarist troops on Jewish villages—
scapegoats for the Russian army's blunders on the Eastern Front—only
further outraged New York's Jews, while also making liberal Gentile
advocates of the Allied cause squirm. Harry Golden, a young boy
selling Yiddish papers on a Lower East Side corner, knew how to lure
customers with breaking war news sent from Eastern Europe: "No matter what the outcome of the skirmish I shouted 'Russians retreat again!'
I shouted it even if the Russians advanced." Moreover, the kaiser's
main ally, the Austro-Hungarian emperor Franz Josef, was a known foe
of anti-Semitism. "Franz Josef was the old reliable," Harry Golden recalled. "The East Side Jews adored him." Russian bigotry and Austrian
tolerance made it hard to view the Allied cause as a clear-cut crusade
of "democracy" against "autocracy." Shrewdly, Viereck's *Fatherland* celebrated Franz Josef with a lavish cover portrait, while on another cover
a cartoon depicted the cruel, sword-wielding czar intimidating a Jewish
captive.[17]

"There is no room in this country for hyphenated Americanism," former president Theodore Roosevelt announced to an auditorium full
of New York's Knights of Columbus in October 1915. Roosevelt repeated his message in numerous speeches and interviews, specifying
his main target: "those professional German-Americans who seek to
make the American President in effect a viceroy of the German Emperor." Roosevelt had become the most visible spokesman for Preparedness, a nationwide movement sponsored primarily by wealthy
businessmen and professional men in New York, Chicago, and other
large cities. Preparedness men urged the need for rearmament and a
national draft. Most in the movement's organizations—the National
Security League, the American Defense Society, and the American
Protective League—were openly pro-Allied and anti-German. They
were also profoundly anxious about ethnic pluralism and the complex
loyalties it implied.[18]

Preparedness advocates sought to alarm and awaken their countrymen by pointing to the dire vulnerability of their nation's largest metropolis. In a 1915 book entitled *America Fallen!* J. Bernard Walker, a
former *Scientific American* editor, argued that the new long-range guns
the government had been placing since the 1890s in the six forts now

guarding New York harbor might, in fact, fail to deter a German invasion, even though the guns made New York the most heavily defended place in the country. Evading their shells, enemy submarines could take Fort Hancock on Sandy Hook, Fort Hamilton at the Narrows, and the Brooklyn Navy Yard under the cover of night. The German surface fleet could then bombard Manhattan's signature skyscrapers—the Woolworth Building, the Singer Building, the Municipal Building—to terrify New Yorkers into submission and extort a $5 billion ransom from them. *The Battle Cry of Peace*, a popular 1915 silent film produced by a Briton, J. Stuart Blackton, and endorsed by Preparedness groups, portrays "an unnamed foreign power" using ships and planes to bomb and shell lower Manhattan—a feat made easy after secret agents gain control of the city's pacifist movement and lull naïve New Yorkers into a state of utter defenselessness. Walker and Blackton unwittingly echoed the very invasion plans the German high command had shelved a few years earlier. (They also echoed forgotten concerns from the 1880s and 1890s, when mass-circulation papers like *Frank Leslie's Illustrated Weekly* and Joseph Pulitzer's New York *World* warned of the port's vulnerability to another potential threat, an artillery bombardment by Spanish warships, although an attack on New York does not seem to have been on the Spanish agenda, even during the Spanish-American War of 1898.)[19]

But proponents of Preparedness were also doing something new: they were calling on all Americans to worry about the fate of a city many of them distrusted or even despised. Manhattan, with its bankers and immigrant masses, had come to seem a malevolent foreign force to many; by the 1890s, some Americans openly viewed Wall Street and Ellis Island as national threats. But some of the Preparedness visionaries of 1915 saw these attitudes as mistaken and dangerous. While millions viewed New York as an alien excrescence, the reality, they implied, was that New York was the essence of America: a rich, powerful, yet utterly vulnerable place, oblivious to how its own self-indulgence and softness lay it open to enemy assault. A successful attack on New York would be an attack on America, an attack the slumbering nation might not survive if it did not arm itself in advance.

On the other hand, some Preparedness lobbyists did harbor agendas that implicated New York and other large cities as threats to national security in and of themselves. While there was room in the movement

A long-range gun at Fort Wadsworth on Staten Island, guarding New York from naval attack, c. 1908. GEORGE GRANTHAM BAIN COLLECTION, LIBRARY OF CONGRESS.

for liberals who viewed Prussian militarism as a menace to world progress, many Preparedness activists were wealthy Anglo-Saxons of deeply conservative views. To these men, military preparation would not only defend America against the external foe, Germany, but also foster a national unity that would help combat internal enemies— labor unions, activists who favored an eight-hour workday, leftist radicals, and recent immigrants who allegedly harbored divided loyalties.

Fear of internal enemies was already well embedded in the consciousness of New York conservatives. After the Civil War, National Guard regiments in New York and other American cities—often composed mainly of wealthy volunteers for whom membership represented a mark of status as well as patriotism—began constructing armories. These imposing castle-like fortresses housed weapons, provided space for regimental drills, and served as citadels steeling the city, in the words of the editor George W. Curtis, "not only against the foreign peril of war, but the domestic peril of civil disorder." New

York's sprawling slum and sweatshop districts harbored threats to the safety of the city's propertied classes, Curtis and the Guardsmen believed. The Draft Riot, the Paris Commune of 1871 in which radicals seized control of the French capital, the rise of a vigorous American labor movement challenging the prerogatives of capitalists, the violent strikes that paralyzed American railroads in 1877, and the calls of a small but vocal array of immigrant anarchists for class war all figured in the thinking of armory builders. (So, perhaps, did apocalyptic novels like Joaquin Miller's *Destruction of Gotham* [1886] and Ignatius Donnelly's *Caesar's Column* [1890], which pictured New York conquered and ravaged by an enraged, brutalized working class.) Behind brick and granite walls, they stockpiled guns and ammunition to protect the established social order and prevent revolution.[20]

With their Gothic towers and crenellated ramparts, armories became visual tokens of the social stresses besetting New York and other cities. While leftists like Boston's B. O. Flowers denounced armories as "great storehouses of death" and "Plutocracy's Bastilles," journals of middle-class opinion, such as New York's *Independent*, viewed them as necessary bastions against strikers who, by forcing other workers to join them, were "worse than wild beasts turned loose upon society." In case of attack by proletarian masses, one reporter suggested in 1887, troops in the Twelfth Regiment Armory on Columbus Avenue at Sixty-First Street could defend its ramparts "in the mediaeval manner with boiling oil and melted lead, or even in the modern manner with musketry fire." Armories became bases for National Guardsmen who sallied forth to quash the Brooklyn streetcar drivers' strike of 1895 and other work stoppages, which appeared to many on both right and left as the first quiverings of an erupting class war. By 1910, some twenty armories—subsidized by the city and by Guardsmen's contributions—loomed over neighborhoods throughout the five boroughs; the five-acre Kingsbridge Armory in the Bronx, completed in 1917, was the nation's, and possibly the world's, largest such structure. Over time, the city's armories would serve a wide range of purposes—as banquet halls, galleries for pathbreaking avant-garde art, showrooms for antiques, and homeless shelters, among others. But for Preparedness advocates in the mid-1910s, they continued to serve their original purpose, as forts arming those "ready to march forth for the defense of our homes and the up-holding of the law," as a Brooklyn Guardsman had once put it, espe-cially if foreign agents stirred the pot of domestic discontent.[21]

While Preparedness advocates worried about class warfare, some among them went further, suggesting that the country's national and racial heterogeneity was itself a threat, especially in a time of global crisis. In his 1916 book, *The Passing of the Great Race*, Madison Grant—Park Avenue lawyer, amateur anthropologist, Preparedness advocate—argued that the superior Nordic race in America (a group in which he included Anglo-Saxons and Germans) were being chal-lenged for dominance by the oncoming swarm of inferior peoples from the far reaches of Europe: "Alpines," "Mediterraneans," and worst of all, Russian Jews, who now infested New York's slums. [22]

Too often, the calls for Preparedness were barely concealing visions of a society in which "dangerous" Americans—immigrants, laborers, dissenters, racial and ethnic minorities—would be forced to obey the commands of a saving remnant of wealthy purebloods. Even Teddy Roosevelt—once celebrated as the immigrant's friend and the foe of privilege—now barked out threats at "professional pacifists, poltroons, and college sissies who organize peace-at-any-price societies" and in-sisted that "the Hun within our gates is the worst of the foes of our own household."[23]

The appeal of the Preparedness movement steadily grew in New York and across the country. When, on Flag Day in June 1916, 125,000 New Yorkers paraded down Fifth Avenue, they marched past a large electric sign that read, "Absolute and Unqualified Loyalty to our Country." By that date, President Wilson—once so insistent a voice for moderation and reason—was also heartily endorsing Preparedness and something called "One Hundred Percent Americanism." New Yorkers who still dared to champion Germany, or even to espouse neu-trality and peace, watched somberly and tensely from the sidelines.[24]

By then, however, many New Yorkers had compelling practical rea-sons for being thankful for the war and for the Allied cause. During World War I, as in earlier conflicts, war was big business for New York. In 1915 and 1916, the Allied war machine became a great engine for American economic prosperity, with New York's financial district the

conduit making it possible. The austere marble edifice at 23 Wall
Street that housed J. P. Morgan and Company became, quite simply,
the most important building on the face of the earth for the Allied
war effort; New York had become as vital to the Allied cause as London and Paris were.

The "House of Morgan" was already one of the most powerful entities in the American economy, and one of the most pro-English, well
before the outbreak of the Great War. The bank prided itself on its
Anglo-American persona, forged in the nineteenth century, when Ju-
nius Morgan and his son J. Pierpont linked Wall Street and the City
of London, enabling British investors to fund America's expanding industrial economy. It went without saying that the bank's current head,
J. P. Morgan Jr., would aid wartime Britain in its hour of need. "We
were pro-Ally by inheritance, by instinct, by opinion," Morgan partner Thomas Lamont later admitted. Morgan, a steadfast Preparedness
man, described Germans as "Huns" and "Teuton savages" during the
war, his animosity fueled by disdain for Jacob Schiff, Henry Goldman,
and other German-Jewish rivals on Wall Street, some of whom were
openly anti-Russian or pro-German.

Sympathies aside, Morgan and other Wall Street bankers soon anticipated great gain. Trench warfare consumed gunpowder, shells, bullets, guns, fuel, and food at a ferocious rate, and the English and French
armies repeatedly faced shortages that threatened their hold on the
Western Front. Wall Street loans proved to be the fuel that kept the
English, French, and Russian war machines running. In 1915, Morgan
organized the largest bond-underwriting syndicate ever created in order to raise $500 million in loans for the English and French govern-
ments. The bond issue foreshadowed even more massive American
lending to the Allies, most of it by the US Treasury with Wall Street
help, later in the war. By the war's end, Wall Street had reversed the
traditional flow of capital across the Atlantic; for the first time, England became the debtor and America the creditor nation.[25]

The loans initially troubled Woodrow Wilson, bent on maintaining
neutrality in thought and deed. But the president soon understood that
the loans promised to lift the American economy out of recession, as
England and France used the credit to go on a transatlantic spree, purchasing Yankee shells, rifles, gunpowder, locomotives, steel, oil, grain,

horses, mules, and a thousand other commodities. The money loaned abroad was coming back home to put Americans to work, a fact not lost on Wilson, busy contemplating a 1916 reelection bid. So the bond issue was permitted, despite its awkward ramifications for American neutrality.[26]

The Wilson administration also allowed Morgan to become the official purchasing agent for the English and French governments (and indirectly for the Russians, who used the English to buy for them). From the DuPont chemical plants in Delaware to steel mills in Ohio and Pennsylvania, from Montana wheat fields to Connecticut arms factories, the distant war started putting Americans to work. From his office at 23 Wall, Morgan purchasing czar Edward Stettinius sent forth an army of 175 agents to sign contracts throughout the country, while also negotiating with a daily flock of Manhattan agents for far-flung suppliers. By late 1915, war contracts were driving a vigorous bull market on the New York Stock Exchange. "The very atmosphere of Manhattan Island seems impregnated with 'war contractitis,'" one journalist wrote. "We breathe it, we think it, we see it, we talk it. . . . Some have even slept it, the disease taking the shape of a nightmare."[27]

War prosperity also lifted the fortunes of many on the lower rungs of the city's economy. In the winter of 1914–1915, an estimated 398,000 New Yorkers—16 percent of the city's workforce—were jobless, many of them inundating free soup kitchens and sleeping in cheap flophouses. But over the following year, factories and workshops began humming again; by October 1915, a reporter speculated that "every machine shop in New York and vicinity which can turn a few lathes must be engaged in making projectiles." By mid-1916, three-quarters of all American munitions destined for Europe were being put aboard ship within a five-mile radius of New York's City Hall. Clerks, warehousemen, truck drivers, longshoremen, and boatmen scurried around as thousands of tons of munitions and supplies poured off boxcars at Jersey City and Hoboken into storage pens and then onto barges for the excursion across the Upper Bay to the waiting holds of freighters bound for Liverpool, Le Havre, and Archangel. New York harbor, the Western Hemisphere's busiest port, had become the principal outlet through which the material bounty of America reached the killing fields of Europe.[28]

But as always during New York's wars, prosperity had a way of distributing itself unevenly. War contracts did not reach many corners of the metropolitan job market. In seasonal industries like garment production, and in families where illness or disability wreaked havoc on household budgets, poverty remained very real. "War contractitis" also drove up the costs of daily staples, while spurring suspicions that speculators were artificially inflating prices. By February 1917, working-class housewives had reached the limits of their endurance. Steeply rising prices for chicken, fish, eggs, milk, flour, and vegetables in open-air pushcart markets and shops prompted boycotts by thousands of women, many of them wives of garment workers, outraged by what they saw as illicit gouging by local retailers. In Brownsville, the Bronx, and on the Lower East Side, they overturned vendors' carts, smashed store windows, and even physically attacked grocers. Most of the demonstrators were Jewish, but the "food strike" appealed to some Irish and Italian women as well. A Mothers' Anti–High Price League, organized by the Socialist Party, demanded that the city and state sell food at cost to working families. Believing that New York governor Charles Whitman was staying at the Waldorf-Astoria, hundreds of female and male protestors battled policemen at the hotel's entrance while shouting, "We are starving" and "Give us bread." The boycott temporarily reduced prices in some neighborhoods, and the demonstrations ended. But little was done to alleviate the plight of families who felt mired in a recession that simply would not end.[29]

"Morgan's war," some called it—a war that made the rich richer, left too many poor, kept Ireland in chains and the czar on his throne, and slaughtered untold thousands of young Europeans. That war remained less than popular among many in the tenements and sweatshops of New York; even in prosperous districts it could pit brother against brother and neighbor against neighbor. Such was not a vision to make Theodore Roosevelt, Madison Grant, or—increasingly—Woodrow Wilson confident in the success of "One Hundred Percent Americanism." Nor was it a vision to guarantee peace between New Yorkers as the distant war dragged on.

At 2:08 on the morning of Sunday, July 30, 1916, a deep roar "like the discharge of a great cannon" filled the air over New York harbor and resounded for miles in every direction. Carl Ramus, a doctor treating immigrants on Ellis Island, watched through opera glasses as "a great light went up. . . . From that great mass of fire there seemed to shoot out thousands of little stars." Within seconds Ramus was running for cover, dodging "thousands of pieces of wood, pieces of sheet metal and a heavy muddy rain." Falling shrapnel pockmarked the Statue of Liberty's copper surface. The blast awakened the populations of Jersey City, Brooklyn, and Manhattan, where shock waves shattered thousands of windows. In Brooklyn, pedestrians were knocked off their feet. Phone service between New York and New Jersey went dead. The sound of breaking glass mingled with the bells of burglar alarms that went off automatically. Customers in an all-night restaurant near South Ferry were cut by fragments from mirrors and windows. Falling glass hurt people at Third Avenue and Eighty-Ninth Street. Scared, half-dressed guests filled lobbies and wandered into the streets outside hotels in midtown and Brooklyn Heights. Like a Fourth of July fireworks display gone awry, intermittent exploding rockets filled the southern sky with bursts of blinding light and sent peals of thunder rolling down the city streets. Newspapers claimed that as far away as Philadelphia and Maryland people called the police, asking about the strange vibrations they felt rattling their homes.[30]

Fire trucks, police cars, and pedestrians converged on Manhattan's tip, where spectators grasped that the focal point of the explosions was Black Tom, a peninsula jutting out into the harbor from the Jersey City shore. Black Tom was the Lehigh Valley Railroad's freight depot, where artillery shells and gunpowder arriving from factories across the Midwest and Northeast were unloaded from trains and then barged out to waiting merchant ships anchored in the Upper Bay. Over the previous year, nearly three thousand rail cars and barges had hauled ammunition to or from the facility's ten piers. It was the largest transfer point in the country for supplying the Allied armies an ocean away—a warren of boxcars and sheds piled high with crates of foodstuffs, hardware, dry goods, guns, and shells intended for the English and French trenches of the Western Front and the czar's armies on the Eastern Front.

By daylight on Sunday, fireboats had extinguished flames that threatened to ignite explosives on two hundred remaining rail cars.

Investigators, scrambling through the smoking wreckage, found the flattened ruins of six piers and thirteen warehouses. In the yard where over eighty dynamite-filled freight cars had stood the previous day, they now looked down on a water-filled crater 300 feet long and 150 feet wide. A barge holding one hundred thousand pounds of TNT had also vanished into thin air. Smoldering piles of grain and sugar filled the harbor air with acrid smoke for a month.

Insurers tallied total property losses at about $20 million, a figure that included $300,000 for New York City's broken window glass. The late hour of the explosion had spared many lives. The final death toll was announced as five: a barge captain, a Jersey City policeman, the Lehigh's security chief, an unidentified man, and an infant thrown from his crib in Jersey City. Other casualties may have gone unreported among hundreds of poor families living on houseboats and barges nearby.[31]

Authorities considered the possibility of sabotage. Indeed, by the summer of 1916, New York police and federal agents had had ample experience of German plotting. Within weeks of the war's outbreak, Ambassador von Bernstorff's key subordinates, including commercial attaché Heinrich Albert and military attaché Franz von Papen, had embarked on a campaign to hinder the aid flowing to the Allies from North America. From his office in the Hamburg-Amerika Building at 45 Broadway, Albert ventured forth with von Papen to find operatives within the nation's largest German population. At the Hofbrau House on Twenty-Ninth Street and the German-American Club on Central Park South, they screened possible recruits—young immigrants loyal to the fatherland, reservists angered by their inability to get back to Germany, seamen from German ocean liners immobilized on the Hoboken and Brooklyn waterfronts, where they would not have to face the Royal Navy's guns.[32]

Several of these German efforts played out as comic opera. Von Papen himself blundered by trying to buy American and Norwegian passports from jobless sailors and Bowery derelicts. He intended to have them doctored and given to German reservists, who might then sail from New York as neutrals and pass muster with Royal Navy boarding parties on the Atlantic. But the Justice Department's New York office soon got wind of the scheme and dispatched Secret Service men to

trail von Papen and his associates around Manhattan. They hit the
jackpot on July 24, 1915, when a federal agent stole a portfolio of documents from a dozing Heinrich Albert on a Sixth Avenue elevated
train. The documents, turned over to Treasury Secretary McAdoo,
showed how Germany was paying to disseminate propaganda throughout the United States and detailed Albert's efforts to set up a munitions plant in Connecticut for the purpose of siphoning munitions
materials away from the Allies. While embarrassing to Germany, the
documents did not prove illegal acts. Wilson's advisor, Colonel Edward
House, suggested that the administration leak the documents without
attribution to Frank Cobb, editor of the New York *World*, the city's
staunchest pro-Wilson paper. In mid-August, headlines decried a plot
by "Secret Agents" on American soil to "Block the Allies." Wilson demanded that Germany recall von Papen in December. The attaché
went home, where he would later play a crucial role in helping Adolf
Hitler to power.[33]

Not all of the schemes hatched by von Bernstorff's operatives,
however, were failures. By early 1915 one of von Papen's contacts, an
admiralty staff officer from Berlin named Franz von Rintelen, was busy
enlisting and paying Irish longshoremen on the West Side docks to
launch a series of dockside strikes and slowdowns to delay the loading
and departure of ships bearing desperately needed munitions to the
Allied Western Front. Meanwhile, Frederick Hinsch, a Maryland
agent of von Rintelen's, hired black Baltimore stevedores to inject
draft animals destined for the Allied armies with deadly glanders and
anthrax germs supplied by a German American chemist in Chevy
Chase. One of the stevedores, Edward Felton, came north to the
Bronx, where he wandered, unwatched, among horses corralled in
Van Cortlandt Park and jabbed them with the anthrax bacillus.[34]

Most ominously, in spring 1915 the cargo holds of ships bound
from New York to England, France, and Russia began unaccountably
to burst into flames, causing hundreds of tons of goods to be ruined
when captains flooded their holds to quench the fires. The mystery
was soon explained. When the steamer *Kirk Oswald* docked in Mar-
seilles with sugar and grain, French stevedores discovered strange
metal "cigars" in her hold. Before leaving New York, the *Kirk Oswald*

had been tied up next to the German liner *Friedrich der Grosse* at the foot of Thirty-First Street in South Brooklyn. Inspector Thomas Tunney of the New York City Police Bomb and Neutrality Squad put the missing pieces together. They led to a Hoboken chemist, Dr. Walter Scheele, whose house turned out to be a bomb factory. Working for von Rintelen, Scheele was filling one end of small lead pipes—the "cigars"—with picric acid and the other end with sulfuric acid. When the acids ate through a time-delay disk placed between them in the middle of the tube, they ignited a blaze that could fill a cargo hold with flames. German sailors stuck on board the *Friedrich der Grosse* were using the vessel's machine shop to cut the tubes and disks for Scheele; von Rintelen's Irish longshore friends, glad to strike a blow against England, placed the bombs in the ships they were loading. Scheele ended up in the Atlanta penitentiary. Von Rintelen tried to slip back to Europe aboard a Dutch liner but was arrested by British agents when the ship touched at Dover.[35]

In 1916, however, after Black Tom, investigators ultimately concluded that the blast was probably a careless accident, and they accused the depot's owners of criminal negligence. Legally, the Lehigh Valley Railroad was supposed to move explosives out of Black Tom within twenty-four hours of arrival, regardless of the war-induced bottleneck that slowed the port's traffic. Authorities determined that a discarded cigarette, or possibly a fire set by night watchmen to keep mosquitoes away, had ignited a depot crammed with far more than its safe capacity of ammunition. Jersey City police arrested several Lehigh Valley Railroad officials for manslaughter and threatened to arrest E. B. Thomas, the line's president. "It is not right for millions of people to be imperiled for the benefit of foreign warring nations and for the profits of munitions dealers," declared Robert Hudspeth, Hudson County's prosecutor. Even after the Black Tom explosion, there were still enough explosives left on the Jersey City shore "to blow New York to pieces."

Despite the arrests and allegations, munitions continued to flow from the harbor's docks and rail yards onto waiting ships. As the *New York Times* noted, any plan to remove "the thousands of tons of condensed destruction . . . would divert millions of dollars from New York." E. B. Thomas, none too worried about the posturing of prosecutors, announced in August that Lehigh had earned an unprecedented $7.6 million over the past year and spoke of "the encouraging outlook for a continuation of the heavy volume of traffic." Charges against Thomas and his colleagues were not pressed. Business, and lax safety conditions, went on pretty much as before. Most believed with the *Times* that, while the explosion "must prove cheering news to Berlin and Vienna," the event was an unfortunate freak accident. To Woodrow Wilson, it was "a regrettable incident at a private railroad terminal."[36]

Only after the war did investigators uncover what really took place at Black Tom. In 1916, Frederick Hinsch had used a brownstone at 123 West Fifteenth Street in Chelsea as a safe house to plan the Black Tom attack. Two of the depot's night watchmen had been bribed to look the other way. Under cover of darkness, Hinsch's recruits—probably an immigrant from Austrian Slovakia named Michael Kristoff, a naturalized US citizen named Kurt Jahnke, and Lothar Witzke, a German naval cadet—snuck into the depot and set off detonators, making their escape before the stored ammunition exploded.[37]

In 1939, a joint US-German Mixed Claims Commission ruled that Germany owed $21 million in damages to the American claimants in the Black Tom and other sabotage cases, including the Lehigh Valley Railroad and Black Tom's insurers. Adolf Hitler was in no mood to pay out money to Americans, and the Nazi government "boycotted" the commission's decision. Following another war, the West German government made good on the claims, paying them on the installment plan. Not until 1979 were the reparation payments owed for the events of July 30, 1916, completed.[38]

Von Bernstorff's agents had scored a victory. Not only had they destroyed tons of munitions that would have been used against the kaiser's troops, but they had disabled the key depot and gotten away with it. Yet their momentary success could not stop the flow of exports. The real casualty of their tactics was the security of the vast majority of German Americans who had nothing to do with such skullduggery. The kaiser's officers and diplomats had been willing to sacrifice their American cousins in a vain attempt to limit the flow of American aid to their enemies. In New York and throughout the country, headlines about Albert's portfolio and Scheele's bomb lab raised doubts about the loyalty of anyone bearing a German name.

Months before the Black Tom explosion, President Wilson himself had pointed the finger of blame at German Americans without naming them directly. In his December 1915 State of the Union address, delivered a week after he demanded von Papen's recall, Wilson had lauded those "virile foreign stocks" whose peoples had enriched the nation over recent decades. But he also blasted "infinitely malicious" foreign-born US citizens, "who have poured the poison of disloyalty into the very arteries of our national life" and sought "to destroy our industries" for the sake of "foreign intrigue." Treachery, the president insisted, would not be tolerated. But how were Americans to tell the difference between manly, patriotic newcomers and disloyal intriguers? Here Woodrow Wilson offered his people no guidance.[39]

June 5, 1917, dawned fair and cool in New York. Through the morning and afternoon, thousands of men lined up outside neighborhood schools, barbershops, and storefronts to register for Selective Service. America had finally joined the Allied war against Germany. President Wilson had asked Congress to declare war in April, after the Germans resumed unrestricted U-boat warfare against all vessels, including American freighters and passenger ships, heading for Allied ports, and after British naval intelligence divulged intercepted cable messages that proved that German foreign minister Arthur Zimmermann was secretly trying to lure Mexico and possibly Japan into a surprise attack on the United States. America's war, Wilson intoned, would be a war "to make the world safe for democracy."[40]

Now the test had come. Would America's population of immigrants and their sons step forward to register for the nation's first mandatory draft since the Civil War? Somewhat nervously, the *New York Tribune* recalled the Draft Riot of 1863. People recognized that neither Congress nor the public unanimously supported entry into the war. But the day passed without major problems. Although thousands of "slackers" failed to appear as summoned, six hundred thousand New Yorkers and over nine million others nationwide came forward to register.[41]

Never far below the surface, the city's ethnic tensions caused scattered incidents, as thirty-eight thousand registrants were picked by lottery for the draft during the summer. While standing in line for his draft board physical, Russian Jewish immigrant Meyer Siegel joked about a gruff policeman nearby. "What did you say about me, you dirty kike?" the policeman shouted as he arrested Siegel for disturbing the peace. But a judge threw the case out of court, and Siegel was able to share the mix of excitement and bewilderment felt by millions of other young draftees. "Here I am," he wrote, "one day, a student of law; the next day, learning how to kill my adversary and be killed. Some change-over!"[42]

Sixty miles east of Manhattan, in the woods of Yaphank, Long Island, thousands of drafted New Yorkers were training at the army's newly built Camp Upton by the fall of 1917; other draftees occupied barracks at Camp Merritt in northern New Jersey. By the time Upton's and Merritt's troops started boarding transport ships at the Hoboken docks over the winter and spring for the passage to France, ethnic pride as well as American patriotism infused the esprit de corps of new units and traditional regiments alike. In addition to the Upper East Side "blue bloods" of the National Guard's Seventh Regiment, and the tough Irish teamsters and stevedores from Hell's Kitchen in the Fighting Sixty-Ninth, a mix of Jews, Catholics, and Protestants, Slavs and Italians, natives and immigrants filled the ranks of the Seventy-Seventh, or "Melting Pot" Division, whose insignia bore an image of the Statue of Liberty.[43]

Flag-waving crowds cheered the "hardy back woodsmen from the Bowery, Fifth Avenue and Hester Street" as they marched through Manhattan in preparation for the voyage to Europe. Among them were many bearing German names and some who spoke with a German accent. Immigrants set aside their reservations about joining the Allies. "I figured this country was different from Russia," concluded Morry Morrison, a Jew from Brooklyn. "It was worth fighting for." On Broadway, theatergoers hummed along with the war's two signature songs, "Over There" by George M. Cohan, grandson of a County Cork emigrant, and "Oh, How I Hate to Get Up in the Morning," by the Seventy-Seventh's own Sergeant Irving Berlin, who had passed through Ellis Island as a boy named Israel Baline. Perhaps, Preparedness advocates and liberal reformers both hoped, entry into the war was achieving the "Americanization" and unity they had long desired.[44]

With the federal government now putting its own money into the war effort, military contracts brought new jobs. Over eighteen thousand workers flocked to the Brooklyn Navy Yard, where they built dozens of antisubmarine boats, barges, and scows, and serviced ships that would convoy the "doughboys" to France. Factories making gas masks and airplane motors opened in Queens. With drafted men leaving their jobs, women filled positions as trolley conductors and assembly-line laborers "for the duration." Backed by the Wilson administration, which prized workplace harmony as a key to efficient war production, labor unions won higher pay and the right to organize, a circumstance many businesses accepted because the government also guaranteed cost-plus profits on war contracts. "We are all making more money out of this war than the average being ought to," a steel manufacturer admitted.[45]

But as local factories churned out equipment for General Pershing's American troops in France, and as patriotic New Yorkers bought "Liberty Loan" war bonds and observed meatless and wheatless days to save foodstuffs needed on the Western Front, a nervous, angry current ran under their flag waving. The battle for pro-Allied loyalty and unity, many believed, had yet to be won. The Rialto, the Broadway, and other midtown movie houses showed silent films with titles like *The Claws of the Hun*, *The Prussian Cur*, and *The Hun Within*, melodramas that portrayed German soldiers as brutish villains. Were wartime atrocities the result of the kaiser's militarism, or did they reflect innate traits in German "racial" character, as pernicious on the Hudson as on the Rhine? The movies did not always provide a clear answer. "German agents are everywhere," warned ads placed in popular magazines by the Committee on Public Information, the federal government's new war propaganda agency. "Report the man who spreads pessimistic stories . . . cries for peace or belittles our efforts to win the war." CPI director George Creel justified such tactics by citing the need to mold the American people into "one white-hot mass" committed to the war with "deathless determination." Like others in the Wilson administration, Creel feared that patriotism might not be enough; outrage, hatred, and suspicion were necessary tools for the enforcement of loyalty.[46]

As Creel and Wilson both knew, the war continued to divide Americans, nowhere more obviously than in New York. The city's intelligentsia, the vanguard of the nation's liberal opinion, split bitterly over the war. The *New Republic*'s Walter Lippmann saw in the call to

arms against the kaiser the rise of a democratic global order, "the Federation of the World," and a renewed crusade against "our own tyran-
nies . . . our autocratic steel industries, our sweatshops and our slums."
But the Greenwich Village writer Randolph Bourne was appalled by
how eagerly pro-war liberals agreed to march in lockstep "with the
least democratic forces in American life"—the reactionary Preparedness men, the zealots who detected a "Hun" in every individual who
chose not to buy a Liberty Bond.[47]

Activists in various causes found the war to be a source of division
and conflict. While some of the city's woman suffragists remained committed pacifists, Carrie Chapman Catt of the National American
Woman Suffrage Association, seeing in the war an opportunity to win
over Wilson and Congress, now denounced "every slacker . . . every
pro-German" who could vote while loyal women could not. Dishar-
mony was equally evident in Harlem, the community rapidly becoming
the nation's "Negro Mecca." From the pulpit of St. James Presbyterian
Church, the Reverend F. M. Hyden declared that military service
would be "the noblest appeal for political and economic rights which
colored men could present to the nation." Harlem's foremost intellectual, W. E. B. Du Bois, also came to endorse the war, urging African
Americans to "forget our special grievances and close our ranks shoulder to shoulder with our own white fellow citizens." But others disagreed. In the pages of their monthly *Messenger*, two young Harlem
socialists, A. Philip Randolph and Chandler Owen, exhorted their fellow blacks to reject participation in Wilson's war. "No intelligent Negro is willing to lay down his life for the United States as it now exists,"
the *Messenger* declared. Those black leaders who were shouting, "first
your country, then your rights," were nothing but "hand-picked, me-
too-boss, hat-in-hand, sycophant, lick-spittling Negroes." Few, however, were willing to risk the draft resistance the *Messenger* seemed to
counsel. Harlem's men duly registered for the draft and went off to
serve in a segregated army under white officers. But many did so with a
determination to press the fight for freedom on both sides of the Atlantic. On July 28, 1917, eight thousand African Americans, including
many draft registrants, marched silently down Fifth Avenue in protest
against lynch law and racist violence. "Make America Safe for Democracy" read the banner under which they walked.[48]

Other groups in New York—Socialists, anarchists, the "Wobblies" of the Industrial Workers of the World—more uniformly opposed American entry into the war. Most formidable was the Socialist Party, which had garnered nearly a million votes nationally for its presidential candidate, Eugene Debs, in 1912, and which adopted an antiwar platform in 1914. New York's immigrant Jewish garment unions made the city one of the national party's bastions. To Morris Hillquit, the party's leader in New York, the war was "a cold-blooded butchery for advantages and power" benefiting "the ruling classes of the warring nations." In the November 1917 mayoral election, Hillquit, the party's candidate, lost to Democrat John Hylan and came in behind John Purroy Mitchel, the sitting mayor and candidate of the pro-war, independent "Fusion" ticket. But Hillquit ran a formidable campaign, winning 142,000 votes, more than the Republican candidate got. The Socialists quadrupled their usual vote in the city. Hillquit's platform, with its calls for public housing and school lunches, spoke to those still left behind by the war boom. But the turnout, which also sent Socialists to the State Assembly and the city's Board of Aldermen, was clearly a protest against American involvement in Europe's conflict. Both friend and foe interpreted the results as evidence of a strong antiwar groundswell in the city's electorate.[49]

To Theodore Roosevelt, the meaning of the Socialist campaign was clear: Hillquit was a "Hun . . . inside our gates." Such invective was becoming common in New York, where the private Preparedness groups echoed Roosevelt and the CPI in their demands for absolute loyalty. Increasingly, anyone who questioned the war—religious pacifists, leftists, those who continued to view neutrality as serving the national interest—found themselves publicly denounced as allies or even agents of Germany. The New York Times blasted "half-baked disciples of socialism, internationalists, pro-Germanists" among the city's public school teachers and demanded the dismissal of any teacher who corrupted students by opposing the war or who didn't "believe in Liberty Bonds."[50]

The Wilson administration looked on without censure. The president and some of his cabinet officers offered verbal reassurances to "loyal" dissenters that their civil liberties would be protected, but in practice they drew few lines between legitimate opposition and disloyalty. "The military masters of Germany," Wilson reminded the public in a June 1917 address, "filled our unsuspecting communities with vicious spies and conspirators and sought to corrupt the opinion of our people." By implication, such efforts were continuing—although in reality, von Bernstorff and his saboteurs had left the country, and propagandists like Viereck had lost credibility.[51]

In 1917 and 1918 Congress, urged on by Wilson, passed several laws, including an Espionage Act and a Sedition Act, which sharply curtailed freedoms of speech and the press for the war's duration. Any person acting, speaking, writing, or publishing so as to "cause insubordination, disloyalty, [or] mutiny," or to obstruct the draft, could be tried, fined, and imprisoned, with jail terms running up to twenty years. According to Wilson's postmaster general, Albert Burleson, who played a key role in monitoring and prosecuting mailed publications that violated the Sedition Act, any public allegation that "the Government is controlled by Wall Street or munitions manufacturers" was seditious, as was any statement "attacking improperly our allies." While cautioning that "criticism, honest criticism, ought not to be muzzled," the New York Times applauded the Sedition Act for giving federal prosecutors "latitude to frame indictments against traitors." By the war's end, the government had arrested over 3,600 Americans for sedition or for allegedly "disrupting" the war effort; 1,055 were convicted for antidraft speech or activity under the Espionage Act.[52]

New York's unbridled talkers, writers, and thinkers—beneficiaries and benefactors of the city's rich heritage of public discussion and debate—were favored targets. Federal agents raided the offices of Viereck's Fatherland and shut down Jeremiah O'Leary's anti-British Bull. Burleson denied mailing privileges to dozens of antiwar periodicals, including the socialist Call, Emma Goldman's anarchist Mother Earth, and The Masses, organ of the Greenwich Village avant-garde. Brooklyn butcher Stephen Binder received a two-year jail sentence for publishing an antiwar book. In Queens, Peter Grimm went to jail for saying, "America ought never to have gone to war with Germany. It is only a war of the capitalists." True, the government did not go the extra step to deprive antiwar groups of their right to assemble or to keep their candidates from running for office. But everywhere Morris Hillquit spoke during his mayoral campaign, his steps were dogged by Justice Department stenographers, taking down his every word, waiting to catch him out in a "seditious" utterance. Hillquit, a seasoned lawyer, watched what he said.[53]

On the morning of September 3, 1918, officers stood vigilantly at the doorways of Grand Central Terminal, Penn Station, and the city's ferry landings, stopping every male who appeared to be between the ages of twenty-one and thirty-one and demanding to see their draft registration cards. The Justice Department's New York "slacker raid" was under way. As the day wore on, "slacker patrols" pulled young men off city streetcars and street corners and confronted them in restaurants and theaters. Those "suspects" who could not produce a card were detained and taken to the city's National Guard armories, where they were held for hours, interrogated, and made to fill out a questionnaire about their draft status. By the end of the raid two days later, the investigators had stopped over sixty thousand men. Most turned out to have valid draft exemptions or were not carrying their cards when detained. About two thousand were ruled to be "seriously delinquent"; hundreds were sent to the army's headquarters on Governors Island or to Camp Upton.[54]

Some twenty-five thousand men took part in the draft-enforcing patrols, including Justice Department agents, soldiers, sailors, and several thousand members of New York's American Protective League, a private Preparedness group, equipped with official badges or certificates. Wilson's Justice Department was strapped for funds and gladly accepted APL men as volunteers. Private citizens reveled in the opportunity to strut, intimidate pedestrians, and interrogate "suspects," all with government sanction and minimal oversight. Preparedness men who were themselves exempt from the draft because of age, infirmity, or work status relished their role as the city's vigilantes. During 1917 and 1918, members of such groups, sometimes aided by soldiers or sailors, heckled speakers and broke up public meetings sponsored by socialists, anarchists, and pacifists. Auditorium owners refused to rent their halls to leftists out of fear of reprisals. In New York, it seemed, the 100 Percenters had the "slackers" on the run.[55]

The "slackers," however, tried to fight back. Liberal lawyers took up the cause of radicals convicted under the Sedition and Espionage acts, arguing their cases all the way to the Supreme Court (which, however, handed down rulings in 1919 upholding Wilson's war measures). A young pacifist named Roger Baldwin founded the National Civil Liberties Bureau to defend those harassed under the onslaught against the First Amendment. Despite raids by federal agents searching for evidence of "sedition" in the files of Baldwin's Fifth Avenue office, his bureau survived to become the American Civil Liberties Union. The liberal journalist Oswald G. Villard, once a Wilson admirer, challenged the president's record: "If he loses his great fight for humanity, it will be because he was deliberately silent when freedom of speech and the right of conscience were struck down in America."[56]

One group in New York, however, found that fighting back was impossible. The city's German Americans, once so openly proud of their dual heritage, could do no right. To defend the kaiser's war effort was now taboo. But when they insisted on their loyalty to the United States, they were met with scornful suspicion. "Beware of the German-American who wraps the Stars and Stripes around his German body," a New York paper warned. The humor magazine *Life* ran cartoons of a rotund, walrus-mustached German American, stolen "Plans of Forts" sticking out of his pocket, who sang his own anthem:

> *My country over sea,*
> *Deutschland, is sweet to me;*
> *To thee I cling.*
> *For thee my honor died,*
> *For thee I spied and lied,*
> *So that from every side*
> *Kultur might ring.*[57]

As elsewhere throughout the country, New York's public and private authorities did their best to erase German influences from the city's daily life. The Metropolitan Opera stopped performing Wagner, while the American Defense Society informed concertgoers that German music was "one of the most dangerous forms of German propaganda." With the National Security League demanding that schools "Throw Out the German Language and All Disloyal Teachers," the New York Board of Education, the largest school district in the nation, decided in the spring of 1918 to eliminate German instruction

The "Enemy Alien Menace" looms over the Woolworth Building and lower Manhattan in a *New York Herald* editorial cartoon, 1918. Cartoon by W. A. Rogers, *The Breath of the Hun,* in *New York Herald,* March 28, 1918. LIBRARY OF CONGRESS.

from the elementary schools, to cut back on high school German courses, and to ban nine German textbooks. Educators even debated whether to eliminate the word "kindergarten."[58]

Pain, humiliation, and fear were real in the German American households of New York. "I did expect from my neighbors and fellow citizens a fair estimate and appreciation of my honesty and trustworthiness," lamented merchant Theodore Ladenburger, who had been a

New Yorker for a quarter century. "It had all vanished." "You couldn't walk the street with a German paper under your arm," Helen Wagner, a young girl living on the Upper East Side, later recalled. "You'd be abused from one end of the block to the other. . . . We kept speaking German at home, but we avoided it on the street." The golden age of German New York was over.[59]

Late in the afternoon of June 2, 1918, Mrs. Clarence Westbrook of West Fifty-Eighth Street, one of 217 passengers aboard the steamship *Carolina* bound from Puerto Rico to New York, was sitting on the ship's deck when she noticed something strange breaking the surface of the water. "There comes a submarine," she said to a fellow passenger. A minute later, a six-inch shell sent a plume of water skyward just astern of the steamer. Terrified passengers stumbled out of the ship's dining room as three more warning shells hit the water. The German U-151 approached, flying the "Abandon Ship" pennant, its crew manning the submarine's deck guns. Soon nine lifeboats and one motor launch, carrying the *Carolina*'s passengers and 113 crewmen, were pulling away from the steamer. "Is everybody off your ship?" an English-speaking officer asked Captain T. R. D. Barbour from the U-boat's deck. "I'm going to shell her." As the boats pulled toward the New Jersey shore forty miles away, six shells shattered the *Carolina*'s hull, sending it to the bottom with a cargo of sugar, forty thousand letters, and fifty-four sacks of parcel post. Two days later, a marching band of Shriners on the Atlantic City boardwalk faced the ocean and played "The Star-Spangled Banner" as vacationing bathers helped twenty-nine exhausted survivors onto the beach from one of the *Carolina*'s boats. Germany had brought the war to the waters off New York.[60]

The *Carolina* was, in fact, the last of U-151's prey on June 2. All day long, frantic wireless messages had been arriving at the Brooklyn Navy Yard and other coastal stations from vessels claiming they were under attack from a German submarine. By the time the U-boat's gunners shot and sank the *Carolina*, they had already dispatched two cargo steamers and three schooners, all American, in the waters fifty miles off Barnegat Light, New Jersey. Captain Kenneth Lowry of the freighter *Texel* had been shocked when a German officer—perhaps the same man who would later hail the *Carolina*—boarded his ship, shook hands, and then announced in faultless English, 'I'm sorry I have to do this, Captain, but this is war, you know. Get your men off as quickly as possible."[61]

Over the previous week, the submarine had laid floating mines in the busy shipping lanes off the mouths of the Chesapeake and Delaware Bays and near the Ambrose Channel into New York, and had used a scissor-like device to cut the underwater telegraph cables linking New York to Nova Scotia and Panama. Now, on June 2, Captain Heinrich von Nostitz ordered 448 people (and Micky, the *Texel's* cat) into eighteen lifeboats. Over the next two days, survivors landed on New Jersey beaches or were rescued at sea by ships that brought them into Delaware, Boston, Hoboken, and New York. By then, thirteen of the *Carolina's* passengers and crew had drowned when a storm overturned the ship's motor launch.[62]

U-151 was one of six submarines dispatched by the German admiralty in the late spring and summer of 1918 to wreak havoc along the American East Coast. The American troops and supplies pouring into France were fortifying the Allies to score the war's knockout blow. By the summer of 1918, ten thousand American men a day boarded troop transports, most of them embarking at Hoboken on the makeshift flotilla of British cargo ships, US Navy vessels, and converted ocean liners that made up the "Atlantic Ferry." Every possible corner of these floating barracks was crammed with doughboys; one private aboard the steamer *Kashmir* described his berth as "the blackest, foulest, most congested hole that I ever set foot into." The liner *Aquitania* carried six thousand troops; the *Leviathan* could carry over ten thousand. U-boat raids, Berlin decided, might daunt the Americans and temporarily halt their transatlantic traffic, giving the German army breathing space for a counteroffensive. While most transports sailed in convoy, escorted by vigilant American and English cruisers and destroyers, a crafty U-boat captain might get lucky. If submarines torpedoed a large transport, the loss of life could dwarf that of the *Lusitania* disaster and spread terror up and down the American coast.[63]

As survivors of U-151's rampage straggled across the New York docks and told their stories to waiting reporters, the destroyer *Preble* left the harbor in pursuit of the predator. In the city, most New Yorkers were reasonably sure they were protected from direct submarine attack by a wire cable net strung across the Narrows, by the gunboat *Amphitrite* stationed there, and by small armed boats called "Submarine Chasers" that patrolled the bay and Long Island Sound. They would have been alarmed, however, to learn how close U-151 came to their shores. From the deck of the submarine on the night of May 28, just days before the attack on the *Carolina*, Lieutenant Frederick Koerner later recalled, "we had our first sight of the bright lights of Broadway, the great glow that hangs over New York City after dark. The splendor of the Western metropolis filled us with a restless longing."[64]

What some New Yorkers feared in the wake of the June 2 attacks was a new and terrible weapon, one that could attack from the sky. As they knew, the Germans had used zeppelins and airplanes to drop bombs on London and Paris. The artist Joseph Pennell had unsettled them with a Liberty Loan poster that envisioned a shattered Statue of Liberty and a flaming Manhattan conquered by German submarines and planes. Now, the Arctic explorer Robert Peary and aviator Alan Hawley announced that U-boats might easily carry "seaplanes" to bomb coastal cities. Army aviators taking off from Governors Island surveyed the city at night, noting that the "winding path of lights" on Broadway might guide enemy bombers. Under police orders, the city practiced a nighttime blackout of electric signs and most public lighting, with authorities warning that "New York may know to the full the experience of London, which has total darkness at night." They also installed air raid sirens at factories around the city, encouraged office workers to practice emergency evacuations, and told residents to seek shelter in their cellars in case of an attack. Most New Yorkers saw the threat as remote (it was, in fact, nonexistent, since the Germans had not placed planes on U-boats, despite Peary's and Hawley's claim). But on July 1, a siren drill at a factory sent scared people scurrying into basements throughout the South Bronx. Eight days later, another siren test at the Con Edison plant on East Fortieth Street alarmed thousands in midtown, who asked each other, "Is it an air raid?" A new kind of war had arrived at the city's doorstep, at least as a possibility.[65]

THAT LIBERTY SHALL NOT
PERISH FROM THE EARTH
BUY LIBERTY BONDS
FOURTH   LIBERTY   LOAN

The Statue of Liberty and lower Manhattan are battered by an
imagined German U-boat and airplane attack in Joseph Pennell's poster, 1918. Lithographic poster by Joseph Pennell, *That
Liberty Shall Not Perish from the Earth: Buy Liberty Bonds. Fourth
Liberty Loan*, 1918. LIBRARY OF CONGRESS.

Over the course of six months in mid-1918, U-151 and five other
submarines sank a total of ninety-one American, British, Norwegian,
and other ships worth $25 million in coastal waters from North Car-
olina to Newfoundland. By the time the last U-boat returned to Germany, they had taken 368 lives. The submarines, moreover, had
successfully eluded the US Navy. But the German admiralty could not
really count the raids as successes. Not one troopship had passed before

the crosshairs of a U-boat's periscope. While von Nostitz and his fellow
captains were sinking schooners, nearly 1.5 million American soldiers
crossed safely to France in convoys. The raids were a last gasp of a navy
that, in a matter of weeks, would be facing mutiny and defeat.[66]

The U-boat campaign did have two notable effects, one of them in
Germany itself. Flaunted by German newspapers, the raids brought a
moment of bitter pleasure to a war-weary population. The American
sitting "on the other side of the great herring pond" was now feeling
"the fist of the war lord," the Cologne *Volks Zeitung* crowed. On the eve
of German collapse, propagandists spun fantasies of New York's downfall. Doughboys on the Western Front must have scratched their heads
when they read leaflets dropped from German balloons that described
how "thousands of Brooklynites are sleeping in cellars fearing a night
bombardment. Some of the wealthiest are moving toward Chicago.
The few Wall Street brokers who must remain downtown in Manhattan are engaging cots in Turkish baths in the Woolworth building and
other skyscrapers."[67] Sprung from the fertile imagination of a German
government writer, the leaflet did little to demoralize American troops,
whatever effect its fantasies might have had on German readers.

The other effect of the U-boat raids, felt in New York and along the
coast, was the conviction that "hyphenates" and "pro-Germanists"
surely had played some mysterious role in the attacks. Surely, many
easterners thought, German Americans must have been using local
beaches to flash signal lights to guide the subs to their targets. Some allegations were even more outlandish; a seaman swore to reporters that
he had glimpsed an officer from the U-140, which had sunk his tanker,
in a New York saloon—no doubt sheltered by his immigrant countrymen. No hard evidence ever surfaced to implicate German Americans
in the U-boat attacks, but this did not prevent the navy from prohibiting anyone of German or Austrian birth from entering a new "barred
zone" running the entire length of the Atlantic coast. Although a few
German-born drivers of milk trucks were arrested for entering the zone
along the Hudson River, most German New Yorkers, accustomed to
such treatment by now, responded with sullen compliance.[68]

Armistice Day, November 11, 1918, arrived in New York to the accom-
paniment of church bells, sirens, foghorns, and singing in the streets.

On the Lower East Side, the day became "a great block party," resident Lewis Feuer later recalled. "The Kaiser in effigy was berated, while American flags and banners waved from lines strung from houses across the street. The children sang 'Over There' and 'My country, 'tis of thee'; the men in uniform were heroes." Other festive days followed, as the Atlantic Ferry started running in reverse and transport ships began to disgorge thousands of new veterans onto the harbor's docks.[69]

It was a delirious, exciting moment for New Yorkers. Doughboys were returning to a city the war had transformed into the world's leading creditor, the world's busiest port, and the cultural capital of what would soon be dubbed the Jazz Age. Men who had left New York feeling they had something to prove came back proudly, with memories and stories of their friends who had fallen dead or wounded on the battlefield. Irish New Yorkers reveled in the prowess of their Fighting Sixty-Ninth and its scrappy chaplain, Father Francis Duffy, whose bravery and leadership under fire earned him more decorations than any other clergyman in the army's history. Manhattan Italians helped reelect one of their own, a gallant young army aviator named Fiorello La Guardia, to Congress. Abraham Krotoshinsky was no longer just a Polish Jewish barber on Park Row; he was also a decorated hero who had helped rescue the Seventy-Seventh Division's "Lost Battalion" during the Meuse-Argonne Offensive. He returned to a city where many of his brethren had come to embrace the Allied cause, encouraged by the overthrow of the czar by Russian revolutionaries and by British promises of a Jewish state in Palestine. Black New York's own 369th Infantry, the Harlem Hellfighters, marched home with the bitter knowledge that most black enlistees had been consigned to menial labor by the US Army. But they could take pride in the combat role their unit had been allowed to play by the French army and in the Croix de Guerre awarded to their members. "We return," W. E. B. Du Bois wrote for the black veterans. "We return from fighting. We return fighting."[70]

While the war had given New York's diverse ethnic groups opportunities for self-assertion and pride, One Hundred Percent Americanism had also gained a momentum that carried it beyond the war's end. Preparedness found a new target: those who supported the Bolshevik Revolution in Russia and, by extension, the radical subversion of American society. As veterans and other workers struggled with postwar inflation and an uncertain job market, employers denounced labor unions as "nothing less than bolshevism." A new organization, the American Legion, demanded the deportation of foreign-born radicals, "this scum who hate God, our country, our flag." The war's strident mood persisted, sustained in part by senseless, terrifying acts committed by isolated radicals. Anonymous pipe and letter bombs targeted prominent businessmen and conservative politicians.[71]

Much as the German government had tainted German America with its wartime sabotage, radicals who resorted to terrorism to advance their causes served only to provoke a backlash against the entire American left. On May Day 1919, roving bands of soldiers and sailors tried to break up a peaceful meeting of garment trade unionists at Madison Square Garden and attacked the office of the socialist newspaper the *Call*, driving staff members into the street and beating them. Seven months later, the New York Police Bomb Squad and federal agents raided the Union of Russian Workers on East Fifteenth Street and rounded up 200 suspected "reds" and "criminal anarchists." In December 1919, a steamship would carry 249 deported foreign-born radicals, including members of the new Communist and Communist Labor parties and the famed anarchist Emma Goldman, from Ellis Island to Europe.[72]

Antiradical agents targeted New York's Jewish community for special surveillance. Despite the sympathy of many Jewish leftists for the new Soviet regime, the city's Jews as a whole were divided on the merits of the Communist experiment. But by 1919, Captain John B. Trevor and others in the New York office of the army's Military Intelligence Division were convinced that "Bolshevism is an international movement controlled by Jews." Trevor's anti-Semitism had bolstered his wartime conviction that Jews were allies and agents of the kaiser; now he feared a mass radical uprising starting in New York's " congested districts chiefly inhabited by Russian Jews." In May he outlined a secret plan for using army machine gun units to cordon off Jewish neighborhoods in the event of revolution. In response, army headquarters in Washington sent him six thousand Springfield rifles to use against the Jewish Bolsheviks of the Lower East Side. But the revolution did not come, and the "Red Scare" petered out as politicians and journalists increasingly questioned the "Americanism" of midnight raids and wholesale deportations. Millions of New Yorkers were happy to put the war and the witch hunt behind them.[73]

But there were other legacies of New York's war. German Americans never fully regained their communal confidence; their once-vital presence in the city's public life receded, almost melted away. When Congress took up the question of postwar immigration, consultants Madison Grant and John B. Trevor were among those redrawing the terms of admission into the United States. The law that resulted, the National Origins Act of 1924, would end a century of unimpeded European immigration. The law limited the number of arriving Southern and Eastern Europeans, including Jews, defining them as undesirables to be kept out of the nation. The new orthodoxy propounded by Grant and other "experts," and embraced by many American voters and congressmen, sounded few warnings about "Nordic" Germans but instead focused on Jews, Italians, and Slavs as racially inferior and as importers of European radicalism. Thus millions of would-be immigrants, many the kin of New Yorkers, were denied the Statue of Liberty's welcome and left behind in a Europe torn apart by the Great War's dark aftermath. Woodrow Wilson's war to make the world safe for democracy had brought to a climax fears of social contamination that New York most vividly symbolized. Enemies already within the gates—"Huns" in all their threatening guises—would no longer be joined and inflamed by masses of new "enemies" arriving at Ellis Island from distant shores.[74]

CHAPTER 8

Tempting Target

Global Conflict and World War II, 1933–1945

The squadrons of enemy twin-engine bombers roared through the morning sky over Long Island, heading for their targets on the western horizon. The planes had encountered no resistance as they made their turn toward the distant Manhattan skyscrapers. But now, thousands of feet below them on the ground, civilians trained their binoculars skyward from dozens of observation posts scattered across the landscape. Soon hundreds of calls flooded into the telephone filter stations at Hempstead, White Plains, and New Haven, where evaluators sent the spotters' reports through to the Army Information Center in the New York Telephone Building on West Street in lower Manhattan. Here, telephone operators and army personnel plotted the reports of the bombers' progress on large table maps, enabling dispatchers to call up Army Air Corps fighter squadrons based at Garden City and Quogue on Long Island. Within minutes, Curtiss P-40 fighter planes took to the air and came up from behind on the attackers.

At over three hundred miles per hour, the P-40s flew much faster than the lumbering bombers, and the fighters soon made short shrift of most of the enemy. But New Yorkers were about to learn the lesson Londoners had so recently learned: "Some bombers always get through," the *New York Times* conceded. As spotters watched from their post atop the Empire State Building, the paper went on to report, "4,000-pound aerial mines blasted at the foundations of New York's skyscrapers. . . . 'Aerial torpedoes' smashed at their sides and upper floors." At night the raids continued, the *Times* explained, but the Sixty-Second Army Coast Artillery swept the skies with searchlights installed at Coney Island, Rockaway, and Fort Totten in Queens, and the unit's antiaircraft fire prevented the bombers from destroying the Brooklyn Navy Yard.

The next day "there was a 'truce' at noon," the *Times* informed its readers, "when both bombers and pursuits returned to Mitchel Field [at Garden City] for lunch." The bombs, of course, were imaginary. So were the enemy aircraft carriers supposedly cruising off Jones Beach on these cold days and nights in January 1941. The "air raid" was part of a four-day exercise organized by the army's recently established Air Defense Command, the first major test of civilian ground-to-air plane spotting for national defense. While thirty-five B-18 bombers and twenty-one P-40s really did crisscross each other in the skies, they fired no bullets and dropped no "aerial torpedoes." Nor did the Sixty-Second Regiment actually use its antiaircraft guns, although its powerful searchlights did sweep the skies.

On the other hand, the plane spotters spread across eastern New York and lower New England were very real. Some ten thousand civilian volunteers and Coast Guardsmen, the former organized in relief relays by the American Legion, manned seven hundred observation posts throughout the Northeast during the test. Nine of these posts were in the city itself. The observation deck of the world's tallest building, the Empire State, provided a vantage point for scanning the skies. So did a hotel roof in Coney Island, a dock at City Island, and an Elks Club in Elmhurst. World War I veterans, the mainstay of American Legion membership, manned most of the observation posts, but other civilians, including women, took part as well.

The army generals who had organized the operation conveyed a mixed message about its outcome. Yes, the system worked: spotters had phoned in sightings in time to permit fighters to take off in successful pursuit. But there had also been problems. Numerous spotters called in inaccurate sightings, even though they had been trained to jot down the direction and altitude of the incoming bombers. Further training and drills, the *Times* averred, would surely strengthen the system, for the army had announced its intention of making civilian observation permanent and extending it up and down the East Coast and to other parts of the country.[1]

The world was a dangerous place in early 1941. Adolf Hitler's Blitzkrieg had created a new German empire stretching from Poland to France. Nazi Germany and Soviet Russia had signed a nonaggression pact; only Great Britain stood against the Nazi domination of Europe. The German Luftwaffe, the air force that had reduced Guernica and Rotterdam to rubble, now was busy trying to do the same to London and other English cities. Germany's Axis partners were also at war. Italian Fascist soldiers and airmen had already given Ethiopia and Albania to Mussolini and with their Nazi counterparts had helped Francisco Franco overthrow the Spanish Republic; now they fought to conquer Greece. Josef Stalin, for the moment Hitler's ally, had thrown the Red Army into eastern Poland, Finland, and the Baltic republics. In Asia, the Japanese Empire continued its bloody, intermittent offensive in China and had begun to move troops into French Indochina.

Many New Yorkers continued to see Europe's and Asia's wars as distant conflicts, somebody else's bad dream. The brief U-boat attacks and air raid drills of 1918 were long forgotten. The city's very vastness seemed to render it invulnerable. Hard hit by the Great Depression (with four hundred thousand men and women still unemployed in 1941), New York not only remained *the* American metropolis, the hub of the nation's financial and cultural life, but was also the world's second largest city, after London. New York's 7.5 million people inhabited a space that stretched across 322 square miles. In the shadow of its skyscrapers, in its residential districts that filled thousands of blocks, many felt insulated by the sheer solidity and size of the city.[2]

New York's military defenses offered extra reassurance to those who needed it. Long-range guns installed during or after World War I faced the Atlantic from the shores of New Jersey and Long Island, defying any invasion fleet bent on taking New York. On Sandy Hook, Fort Hancock's twelve-inch guns had a range of almost 20 miles; the massive sixteen-inch guns at Fort Tilden near Rockaway Beach could hurl a one-ton shell nearly 28 miles out to sea. Forts Terry, Wright, and Michie at the eastern tip of Long Island would prevent an attack by way of Long Island Sound. From Miller Field on Staten Island and from the Long Island fields, radio-equipped Army Air Corps planes patrolled out to sea, reporting on incoming vessels and, if need be, helping coastal artillery spotters to optimize the accuracy of their fire. The Sixty-Second Regiment based at Fort Totten in Queens could move its mobile antiaircraft guns and spotlights around the city by truck as needed. The *New York Times* noted confidently that, in the event of a real war, "the Army's new and secret aircraft detector" would warn of enemy planes 150 miles out to sea. Indeed, by 1942, radar antennae faced seaward from Fort Hancock, affording New York City an early-warning system akin to the one that helped defeat the Luftwaffe over England.[3]

As ever, the city's remoteness from Europe's battlefields seemed the strongest guarantee of safety. (As for the Japanese threat, that was the concern of West Coast cities facing the Pacific, and New Yorkers worried less about an attack from that direction.) Because no bomber could carry enough fuel to cross the Atlantic, make its attack, and return, the *Times'* military expert, Hanson Baldwin, contended that the worst East Coasters might expect would be "a small surprise raid, which could do little damage . . . undertaken by a plane or two from a ship at sea." Baldwin deemed even this unlikely, given the vigilance of navy, air corps, and coast guard patrols.[4]

For many New Yorkers, however, the danger remained real, even when they tried to push it out of their minds. A suppressed anxiety came pouring out of people when the right button was pressed. On Halloween Eve, 1938, Orson Welles's Mercury Theatre on the Air dramatized H. G. Wells's *War of the Worlds* and managed to convince at least one-fifth of an estimated six million listeners that the Northeast was under attack. In Manhattan, frightened people crowded police stations and public parks, snarled traffic on Riverside Drive in an effort to flee, and flooded the *New York Times* switchboard with frantic requests for information. Some, perhaps, fled their homes to save themselves from the Martian advance through central New Jersey that Welles's actors conveyed so grippingly. But others had a different threat in mind. Running out into the street, a Newark housewife shouted, "New Jersey is destroyed by the Germans—it's on the radio!"

That fall, after all, Hitler had brought Europe to the brink of war during the Munich Crisis, when he demanded—and ultimately got—the Sudetenland region of Czechoslovakia for the Third Reich. Such fears proved prescient; ten days after Halloween, on "Crystal Night," Nazi mobs would rampage through the cities of Germany and Austria, burning synagogues and beating and killing Jews.[5]

By the time of the mock "air raid" in January 1941, New Yorkers and other Americans had entered an even tenser period than that which preceded the outbreak of war in Europe. Hitler now controlled Western Europe and threatened to conquer Britain. Despite the opposition of isolationists, Franklin Roosevelt had managed to commit the nation to a program of pro-British military preparedness. Congress enacted the first peacetime draft in American history in September 1940, and sixteen million men had registered. Meanwhile, the Lend-Lease Program and the direct sale of American arms and supplies were helping to keep Britain in the war. Was the country—and its largest city—on an irrevocable collision course with Germany?

Anticipating such a collision, officials called for both preparedness and the avoidance of panic. "New York City is the logical and most attractive and tempting target for a foreign enemy," Mayor Fiorello La Guardia declared in June 1941. He was echoed by New York State's lieutenant governor, Charles Poletti: "Who can say that 3,000 miles of ocean are sufficient insulation against attack by those who, we know, hate America?" Despite the distance, New York's leaders warned, the attack—however minimal the possibility—might come. As early as the previous summer, after France fell to the Germans, La Guardia had revamped the city's Disaster Control Board, turning it into a preliminary coordinating group for defense planning. In March 1941, President Roosevelt appointed him director of a new nationwide Office of Civilian Defense. Corralling city councilmen; the police, fire, and health commissioners; and representatives of the utility companies and mass transit lines, La Guardia sought to make New York a national showcase for effective civil defense.[6]

In June 1941, the mayor announced the formation of the city's Air Raid Warden Service, a voluntary organization for men and women exempt from the draft. With bases of operation in each of the city's eighty-two police precinct houses, the service would carve up the city into districts staffed by volunteers who would enforce blackouts, direct civilians to safe shelter during raids, report all bombings and fires, administer first aid, and help people trapped in damaged buildings. By September 1941, one hundred thousand New Yorkers had voluntarily joined the Air Raid Protection Services in one capacity or another.[7]

La Guardia urged calm, repeatedly asserting that there was only a 3 to 5 percent chance of an aerial attack on his city. (The mayor neglected to explain how he had arrived at this very precise-sounding percentage.) But throughout 1941, an array of institutions reinforced the mayor's broader message. New York firemen just back from a fact-finding tour of London publicly demonstrated the proper technique for rescuing residents from burning tenements during an incendiary attack. As the city's public schools began conducting air raid drills, the Upper East Side's elite, private Dalton School "evacuated" one hundred students and fifteen teachers to Connecticut to "test the possibilities of carrying on school work in the suburbs while New York City is theoretically the target of bombers."[8]

Much of New York's preparation was playacting, to be sure. But such double vision—a sense of the city as probably safe but possibly at risk—had been the response of countless New Yorkers during earlier wars. As in those bygone conflicts, some—probably a minority—worried about an attack, others dismissed such fears as groundless, and still others leaned one way or the other as global and personal circumstances moved them. Over the next five years, this dual awareness of safety and risk would shape the way New Yorkers experienced a new world war. As their city became the outlet for Franklin Roosevelt's "great arsenal of democracy," as it became a port of embarkation for three million Americans bound for the battlefields of North Africa and Europe, New York's people measured in their mind's eyes the vast stretches of ocean and sky—vast *enough*, they hoped—separating them from Hitler's fleets and planes.[9]

As New Yorkers looked eastward across the ocean, the rise of dictators and new wars in Europe and Asia generated tense undercurrents that divided city dwellers from each other. In the years before the United

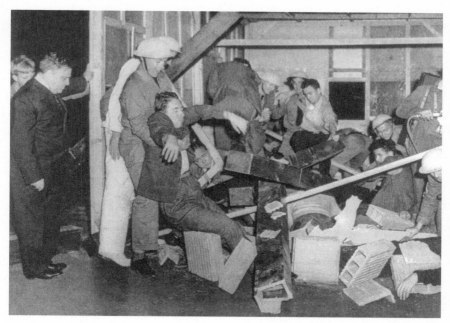

Mayor La Guardia (left) watches as city air raid wardens demonstrate the removal of casualties from a mock bomb site, c. 1941. PHOTO BY FOX PHOTOS / GETTY IMAGES.

States entered World War II, ethnic loyalties and new ideologies—sharpened by harsh economic times—brought the city's people into collision, once more raising the prospect that New Yorkers themselves were importing distant conflicts. Though the National Origins Act of 1924 had drastically reduced immigration into the country, in 1940 some 2 million New Yorkers had been born abroad; another 2.7 million claimed at least one foreign-born parent. This also meant that millions of New Yorkers had living relatives in Europe. By the mid and late 1930s, well before Hitler's troops marched into Poland, the tensions dividing Europe had reached New York's street corners. The rallying chants of clashing allegiances resounded down the avenues and through the parks.

The most provocative of the militant groups in Depression-era New York was the German American Bund, the American version of the Nazi Party. In marches through Yorkville on the Upper East Side, at banquets in Ebling's Casino in the Bronx, and during rallies in their

compounds at Camp Nordland in New Jersey and Camp Siegfried on
Long Island, Bundists unfurled the swastika next to the stars and
stripes. New York's first Nazis had organized in the Bronx in 1922,
only three years after German extremists formed the party in Munich.
By 1936, various splinter groups had consolidated under the leadership of Fritz Kuhn, an immigrant chemist who ran his nationwide
Bund from offices on East Eighty-Fifth Street in Yorkville. Estimates
of Bund national membership ranged from 8,500 to 25,000. The one
indisputable fact was that more Bundists lived in the New York metropolitan area than anywhere else.[10]

Parroting his German role model, the führer of East Eighty-Fifth
Street urged "Aryan (White Gentile) Americans to stamp out Jewish-
Atheistic Communistic International Outlawry!" New York Nazis also
warned of the "Black Danger"—the masses of "subhuman" African
Americans who did the Jews' dirty work. In his speeches and in the
pages of the bilingual Bund newspaper, the *Deutscher Weckruf und
Beobachter*, Kuhn demanded that the United States remain neutral
while Hitler extended the boundaries of "the New Germany."[11]

For many German New Yorkers, the Bund was an uncomfortable
presence. The German Workers Club openly denounced the American Nazis, warning that "democracy . . . will be destroyed in Yorkville,
if the people of Yorkville are not vigilant." Others maintained a careful public silence. Whatever they might have thought of Nazi racism
and the rise of the one-party state, it was hard for many German
Americans not to feel pride in the resurgence of their homeland.
Above all, however, they feared a return of the anti-"Hun" fervor of
1917–1918, and consequently most avoided any overt identification
with Kuhn's and Hitler's New Germany. The majority of Kuhn's recruits remained recent émigrés, young down-and-out Germans who
had taken advantage of the relatively generous quota accorded them
under the National Origins Act to flee financial turmoil in Weimar
Germany. Frustrated by New York's Depression economy, they felt no
stigma in looking homeward for political inspiration.[12]

In their jackboots and armbands, the Bundists were out to get
attention—and they certainly succeeded with the city's Jewish population. Many of New York's two million Jews had expressed their out-

Stars, stripes, and swastikas. German American Bund marchers on East Eighty-Sixth Street, October 30, 1939. NEW YORK WORLD-TELEGRAM & SUN NEWSPAPER PHOTOGRAPH COLLECTION, LIBRARY OF CONGRESS.

rage from the very beginning of Hitler's accession to power. On May 10, 1933, for example, one hundred thousand people marched from Madison Square to the German consulate at the Battery to protest the new Nazi government's forced retirement of Jewish civil servants, its establishment of restrictive quotas on Jewish enrollment in German high schools and universities, and its call for all Aryans to boycott Jewish businesses. Mayor John O'Brien reviewed the march from the steps of City Hall, and numerous Christian politicians and clergymen took part. But most marchers were members of Jewish organizations and Zionist clubs; the Jewish Undertakers' Union brandished a banner reading "We Want Hitler."[13]

Already underway was a boycott against businesses selling imported German goods. Various Jewish community and veterans' groups had called for the boycott in March; soon it was endorsed by Rabbi Stephen

Wise's American Jewish Congress, and volunteer activists confronted shoppers with leaflets and picket lines outside offending stores. But the boycott actually divided New York's Jews. Many among the city's German-Jewish businessmen and civic leaders feared the protest would further inflame the Nazi regime and consequently refused to endorse it. As if to confirm their fears, Bundists—aided, this time, by the German consulate in New York—eventually launched a counter-boycott. On Yorkville street corners, they handed out fliers urging consumers to "Patronize Gentile Stores Only!"[14]

After January 1, 1934, anti-Nazis could rely on the city's leading public official for wholehearted aid. Fiorello La Guardia had earned a reputation as one of the nation's most liberal congressmen. Now, as mayor, La Guardia recognized that his political future depended on the support of progressive Jews as well as proud Italian Americans. To ensure the allegiance of the former, anti-Nazism was good politics. But the mayor's heart was also in it. When he had joined the National Conference Against Racial Persecution in 1933, he publicly labeled Hitler "a perverted maniac." Two years before the opening of the 1939 New York World's Fair, the mayor told a Jewish women's group that the fair ought to include a "Chamber of Horrors" with a wax figure of "that brown shirted fanatic who is now menacing the peace of the world." Speaking in Yiddish, La Guardia shared his opinion of Hitler, Mussolini, and Stalin with a Jewish audience in 1937: *"Ich ken die drei menschen, die schlag zoll zei trefen"* ("I know these three men; the Devil take them").[15]

La Guardia delighted in making such statements, which invariably elicited press coverage. Just as delightful was the fact that his statements got under the skin of the Reich leadership in Berlin. After it became public knowledge in 1937 that La Guardia's Italian-born mother was Jewish, Josef Goebbels's propaganda ministry derided him as "a dirty Talmud Jew," and the Nazi press ran a photograph allegedly showing the "pimp" La Guardia pinching the backsides of scantily clad young women (in fact, the picture showed the New York nightclub owner Billy Rose surrounded by showgirls). With ominous specificity, Hermann Goering suggested that his Luftwaffe might bomb Manhattan from Governors Island to Rockefeller Center—the heart of the downtown and midtown business districts, and of the city's internationally renowned skyline—to "stop somewhat the mouths of the arrogant people over there."[16]

La Guardia's sparring with the Nazis clearly gratified the man in the White House, who could not publicly indulge his own anti-Nazi sentiments so bluntly. When the German government protested La Guardia's "Chamber of Horrors" remarks to Secretary of State Cordell Hull, Roosevelt told Hull, "We will chastise him like *that*," lightly tapping his own wrist with two fingers. The next time the mayor was a guest in the Oval Office, Roosevelt greeted him with the Hitler salute. "Heil Fiorello," he said, grinning. "Heil Franklin," the mayor responded with the same salute.[17]

Holding that the Bill of Rights must be maintained in New York, La Guardia permitted the Bund to hold a mass rally in Madison Square Garden on Washington's birthday, 1939. Addressing an audience of twenty-two thousand, which included reporters and hecklers as well as Bundists, Fritz Kuhn lambasted Roosevelt and his Jewish Treasury secretary, Henry Morgenthau, for turning America into a "Bolshevik paradise." Dwarfed by a thirty-foot-high portrait of George Washington and banners reading "Stop Jewish Domination of Christian America," Kuhn warned that only Nazism could rescue "Americanism." "The time will come," he insisted, "when no one will stand in our way."[18]

Outside, however, thousands were ready to stand in the Bundists' way. While 1,700 policemen ringed the building, ten thousand Jewish veterans, American Legionnaires, African American protesters, and members of the Socialist Workers Party chanted, "Keep the Nazis Out of New York." Inside, fistfights broke out throughout the hall as a young Jew, Isadore Greenbaum, rushed the stage. Bundists threw him to the floor. By evening's end, police had arrested Greenbaum and twelve other demonstrators for disorderly conduct. German propaganda sheets soon reviled "the Jew Greenbaum," confirming that Nazi hatred of Jews was now a transatlantic affair, bridging the ocean between Berlin and New York.[19]

Bundists were not the only group denouncing a "Jewish conspiracy" in Depression New York. In Irish neighborhoods, an aspiring middle class of teachers, lawyers, and civil servants saw Jews as rivals for a dwindling supply of Depression-era jobs. Accustomed to controlling Tammany Hall, Manhattan's Democratic Party machine, many Irish New Yorkers resented La Guardia's successful "Fusion" movement of liberal Republicans and anti-Tammany Democrats, which appeared to be putting Jews, Italians, and Protestants into traditionally "Irish" civil service posts. Additionally, the Irish-dominated Catholic Church in New York, deeply conservative in its leadership and official teachings, warned parishioners that the True Faith was under siege from the forces of modernity, liberalism, leftism, and atheism—in Soviet Russia, in anticlerical Mexico, in the godless Spanish Republic, and in New York City. Jews appeared to be in the vanguard of these ideological threats. (In truth, while the vast majority of New York's Jews were not Communists, the city's Communist Party, claiming over thirty thousand members, was heavily Jewish). Underpinning these various resentments and fears was a vernacular folk Catholicism, brought from Europe by generations of immigrants (and sustained by some priests and nuns), which nurtured the image of the Jew as "Christ-killer."[20]

In combination, these volatile elements predisposed thousands of the city's Catholics, particularly Irish Americans, to the nationwide messages broadcast in the late 1930s by Michigan's "Radio Priest," Father Charles Coughlin. Increasingly, Coughlin joined an unabashed anti-Semitism and pro-Nazism to his populist economic message. Coughlin defended Berlin after the Crystal Night pogroms and repeatedly denounced Jews and Communists as if the two were synonymous. Rather than disavow Coughlin, the *Brooklyn Tablet*, official paper of that borough's diocese, argued that the charge of anti-Semitism was "nothing more than a 'Red' herring used by Communists and their 'liberal' dupes and stooges to spread strife, discord and confusion." To be sure, numerous Catholics attacked Coughlin, and Professor Emmanuel Chapman of Fordham University founded the Committee of Catholics to Fight Anti-Semitism. But while some official church periodicals offered condemnations of anti-Jewish bigotry, the church hierarchy proved reluctant to chastise the popular Coughlin.[21]

Among those stirred by Coughlin were young working-class and lower-middle-class men for whom passive radio listening was not enough. By 1938, orators were mounting soapboxes in Manhattan's Columbus Circle and Washington Heights, Brooklyn's Flatbush, and the South Bronx, hectoring passersby to join the Christian Front, a Coughlin-inspired movement pledging "to defend Christian civilization." Recruiting primarily in mixed Irish-Jewish neighborhoods or at the borders between Irish and Jewish blocks, Fronters declared that "the Jews have all the good jobs" and that Franklin Roosevelt was at the helm of a plot to hand over the nation to Jewish Communists. Boycotting Jewish businesses and keeping America out of a war for England and Jewry were imperative. Even more militant were the Christian Mobilizers, a splinter group led by a Protestant named Joe McWilliams ("Joe McNazi" to his foes), who judged Hitler to be "the greatest leader in the history of the world" and who cultivated ties with Kuhn's Bundists. By decade's end, fistfights between Irish and Jewish New Yorkers were a common occurrence in the streets and in front of the offices of WMCA, the local radio station that broadcast Coughlin's tirades.[22]

In early 1940, the FBI broke up an outlandish plot by eighteen New Yorkers—including eleven Irish Americans and five Germans, one of them a Bundist—to foment a "Christian uprising" by blowing up Jewish businesses and the offices of the Communist *Daily Worker* and assassinating prominent Jews. The conspiracy may have been more fantasy than reality; the trial resulted in acquittals, dismissals for lack of evidence, and a mistrial for three of the defendants. But the hatred underlying such dreams of destruction was very real. "New York is a veritable powder keg," William J. Goodwin, a prominent Coughlinite and isolationist, warned in February 1941. "Our entry into the war might touch it off."[23]

For another of the city's largest ethnic groups, responses to international events took on the character of an internal civil war. After his rise to power in 1922, Benito Mussolini's Fascist regime elicited widespread enthusiasm among the one million denizens of "the biggest Italian city in the world." Indeed, Italians were not Mussolini's only New York fans: numerous Anglo businessmen and pundits lauded Fascism as a pragmatic solution to Italy's problems, and Thomas Lamont, partner at J. P. Morgan, enthusiastically arranged a $100 million loan to Italy in 1926. But Il Duce's ambition to revive ancient Rome's glories resonated most fully in the tenements and social clubs of Mulberry Street, East 116th Street, and Arthur Avenue. Blackshirts strutted through

Italian East Harlem, practicing the Fascist salute. Mussolini sparked community pride and patriotism in people who had long endured the epithets "wop" and "dago." As one anti-Fascist woman admitted, the dictator "enabled four million Italians in America to hold up their heads, and that is something."[24]

Faith in a homeland seemingly reborn under Fascism united many Italian New Yorkers. The community's *prominenti*—its leading business-men and spokesmen—included many who cultivated intimate ties with Fascist Rome, none more powerful than the publisher and Democratic politician Generoso Pope, whose daily *Il Progresso Italo-Americano* covertly received direct cables from the Italian foreign ministry until 1940. Rich and poor rallied together when Italy invaded Ethiopia in 1935. To help pay for the invasion, Italian American women sent their gold wedding bands to Rome by the thousands (in return they received steel rings blessed by a parish priest). Fiorello La Guardia considered Mussolini "a barbershop bully," but he watched his step and his words when it came to developments in the mother country. The mayor never publicly blasted Fascism the way he lambasted Nazism. To do so would be to risk his electoral base among New York's Italians.[25]

A vocal and vigorous minority of anti-Fascists, however, also in-habited the Italian community. Their most colorful figure was the anarchist Carlo Tresca. A man of great charm and gusto, Tresca was equally at home conversing with his friend the philosopher John Dewey, blasting Mussolini in his weekly *Il Martello* (the Hammer), and leading fellow Italian leftists armed with daggers and baseball bats into battle against Fascists in the streets of New York. Pro-and anti-Fascists clashed repeatedly, leaving a trail of bloodied heads, and sometimes corpses, behind them. On the Fourth of July, 1932, hun-dreds battled at the Garibaldi "shrine" at Rosebank on Staten Island, where the great nineteenth-century Italian liberator had once lived in exile. Although outnumbered, Tresca's men claimed victory over their enemies. Salvatore Arena, a Brooklyn member of the Duce Fascist Al-liance, was shot and killed; his murderer was never caught.[26]

In 1935, another population confronted and challenged the city's Fas-cists, adding racial tensions to political ones. The Christian kingdom of Ethiopia had long been a focal point of pride for New York's black nationalists. When the Italian army invaded Ethiopia that year, the specter of arrogant Europeans slaughtering poorly armed Africans sparked a groundswell of indignation throughout Harlem. Thousands—conservative churchmen, Communists, followers of Marcus Garvey—crowded into the Abyssinian Baptist Church for meetings of the Provisional Committee for the Defense of Ethiopia. Some began training as a "Black Legion" with the aim of reaching Africa to fight Mussolini's troops. Aviator Herbert Julian, Harlem's "Black Eagle," trained for battle at Roosevelt Field on Long Island. When he reached Ethiopia, that nation's leaders consigned him to the task of training ill-equipped ground troops.[27]

Back in New York, the proximity of Italian East Harlem and black Harlem generated friction. When Ethiopia fell in May 1936, jubilant parades filled the streets of Italian neighborhoods. A few days later, Rome announced a policy of strict racial segregation in its new colony, and news arrived of Italian massacres of Ethiopian prisoners. Four hundred black demonstrators marched on Lenox Avenue, broke the windows of two Italian American groceries, and fought with policemen, one of whom shot and wounded an African American. Bitter feelings continued after the war ended. "No black man could, in good conscience, go into most Italian bars in Harlem," black nationalist James R. Lawson recalled later. "Mussolini's picture hung over almost every Italian cash register up there."[28]

With Ethiopia under Fascist control, African Americans resorted to the symbolic satisfaction of sports. They exulted in June 1935 when the "brown bomber," Joe Louis, knocked out Italy's heavyweight champion, Primo Carnera, before an interracial audience of sixty thousand in Yankee Stadium. Aware of Nazi Germany's racism, they were mortified less than a year later, when Louis fell to the punches of the German heavyweight Max Schmeling in the very same ring. Walking on Seventh Avenue in Harlem, the poet Langston Hughes saw "grown men weeping like children, and women sitting on the curbs with their heads in their hands." Two years later, sweet redemption: in a rematch, again in Yankee Stadium, Louis sent Schmeling to the canvas in the first round. The German champion didn't regain his feet. Blacks, Jews, and other anti-Nazis celebrated throughout the city. As the news came over the radio in Harlem, tens of thousands poured into the streets.

"With their faces to the night sky," reported the novelist Richard Wright, "they filled their lungs with air and let out a scream of joy that it seemed would never end, and a scream that seemed to come from untold reserves of strength."[29]

Uptown, Africa's war aroused black Harlem; downtown, Asia's war stirred the people of Chinatown. Japan's invasion of Manchuria in 1931 had led to a brutal, protracted conflict in China, pitting Chiang Kai-shek's Nationalists and Mao Tse-tung's Communists against the Japanese—and often against each other. These conflicts echoed on Mott, Bayard, and Pell Streets, where perhaps ten thousand immigrants, mostly men, filled tenements that had first become a recognizable Chinese district in the late nineteenth century. Elite businessmen allied with Chiang's Nationalist Party dominated Chinatown's affairs, but many residents were restaurant and laundry workers who sympathized with Mao's movement. Chiang's attacks on the Communists and his failure to back up his own generals against the Japanese kept political tensions high in Chinatown throughout the 1930s.

Opposing factions sponsored their own newspapers, clubs, and rallies; threats, name-calling, and occasional bloodshed ensued. But at times the opponents managed to submerge their differences long enough to cooperate for the greater good of the homeland. The Chinese Women's Patriotic Association held fund-raising auctions and charity balls. Residents feted the war hero General Tsai Ting-Kai on his New York visit in 1934, and they cabled money and encouraging messages to Shanghai and other strongholds of anti-Japanese resistance. In November 1937, two thousand Chinese New Yorkers paraded through lower Manhattan with a dragon float and a banner reading, "Fight Against Japan to the Very Bitter End to Save China." But this sentiment found no outlet in local violence. Only a few thousand Japanese businessmen, consular agents, and domestics lived in New York, and they were scattered. Chinatown residents had no Little Japan against which to vent their outrage.[30]

Long ignored by the city's politicians and civic leaders, caricatured by journalists and entertainers, the Chinese broke out of their ghetto to command white attention during the Sino-Japanese conflict that preceded—and ultimately bled into—the global war. They did so on their own terms and for the first time in the community's history. By 1938 a widespread boycott of Japanese silk was underway in New York, and politically enlightened women traded their silk stockings for lisle cotton ones. Merchant seamen picketed ships carrying scrap iron to Japan. A war seven thousand miles away had arrived on the city's streets and piers, much as events in Germany, Italy, and Ethiopia pitted New Yorkers against each other in a seemingly endless round of marches, speeches, boycotts, and brawls.[31]

In the years before the Japanese attack on Pearl Harbor in December 1941, international politics made strange bedfellows in New York. Movements like the America First Committee, opposed to any American entanglement in foreign wars, included liberals, pacifists, and pro-Nazi allies of Father Coughlin. Support for Roosevelt's efforts to aid an embattled England came from Democratic internationalists, but also from the Republican businessmen of the Fight for Freedom Committee, who called for an American declaration of war on Germany.

Through the 1930s, however, it was leftists who warned most vigorously of the rise of Nazism, Fascism, and Japanese imperialism—and in the Depression era, Communists superseded Socialists as the city's most dynamic and conspicuous left-wing party. The Communists' national headquarters faced Union Square, which became the setting for mass rallies protesting Washington's alleged indifference to the rise of the belligerent right-wing dictatorships. Emboldened by the Soviet Union's role as a bastion against Fascism, New York Communists took to the streets to put their beliefs into action. In July 1935, Bill Bailey, a young merchant seaman raised in the Irish slums of Hell's Kitchen, along with Adrian Duffy, "Low-Life" McCormick, and two other comrades, fought their way onto the deck of the German ocean liner *Bremen*, docked at the foot of West Forty-Sixth Street. As Nazi sailors and New York policemen tried to stop them, they ripped the swastika flag off the ship's pole and threw it overboard, where, in Bailey's words, "it just floated down into the dirty Hudson." After they were arrested, they explained that they had acted to avenge the recent mistreatment of New York Communist seamen by Nazis in the port of Hamburg.[32]

With the outbreak of the Spanish Civil War in 1936, some three thousand Americans—between one-fifth and one-third of them from

New York City—joined the Abraham Lincoln Battalion and sailed off to help defend the Spanish Republic against Franco's, Mussolini's, and Hitler's armies. Most "Lincolns" (Bailey and McCormick among them) were Communists, but their ranks also included others stirred by Moscow's call for an international Popular Front against Fascism— Socialists, anarchists, liberals, and blacks avenging Ethiopia. "As a Jew and a progressive, I would be among the first to fall under the axe of the fascists," Hyman Katz explained in a letter from Spain to his mother in New York in November 1937.[33]

Back home, leftists recognized that the Iberian conflict was a prelude to something bigger. "For the duration of the Spanish agony," the novelist Albert Halper later wrote, "New York was a city of stirring mass meetings, rallies, and fund raisings. . . . One returned to one's room or apartment, drained, sickened, unable to sleep." New York labor unions and left-wing clubs sent several ambulances and thousands of tons of food, clothing, and medicine to the dying Republic (while conservative Catholic groups dispatched funds and supplies to Franco's victorious rebels). When the survivors of the defeated Lincoln Battalion sailed back to New York in 1938 and 1939, they were greeted as heroes by welcoming crowds on the West Side piers.[34]

Yet the flow of international events kept shifting the ground under New Yorkers. When Berlin and Moscow announced their nonaggression pact in August 1939 and proceeded to carve up Poland, Communists abruptly abandoned the Popular Front and blandly argued that Germany's imperial ambitions were no worse than England's or France's (a position they would maintain until June 1941, when Hitler's tanks rolled into Russia). Disgusted Socialists in the midtown garment district greeted their Communist coworkers with shouts of "Heil Hitler." In truth, many rank-and-file Communists were shaken by Stalin's about-face, although most hewed to the party line. Some surmised that the pact was a temporary expedient, merely delaying a collision between Germany and Russia. Beyond that, who could say how far the war would spread? By the summer of 1941, 72 percent of American respondents to a *Fortune* magazine poll believed Hitler to harbor global, including transatlantic, ambitions. Millions of people in New York and throughout the country, of widely varying political viewpoints, shared a fear Hyman Katz had voiced four years earlier: "If we sit by and let them grow stronger by taking Spain, they will move on to France and will not stop there; and it won't be long before they get to America."[35]

Across the Atlantic, Nazi leaders were indeed looking westward. In 1938, a Focke-Wulf prototype commercial liner flew nonstop from Berlin to New York, a distance of some 3,900 miles. That same year the Luftwaffe drafted secret guidelines for future long-range bombers. With the outbreak of war in September 1939, Luftwaffe commander in chief Hermann Goering, anticipating the eventual entry of the United States, brought up the possibility of "nuisance raids" by his bombers along the American East Coast, although some of his staff were skeptical. During 1940, the Junkers, Messerschmitt, Heinkel, and Focke-Wulf firms all began preliminary work to design long-range four-engine bombers that would have the fuel capacity to make round-trip sorties from Brest in occupied France to New York and back. The Luftwaffe recognized that such raids would most likely involve a small number of bombers that would have to return immediately after dropping their bombs. Yet such raids might require the Americans to devote inordinate resources to protecting their coast.[36]

Delighted by the Luftwaffe's plans, Hitler was forthright about his ambitions for such raids. He rhapsodized to his architect Albert Speer about New York "going down in a sea of flames," with its skyscrapers turned into "towers of flame." In March 1941, after Roosevelt signed the Lend-Lease Pact with Britain, Hitler lamented "that we had no aircraft capable of bombing American cities." Two months later, at a conference with his naval war staff, Hitler emphasized the need to occupy the Portuguese Azores and the Spanish Canary Islands as bases from which to attack the United States. Such bases would provide airfields hundreds of miles closer to the American East Coast, cutting flight distances and fuel needs for bombers. While the Germans never occupied the islands, Hitler retained a vivid sense of what he wanted to do to Manhattan.[37]

Hitler's animosity toward New York was not merely due to its identity as the largest Jewish city in the world, but also fit a more sweeping Nazi hostility toward the United States. Neither Hitler nor any of the other top Nazis had ever been to America, and they were free to concoct fantasies shaped by their consumption of popular stereotypes. Franklin Roosevelt noted shrewdly in 1939 that what impressed Hitler about America was its size and wealth; a combined hatred and barely suppressed envy of American financial might and material abundance ran through Nazi propaganda. At the same time, Hitler and his leading ideologues, Alfred Rosenberg and Joseph Goebbels, saw America as a degenerate society contaminated by the "mongre-lized" mixing of diverse races and by effete democracy. "What is America," Hitler asked a friend, "but millionaires, beauty queens, stu-pid records and Hollywood?" Yet this "half-Judaized, half-Negrified" culture—purveyed throughout the world via movies, magazines, and jazz—constituted an insidious international threat, one that could even seduce pure Aryans. "Transfer [a German] to Miami," warned Hitler, "and you make a degenerate of him—in other words—an American." The führer might have been thinking of his nephew, English-born William Patrick Hitler, who lived in New York City and publicly denounced his uncle as "a menace" in 1939.[38]

For Hitler and Nazi ideologues, these assessments of American power and weakness converged in their image of New York City. Manhattan and its famed skyline embodied a rotten culture that needed to be destroyed before it contaminated the rest of the world—not least because the skyline's message of American glamour, power, and prosperity proved so seductive to Europeans, including Germans. At the same time, because Americans were decadent and corrupted, Manhattan was really a flimsy Hollywood movie set that could be knocked over to reveal the impotence behind it. The Luftwaffe would easily topple the towers after turning them into "blazing bundles of firewood"—provided they could reach New York with adequate fuel reserves. Thus, while Washington, DC, and various industrial targets also loomed in Luftwaffe discussions, New York remained the prime fixation of Nazi fantasy.[39]

Following American entry into the war, the German air force and its contractors continued to work in earnest on transatlantic bombers with sufficient fuel to reach New York and return safely. The German high command may have fantasized about destroying New York, but, as during the previous war, some Berlin functionaries saw New York as useful, a metropolis whose still sizeable German community provided cover for espionage. By 1935, the Abwehr (German military intelligence) had managed to establish spies in New York. Over the next five years, operations expanded to include several rings of agents across the country, consisting of German émigrés, many of them naturalized US citizens, and a few Americans of German descent. The Little Casino Restaurant on Yorkville's East Eighty-Fifth Street—close to Fritz Kuhn's national Bund headquarters—became a center of operations for agents.

It wasn't long before Germany's network of New York spies began proving its utility. Otto Voss, a mechanic at the Seversky Aircraft plant in Farmingdale, Long Island, smuggled out plans of new fighters being developed for the Air Corps. Rene Froehlich, a soldier stationed at Fort Jay on Governors Island, collected information on troop and ship movements. On a visit to Germany, Queens resident Hermann Lang transmitted plans of a top-secret aerial bombsite from his workplace, the Carl Norden plant on Lafayette Street. Kurt Ludwig drove up and down the East Coast, photographing factories and army bases; sometimes he took along eighteen-year-old Lucy Boehmler from Maspeth to flirt with soldiers and coax information from them. One operative even provided a map showing fifty-two Long Island golf courses, "ideal landing places for German aircraft." Crewmen on German ocean liners carried documents and photographs from the West Side piers to Abwehr offices in Hamburg and Bremen.[40]

Often, however, the spies were amateurish and sloppy, more interested in Abwehr payments than in being discreet. Some bragged openly in bars and restaurants about their work for the Reich. Bronx resident Guenther Rumrich, who offered his services to the Nazis after reading about World War I spies in the New York Public Library, blundered in 1938, when he tried to secure fifty blank passports from the State Department under false pretenses. Trailed by federal agents and New York police, Rumrich was arrested and named his fellow agents. He and three coconspirators were convicted of violating the 1917 Espionage Act and sent to prison.[41]

Even more spectacular was the error in judgment made by the Abwehr itself in 1940, when its officers forced German-born William Sebold, an American on vacation in the fatherland, to agree to become a spy when he returned to New York. Gestapo agents threatened to

kill him if he refused. But Sebold promptly went to the FBI and became a double agent. Over the course of sixteen months, FBI agents
filmed from behind a "mirror" in Sebold's West Forty-Second Street
office, as Lang and others boasted about their exploits; a shortwave radio set up in a house in Centerport, Long Island, sent false espionage
reports in Sebold's name back to Germany. In June 1941, in what
J. Edgar Hoover called the "greatest spy roundup in U.S. history,"
thirty-three German agents were arrested and tried in a Brooklyn
courtroom, with Sebold as key prosecution witness. All thirty-three
were convicted and imprisoned. (Still fearing the Nazis, Sebold assumed a new identity and left New York under an early version of the
federal witness protection and relocation program.) Committed to
cultivating pro-Allied public opinion without violating official American neutrality, President Roosevelt used the evidence of Nazi espionage to advance his case that Hitler posed a threat on both sides of
the Atlantic, a threat Americans had to prepare for.[42]

Sunday, December 7, 1941, dawned cold and clear in New York City.
New Yorkers perusing their *Times* over breakfast learned from Tokyo
correspondent Otto Tolischus that "the Japanese people as a whole
are normally friendly and polite" but that they blamed American
diplomatic intervention for delaying Japanese victory in their war
with China. That afternoon, many New Yorkers listened to their ra-
dios, following the New York Giants–Brooklyn Dodgers football game
at the Polo Grounds on the Mutual Broadcasting System. At about 2
PM, an announcer's voice broke into the game: "We interrupt this
broadcast to bring this important broadcast from United Press: Flash!
The White House announces Japanese attack on Pearl Harbor!" From
New Jersey, a disbelieving man called the Mutual switchboard operator and told her, "Ha! You got me on that Martian stunt; I had a
hunch you'd try it again."[43]

Mayor La Guardia immediately placed the officers of New York's
Japanese consulate under police supervision. Starting on the evening
of December 7, the police and the FBI began rounding up 2,500 Japanese New Yorkers and transporting them to Ellis Island for precautionary internment. Agents also seized the briefcase of Morito Morishima,
the city's Japanese consul general, at his office in Rockefeller Center

and found in it several strips of film with photographs of the Washington Monument, the Manhattan skyline, and various bridges in the Washington and New York areas; apparently, the threat of Japanese attack or sabotage was not limited to the West Coast, after all. The shock waves of disbelief, confusion, and even relief that the expected crisis had finally arrived reverberated through the city.[44]

That night a teleprinter in Lorient, on the Atlantic coast of occupied France, delivered the news of Pearl Harbor to Admiral Karl Doenitz, U-boat commander in chief. The report caught Doenitz (as well as Hitler) completely off guard, as Tokyo had not shared its plans for the surprise attack with its allies in Berlin. Doenitz walked to his Situation Room, where a three-foot-diameter world globe allowed him to plot the courses of the submarines that had been ravaging Allied shipping for over two years. He now plotted the distance between his U-boat pens at Lorient and various potential target zones in the Western Hemisphere. Of pressing interest to Doenitz was the fact that the distance from Lorient to the waters off New York City, three thousand nautical miles, would permit each of his long-distance U-boats a total of between six and fifteen days to torpedo ships approaching or leaving New York harbor, before having to refuel. The admiral waited a mere four days for Hitler's impulsive declaration of war against the United States on December 11, at which point the American coast became fair game. In the days to follow, Doenitz would put his Operation Paukenschlag ("Operation Drumbeat") into play, with dire consequences for seamen working the waters off the Atlantic coast of the United States. New York City's real war was about to begin.[45]

As the torpedo slammed into the hull of the *Coimbra*, it ignited the tanker's eighty thousand barrels of oil and sent a blinding sheet of fire boiling up into the night sky. Surveying the blaze from the bridge of U-boat 123 a quarter of a mile away, *Kapitanleutnant* Reinhard Hardegen estimated its height as over six hundred feet above the Atlantic's choppy surface. Somehow, crewmen aboard the stricken British tanker managed to ready a gun on the stern deck to fire at their attacker. Hardegen promptly ordered a second torpedo. This one sent the *Coimbra* to the bottom, taking thirty-six men with her. Several others, some of them wounded, boarded a raft and a dory and began the long row toward the shore of eastern Long Island, some twenty-seven miles distant, in the early morning hours of January 15, 1942.

Hardegen exulted at this, his third "kill" since leaving the German submarine base at Lorient, France, three weeks earlier. Already, U-123 had torpedoed and sunk a British steamer three hundred miles east of Cape Cod and a Norwegian tanker sixty miles southeast of Montauk, Long Island, with a combined loss of over eighteen thousand tons of shipping, seven thousand tons of general cargo, twelve tons of fuel oil, and 110 lives. U-123 was the lead vessel of Admiral Doenitz's Operation Paukenschlag. The admiral recognized that if a concentrated U-boat onslaught sank Allied vessels faster than they could be built, the toll on shipping would effectively cut the transatlantic supply line to Britain. With its economy throttled, England could never become the launch pad for an Allied invasion of continental Europe. The U-boats' chokehold would leave the island's people nearly starved and its factories and vehicles bereft of oil; Winston Churchill would be driven to his knees, enabling Germany to fight a one-front war against Russia. Paukenschlag was Doenitz's demonstration to Adolf Hitler that U-boats must be concentrated off the American coast in order to win the war.[46]

A few hours before sinking the *Coimbra* on January 15, Hardegen had ventured near the acknowledged target for the raid. "My mission was to get to New York," he later wrote. When Hardegen had unsealed his instructions at sea, two American guidebooks to New York City tumbled out of the envelope. The brightly colored cover of one showed skyscrapers and the Statue of Liberty towering over a scene of colonial Dutchmen trading with Indians and bore the legend "1626—Bought for Twenty Four Dollars. 1939—Valued at Twenty Four Billion!" More germane to Hardegen's task, the guidebooks included fold-out tourist maps of the city—maps that showed the location of the Ambrose Channel leading into the port.[47]

As a young naval cadet, Hardegen had visited New York during a round-the-world German training cruise nine years earlier. Like many tourists, he had ventured to the top of the Empire State Building and gazed out on the bright lights, skyscrapers, distant factories, piers, and moored ships spread before him. Hardegen and Doenitz both knew that New York harbor, the world's busiest, was destined to play a crucial role in the war. On the evening of January 15, the commander brought U-123 in for a close look.[48]

Due south of Rockaway Beach, U-123 bobbed on the surface. The submarine was so close to shore that *Leutnant* Horst von Schroeter "could see the cars driving along the coast road, and I could even smell the woods." But the real attraction was to the west: clearly silhouetted against the sky were the three-hundred-foot Parachute Jump and the Wonder Wheel, the world's largest Ferris wheel, both at Coney Island, and beyond them the red lights of a radio beacon on Staten Island. And behind them all was a glow in the night sky—the reflected gleam of Manhattan's millions of lights on the clouds above. Hardegen found himself musing whether the Broadway shows were letting out just over the horizon, and the jazz clubs tuning up for a night of revelry. Already, on the wireless below, his men had been listening to the Gramercy Chamber Trio, broadcast by Manhattan's WNYC, after passing up WOR's "The Goldbergs," a popular comedy about a Bronx Jewish family.[49]

Hardegen turned back to business. While the camouflage-gray hull of U-123 was surrounded by a medley of oblivious fishing smacks and tugs on the harbor's outer reaches, a worthy prize—a big tanker or cargo ship heading into or out of New York—was nowhere in sight. As tempting as the Ambrose Channel and New York harbor might have been, Hardegen knew that once he entered and wreaked havoc, he might not get back out alive. Instead he turned his vessel east, sinking the *Coimbra*. From there he ventured south and found rich hunting grounds along the coastal route favored by freighters and oil tankers shuttling between New York, Philadelphia, and the Gulf Coast ports. Off Cape Hatteras he sank three more ships. He was soon joined by the five other U-boats of Paukenschlag. Over the next four weeks, the six submarines sank twenty-one Allied cargo ships in the waters between Newfoundland and South Carolina. So commenced what the submariners called "the great American turkey shoot."[50]

What shocked Hardegen was the utter negligence of New Yorkers and other Americans in the face of a war that was now over a month old. "I assumed that I would find a coast that was blacked out . . . ," he later recalled. "I found a coast that was brightly lit. . . . Ships were sailing with navigation lights." For Hardegen and other U-boat commanders who followed, "the glow of New York on the clouds" became emblematic of a stubborn American denial of the reality of war.[51]

In New York and Washington, people sought to piece together what was happening in the wake of the sinkings. With the Coimbra's oil and life preservers washing up on Long Island beaches, and survivors reaching shore, a news blackout was impossible. While navy spokesmen reassured the public that they had the situation in hand, the truth was that Admiral Ernest King, commander in chief of the US fleet, had not taken seriously the risk of U-boat attack—this despite urgent warnings from British admiralty cryptologists who were deciphering wireless transmissions between Doenitz's headquarters and his vessels at sea.[52]

King's preoccupation with the Pacific war, his conviction that a coastal raid was unlikely, and a shortage of antisubmarine vessels had all impeded precautionary measures. While the army air corps had been urging people on the East Coast to look skyward, the navy had grown accustomed to viewing the Battle of the Atlantic as a conflict being fought far from American shores. For over six months prior to Pearl Harbor, the navy (with FDR's blessing) had been fighting an undeclared war in the North Atlantic against U-boats, bringing the two nations to the brink of open war. German submarines had torpedoed four American merchant ships (including the Robin Moor and the Sagadahoc, outbound from New York), two American destroyers, and a navy tanker, with a total loss of 164 lives. But the confrontations had taken place hundreds of miles from America, and the continuing political strength of isolationists deterred Roosevelt from declaring war. The navy, in short, was the one service that was already in active combat—and the one service that seriously neglected to prepare for an attack.[53]

The navy now took action, albeit slowly, following the Coimbra sinking, coordinating its efforts with the coast guard, the army, and the army air force. As during the last war, an antisubmarine net and boom had already been stretched across the Narrows, with a nine-hundred-foot gate to admit friendly vessels. Acoustic hydrophones placed in local shipping channels would detect approaching U-boats; strategically placed mines would sink them. By the spring of 1942, the navy required coastal cargo vessels to sail in convoys of forty or fifty ships, usually under the protection of cutters, patrol boats, and antisubmarine trawlers lent by the British. Planes from the army's First Air Support Command at Mitchel Field, Long Island, and seaplanes from the Naval Air Station at Floyd Bennett Field in Brooklyn covered the passage of convoys along the coast.[54]

The military command also accepted the services of volunteer pilots in the Civil Air Patrol, and of boatmen in a newly formed Coastal Picket Patrol. The latter, soon nicknamed the "Hooligan Navy," consisted of hundreds of motorized yachts and other small craft owned by fishermen and amateur sailors eager to serve. Hooligans like Jakob Isbrandtsen, a young steamship company clerk, plied the waters off New York armed with Springfield rifles and Lewis machine guns. Navy men might grin or grimace, but like their predecessors in the Sea Fencibles in 1812, the boatmen played an effective role, exasperating the U-boat captains. The risk of being spotted by a yacht that could radio for a navy depth-charge attack or air force bombing run kept U-boats submerged and away from the convoys. By the spring, Doenitz, convinced that the East Coast was now less vulnerable than the Gulf Coast and Caribbean, shifted most of his U-boats to more southerly climes.[55]

The submarines had not left the New York region entirely, however, and for the remainder of the war, U-boats in local waters would remain on the minds of New Yorkers. "In New York, the front was at the sea buoy," one merchant seaman later recalled. Even as the navy had pondered what to do in the wake of the attack on the *Coimbra*, U-130 sank a Norwegian tanker off the New Jersey coast in late January 1942, and U-404 sent an American freighter to the bottom in March, silhouetted against the glimmering lights of Atlantic City. When New Yorkers started to forget about U-boats, the Germans reminded them. On the night of November 10, 1942, U-608 laid mines in the waters just off the Ambrose Channel. One was discovered three days later, and for the only time during the war, the port of New York was closed for forty-eight hours, as minesweeping vessels collected and detonated five German mines. On May 5, 1945, with Hitler already dead and the Red Army in control of Berlin, U-853 sank a coal boat at the eastern end of

Long Island Sound, only to be depth-charged and sunk in turn by a navy and coast guard patrol.[56]

"The losses by submarines off our Atlantic seaboard and in the Caribbean now threaten our entire war effort," General George Marshall had warned in June 1942—a view shared by Churchill and others. True, by the following month, eight enemy subs had been sunk off American and Canadian shores. But in the six months following the initiation of Paukenschlag, U-boats destroyed nearly 400 Allied vessels in North American and Caribbean waters (171 of them off the East Coast), with a loss of some 2,400 lives.[57]

When measured against the war-winning goal Doenitz had propounded in December 1941, however, the total results of Paukenschlag were disappointing. Hitler never saw fit to concentrate U-boats off American shores, choosing to place his naval and other strategic priorities elsewhere. Doenitz was forced to refocus his efforts to the North Atlantic after mid-1942. Germans were left to ponder the fleeting vision of an alluring and seemingly vulnerable America offered by Reinhard Hardegen in a book for wartime readers, in which he echoed the comments made by U-boat officer Frederick Koerner twenty-four years earlier. "I cannot describe the feeling with words, but it was unbelievably beautiful and great," the *Kapitanleutnant* wrote of gazing at New York's glow on the night clouds overhead. "I would have given away a kingdom for this moment if I had had one. We were the first to be here, and for the first time in this war a German soldier looked out upon the coast of the U.S.A." But it would not be the last time.[58]

In truth, New York's unfolding war was very much a maritime affair, and Hitler missed an opportunity to inflict severe damage, if not to win the war, when he turned his attention from the city and its surrounding waters. Already the world's busiest port, New York now became the great American terminus for the "bridge of ships" linking Franklin Roosevelt's "arsenal of democracy" to Britain, Russia, and the fronts that would be opened in North Africa and Europe. A continuous armada of vessels laden with weapons, ammunition, and supplies steamed out of the Narrows and Long Island Sound to destinations as far flung as the Texas oil ports, Liverpool, Falmouth, and Glasgow in the British Isles,

Casablanca in Morocco after the American landings there, and Murmansk and Archangel above the Arctic Circle in Russia.[59]

The transatlantic convoys—clusters of thirty to eighty cargo ships and oil tankers, guarded by escorts of several navy destroyers, corvettes, and cruisers—became the lifeline of the European war, and New York soon became their most important nexus. Learning from British example, the navy knew that merchant ships traveling en masse and guarded by armed escorts had a better chance of repelling and surviving U-boat attacks. Philadelphia, Boston, and other ports also dispatched convoys, and initially Halifax, Nova Scotia, was the main assembly point for the Atlantic runs. But after September 1942, when New York replaced Halifax as the key western terminus, the harbor became the greatest marshalling yard for vessels arriving from the Gulf oil ports, the West Indies, Africa, and even India via the Panama Canal, all in preparation for the Atlantic trek. By the end of the war, a total of 1,462 convoys, consisting of 21,459 ships carrying over sixty-three million tons of supplies, had sailed from New York to sustain the Allied war effort.[60]

An air of secrecy, meant to defeat spies, surrounded the departure of these flotillas from New York. Vessels shuttled back and forth across the harbor, loading petroleum at the New Jersey refineries behind Staten Island; or picking up locomotives, electric generators, and refrigerated blood plasma at the world's largest warehouse, the Brooklyn Army Terminal in Sunset Park; or powdered eggs, flour, and crated airplanes at Hoboken's piers; or tanks and trucks at Bayonne's Port Johnson Terminal. Hilda O'Brien, a Columbia University graduate student sharing an apartment on Riverside Drive with several other single women, watched the ships come and go: "We were always curious that at night the Hudson River would be filled with gray boats of all sizes and shapes and the next morning they'd all be gone."[61]

In the waters just past the Ambrose Channel, freighters and tankers arrayed themselves in long columns or in a vast square, several miles across, with US and British naval vessels on the periphery and a trawler trailing behind to pick up survivors should disaster befall the ships. After being joined by additional vessels in Nova Scotia or Newfoundland, the convoys would press as fast as they could across the Atlantic to

Iceland, England, or Scotland, in whose waters the Royal Navy took over escort duty from the Americans. Some continued on the Murmansk run to the Soviet Union's arctic ports.

The cargo ships and tankers were manned by merchant seamen: professional sailors whose vital work earned them draft deferments. At the National Maritime Union hiring hall on West Seventeenth Street in Manhattan's Chelsea, seamen from New York and all over the country lined up to take berths on board the convoy vessels. High wartime pay was an incentive, but most crewmen also were deeply committed to the war's cause. Moray Epstein, a young seaman from New Jersey embarking on the freighter *John Walker* for Russia in August 1942, wrote expectantly to his future bride, Sylvia, about seeing the land of his parents' birth and about his duty. "I know that someone has to sail these ships, and that the work we are doing is work that must be done. But it could be so easy," he added, "so tempting to give this up just to be able to walk with you in East River Park."[62]

Seamen were aware of the risks they faced. Many convoys arrived at their destination with six or a dozen ships missing. In March 1943, thirty-eight U-boats converged on two convoys outbound from New York in the mid-Atlantic. Over four days, in a battle zone stretching across six hundred miles of stormy seas, the submarines sank twenty-two out of a total of eighty-nine cargo vessels, despite the defense put up by British escorts; 379 crewmen lost their lives. Most daunting of all was the "Bomb Alley Run" to Murmansk or Archangel, during which convoys braved attacks by subs and bombers from Nazi-occupied Norway.[63]

Surviving a convoy run could be both harrowing and exhilarating. On board the freighter *Richard Henry Lee* off Norway in May 1942, seaman Sam Hakam from Brooklyn watched as German bombers sank a sister ship: "You could see a lot of blackened heads—the heads of men still alive—on the water. The heads looked like floating bowling balls. Many of those boys weren't rescued." Survival occasioned pride as well as relief. "Ambrose Light. Excitement and tension rose," Moray Epstein jotted down as the *John Walker* returned intact from Archangel in February 1943. "We passed Coney Island. Emotion washed over me when I saw the Statue of Liberty, the symbol that gives meaning to our voyage. I wanted to cry. . . . Did my mother have the same feelings when she came to America?" Epstein mused. "I shall never forget this homecoming."[64]

The nautical chain between North America and Europe was vitally important to the Allied war effort, and the men and communities involved paid a heavy price to sustain it. About one in every twenty-six US merchant seamen lost his life, a higher mortality rate than that of any other American armed service during the war. The convoys manned by these men and boys (many were still teenagers) won the war on the western front by bringing America's industrial might to bear against Hitler. The four hundred Sherman tanks and engines carried by two New York convoys to Suez in July and August 1942, for example, arguably enabled Montgomery's British Eighth Army to beat Rommel's Afrika Korps at El Alamein. New York convoys also provisioned Allied troops in Britain in preparation for D-Day and continued supplying them as they fought their way across Europe. With up to 540 ships docked or anchored at any one time, and a vessel arriving or departing every fifteen minutes, the port of New York remained a logical target for U-boats and Luftwaffe planning, and for New Yorkers' apprehensions of sabotage and attack.[65]

While supplies and armaments flowed day and night, so did GIs. "Liner Row"—the series of piers built during the 1930s between West Forty-Sixth and West Fifty-Fourth Streets to berth luxury ocean liners—became the nation's prime departure point for GIs embarking on troop transports to Britain and elsewhere. The ships that carried them were liners converted into troop carriers: floating cities like the *Queen Mary*, the *Queen Elizabeth*, the *Aquitania*, and the *Nieuw Amsterdam*, each of which could hold between eight thousand and sixteen thousand soldiers and their gear—more human beings than had ever before sailed on a single vessel. Regiments readied at Camp Shanks in Rockland County, Camp Kilmer in New Jersey, and Fort Hamilton in Brooklyn often arrived directly at the piers by ferry and poured up the gangplanks onto the liners. "There was humanity from end to end," one awed soldier noted. The fastest ships afloat, these transports counted on their speed (about twenty-eight knots) to outrun U-boats and sailed alone without escort protection. None sank during the war, and by V-E Day they had conveyed over three million American troops from the Hudson River to

Europe. No other port came close in manning the Allied North African, Italian, and western fronts. Men slept in steel and canvas bunks often stacked eight high. Seasickness, claustrophobia, and fear of sinking made the voyage miserable for many young soldiers. During a stiff mid-Atlantic storm, a British sailor on the *Queen Mary* listened as GIs screamed "in absolute fear and terror." But the passage was over in five or six days.[66]

With a city full of German Americans and Italian Americans just beyond the docks, fears of maritime sabotage and espionage were inevitable. "New York is full of loose talk," a Canadian seaman complained to reporters after the *Coimbra* sinking. When the majestic French liner *Normandie* burst into flame and capsized at the foot of West Forty-Eighth Street in February 1942, saboteurs were suspected, although the true cause proved to be a fire ignited by workmen busy converting her into a troop carrier. One rumor had it that spies were attaching messages for U-boat captains to the undersides of lobster buoys floating off Long Island. Others worried that the Italian fishermen who brought their boats into the Fulton Fish Market might be loyal to Mussolini, and hence aiding the German raiders. The Office of Naval Intelligence actually enlisted Joseph "Socks" Lanza, the market's Mafia capo, to help scrutinize the activities of the fishing crews for evidence of disloyalty. But the bleak reality was that by following the shipping lanes and receiving deciphered Allied wireless messages from Doenitz's headquarters, U-boats cruising offshore didn't need spies to tell them where to find their prey.[67]

The city's material bounty, flowing in ever-greater quantities eastward across the Atlantic, signified just how vital New York was becoming to the Allied war effort. Even before Pearl Harbor, federal spending on military preparation was funneling billions of dollars in war contracts to shipyards, automotive plants, and aircraft factories across the country, putting millions of Americans to work. Alarmed city officials saw that the big contracts were bypassing New York's thirty-five thousand workshops with their specialized parts manufacturing and going instead to the vast assembly-line factories converting to war production—places like the Ford plant at Willow Run, Michigan, and the aircraft assembly lines of Curtiss-Wright in Buffalo and Grumman on Long Island. By mid-1941, the New York State Division of Commerce was lobbying in Wash-

The capsized liner *Normandie* in its berth, West Forty-Eighth Street, February 1942.
PHOTO BY HULTON ARCHIVE / GETTY IMAGES.

ington to ensure that the state and the city got their share of war largesse. By August, the division was also sponsoring "production clinics" in city hotels where major contractors like Connecticut's Pratt & Whitney, Pennsylvania's Baldwin Locomotive, and Long Island's Republic Aviation could link up with those the *New York Times* described as "the little fellows"—subcontracting firms like the Duro Brass Works on Lafayette Street, which employed fifteen workers, or the S. & W. Sewing Machine Attachment Company on Sixth Avenue, whose twenty employees could shift into making wrenches and other tools for engine production. President Roosevelt, too, belatedly did his part, ensuring in 1942 that his home state's dominant city—a crucial Democratic electoral bastion—would get a healthy share of war contracts.[68]

Larger plants, like Brooklyn's Murray Manufacturing, Sperry Gyroscope, and Pfizer Pharmaceuticals, were soon benefiting along with "the little fellows" from wartime demand, hiring thousands, including many women, to make trench mortar shells, instruments for air force bombers, and penicillin. At the block-long Bell Telephone Laboratories in the West Village, the nation's largest industrial research complex, scientists designed over one hundred different types of radar equipment for navy and air force use, developed a sonar device for detecting U-boats, and created torpedoes that could seek out Doenitz's vessels by homing in acoustically on their motors. Out of the factories and warehouses the armaments, drugs, and appliances flowed onto the ships bound for Liverpool, Casablanca, Archangel, and Normandy; into the pockets of their makers flowed government pay. By 1943, the city had attained something approximating full employment, making the last three years of the war a boom time for New Yorkers. In 1945, 1.7 million city residents would be working in factories and war plants.[69]

For New Yorkers, it was the Brooklyn Navy Yard—a city unto itself—that most dramatically exemplified the city's role in fighting the war. By 1944, over seventy thousand men and women labored around the clock in ten-hour shifts in a two-hundred-acre complex containing three hundred buildings, thirty miles of railroad track, several dry docks, massive cranes for hoisting gun turrets, and twin thousand-foot-long trenches that served as launching ways for warships. It had become the nation's—and probably the world's—biggest and busiest shipyard. During the war the yard's workers built five aircraft carriers and three battleships, including the *Missouri*, upon whose deck the Japanese would surrender in September 1945.

The yard's main task was to alter, fit out, and repair vessels by the thousands. Workers converted over 11,000 transport and patrol vessels for naval service, assembled 3,581 landing craft, and repaired over 5,000 vessels. In total, the wartime yard churned out more ships than Japan did. It also became a focal point for an unprecedented influx of women into heavy industry, as males were drafted away from manufacturing in large numbers. By war's end, six thousand women would be working there. Women never obtained equal pay in the yard, but union pressure led to opportunities for promotions and wages that seemed a godsend by Depression standards. After three and a half years in the yard, Ida Pollack remembered, "I had become a first-class welder, and I made more money than my father." "I guess I was filled with the spirit of helping to win the war against Fascism," her friend, shipfitter Lucille Gewirtz Kolkin, later recalled. "I loved the toughness of it, the patriotism of it, the romance of wearing work clothes and having dirty hands and usually a dirt streak across my face."[70]

As the war pulled the city out of the Depression, two thousand steel drums sat in a Staten Island warehouse, casting a long shadow into the future. The drums had arrived in the fall of 1940, imported by an émigré Belgian mining executive named Edgar Sengier. They contained uranium ore from mines in the Belgian Congo. More than a year and a half earlier, on January 25, 1939, Professor John Dunning and a team of Columbia University physicists working in the basement of Pupin Hall at Broadway and 120th Street had split a uranium atom. "Believe we have observed a new phenomenon of far reaching consequences," Dunning jotted down that day, in one of history's most loaded understatements.

The experiments on upper Broadway were part of an unprecedented arms race. Dunning, his colleague Enrico Fermi, Albert Einstein, and other physicists had become aware that German scientists were making breakthroughs in atomic physics that might arm Hitler with a weapon enabling him to dominate the world. By January 1940, with Roosevelt's support and government funding, the ultrasecret Manhattan Project was underway in Pupin Hall, its goal to beat Hitler to the nuclear bomb. Two years later, in need of ever-greater space, the project moved to the University of Chicago, where by the end of the year Fermi, still on Columbia's payroll, produced the world's first self-sustaining nuclear chain reaction.

Manhattan Project officials turned back to New York to fuel further development. By the time of Fermi's breakthrough, Brigadier General Leslie Groves, bent on securing an ample ore supply so the project could continue, had learned of Edgar Sengier and sent an emissary to Sengier's Broad Street office. The anti-Nazi Belgian businessman, alert since before the war to the military potential of atomic research, now signed over his 1,250 tons of uranium to the US government and guaranteed further imports from the Congo. Thanks to the Columbia experiments and the Staten Island uranium, New York City can lay claim to being the cradle of the atomic bomb. [71]

The war brought a peculiar dual consciousness to New York, a sense of global conflict as both utterly remote and omnipresent. Nowhere was this truer than in Manhattan's symbolic town center, Times Square. A visitor to the district, with its dizzying medley of playhouses, movie theaters, nightclubs, bars, shooting galleries, billboards, and neon signs, and its round-the-clock throngs of sightseers, might be excused for momentarily forgetting that the city was engaged in history's most cataclysmic military struggle. On a given night, a young Frank Sinatra might be crooning to a wall-to-wall crowd of screaming bobby-soxers at the Paramount on Broadway at Forty-Third Street, while on other evenings couples jitterbugged there to the swing tunes of Benny Goodman's and Harry James's bands. A few blocks away, in clubs on Fifty-Second Street like the Onyx and the Three Deuces, the black musicians Dizzy Gillespie and Charlie Parker were pioneering a new, joyously frenetic jazz called bebop. Cocktails flowed freely into the wee hours at El Morocco on East Fifty-Fourth Street, at Billy Rose's Diamond Horseshoe on West Forty-Sixth Street, and in a score of other midtown clubs.[72]

Despite Times Square's carnival atmosphere, a quick double-take would have convinced any visitor that New York itself was very much at war. A gigantic cash register, joined later by a fifty-five-foot-tall replica of the Statue of Liberty, towered over Forty-Third Street at the Square, both advertising the sale of War Bonds. For eighteen months in 1942–1943, although interiors remained lit, the Great White Way (along with the rest of the city) was darkened at night by an official "dimout" that extinguished Broadway's marquee and billboard bulbs. The measure was meant to deprive U-boats of the nocturnal coastal glare that could help them target vessels—a belated acknowledgment of the hazard that had so surprised U-boat commander Hardegen—as well as to conserve energy (the nightly dimout was later replaced by a "brownout," permitting some low-intensity exterior lighting, as the threat from the sea seemed to wane). But the nightly crowds still converged. The fact was that midtown, like the rest of the city, was riding on a flood tide of war prosperity. Gasoline, sugar, coffee, and meat were being rationed, and rental housing was in short supply, but entertainment was not, and war workers with pay in their pockets flooded into the nightclubs and bars to enjoy what the city had to offer.[73]

If New Yorkers reveled in the hubbub around Broadway, so did a continuous stream of servicemen and women and merchant seamen from every Allied nation. Soldiers from Camp Shanks on twelve-hour passes; GIs arriving at Penn Station from camps across the country; some of the 150,000 British seamen who passed through New York during the war: all crossed paths in Times Square. War seemed inescapable in the midtown hotels. When George Goldman and forty of his fellow seamen survived the sinking of their tanker by a U-boat, they found themselves back in New York, put up in the Hotel Woodstock by their employer, the Sinclair Oil Corporation. "We were all bearded and burnt black with the sun and we walked into the dining room of this hotel and had a nice steak dinner, everyone was looking at us, we looked like Captain Hook's men." The next morning, Goldman remembered, "we walked up to Rockefeller Center where the company's office was. . . . Nobody stuck their hand out and said, you did a good job, do you need any help. . . . They just gave us our pay, and so long, and we made our way down to the Union Hall and registered for another ship."[74]

Many soldiers and seamen came to New York looking for more than just a drink and a show. "The wolf-whistle sounded now in the streets of midtown," Jan Morris later wrote. "Lean and rangy servicemen shifted their gum to the other cheek as they eyed the sidewalk broads." For some men and women, wartime New York offered a particular kind of freedom. Accosting groups of soldiers and sailors in Times Square, the young Tennessee Williams recalled making "very abrupt and candid overtures, phrased so bluntly that it's a wonder they didn't slaughter me on the spot." Sometimes his overtures were successful. Gay New York at war had its own covert geography: the Hotel Astor bar and the Plaza Hotel's Oak Room, where soldiers could meet civilian men; gay brothels alongside straight ones on Sands Street near the Brooklyn Navy Yard. But the city also afforded opportunities for lasting relationships. At war's end, a number of gay men and lesbians formed the Veterans Benevolent Association and held regular meetings in rooms on Houston Street near Second Avenue. Despite its low profile, the VBA was one of the nation's first gay rights organizations and presaged New York's role as one of the world's crucial gay cities.[75]

"New York in wartime was the sexiest city in the world," recalled Arthur Laurents, at the time a young soldier. "*Everybody* did it—in

numbers. And everybody drank." Times Square's giddy freedom embodied how the war was setting millions of young Americans in motion,
releasing them from the scrutiny and inhibitions of their home communities and families. But it also revealed something more frantic, the
carpe diem energy of young people with money in their pockets, a few
hours to enjoy, and great uncertainty as to whether death on a distant
battlefield might await them.[76]

Some 891,900 New Yorkers—over one-tenth of the city's
population—enlisted or were drafted during the war, and for their
loved ones back home, the battlefront was never too remote a presence. Husbands, fathers, sons, and brothers were sent across the country or overseas in numbers never approached in previous wars. "One of
our [Navy Yard] friends," Ida Pollack recalled, "her husband was killed
in the Battle of the Bulge. . . . It wasn't a lark." Ultimately 16,106 New
Yorkers would be killed, mortally wounded in combat, die of other
causes, or go missing. By 1944 and 1945, many caskets would arrive on
ships that unloaded their somber cargoes at the Brooklyn Army Terminal, from which they would be conveyed to mourning families
throughout the city and beyond.[77]

Just as the city offered both distractions from and reminders of the war,
there was also a dual quality to the ways in which New Yorkers reacted
to the possibility of a German attack. Such an assault was still usually
envisioned as airborne. "Enemy Planes!" barked Civil Defense posters
from walls and billboards. "Will you be asleep . . . Or helping your neighbors?" Many found the prospect of a Luftwaffe raid hard to take seriously.
Cathleen Schurr, an Englishwoman who had survived the U-boat sinking of a passenger liner, felt New Yorkers were merely playing at war.
"We lived in Greenwich Village, and you barely knew we were at
war. . . . We had sirens going from time to time, and we had signs up
saying where the shelters were. A lot of people went around complaining. I never could understand what they were complaining about." But
others worried. "I remember one fellow on the *Times*, a reporter about
my age, was scared to death," newspaperman George Garrott remembered. "He lived in Greenwich Village in an apartment on the top floor
of his building, and he immediately canceled his lease and moved into a

cellar right after we got in the war. I knew a few other people who did that kind of thing. . . . Personally, I just felt, when it comes, it comes."[78]

Many New Yorkers did what they could to prepare for the eventuality of an enemy attack. By war's end, four hundred thousand men, women, and adolescents—more than one out of every twenty New Yorkers—had become Civilian Defense Volunteers. Some found the whole operation comical or annoying ("people running around in hats, getting in everybody's way," Garrott remembered). But for those exempted from the draft—women, teenagers, overage or disqualified men—Civil Defense was a way to contribute to the war effort. In the Jewish neighborhood of Borough Park, Brooklyn, teenager Norman Dworkowitz became an air raid messenger, carrying messages between observation posts during air raid drills. "I remember taking the job very, very seriously. . . . We even talked about what would happen if we were bombed and how we would get people to hospitals. . . . In my mind, anyway, it was a very clear and strong threat that something like an air raid could happen, and we tried our best to prepare for it."[79]

From the summer of 1942 onward, New Yorkers were kept on their toes by what proved to be the most dramatic Nazi "invasion" of the United States. In the early morning hours of June 13, 1942, John Cullen, an unarmed member of the Coast Guard patrolling the fog-shrouded Atlantic shore at Amagansett, Long Island, came upon a strange scene: four men, one of them wearing a bathing suit and dragging a canvas bag, another in dungarees and a brown fedora hat, at the water's edge. "Look, I wouldn't want to kill you. You don't know what this is all about," the man in the fedora told Cullen and then pushed $260 into his hand. By the time Cullen had run back to the Amagansett Lifeboat Station to rouse his comrades, the four men had disappeared into the fog. Combing the beach the next day, Coast Guard investigators discovered a hastily buried cache of detonators, TNT blocks, and fountain pens full of sulfuric acid for igniting explosives.[80]

Six days after the explosives were discovered, a man named George John Dasch turned himself in at FBI headquarters in Washington, DC, and told a remarkable story. Dasch claimed to be one of a group of eight men trained in Germany to undertake sabotage missions against key American sites, including aluminum plants in Tennessee and upstate

New York, the Pennsylvania Railroad station in Newark, New Jersey, the Hell Gate railroad bridge over the East River, and, if enough explosives were left, Jewish-owned department stores. Dasch (the man in the fedora) and three others had landed at Amagansett from a U-boat; the other four saboteurs were dropped four nights later on a beach near Jacksonville, Florida, by a second submarine. After their encounter with Cullen, the Long Island group had traveled by train to Manhattan, where they booked themselves into midtown hotels under assumed names. But Dasch—along with Ernst Peter Burger, who would stay in Manhattan when Dasch later traveled to Washington—had had second thoughts. Dasch divulged the likely whereabouts of the others to the FBI, and within days his coconspirators had all been arrested in New York and Chicago and jailed in Washington, along with Dasch himself.

J. Edgar Hoover crowed to the press about how his agents had broken a dangerous Nazi sabotage ring, but the actual plot was deeply flawed from the start. Walter Kappe, an officer in the Abwehr and a former German American Bund officer in Chicago and New York, had recruited the eight agents from among repatriated Germans who had once lived in the United States. Dasch, for example, had been a waiter in Manhattan, and Edward Kerling had packed meat in Brooklyn. But the eight turned out to be an unreliable crew. Several were lukewarm Nazis at best, and few seemed to master the explosives training they received in a secret camp near Berlin. Dasch lost his forged American ID papers, including a Social Security card, on a train. In a stopover in Paris en route to the German U-boat base at Lorient, Heinrich Heinck (a "typical German spy, dumb and big mouthed," Dasch later complained) got drunk and told a barroom full of strangers that he was a "secret agent." As they crossed the Atlantic toward Long Island, Dasch and Burger were getting cold feet. Later, in the mission's most surreal episode, Dasch dropped in on a Forty-Ninth Street waiters' club and played a thirty-six-hour pinochle marathon against a Jewish friend he had worked with years before. Queried by former colleagues surprised to see him, Dasch responded, "I'm here—what difference does it make how I came?" He left for Washington a day later.[81]

None of the eight saboteurs ever got close to their designated targets, but President Roosevelt resolved to make examples of them. A quickly convened military commission found all eight guilty of intent to commit sabotage and espionage. With unusual (and, in the eyes of later legal scholars, unconscionable) haste, the Supreme Court struck down a defense challenge to the proceeding's constitutionality, specifically its denial of habeas corpus and a civil trial to the defendants. On August 8, six of the men died in the electric chair in a Washington jail. Dasch and Burger received long prison terms; President Truman pardoned them and deported them to Germany in 1948. Six decades later, the Bush administration would cite the tribunal and the Supreme Court ruling as precedents for its own military trial of noncitizens, including Guantanamo Bay detainees, implicated in the September 11 attacks.[82]

For all of the mission's clumsiness, it fueled wartime anxiety. ("We don't want to be alarmists," one Manhattanite wrote to J. Edgar Hoover that summer, "but please investigate 306 West 99th Street. . . . Lets men with shortwave sets keep them on all night.") The sabotage plot also confronted officials with the delicate task of encouraging vigilance while not drawing attention to the porousness of the long American shoreline. Sure enough, in November 1944, the Abwehr tried again, using a U-boat to drop two agents on the Maine coast, with naïve instructions to ferret out American military secrets and transmit them by radio to the fatherland. Recent history repeated itself: once ensconced in the anonymity of the nation's largest city, William Colepaugh turned himself and fellow spy Erich Gimpel in to the FBI. A military tribunal convened on Governors Island sentenced both to death, but President Truman commuted their sentences to life imprisonment.[83]

While they fretted about the dangers of German spies in their midst, New Yorkers remained unaware of another, more ominous reality, one that jibed more closely with the warnings voiced by La Guardia and his wardens. Hitler's vision of Manhattan going up in flames continued to inspire German leaders and engineers until the very end of the war. In October 1943, contemplating the propaganda and morale value of an attack on New York, Hermann Goering blurted out, "If only we could reach it! With just a couple of bombs we could force them to black out." Designers worked on prototypes for a transatlantic "America bomber," an aircraft trailing extra fuel tanks or perhaps capable of being refueled in midair by another plane. By 1944, a model Messerschmitt 264 equipped with four BMW engines was undergoing flight tests in Germany. Another plan envisioned a squad of seaplanes refueling from a U-boat tanker off the East Coast and then bombing New York; Luftwaffe Colonel Viktor von Lossberg suggested either "the Jewish area or the docks" as the prime target. Still another idea, one which engaged Wernher von Braun, posited a rocket launcher towed across the Atlantic by a U-boat, permitting the dreaded V-2 rocket, the scourge of London and Antwerp in 1944, to be aimed at New York. Most visionary of all was the scheme of Dr. Eugen Sanger, who proposed building a rocket-propelled, two-seat "space bomber," which could rain death on America from 160 miles up in the earth's atmosphere. But the technical difficulty of these projects, and the depletion of the Luftwaffe's resources as the war dragged on, consigned them to failure.[84]

Equally unsuccessful were plans by Germany's partners, Japan and Italy, to bring the war to New York in order to intimidate America and to build morale on the Axis home fronts. Following Pearl Harbor, the Japanese navy had begun developing a prototype submarine, the I-400, large enough to carry planes for bombarding American coastal targets and the Panama Canal. The I-400, in fact, was the world's largest submarine at the time. One Japanese plan envisioned a fleet of I-400s approaching the West Coast, launching the bombers to attack coastal cities and then rounding Cape Horn and dispatching the refueled planes against New York and possibly Washington. Admiral Isoroku Yamamoto, the mastermind of the Pearl Harbor attack, believed the attacks might sow such panic that Americans would lack the will to mount a full-fledged war in the Pacific. However naïve that expectation may have been, three of the massive submarines were actually built. By the time they were seaworthy in 1944, however, the Japanese navy was fighting a defensive war, and the American coasts were beyond their range.[85]

Meanwhile, in 1943 the Italian navy began training crews for attacks on New York harbor. In one plan, a transatlantic submarine would release midget subs to slip through coastal minefields to torpedo shipping in the Upper Bay. In another scheme, special torpedoes manned by divers—already used to devastating effect by the Italians against British ships in the Mediterranean—would be dispatched from submarines or Cant Z.511 transatlantic seaplanes flying from the German-occupied French coast. Undeterred by the defensive gate at the Narrows (their comrades had shepherded torpedoes through a similar gate in the harbor of Alexandria, Egypt, and sunk two British battleships), the divers would steer the torpedoes into New York harbor on or near the sea's surface at night. The Italians would attach the torpedoes' warheads and timed detonators to the hulls of ships before swimming away to safety on the shore, either to hide or surrender. Refueling from a German U-boat off the south shore of Long Island, the seaplanes would return to Europe. Not to be outdone, Mussolini's air force also drafted plans to use the Savoia-Marchetti SM.95, an Italian equivalent of the prototype German long-distance bombers, to drop small bombs on Manhattan to terrify America. The withdrawal of Italy from the war in September 1943 put an end to these dreams. For both the Japanese and the Italians, the lure of bringing war to America's (and arguably the Allies') most powerful city, of puncturing its bubble of apparent invulnerability, proved tantalizing enough to send military engineers to their workshops and secret combat teams to their training grounds.[86]

In the war's final months, the threat of transatlantic attack did provide Nazi leaders with propaganda to bolster the morale of their war-weary, nearly defeated population. In November 1944, the US Navy received reports from spies in Europe suggesting that U-boats might soon carry rockets and missiles on their decks to bombard America. Then in early December, Albert Speer, head of Hitler's war production, announced that a new intercontinental rocket, the V-3, would soon "be ready for firing against New York." Speer's lie alarmed American intelligence officers. In January, Admiral Jonas Ingram, commander in chief of the Atlantic Fleet, caused a sensation when he announced from his Manhattan headquarters that an impending German "attack on New York or Washington by robot bombs," launched from U-boats or long-distance planes, was a probability. "The thing to do is not to get excited about it," Ingram told reporters. "It might knock out a high building or two. . . . It would certainly cause casualties in the limited area where it might hit." The *Times* found the city full of "talk of robots, buzz bombs, rockets, V-3's," and noted that conflicting alarms and reassurances from officials and scientific experts were confusing the public. The *Times'* editors worried about the fate of treasures in the Metropolitan Museum of Art and the Morgan Library—masterworks that had been removed from the city for safekeeping after Pearl Harbor, but that had recently been returned to their institutions. "It is just as well to assume that an attack may be made even though the amount of damage would be small," the *Times* advised its readers.[87]

When, in April 1945, during the European war's final weeks, British intelligence reported that six U-boats were heading west across the Atlantic, Admiral Ingram was ready for them and for the rocket attack he believed they might launch. He dispatched two aircraft carriers and some twenty destroyers from Newfoundland, and the ships tracked down and sank three of the submarines in mid-ocean. Taken to the naval base at Argentia, the surviving captain and several crewmen of one of the U-boats were repeatedly beaten (in at least one case, with rubber truncheons) by American interrogators bent on extracting the truth about the planned rocket attacks they believed imminent. But the prisoners could tell them nothing: the six U-boats had been on a routine mission to sink convoys.

The plan to bombard New York remained what it had always been, an unrealized fantasy. New Yorkers survived the war without the air raid many of them at least half-feared. The city's only major airborne disaster would come in July 1945, when an American B-25 bomber accidentally crashed into the seventy-ninth and eightieth floors of a fogbound Empire State Building, killing fourteen.[88]

But what of the ethnic and political "powder keg" William Goodwin had warned of in 1941? In truth, the war became a great harmonizing force on New York's home front, as elsewhere. As Norman Dworkowitz ran messages to plane spotters in Borough Park, boys in Little Italy, Yorkville, and Harlem were doing the same. New Yorkers of every ethnic group and social class participated in patriotic scrap metal and rubber collection drives, and in practice blackouts, meant to test the city's ability to elude Luftwaffe "night marauders." Fritz Kuhn's Bund had been eviscerated by prosecutions targeting financial fraud within the organization, and Kuhn himself had been in prison since 1939 for embezzling funds. Stunned when Mussolini declared war on America after Pearl Harbor, most Italian Americans immediately pledged themselves to the American and Allied war effort. "Now we know where we stand. We are all together, this unites us all," declared grocer Al Cazazza.[89]

There were darker aspects of the city's response to the war, to be sure. Some Japanese, suspected of being spies or saboteurs, remained imprisoned on Ellis Island. Although the mass internments that took place on the West Coast never happened in New York, La Guardia refused to let Japanese Americans participate in "New York at War," a patriotic parade up Fifth Avenue in 1942, or in other civic events. Italian emigrants who were not U.S. citizens had to carry humiliating identification cards until October 1942, when the Justice Department decided the threat of their "disloyalty" was negligible. But more conspicuous than the arrests and restrictions were the enthusiastic War Bond rallies in Italian neighborhoods, the parties for German-American draftees bound for basic training, and demonstrations by small groups of Nisei and Issei who renounced their homeland's imperialism. The city's leading Italian American did his part as well. "This is your friend La Guardia speaking," the mayor announced in Italian in anti-Fascist radio broadcasts transmitted from New York into Italy by the Office of War Information.[90]

Yet if the simmering pot did not explode, it did boil over in episodes fueled by anger and resentment. The city's African Americans, for example, waited restlessly for the wartime economic boom to reach their burgeoning communities in Harlem and Bedford-Stuyvesant. But jobs for blacks were slow in coming. Numerous defense plants (including Sperry Gyroscope) turned blacks away or found ways to discourage their applications; when blacks were hired, pay and conditions were often less than equivalent whites enjoyed. Black trade unionists managed to persuade Sperry to embrace a racially egalitarian hiring policy for the war's duration, and A. Phillip Randolph, the World War I dissenter who now headed the Brotherhood of Sleeping Car Porters, launched a successful drive from his Harlem headquarters to pressure FDR to establish a federal Fair Employment Practices Committee (FEPC) to guarantee equal hiring in war industries for all Americans, regardless of race, creed, color, or national origin. But wartime bigotry persisted, exacerbating the Depression-era poverty and joblessness that burdened black neighborhoods more harshly than white ones. If the FEPC rectified instances of discrimination, it did not create an egalitarian workplace. Although several hundred black men and women were hired in the Brooklyn Navy Yard, Lucille Kolkin recalled that "there were a lot of racist remarks and it was almost impossible for a non-white to receive a promotion."[91]

While fifteen thousand Harlem residents volunteered as air raid wardens, the columns of black newspapers bristled with reports of insults and violence suffered by black soldiers across the country. From Camp Stewart, Georgia, members of the all-black 369th Engineers wrote home to Brooklyn, describing how white authorities demanded that their visiting wives and girlfriends carry passes certifying that they were not prostitutes. Closer to home, at Fort Dix, New Jersey, German POWs enjoyed the privilege of sharing a chow line with white soldiers, while black GIs did not. White soldiers and civilians beat, shot, and killed black servicemen in confrontations on and near base camps. In a letter to the New York Age, a black paper, one soldier blasted "these part-time Americans who . . . are tearing to tatters and ripping to rags the American flag's meaning of equality." In 1943, the liberal magazine Nation averred that Harlemites "have asked the question, 'What will the war bring us?' The answer, as most of them see it, is 'Nothing.'"[92]

The tinder box needed only one spark. On August 1, 1943, when a white policeman shot and wounded a black serviceman after an altercation in the Hotel Braddock lobby on West 126th Street, a false rumor spread through Harlem's streets that the soldier had been killed. By night, furious mobs were smashing store windows, overturning and burning cars, and hurling stones at police and firemen. La Guardia, well liked in the black community, made a police precinct house on 123rd Street his base of operations for mobilizing Harlem leaders to help him end the mayhem. Riding through Harlem in a sound truck, NAACP head Walter White found that pleas for calm were "greeted with raucous shouts of disbelief." By the time the riot ended the next day, over $3 million in property had been destroyed or looted from stores, 606 people were under arrest, 189 injured, and 6 blacks were

An overturned vehicle burns on a Harlem Street, August
1 or 2, 1943. THE GRANGER COLLECTION, NEW YORK.

dead, most of them shot by police. The young James Baldwin, a witness
to the riot's aftermath, moved "through a wilderness of smashed plate
glass. . . . The spoils of injustice, anarchy, discontent, and hatred were
all around us."[93]

New York's Jews experienced their own frustrations during the war. True,
the United States had finally committed itself to the war to vanquish
Hitler, and the city had become a sanctuary for Hitler's foes and victims.
Throughout the 1930s and early 1940s, tens of thousands of European
refugees found safe haven in the city, creating enclaves in Washington
Heights and elsewhere. Their numbers included some of the world's
great artists, scientists, and thinkers, including the Jews Claude Levi-
Strauss, Hannah Arendt, Leo Szilard, Erich Fromm, Kurt Weill, and
Marc Chagall, and the anti-Nazis Jacques Maritain, Enrico Fermi, Ber-
tolt Brecht, Béla Bartók, Andre Breton, and Piet Mondrian. "Hitler is
my best friend," quipped Walter W. S. Cook, director of the city's Institute of Fine Arts: "He shakes the tree and I collect the apples." This

intellectual migration would help make New York the world's postwar arts capital, supplanting Paris. "If Aristotle were alive today he would be a New Yorker," the columnist Max Lerner proclaimed proudly.[94]

For all the US government's willingness to take in limited numbers of refugees, New York's Jewish leaders were exasperated by Washington's unwillingness to do more. Immigration policy remained guided by the National Origins Act of 1924, which intentionally restricted the number of Eastern Europeans who could legally enter the country. The State Department also limited the number of visas awarded to German and Austrian refugees. While Roosevelt openly deplored Nazi anti-Semitism, he did little to widen the entryway for its victims. Opinion polls showed that a majority of Americans, Depression-weary and suspicious, opposed taking in a flood of new émigrés.

Increasingly, leaders of Jewish organizations faced a dreadful truth: the Nazis intended to wipe European Jewry off the face of the earth. In August 1942, Stephen Wise, rabbi of the Free Synagogue on West Sixty-Eighth Street and president of the American Jewish Congress, received from a Jewish activist in Switzerland a telegram that warned that the Nazis appeared to be implementing a systematic extermination plan "to resolve once for all Jewish question in Europe." When the State Department finally permitted Wise to make the news public in November, it galvanized Jewish leaders, although they disagreed on a course of action. Some feared that pushing too hard would merely increase domestic anti-Semitism. But Wise and his allies pressed the Roosevelt administration to take an assertive role. Surely, with American newspapers publicizing German atrocities, something would be done. (In early 1943 a *New York Post* headline screamed: NAZI FRENZY THREATENS MURDER OF 5,000,000 JEWS BY END OF YEAR.)[95]

Yet the efforts of Jewish leaders to elicit government action on behalf of their European brethren seemed fruitless. In October 1943, four hundred rabbis, many from New York, journeyed to Washington to present a petition to Vice President Henry Wallace calling on the United States and the Allies to save Europe's Jews and ease immigration to British Palestine. Their effort helped convince Treasury Secretary Henry Morgenthau to press for the creation of the War Refugee Board, an organization that helped save tens of thousands of lives in

1944–1945. But for many New York Jews, especially those with loved ones stuck on the other side of the Atlantic, it was too little, too late. Combating genocide failed to become a priority for the American and Allied war effort.[96]

Frustration with Washington was matched by trouble at home in New York. The war saw a nationwide upsurge in anti-Semitism as many Gentiles (seemingly forgetting Pearl Harbor) blamed Jews for entangling America in a war against the Axis. "We do not hire Jews," some New York employers admitted, and Jews outnumbered blacks in lodging FEPC job discrimination reports. Embittered by the social stresses of the war, a minority within the Irish population targeted Jews. In Washington Heights, Fordham, and Tremont, gangs of mostly Irish teens and young men threw stones at families leaving Sabbath services, painted swastikas on synagogue doors, and broke shop windows while yelling "Kill the Jews." For every group of Irish neighbors disgusted by the attacks, Jewish community spokesmen charged, there seemed to be a policeman looking the other way. "We are damned sick and tired of watching the sick Hitler-like grin" on the face of "Captain McCarthy (or O'Brien) . . . and hearing the usual answer: 'Ah, the boys are just playing.'" By January 1944, one Brooklyn Jewish periodical asserted that "the streets of New York have become unsafe for Jews and—who knows?—pogroms might be in the making."[97]

Adina Bernstein was the young widow of a rabbi, a US Army chaplain killed in North Africa in 1943. One day she sat in a northern Manhattan park near "two Irishwomen" who "were complaining that over in Europe Christian boys were fighting to save the Jews in Germany. It went on and on and on and on, Christian blood being spilled. Finally, I couldn't take it, and I said 'Did you lose anybody in the service?' 'No.' 'Well, I did. Do me a favor and just go away so that I don't have to hear you or see you.' They got up, but she had the last word. 'It's still a goddamn Jewish war.'"[98]

Around 7 PM on August 14, 1945, the news flashed along the electric ribbon encircling the New York Times Building at Forty-Second Street and Broadway: "Japan Surrenders." Within minutes, the intersection was jammed with a throng of thousands, bringing traffic to a halt in every direction. Confetti and streamers rained down from office buildings. Within two hours, the *Herald Tribune* reported, "two million yelling, milling celebrants of peace were jammed into the area bounded by Ninth and Sixth Avenues and Fortieth and Fifty-Third Streets." That spring, New Yorkers had experienced over the course of three weeks the death of Franklin Roosevelt, the execution of Benito Mussolini, and the suicide of Adolf Hitler, followed a week later by Allied victory in Europe. Already the troop ships were disgorging servicemen and women onto the West Side piers by the hundreds of thousands. Now the long war was finally over. In Times Square, *Life* magazine's Alfred Eisenstaedt, watching as a sailor engulfed a nurse in a rapturous kiss, snapped the moment's signature photograph. That night, as the citywide party continued, thousands flocked into churches for services of thanks and remembrance.[99]

Once again, New York had escaped the full brunt of a catastrophic war. True, tens of thousands of its servicemen and merchant seamen had lost their lives or been wounded in Africa, Europe, the Pacific, or the Atlantic. But the city itself was spared, despite the fears of many of its people and the intentions of the Luftwaffe, the Kriegsmarine, the Abwehr, and Hitler himself. The city's ethnic and political tensions, inflamed as always by global conflicts, erupted in sporadic moments of violence, but the unifying momentum of the war effort and of renewed prosperity had prevented a reprise of anything akin to the Civil War Draft Riot.

The end of the war left New York stronger and more important than ever. With Europe's great cities in rubble, Manhattan was now definitively the global capital of commerce, finance, and culture; emblematic city of the world's richest and most powerful country; and a fitting home for the new United Nations (which opened in temporary quarters at a Sperry Gyroscope plant on Long Island in 1946, before moving to its permanent site along the East River five years later). New York lawyers, financiers, and labor leaders—Henry Stimson, John McCloy, Averell Harriman, Bernard Baruch, and Sidney Hillman—had played pivotal roles in mobilizing Roosevelt's Washington and the nation for global war; Wall Street once more had been crucial to funding the war effort. A distinctive New York style of liberalism, one in which politicians, union heads, and businessmen embraced or at least accepted an expansive vision of government intervention to improve urban con-

ditions, carried the impetus of the New Deal through the war and beyond. With support from Washington and Albany, Fiorello La Guardia
had presided over the construction of new public housing for union
members and minorities and a health insurance plan that provided
medical coverage to thousands of city residents. Federally mandated
rent control implemented during the war continued into the postwar
years. As veterans availed themselves of GI Bill benefits to go to college
and buy homes in the outer boroughs or suburbs, the postwar depression many had feared failed to materialize—even as many women and
African Americans lost their wartime factory jobs to returning white
veterans deemed to have seniority. Factories that had cranked out mortar shells resumed production of consumer goods; vacationers replaced
GIs on the floating hotels steaming in and out of Liner Row.

But New York also entered a postwar era soon defined by the momentous technological breakthrough the city itself had helped to
spawn. Few of those crossing the intersection of Broadway and 120th
Street yet gave much thought to the cataclysmic weapon that had had
its cradle there or to how that weapon, the bomb that had ended the
war, would soon be hanging over their daily lives.

CHAPTER 9

Red Alert

The Cold War Years, 1946–1982

The sirens began wailing at 8:30 AM, at the height of the morning rush hour. Prodded by policemen and civil defense wardens, tens of thousands of New Yorkers abruptly halted their daily commute to crowd into the lobbies of office buildings and down into subway stations. Drivers on the streets and highways pulled over and turned off their ignitions. Nurses escorted patients into hospital recesses, away from windows. Within minutes, the *New York Times* reported, New Yorkers had "created a ghost city out of a buzzing metropolis." An eerie silence descended on Times Square and Herald Square, empty but for a few policemen mounted on horses. At 8:45, the sirens sounded the "all clear" signal, and the city's people resumed their interrupted journeys to work and school. It was December 13, 1952, and New Yorkers had just undergone the "red alert" that officials had prepared them to expect that morning.[1]

Most New Yorkers took the exercise in stride; they had already proven their ability to clear the streets in a similar drill in 1951. And they would do so again and again, in annual drills christened Operation Alert by President Eisenhower's Federal Civil Defense Administration (FCDA), the agency founded in 1950 to help civilians prepare for the possibility of nuclear attack. For those remembering the camaraderie of the home front against Germany and Japan, the exercise might even trigger a twinge of nostalgia. The new threat, however, differed in ominous ways from those once posed by Nazi bombers and U-boats.

Waiting for the all-clear siren during an air raid drill, Wall Street,
November 28, 1951. © ARTHUR AIDALA, BETTMANN / CORBIS.

The 1952 drill posited a lone Russian bomber hovering over the intersection of Boston Road and Southern Boulevard in the Bronx, dropping a single atomic bomb. As the hypothetical blast and ensuing fires
devastated block after block of apartment buildings, schools, factories,
and stores, an estimated 203,000 New Yorkers would perish; another
277,000 would be wounded. By the time of Operation Alert 1957, the
hydrogen bomb, and a growing awareness of the effects of radioactive
fallout, had upped the ante: the casualties inflicted by an H-bomb exploding over Governors Island were projected to be 2,339,012 killed
and 2,261,238 severely wounded. No corner of the city would be
spared: 294,000 people would perish in Queens and over 88,000 in the
distant Bronx.[2]

New Yorkers were hardly alone in facing the grim realities of the new nuclear age. Atomic weapons were the great equalizer, and America's erstwhile ally Russia—now the country's rival and foe—was clearly developing an extensive arsenal of them, after testing its first A-bomb in 1949. Flying over the Arctic from the Soviet Union, new long-range bombers or missiles might hit innumerable American targets before fighter squadrons, alerted by Canadian and US radar stations, could intercept them. In an attempt to meet this threat, Operation Alert cast an ever-wider net, involving forty-three American cities in 1954, sixty-one in 1955, and seventy-five in 1956. In 1955, Eisenhower himself and fifteen thousand federal workers temporarily evacuated Washington for "secret relocation centers" in Maryland. Like other Americans, New Yorkers had to stand tough, the *New York Times* asserted in the wake of the 1955 drill. There was "no substitute for a just and lasting peace," an editorial argued, but such a peace could not come "at the price of dishonor, or appeasement, or surrender of principle." A real breakthrough was unlikely, "unless the Soviets abolish their Iron Curtain and amend their program to permit work for real peace." Until then, the newspaper told its readers, Operation Alert would be a crucial yearly reminder of the need for urban civil defense in the face of "the deadly menace that hangs over the world today."[3]

The nuclear menace did not hang lightly over New York. Yes, the Soviets might try to barrage the entire country, but few doubted that New York would attract more Soviet bombs than, say, Iowa City or Atlanta. In the post-Hiroshima age, the writer E. B. White noted in 1948, New York was "becoming the capital of the world." The United Nations was located in New York, not Washington or Europe; Wall Street had supplanted the City of London as prime mover of international capitalism; Manhattan's studios, galleries, and museums, not Paris's, now set the standards for cultural achievement. Josef Stalin doubtless understood all this. "In the mind of whatever perverted dreamer might loose the lightning," White observed, "New York must hold a steady, irresistible charm." A familiar paradox resurfaced, but with far higher stakes: the city's very power and fame as industrial hub, corporate headquarters, and symbol of American ascendancy lay it open to obliteration. "A single flight of planes no bigger than a wedge of geese can quickly end this island fantasy, burn the towers, crumble the bridges, turn the underground passages into lethal chambers, cremate the millions. The intimation of mortality is part of New York now," White explained, "in the sound of jets overhead, in the black headlines of the latest edition."[4]

Federal civil defense spokesmen and their copywriters at the Madison Avenue advertising agency Batten, Barton, Durstine & Osborn insisted that New Yorkers, like other Americans, prepare to survive a possible Russian attack. "We must have a strong civil defense program . . . ," Jean Wood Fuller of the FCDA told audiences across the country in 1954, "to help us get up off the floor after a surprise attack, and fight back and win." The population would have to take measures to survive and restore the government and economy. Indeed, such preparations would deter World War III by persuading the Soviets that a nuclear onslaught could not succeed. Why would the Kremlin risk "mutually assured destruction" if at least some New Yorkers and other Americans would dig themselves out, resurrect the capitalist way of life, and seek vengeance? Civil defense was thus vital.[5]

Despite their preparations, New Yorkers were haunted by the possibility that civil defense wouldn't prevent war. It was hard to conceive how one of the world's most densely populated cities could withstand the blast of atom or hydrogen bombs, or the horror of radioactive fallout. Hiroshima and Nagasaki had prompted an immediate recognition by journalists that a new age had dawned. Three months after the end of World War II, *Life* magazine ran a vivid piece entitled "The 36 Hour War," which embodied the future in a drawing of hooded and masked survivors taking radiation readings on an utterly flattened Fifth Avenue, recognizable only from the lion statues still standing before a demolished Public Library. Envisioning the atomic devastation of Gotham would become a commonplace way to measure the deathly power of the bomb in the popular culture of the late 1940s and 1950s. And, as in previous wars, New Yorkers struggled within themselves as well as fought amongst themselves, turning the city itself into a Cold War arena. [6]

The Cold War had set New Yorker against New Yorker well before the Russians tested their first atom bomb in 1949. By 1946, the year Winston Churchill coined the phrase "Iron Curtain," mistrust was beginning to freeze what only a year before had been a warm outpouring of admiration for the Red Army and its role in vanquishing Nazism. In June 1947, a grand jury sitting in the federal courthouse on Foley Square in lower Manhattan began a year of work to determine whether the Communist Party of the USA was a conspiratorial organization dedicated to overthrowing the US government.

Undaunted by the rising tide of anti-"red" sentiment and policy, twenty thousand New York Communists gathered on May 1, 1948, to parade down Broadway to Union Square in their annual May Day parade. On a midtown block, the novelist Howard Fast stood with "teachers, lawyers, doctors, dentists, actors, writers, editors, publishers—an unbelievable crowd," stretching from Eighth Avenue to Broadway, waiting their turn to join the procession. Fast watched for at least half an hour as "each block, starting at the most uptown block, had been emptying in turn, moving out into the avenue, trade union groups carrying their colorful old banners." For many, faith in a progressive and harmonious postwar world, a world of industrial unionism, racial justice, and friendship between the United States and the USSR, remained fervent. Most May Day participants counted on the peculiar good-humored tolerance that characterized daily life in the city that was headquarters to the American left. When Freedom House, a conservative group, challenged the party's legal parade permit as "an insult to America," Fast observed "a large, wise old Polish cop" explaining the situation to the Freedom House emissary: "'Look . . . on May Day, the left wing of labor marches. On Labor Day, the right wing of labor marches. Why do you want to make trouble?'"[7]

Suddenly, at noon, with Fast's throng still waiting their turn to parade, the doors of a Catholic parochial school on the block swung open, and as Fast later recalled, "about a hundred screaming, cursing, teenage students, armed with everything from brass knuckles to pens, poured into the middle of our huge crowd, their fists flying, shouting their war cry: 'Kill a commie for Christ!'" Chaos ensued as police poured in to separate the two groups and to order Fast and his comrades to start marching. The parade proceeded more or less as planned, although two union functionaries were briefly jailed for resisting arrest, and Fast himself narrowly escaped arrest for arguing with the police. "There's always a next time," one policeman told him.

The remark proved prescient. In July, the federal grand jury in Foley Square would indict twelve members of the Communist Party's national board for conspiring to advocate the overthrow of the US government. Two years later, Fast himself would spend three months in federal prison for refusing to hand over papers of the Joint Anti-Fascist Refugee Committee, an identified "Communist front" group, to the House Un-American Activities Committee (HUAC). "Don't you see how fast things are changing?" his wife, Bette, had warned him before the parade.[8]

With the onset of the Cold War, New York's Communists felt the full brunt of what would eventually be labeled McCarthyism. Many New Yorkers, and not just high school rowdies, took part eagerly. Local Republicans charged that President Harry Truman was "soft" on Communism; Tammany Democrats responded by lauding Truman's 1947 Loyalty Program and the president's full cooperation with FBI investigations of subversives. The wartime truce between the city's Socialists and Communists, common foes of Nazism, unraveled as Socialists and others purged known Communists from the governing boards of local labor unions. A 1949 New York State law led to the interrogation and dismissal of over four hundred of the city's public school and college teachers as suspected Communists. The American Legion, Veterans of Foreign Wars, Catholic War Veterans, and American Jewish League Against Communism picketed performances by "red" actors.

The new Red Scare, like that of 1919, reached beyond the limits of the Communist Party to intimidate and harass countless liberals, civil libertarians, pacifists, non-Communist leftists, and ex-Communists whose real "crime" was commitment to progressive causes that could be denounced as subversive and pro-Soviet. More than any other city in the country, New York remained the hub for a wide spectrum of liberal and leftist organizations. But non-Communist admirers of the Soviet Union and enthusiasts for racial integration, labor unionism, Roosevelt's New Deal, and international disarmament also aroused the ire of many New Yorkers, just as surely as they raised the hackles of FBI director J. Edgar Hoover.

Many Americans believed that, like Hollywood, New York City—with its domination of the performing arts, journalism, publishing, and radio and television broadcasting—was a potential threat to national security, a Trojan horse for seducing and lulling the nation's unsuspecting millions with subtle, red messages. As Hoover put it in 1947, leftist subversives were "termites gnawing at the very foundation of American society," and New York was a city perceived as being particularly infested. From an office on West Forty-Second Street in 1950, an anti-Communist organization called the American Business Consultants issued *Red Channels*, a pamphlet listing 151 mostly New York– and Hollywood-based performers, writers, and directors allegedly responsible for "Communist influence in radio and television." AWARE, Inc., an outgrowth of the American Business Consultants, advised networks, sponsors, theaters, and schools to drop tainted employees, who then endured a shadowy blacklist that few employers admitted existed. The climate of fear, of having to watch what one said and to wonder who might be an informer, seeped in everywhere. Greenwich Villager Morris Jaffe was not the only New Yorker who wrapped books about Marxism in brown paper to conceal their titles from prying eyes—this on the bookshelf in his own apartment.[9]

New Yorkers had more to fear than being blacklisted. To win the Cold War, the government took measures that exceeded the bounds of all but the most paranoid imaginations, using New Yorkers and other Americans as guinea pigs. During the early 1950s, the CIA and military intelligence may have sprayed unknowing New York subway riders with aerosol LSD, a drug being tested as a possible "truth serum" for extracting secrets from Soviet spies; other "vulnerability tests," some performed as late as 1966, entailed releasing airborne bacteria in subway stations to gauge the viability of biological warfare. Such experiments remained top secret until congressional investigations unearthed them during the 1970s.[10]

With the start of the Korean War in 1950, and with thousands of young New Yorkers filing through the army's Induction Station at 39 Whitehall Street and the navy and marine corps recruiting offices at 346 Broadway on their way to basic training and shipment across the Pacific, dissent seemed doubly unpatriotic to many in the city. Those who stayed home donated blood and sent packages to the troops. For most New Yorkers, the Korean War differed in essential ways from World War II. Where the earlier war had rescued the economy, New York's prosperous manufacturing base now sailed along on domestic consumption. True, the Brooklyn Navy Yard's civilian workforce jumped from 9,600 to 20,000 during

the Korean War; jobs also opened up in other shipyards around the harbor and on the twenty piers shipping military cargo. In the nearby suburbs, Nassau County's aviation factories churned out F-84 jets that
dropped bombs and napalm on the enemy and F-9 Cougars that outshot
Soviet-built MIGs over Korea. At least 966 young New Yorkers would
lose their lives fighting Communists in the fields and mountains of Korea
or in the skies above it. Others came back with wounds; Norman Dworkowitz, who had scanned the skies of Brooklyn for Luftwaffe bombers as a
young teenager, returned home from a Korean trench with a fragment of
grenade shrapnel lodged in his face and a Purple Heart. Yet, except for
those anxiously awaiting the return of loved ones serving overseas, the
contained scale of the war compared to the all-out effort of the early
1940s made the new conflict seem more remote. At the same time, the
queasy possibility that the war might escalate into a direct confrontation
with Red China, and into a nuclear World War III, infused the early Operation Alert drills—and the campaign against domestic Communists—
with their own particular tensions.[11]

For all the damage that the anti-Communist witch hunt did to individual lives and to freedom of thought and expression, the city *was* a base
for clandestine Soviet activities. Even before World War II or the Cold
War, the city's centrality, its leftist sympathies, and the anonymity it afforded made New York fertile turf for Soviet moles—or worse. In the
late thirties, as Stalin's purges in Russia sent hundreds of thousands to
their deaths, agents of the NKVD, the Soviet secret police, were active
in New York. After Walter Krivitsky, Red Army chief of intelligence for
Western Europe, defected to New York in 1938, he charged that "Red
Judases"—Soviet assassins or kidnappers—were trailing him around the
city. Krivitsky died in a Washington hotel room in 1941, an apparent
suicide, but friends persisted in raising questions about his death. Even
more alarming was the fate of Juliet Poyntz, a founding member of the
American Communist Party who had also become alienated from
Stalin. Poyntz disappeared into thin air after leaving her West Fifty-
Seventh Street apartment in June 1937. She was never heard from
again. Anti-Soviet observers—including the anarchist Carlo Tresca,
who had rallied fellow leftists against Fascism in the 1930s—charged

that the Kremlin was sending forth its Great Purge to snatch victims from the very streets of Manhattan.[12]

But it was as a meeting place and recruiting ground for spies that New York would play its most important role for the Soviet Union. By 1932, Max Bedacht, a leading figure at Communist Party headquarters in New York, was acting as liaison between the OGPU, Stalin's intelligence service, and the party's "underground" in the United States. In an apartment tucked away on Gay Street in Greenwich Village, Aleksandr Ulanovsky, an officer of the Red Army's military intelligence division, deciphered instructions from the Comintern by dipping letters written in invisible ink into a solution of potassium crystals. Native-born New Yorkers also took part. In 1934, Whittaker Chambers, former editor of the party magazine *New Masses*, became a courier shuttling regularly between Washington and Manhattan, driving back to the city with microfilm and stolen documents collected by secret Communists working in the State Department and other federal agencies.[13]

Chambers handed over the materials to his Soviet handlers, meeting with Boris Bykov and other operatives at secluded spots in Prospect Park and elsewhere in Brooklyn, although as one Russian agent later recalled, the cloak and dagger precautions were unnecessary: "If you wore a sign saying, 'I am a spy,' you might still not get arrested." The most useful information was gathered in the nation's capital, but New York—where functionaries at Communist Party headquarters on East Twelfth Street cooperated with agents posted to the Soviet consulate on East Sixty-First Street—was the natural place for rendezvous, from which stolen secrets could be relayed to Moscow via ocean liner or secret cable transmission.[14]

World War II amplified the city's value to Soviet spies. Indeed, New York was a useful base for various Allied spy services during the war; from offices in Rockefeller Center, members of British Security Coordination, briefly including a young naval intelligence officer named Ian Fleming, provided pro-Allied and anti-Axis propaganda to influential newspaper columnists like Walter Winchell well before the attack on Pearl Harbor lured America into the war. They also broke into the Japanese consul general's office a few floors below theirs and made microfilm copies of the secret Japanese diplomatic shortwave radio code. But these British agents generally carried on with the covert support of federal authorities in Washington. Such was not the case for Soviet agents eager to ferret out military secrets from a nation that was ideologically opposed—if temporarily allied—to their own. Security was often lax in the city's thriving wartime workshops and labs. By 1944, a German refugee physicist named Klaus Fuchs, working for a Manhattan Project affiliate firm in the Woolworth Building on lower Broadway, was meeting with Harry Gold, a Soviet agent, on downtown street corners and passing top secret nuclear research to him. (Fuchs soon moved on to the army's high-security compound at Los Alamos, New Mexico, from where he continued to feed atomic bomb information to the Russians.)[15]

Uptown, a New York-born Communist named Julius Rosenberg, working as a US Signal Corps inspector in the Emerson Radio and Phonograph plant on Eighth Avenue, managed in 1944 to smuggle out one of the explosive detonators being manufactured there for wartime antiaircraft use. Rosenberg handed it, wrapped in a gift box, to Soviet agent Alexander Feklisov in an Automat cafeteria near Times Square. Rosenberg became a key figure in a spy network bent on acquiring US military secrets and passing them on to Russian agents. By a stroke of luck, Rosenberg's brother-in-law, machinist David Greenglass, also a Communist, was assigned to Los Alamos in August 1944. Harry Gold went to New Mexico and returned to New York with Greenglass's sketch of a component used in the making of the atomic bomb's detonator. When Greenglass himself arrived back in the city on furlough in 1945, he brought additional information on the detonator and a list of Manhattan Project scientists at Los Alamos. At least some of the spies, imbued with the conviction that America should share its secrets with its Soviet ally, professed to see no treason in their own actions. "I had no idea about betraying the United States," David Greenglass later maintained. "All I had in mind was helping a guy that was at war fighting the Nazis."[16]

With the onset of the Cold War, the Soviet spy rings in the United States disintegrated. British authorities arrested Klaus Fuchs in London in January 1950. In Philadelphia, the FBI picked up Harry Gold a few months later. Gold's confession allowed the arrest of David Greenglass, Julius Rosenberg, and Julius's wife, Ethel, David's sister, all living on the Lower East Side. The news made front-page headlines, but the true story behind their apprehension remained a secret until the mid-1990s. During the late 1940s, US Army cryptologists working in a station at Arlington, Virginia, managed to break the code Russian diplomats were using in their cables and radiograms back to Moscow. The breakthrough, kept secret in order to lull the Soviets into thinking their covert operations were still safe, enabled the FBI to identify Gold, Julius Rosenberg, and others as spies.

The trial of the Rosenbergs, and the question of their guilt or innocence, divided New Yorkers. Many were persuaded that the couple were spies and traitors. Others argued that the government was framing two guiltless individuals. With the revelation of the so-called Venona decrypts, even the most ardent defenders of the Rosenbergs' innocence have, for the most part, conceded Julius's complicity; historians continue to argue over the nature and extent of Ethel's role and whether it justified her conviction. Whether the secrets passed on to the Soviets actually accelerated the Russian nuclear program is also the subject of debate. Most experts agree that Stalin's scientists would soon have produced a bomb on their own, although some also argue that early access to American atomic secrets emboldened Stalin to permit North Korea to invade South Korea in 1950. At the time, the sentence meted out to the Rosenbergs—death in the electric chair—became a rallying point for Communists and many liberals around the world, and a public relations coup for the Kremlin, which charged that the United States was barbarously martyring the couple because they were party members, not spies. Photographs of ten-year-old Michael Rosenberg and six-year-old Robert, soon to be orphaned by the state, stared sadly from placards carried by Communists in Union Square protest rallies.

President Eisenhower refused to commute the death sentences. "By immeasurably increasing the chances of atomic war," he asserted, "the Rosenbergs may have condemned to death tens of millions of innocent people all over the world." On the evening of June 19, 1953, Julius and Ethel Rosenberg were electrocuted at Sing Sing Prison in Ossining, New York. On West Seventeenth Street, a crowd of five thousand, pushed by police out of Union Square for lack of a permit, held a vigil, many of them lifting signs reading "We Are Innocent" and weeping.[17]

One dimension of the Rosenberg case lingered uncomfortably over the entire Cold War era in New York, the world's largest Jewish city: the fact that Jews were the largest and most conspicuous ethnic bloc within the city's Communist Party, which itself represented at least 40 percent of the party's national membership. To be sure, the dramas played out in the city's courtrooms ensnared numerous Gentiles as well, among them accused spy Alger Hiss and his ex-Communist accuser Whittaker Chambers. But the taint of disloyalty possessed a particularly noxious sting for the city's (and nation's) Jews, especially among the large majority who were not Communists.

The Mississippi congressman and bigot John Rankin spoke the words other Americans were thinking when, during the HUAC hearings of 1947, he read into the record a list of names from a petition sponsored by a liberal group opposed to blacklisting. Rankin implied that the group was a Communist front. Among the signers was "Danny Kaye. . . . We found out his real name—David Daniel Kaminsky. . . . There is one who calls himself Edward [G.] Robinson. His real name is Emmanuel Goldenberg." Rankin went on to list the "aliases" and birth names of other performers. In light of such sentiments, the government went to special lengths to ensure that the ferreting out of accused spies could not be denounced as an anti-Semitic witch hunt. Accordingly, when the Rosenbergs came to trial, their judge was Irving Kaufman, who imposed the death sentence; their prosecutor was Irving Saypol, aided by an ambitious young attorney named Roy Cohn who would soon be making headlines assisting Senator Joseph McCarthy in Washington.[18]

While the two prosecutors and the judge shared the Rosenbergs' religious heritage, no Jew was among the jurors who decided the Rosenbergs' guilt or innocence. Many Jews in New York, of varying political outlooks, greeted the conviction and execution of the Rosenbergs with a mixture of embarrassment, anger, and remorse. "My father took my sister and me to the corner of our block in Brooklyn to watch the Rosenberg funeral procession pass," journalist Sam Roberts later remembered. "Even at the age of six, I was aware that somebody had done something to make us ashamed." The bitterness spawned by the Rosenberg case would linger across years and generations. After the eulogies at the funeral of Judge Kaufman in 1992, the angry voice of an uninvited guest echoed through the synagogue: "He murdered the Rosenbergs. Let him rot in hell."[19]

As the pursuit of domestic spies and subversives crested in the early and mid-1950s, the anxious question lingered: How could the city's population be protected against Soviet nuclear attack? Across the nation, thousands of homeowners built private shelters, often purchased in prefabricated kits, to shield themselves from bomb blast, flame, and radioactive fallout. In Princeton, New Jersey—midway between New York and Philadelphia, another presumed target city—physicist Eugene Wigner, one of the fathers of the Manhattan Project, built a blast shelter for his family. But elsewhere in the Greater New York area, many suburbanites balked. In New Canaan, Connecticut, Marnie Seymour recalled years later, "our neighbors were going to build a bomb shelter, elaborate, well stocked. They wanted us all to go together. We'd be compatible. Harry [her husband] talked 'em out of it. He said, 'You'd be sizzled to death. There'd be nothing to come out to. You wouldn't want to survive. It would be a slow, hideous death.'"[20]

The beau ideal of the shelter effort, encouraged by the FCDA, was the backyard or basement single-family refuge, an innovation well suited to an increasingly suburban nation of freestanding houses, not to the apartment complexes of a large city. A subtle anti-urban bias underpinned much of this effort; it was as if the government itself was writing off the big cities as hopeless casualties in any nuclear strike, with the nation's saving remnant of middle-class suburban businessmen, professionals, and their families posited as the most likely—and implicitly, the most desirable—survivors. With Congress unwilling to appropriate large sums for civil defense on top of the Pentagon's ballooning budget, the FCDA and state agencies encouraged "self-help"—meaning that citizens were left to fund their own private means of survival, a philosophy that defeated the construction of expensive, large-scale urban shelters. In an era that reveled in white-bread conformity, it was Chicago, Detroit, Los Angeles, San Francisco, New York—with their ethnic neighborhoods, their unsightly zones of poverty, and their growing populations of blacks and Latinos—that were shortchanged.

So what were apartment-dwelling New Yorkers supposed to do? Duck and cover. Pamphlets distributed by the FCDA, such as *Survival Under Atomic Attack* (1951), drew no distinction between city dwellers and others but encouraged all to think that the bomb could be survived. With the bomb exploding nearby, pedestrians should huddle next to the foundation of a "good substantial building" or "jump in any handy ditch or gutter." Even radiation was survivable; once back indoors, "you can get rid of all the radioactive dirt you've picked up if you keep scrubbing" during an ordinary bath or shower.[21]

In the city's schools, air raid drills became routine. New York's children, like others across the country, followed the Atomic Age adventures of Bert the Turtle in FCDA animated filmstrips and comic books: "*BERT DUCKS AND COVERS. HE'S SMART, BUT HE HAS HIS SHELTER ON HIS BACK. YOU MUST LEARN TO FIND SHELTER.*" Growing up in the Bronx, Todd Gitlin learned to expect the unexpected: "Every so often, out of the blue, a teacher would pause in the middle of class and call out, 'Take Cover!' We knew, then, to scramble under our miniature desks and to stay there, cramped, heads folded under our arms, until the teacher called out, 'All clear!'" As Gitlin later reflected, the experience bonded an entire generation together—"the first American generation compelled from infancy to fear not only war but the end of days." Across town in Spanish Harlem, kindergartener Mickey Melendez learned a similar lesson: he and his classmates "were meticulously trained to go under our desks to protect us from the bombs that were expected to fall all over the city." In 1951–1952, the Board of Education spent $159,000 to issue metal dog tags to every student attending public, private, or parochial schools in New York. The tags, to be worn around the neck, would ostensibly prevent children from getting lost in the chaos of a nuclear attack. That such tags might also serve to identify charred remains was usually left unsaid.[22]

Some planners proposed jumbo-sized urban versions of the suburban shelters. In the city, such sanctuaries would have to sacrifice individuality and privacy for the collective needs of thousands of apartment dwellers. Civil engineer Robert Panero, a contractor to the US Army Corps of Engineers, revived a World War II idea and seriously advo-

Architect Hugh Ferriss's vision of air raid shelters for New York during World War II, shown here, foreshadowed similar plans during the early Nuclear Age. Hugh Ferriss, *Shelter Equipped for Occupancy*, 1942. CHARCOAL AND CHARCOAL PENCIL, 180 3 250. MILDRED LANE KEMPER ART MUSEUM, WASHINGTON UNIVERSITY, ST. LOUIS. GIFT OF MRS. HUGH FERRISS, 1963.

cated drilling vast tunnels into the hard schist eight hundred feet below Manhattan's streets, a feat he argued would permit the island's entire population to get underground in twenty minutes' time. The softer rock beneath Brooklyn and Staten Island posed challenges Panero never solved, and the whole idea was shelved as impractical.[23]

The city's efforts to create shelters lagged through the 1950s. When federal, state, and city officials asked owners of public buildings to provide basement shelters, they were largely ignored. Civil Defense spokesmen criticized such "apathy," which seemed to reflect the attitude the *New Yorker* magazine had detected as early as 1946, when it described many Americans as dealing with the possibility of nuclear war "by simply refusing to think about it."[24]

It would take the US-Soviet confrontation over Berlin in 1961 to reenergize the urban shelter initiative. Addressing the nation live on television on July 25, 1961, President Kennedy called on Congress to identify fallout shelters and "to stock those shelters with food, water, first-aid kits, tools, sanitation facilities, and other minimum essentials for survival." (Privately, Kennedy told his aide Ted Sorensen, "I don't want the survivors, if there are any . . . to say we never warned them or never did anything to save at least some of their families while there was still time.") An army of civil engineers soon fanned out from federal arsenals and navy yards to identify and mark fallout shelters in public and private buildings across the country. This time, many property owners complied by providing at least token space in basements and storerooms for sanctuary and supplies. Ultimately, over fifteen thousand buildings in New York City would be adorned with yellow and black "Fallout Shelter" signs; landlords stocked basements with thousands of kits, provided by the federal Office of Civil Defense, containing two-week supplies of penicillin, the sedative phenobarbital, an appetite suppressant in candy form, crackers, water drums, portable toilets, a radiation detector, and other items deemed survival essentials.[25]

Although federal inspectors returned regularly until the early 1970s to certify the fallout supplies, many tenants remained ignorant or indifferent. Realism as well as denial undermined New Yorkers' enthusiasm for the program. As early as 1954, many New Yorkers knew that basement storage rooms were unlikely to withstand the new hydrogen bomb, five hundred times more powerful than the Hiroshima blast, or the toxic radiation it would spread. Jim Hulme, a bank teller living on Second Avenue, was typical of those the *Times* interviewed in 1961: "I live in an apartment house. Where could I go? The only thing I could do would be to run to the basement or run under the bomb when it falls. Get it over with quickly."[26]

If fallout shelters were ineffective, what about evacuation? In 1956, the *Bulletin of the Atomic Scientists* asserted that "Run Like Hell" made more sense than "Duck and Cover." Officials came to agree, or at any rate drafted contingency plans for "defensive dispersal" from New York and other large cities. Indeed, the ongoing postwar flight of middle-class city dwellers into suburbia easily dovetailed with Cold War priorities. When the $100 billion Interstate Highway Act passed by Congress in 1956 funded the building of forty-one thousand miles of roadways, President Eisenhower justified the expense in civil defense terms: "[In] case of atomic attack on our key cities, the road net must permit quick evacuation of target areas."[27]

As early as 1955, Mayor Robert Wagner met with New York governor Averell Harriman and the governors of New Jersey and Connecticut to discuss the emergency evacuation of the city. That same year, Lieutenant General Clarence Huebner, New York State's Civil Defense director, presented a plan for the evacuation of New York City, Buffalo, Albany, and nineteen other communities in the event of nuclear attack. A more detailed state plan, drafted in 1958, came with elaborate tables showing the number of New Yorkers who, in the first phase of an evacuation, would be directed by train and highway to Orange County, the Catskills, and the Adirondacks (724,000 people) or to northern and central New Jersey (866,000). Homeowners and businesspeople in these outlying counties would be expected to take in "an average of two persons to a room, with family units being kept intact or as close together as possible." Other urban refugees would be deployed around the region in successive, orderly phases.[28]

But the challenge of moving eight million people on terrifyingly short notice and dumping them in the suburban and rural hinterland was a quixotic proposition, unrealistic even to some civil defense proponents. How much advance notice would New Yorkers have of a bomb falling on them? Mayor Wagner's experts argued optimistically in 1955 that the new radar systems being installed by the Pentagon for continental defense would provide "from two to six hours' warning," sufficient time for an "emergency traffic plan, controlled from helicopters," to be implemented—although up to three million people in Brooklyn, Queens, and the Bronx might have to walk to safety along roads and highways into Nassau and Westchester counties.[29]

By the mid-1950s, analysts correctly assumed that the Russians would soon have intercontinental missiles that would reduce warning times to half an hour at most—hardly time even to prepare a fraction of the city's population to flee. "Getting out of the city on short notice—as any pre-holiday traveler can testify—is no mean feat," Bernard Stengren reminded *New York Times* readers in 1955. And some questions remained unanswered. "Who is to go first," Stengren asked, "school children, mothers with children, families?" Recalling Orson Welles's 1938 *War of the Worlds* broadcast, he suggested that panic might turn any orderly movement into a free-for-all. And would fallout, carried by unpredictable winds, really spare the suburbs?[30]

Then there was the question of how welcoming the suburbs might actually be. In April 1955, William J. Slater, Westchester County's director of Civil Defense, warned New Yorkers against seeking safe haven in his jurisdiction when he declared that he would "mobilize civil defense forces to prevent an evacuation of New York City in the event of an enemy attack." Evidently the vision of millions of city dwellers swarming over the Bronx border into Westchester—a county already beset by tensions over the arrival of Jewish, black, and Puerto Rican migrants from the city—did not appeal to Slater.[31]

City and state administrators tried to prevent outlying communities from shutting their doors to New Yorkers in the case of a nuclear emergency. Indeed, New York City had recently gone toe to toe with Slater, removing a billboard erected on the Hutchinson River Parkway stating that "the boundary would be closed in case of enemy attack." Slater insisted that similar signs posted on the Boston Post Road, the Bronx River Parkway, and the Sawmill River Parkway would remain in place. State officials quickly overrode him, announcing that civilian cars would be permitted to evacuate into and through Westchester. Such confusion—along with numerous science fiction stories depicting gun-toting suburbanites driving nuclear refugees away from their private bomb shelters—must have given many New Yorkers further reason to doubt the realism of evacuation.[32]

If all else failed, the government would try to shoot Russian bombers and missiles out of the sky. In the mid and late 1950s, residents of such New York City suburbs as Huntington, Long Island, and Spring Valley, New York, and Summit, New Jersey, began to encounter barbed wire fences, gated roadways, and even soldiers with guard dogs keeping them out of mysterious compounds in remote corners of their towns. Behind the fences and dogs, army and National Guard troops manned installations equipped with batteries of Nike antiaircraft missiles. By 1961, the city was encircled by a ring of nineteen Nike batteries. New

York was not alone; fifty-six other major cities, air force bases, and power plants obtained Nike batteries.[33]

If Russian Tu-4 bombers managed to elude American fighter jets once they crossed early-warning radar networks strung across Canada and the Great Plains and on "Texas Towers" (modified oil rigs) off the New England coast, Nike bases would use their own radar systems and computers to home in on the bombers. Stored underground in protective magazines, the one-ton, thirty-two-foot long Nike Ajax missiles would be lifted by elevator to their ground level launch rails and fired at a range of about thirty miles to demolish the incoming Russian planes. In 1958, new, more powerful Nike Hercules missiles—armed with forty-kiloton nuclear warheads, equivalent to the Hiroshima bomb—began to replace the Ajax series in order to meet the threat of Soviet intercontinental missiles. Aimed at a cluster of incoming missiles detected by radar, the "Hercs" would theoretically climb to a height of a hundred thousand feet, exploding and destroying the enemy projectiles before they got within seventy-five miles of New York City. By 1959, New York City—Fort Tilden at Rockaway Beach, Queens, to be exact—was home to a battery of operational atomic warheads; nine other suburban bases nearby were also armed with "Hercs."

The families enjoying the summer surf at Jacob Riis Park, a few hundred yards down the beach from Fort Tilden, may have taken some comfort from the presence of such formidable defenses, if they knew or thought about them at all. The army made no attempt to conceal the presence of defensive warheads in the metropolitan area, seeking instead to win over worriers (and, perhaps, discourage the Russians) by holding press conferences and organizing public exhibits. The "possibility of any nuclear explosion occurring as a result of an accident . . . is virtually non-existent," Major General Nathaniel A. Burnell 2nd of the First Region, Army Air Defense Command at Fort Totten, assured reporters in 1957.[34]

But Burnell was wrong. On May 22, 1958, maintenance work being done on a Nike Ajax missile at a base at Middletown, New Jersey, somehow went awry; the missile exploded, detonating others nearby, costing six soldiers and four civilians their lives. Fortunately, the Ajax was not nuclear. But two years later, a nuclear missile at McGuire Air

Nike Hercules missiles stand ready at Fort Hancock, Sandy Hook, c. 1969. NPS / GATEWAY NRA MUSEUM COLLECTION.

Force Base in New Jersey caught fire and leaked melting radioactive plutonium. The accident could not trigger a nuclear reaction, and crews quickly sealed off the contaminated area (it remains off-limits to this day and will be for centuries). Yet when news of the fire reached New York City, at least fifty people placed anxious calls to civil defense offices, pressing for information on the danger of drifting radioactive fallout; McGuire operators had to field a "flood" of incoming phone queries. While officials continued to insist that defense against Russian nuclear assault was crucial, some wondered whether the local "protection" might be more deadly than the foreign threat.[35]

Acknowledging in 1950 that New York would be a "first target" in a nuclear strike, the editors of the liberal Catholic magazine *Commonweal* expressed the resignation that many felt: "A man knows that he is a part of it—these buildings, these streets, these subway crowds . . .

and that if one day they are blasted into nothingness, then he should be there. . . . One stays where one is, hopes for the best and plans to do his part should the worst come." But by the mid-1950s, some New Yorkers were shedding such fatalism and daring to challenge the prevailing assumptions propounded by the government and mainstream press. During Operation Alert 1955, twenty-seven pacifists led by the indefatigable Dorothy Day of the Catholic Worker movement were arrested after refusing to leave City Hall Park to seek shelter once the alarm siren sounded. "We will not obey this order to pretend, to evacuate, to hide . . . ," Day declared in a pamphlet. "We know this drill to be a military act in a cold war to instill fear, to prepare the collective mind for war."[36]

Over the next few years, Day and her fellow pacifists—including A. J. Muste of the Fellowship of Reconciliation and leaders of the War Resisters League such as the black activist Bayard Rustin—led others in public acts of civil disobedience during Operation Alert. They faced fines imposed by hostile judges and physical abuse endured in detention; Day and several others repeatedly served brief prison terms. Day and Muste were seasoned veterans of the struggles to gain conscientious objector status for pacifists during World War II; Muste's New York antiwar activism, in fact, dated back to 1915. In different ways they each embraced a vision of a peaceful Christian and socialist society that rejected the inhumanity of both Soviet communism and American-style capitalism.

But "ordinary" New Yorkers, fearing for the lives of their families, also began to take part in the growing pacifist movement. On April 15, 1959, twenty-four-year-old Mary Sharmat, pushing her young son Jimmy's stroller, sat down on a bench in the center island of Broadway at Eighty-Sixth Street. As the Operation Alert siren sounded, and as hundreds of pedestrians stopped to watch, she quietly explained herself to a civil defense officer: "I cannot take shelter. I do not believe in this." A policeman threatened her with a fine, then smiled, and let her go, to the fury of the civil defense men. Five miles downtown, another young mother, twenty-one-year-old Janice Smith, brought her two- and four-year-old children to Dorothy Day's fifth annual demonstration in City Hall Park. "All this drill does is frighten children and birds," Smith told policemen and reporters. "I will not raise my children to go underground." She was arrested but then released without being charged. Sharmat and Smith quickly linked up, and through phone calls and playground recruitment they mobilized a growing network of young middle-class mothers and their husbands to practice civil disobedience. "PEACE is the only defense against nuclear war," declared a leaflet drafted by Smith and Sharmat's new group, the Civil Defense Protest Committee. The committee's literature looked to Gandhi for inspiration.[37]

On May 3, 1960, one thousand women, children, and men crowded into City Hall Park. As Sharmat recalled, "Many men came down. Our skirts gave them courage. We loaned out extra babies to bachelors who had the misfortune to be childless." Five hundred adults willing to be arrested stayed put as the sirens blared; when a civil defense official mounted a bench and declared them all under arrest, the crowd cheered. The fifteen men and eleven women actually arrested were sentenced to five days in jail. The following year, 2,500 New Yorkers practiced civil disobedience in City Hall Park during Operation Alert. By then, demonstrations were also being held in cities across the country and on college campuses throughout the Northeast.[38]

Operation Alert 1961 was the last such drill. The Kennedy administration, embarrassed by news coverage of the protests and increasingly adverse editorial opinion, quietly canceled 1962's exercise. Just as importantly, the protests—the first large-scale public demonstrations against the prospect of nuclear annihilation—energized middle-class New Yorkers who otherwise might have thought twice about joining radical leftist groups. They filled the ranks of new disarmament organizations such as SANE and Women Strike for Peace, which would play an active role nationwide as the 1960s unfolded. Women Strike for Peace became a proving ground for New Yorkers like the lawyer Bella Abzug, the pacifist Cora Weiss, and other women activists. Their lobbying and public relations savvy helped persuade John Kennedy to sign a limited nuclear test ban treaty in 1963 and also paved the way for their impending roles in national politics.

A new generation coming to maturity—the Duck and Cover generation—began to find its voice in these demonstrations in New York's streets and parks. Inspired by the emerging Southern civil rights movement and exhilarated by the decline of McCarthyism, young New Yorkers sang "We Shall Overcome" and "We Shall Not Be Moved" and courted arrest in City Hall Park. For some, the schoolroom drills began a process of radicalization that would continue to build. Looking back, Robert K. Musil, leader of Physicians for Social Responsibility, found the roots of a new decade in the schoolhouse drills: "The styles and explosions of the 1960s were born in those dank, subterranean high-school corridors near the boiler room where we decided that our elders were indeed unreliable." Duck and Cover veterans from New York City would go on to populate the leadership ranks of the New Left: Mario Savio from Queens became the face and voice of the student free speech movement at Berkeley, Todd Gitlin from the Bronx would be a president of Students for a Democratic Society (SDS) and an antiwar activist, and Mickey Melendez from Spanish Harlem would cofound the militant Puerto Rican organization the Young Lords.[39]

A new youth counterculture, spilling out from Greenwich Village coffeehouses into open-air performances in Washington Square, posited the bomb as a symbol of everything wrong and insane in American society. "People were building bomb shelters everywhere," folksinger John Cohen later recalled. " . . . Here we were in the middle of Greenwich Village like a little pus pimple in the middle of this huge society, saying . . . I'm not going to live my life that way." Yet despite the protests emanating from New York's bohemian quarter, the confrontations between President Kennedy and Russian Premier Khrushchev—over Berlin in 1961, over Cuban missiles in 1962—meant that the Cold War might grow very hot at any moment. "The night of the Cuban Missile Crisis," Cohen remembered, " . . . the general feeling was the world was going to end or something." Walking into the Gaslight Café on Mac-Dougal Street, Cohen saw his young friend Bob Dylan up on stage, singing to a small audience. Cohen joined Dylan to sing the country standard, "You're Gonna Miss Me When I'm Gone." All the while Cohen was thinking, "*who's* going to miss us when we're gone? We're all [going to be] gone! . . . What the hell is this?" Dylan was soon singing one of his own songs, "Let Me Die in My Footsteps," in the Village coffeehouses, an anthem that defied civil defense preparations and embodied the disobedience now linking venerable pacifists, middle-class families, and a growing body of students throughout the country.[40]

The songs, the street rallies, and the acts of civil disobedience would soon have a new focal point, a country nine thousand miles away in Southeast Asia, a place that would soon fill the living rooms of New Yorkers with bloody images and their streets with angry crowds.

On August 8, 1964, a small midtown demonstration foreshadowed the future in ways no New Yorker could predict or realize. Some sixty men and women, mostly of college age, gathered in Duffy Square, at Broadway and Forty-Seventh Street, with placards reading "U.S. Troops Out of Vietnam." They were led by a student organization called the May 2 Movement, and they included members of small leftist groups active on local campuses, mostly Trotskyist and Maoist, including Youth Against War and Fascism and the New York Spartacist Committee. Their chants that day drew connections between the civil rights movement and opposition to American foreign policy. Early August 1964 was the tense climax of Freedom Summer; three hundred Northern students had flocked to Mississippi to help blacks register to vote. Four days earlier, the bodies of white New Yorkers Michael Schwerner and Andrew Goodman and black Mississippian James Chaney had been unearthed near Philadelphia, Mississippi, where local Klansmen had buried the three Congress of Racial Equality activists after murdering them. Three weeks earlier, Harlem had exploded in four days of rioting after a white policeman fatally shot a black teenager. "Protest Police Brutality—Here and in Vietnam," and "Send Troops to Mississippi—Not Vietnam," the Duffy Square demonstrators chanted.[41]

Citing a ban on political demonstrations in midtown, put into effect after a 1962 antinuclear testing rally, Captain John McAllister of the Sixteenth Precinct ordered the Duffy Square protesters to disperse. Many refused. As the group chanted "Fascist Cops! Fascist Cops!" mounted policemen and patrolmen on foot charged into them with nightsticks swinging. A reporter watched as a young woman "went at a patrolman with both fists," and as "a young man in a green T-shirt made himself as stiff as a board and was loaded into a police car." Seventeen were taken to the precinct house by patrol car and taxicab. As the arrestees' friends marched and chanted in a circle outside the precinct on Forty-Seventh Street, anti-Castro Cuban émigrés living in adjoining tenements leaned out their windows, jeered, and poured water on them. As the Cold War grew hot again in a remote region of Southeast Asia, the inhabitants of the nation's most cosmopolitan city once more brought the conflicting passions and ideologies of a foreign war into their own streets.[42]

On August 7, the day before the Duffy Square protest, Congress had passed the Gulf of Tonkin Resolution, giving President Lyndon John-son authority to commit American forces against Communist North Vietnam and Communist guerillas fighting the South Vietnamese gov-ernment. But Vietnam had already gained the attention of New York pacifists a year earlier, when, on the anniversaries of the Hiroshima and Nagasaki bombings, two young Catholic Workers, Thomas Cornell and Christopher Kearns, picketed the residence of South Vietnam's permanent observer to the United Nations, Mrs. Tran Van Chuong, in the East Sixties. South Vietnam's despotic president, Ngo Dinh Diem, himself a Catholic, had sparked international uproar and embarrassed his ally, President Kennedy, by launching a violent persecution of his nation's Buddhist majority. "We demand an end to U.S. military sup-port of Diem's government," Cornell's and Kearns's picket signs read. The strategic advantage of demonstrating in the nation's media capital became clear when ABC News sent a television crew to cover and broadcast a rally by the two men and 250 supporters on the tenth day of their protest.[43]

Religious pacifists and student members of an emerging New Left were fashioning the tactics of an antiwar movement before most Americans were even paying attention to developments in Indochina. By the late summer and fall of 1964, in fact, a coalition of groups and individuals was coming together in opposition to Johnson's accelerat-ing intervention in Vietnam. Demonstrators brought the energy of the nuclear disarmament and anti–civil defense movements to a new cause. At rallies in Washington Square Park, a thousand New Yorkers listened to the octogenarian socialist leader Norman Thomas and the septuagenarians A. Philip Randolph and A. J. Muste—three men who, between them, had given over 150 years of work for progressive change—denounce the war. Muste insisted on the need "to keep the issue of Vietnam before the public, and before the Administration."[44]

More than altruism propelled the new protest movement. By 1965 and 1966, Mickey Melendez and other recent high school graduates faced a new and dangerous world. "Adulthood had arrived, and along with it, the war . . . ," Melendez remembered. "The draft was breathing down hard on all our backs." Pals from the South Bronx neighborhood where he now lived enlisted or were drafted into the marines, the air force, and the army. "My neighbor, Pedro, came back in a body bag with his tags on his big toe. . . . It just didn't make sense. Was there any reason for him to die? The news on the TV, the radio, or the papers did not provide a good answer to that question." Over the course of a decade, thousands of New Yorkers would serve in the armed forces during the Vietnam War. As was true nationally, their ranks were disproportionately filled with the poor, the undereducated, and men and boys of color, as deferments shielded most college students from the draft. By the time the war was over, 1,741 New Yorkers had been killed in Southeast Asia. To Melendez's friends, "War was not popular. Neither was defeat." Such ambivalence—a mix of fear, grief, anger, patriotism, and unwillingness to see the United States lose the conflict—was more widespread than one might glean from the public protests and media coverage that sought neatly to split Americans into antiwar and prowar camps.[45]

Antiwar activists used New York as an organizational center and proving ground during the Vietnam War. Faces of Vietnamese children stared out from photographs on the walls of New York subway stations in 1965, skin twisted and mutilated by napalm. The posters, pasted there by SDS members, were only one sign of the ways in which the distant war was coming home to New Yorkers. With LBJ's bombing of North Vietnam in February, and with over two hundred thousand American troops now on the ground in South Vietnam, the antiwar movement gained momentum and headlines. Bearing nonviolent witness in the Gandhian tradition linked several national organizations that made 5 Beekman Street, across Park Row from City Hall Park, their official home. The building housed the offices of A. J. Muste's Fellowship of Reconciliation, Bayard Rustin and David Dellinger of the War Resisters League, the Catholic Peace Fellowship, the Committee for Nonviolent Action, and the pacifist magazine Liberation, all of which cooperated to oppose the war.[46]

Five Beekman also harbored the new Fifth Avenue Peace Parade Committee, run by Norma Becker, a tireless schoolteacher and Freedom Summer veteran. She oversaw an eager crew of high school and college volunteers who staffed phones, stuffed envelopes, and mimeographed leaflets at all hours of the day and night. Becker's Charles Street apartment became the arena for some of the national movement's most heated bull sessions. Over the next few years, New York stalwarts like Becker, Dellinger, David McReynolds of the War Resisters League, Cora Weiss of Women Strike for Peace, Linda Dannenberg of the Student Mobilization Committee to End the War in Vietnam, and others would provide a coordinating organizational backbone for the antiwar movement. They were not alone; activists from other parts of the country also played key roles in the "Mobe," the National Mobilization Committee to End the War in Vietnam (1967) and its successor umbrella organizations that sought to keep a precariously diverse national movement together. But Dellinger, Becker, and Weiss were ubiquitous in the Mobe's strategic planning and operations. As the setting for marches and confrontations shifted among Washington, Berkeley, Oakland, Chicago, and campuses nationwide, New Yorkers—with their seasoning in progressive organizations, their willingness to fund liberal causes, their ability to mobilize vast numbers and individual celebrities, their street smarts and media awareness, not to mention their stubbornness and chutzpah—played pivotal roles in the movement's genesis and survival.

Across the city, as across the entire country, Vietnam aroused members of the swelling postwar baby boom generation, on campuses where most males were exempt from the draft, and in neighborhoods where the body bags were beginning to return. Pondering the linkages they perceived between capitalism, imperialism, and institutionalized racism, students joined New Left organizations like SDS, now a national entity whose headquarters had moved from New York to Chicago in 1965, partly to cut free from its parent organization, the more moderate League for Industrial Democracy. In a meeting in New York in December 1964, SDS leaders had begun organizing the first mass antiwar march on Washington for Easter 1965. Off the campuses, in poorer neighborhoods, America's Asian war was also becoming a debatable issue. To at least some in

Spanish Harlem and the South Bronx, including Mickey Melendez, "the 'enemy' looked too much like us—Puerto Ricans. American troops were destroying shantytowns in a remote country, which had an eerily similar appearance to the tropical country of our fathers."[47]

On April 15, 1967, in the Spring Mobilization to End the War in Vietnam, the pediatrician Dr. Benjamin Spock and Martin Luther King Jr. led at least one hundred thousand demonstrators—perhaps as many as four hundred thousand—from Central Park across Fifty-Ninth and Forty-Seventh Streets to a rally outside the United Nations. It was, to date, the largest antiwar demonstration in American history. In addition to busloads of marchers from Pittsburgh, Cleveland, and Chicago, the city's disparate constituencies flowed into the massive crowd. The middle-class professional women and housewives of Women Strike for Peace, some of them participants in the anti–civil defense actions of 1960 and 1961, joined the throng. A civil rights movement veteran named Abbie Hoffman helped lead a motley contingent from the East Village, which had burst forth as the East Coast's mecca for hippies and cultural rebels. Hoffman sauntered uptown amid "[Allen] Ginsberg's bells and chants, The Bread and Puppet Theater group, gaily dressed and stoned, a Yellow Submarine, and a lot of people who looked like they had posed for the Sergeant Pepper album cover." "No Vietcong Ever Called Me Nigger," asserted signs carried by protesters from Harlem. Many marchers chanted, "Hell no, we won't go," and "Hey, hey, LBJ, how many kids did you kill today?" Some went further than demanding an end to bloodshed and actively advocated the cause against which the United States was fighting in Vietnam. Marching with several hundred fellow Columbia students, Mark Rudd, a freshman from the New Jersey suburbs, observed militants carrying the red, blue, and gold Vietcong flag. "I felt a secret thrill: Here were people declaring in public what I only dared to say in private." At the same time, Rudd "looked up to see a group of nuns waving at us from a second-floor balcony of their fancy Upper East Side convent. Everyone in New York seemed to be against the war."[48]

Already, however, friction over goals, strategies, and ideologies was straining the broad coalition. Were acts of nonviolent civil disobedience called for, or did rallies have to be strictly law-abiding in order to

attract the largest possible number of Americans? Many religious pacifists welcomed the opportunity to violate the law. Christopher Kearns
and several others had already burned their draft cards in front of the
army's induction center on Whitehall Street in July 1965. *Life* magazine, located five miles uptown, sent photographers to cover the event;
pictures of Kearns's act reached millions of readers across the country.
Ten weeks later, near the same spot, twenty-two-year-old Catholic
Worker David Miller became the first American to violate a new federal law making draft card burning a felony. Several New Yorkers
would serve prison time for destroying their cards; Bronx native Bruce
Dancis, president of SDS at Cornell, spent eighteen months behind
bars. Others, however, like members of the Socialist Workers Party,
which played an active role in the movement, saw illegal acts as alienating more staid members of the working class and thus getting in the
way of an alliance between students and workers, which they hoped
would bring radical change to America, beyond merely ending the war.
Still others saw the movement as a prelude and precipitant to revolution. Divergent aims kept the movement in a state of tension and mutual distrust, continually threatening to erode its unity and its impact.[49]

As elsewhere in America, the mid- and late 1960s were explosive in
New York, and not just because of the Vietnam War. The economic
boom jump-started by federal spending during World War II had permitted a million middle-class, mostly white New Yorkers to move to
the surrounding suburbs. Their places were taken by poor newcomers:
African Americans leaving the South and Puerto Ricans leaving their
island home for opportunity in the north. They arrived in a city that
was losing its manufacturing economy to the cheaper, nonunionized
South and western Sunbelt—a transformation also rooted in wartime
federal encouragement of new industries beyond the traditional smoke-
stack cities of the Northeast and Midwest. Going west and south, too,
were the military contracts and installations that had provided thousands of New York jobs since World War II; the shutting down of the
Brooklyn Navy Yard in 1966 was only the most dramatic of these
losses. The factory and sweatshop jobs that had greeted European emigrants for over a century were missing for the hundreds of thousands of

unskilled or semiskilled rural families arriving by plane from San Juan or by bus and train from the Cotton Belt.[50]

By the mid-1960s, the new urban poor faced racism, housing and job discrimination, decaying slums, a de facto segregated public school system, drug addiction, and crime. The nonviolent civil rights movement gave way to a new, angry Black Power insurgency among many of the young in Harlem, Bedford-Stuyvesant, and Brownsville. Not since the Civil War Draft Riot was race so volatile and tense an issue. Mayor John Lindsay's liberal outreach to minority communities, and his policy of restraining the police in confrontations with black youths, saved New York from the devastating "race riots" that leveled whole neighborhoods in Newark, Detroit, and dozens of other cities. Even so, three black New Yorkers died, dozens of "ghetto" inhabitants and police were injured, and hundreds of stores were damaged by looting and fires during three major riots in Harlem and Brooklyn between 1966 and 1968. "If they [the police] want war, we'll give them war," an eighteen-year-old East Harlemite told Lindsay in 1967.[51]

Liberals and black militants alike warned that, without substantive economic and political change in an increasingly divided city, the powder keg of New York might explode. The black psychologist Kenneth Clark, who had grown up in Harlem, warned in 1965 that "the dark ghettos now represent a nuclear stockpile which can annihilate the very foundations of America." In 1968, the journalist Jimmy Breslin, who had grown up in Jamaica, Queens, asserted that "unless we give the ghettos a chance to work out their own problems . . . you'll see shotguns on Park Avenue." In 1969, the more conservative political scientist Daniel Moynihan, who had grown up in Hell's Kitchen on the West Side, told Richard Nixon that the "social fabric of New York City is coming to pieces. . . . Like a sheet of rotten canvas, it is beginning to rip," and might soon be "in shreds and tatters." National Guard regiments might find themselves facing gunfire and flames in the streets of America's largest city, as they did in Newark, Detroit, Washington, and elsewhere.[52]

In April 1968, three weeks after the assassination of Martin Luther King, one thousand demonstrators, including members of SDS, the Students Afro-American Society, and outside sympathizers, launched a sit-in and occupation of five buildings on the Columbia University campus. The sense of a coming showdown, of a society to be somehow reborn as it came apart at the seams, had increasingly gripped a very vocal and active minority within the interlinked student and antiwar movements, and now this militant cadre was making its presence felt in the heart of upper Manhattan. Their grievances linked local and global issues: protest against an "apartheid" gym to be built by Columbia, which would limit use by and effectively segregate members of the nearby Harlem community; a demand for amnesty for several students disciplined for a recent antiwar demonstration; and insistence that the university sever its ties to IDA, an intercollegiate think tank that provided research on carpet bombing and the defoliant Agent Orange for the Pentagon. Student demonstrator James Simon Kunen noted that IDA had a "secret research facility" in Pupin Hall, "a building which already bears the distinction of having been the birthplace of the atom bomb."[53]

For a week, as Columbia's president Grayson Kirk, fearful of sparking a riot in Harlem, held back the police, students and supporters roamed the occupied buildings and voted on strategy and tactics. On April 30, Kirk finally called in the police. Patrolmen in riot gear dragged 705 students, many through a gauntlet of blows from nightsticks, fists, and feet, out into paddy wagons waiting at the Broadway curb. Over one hundred people, including fourteen police officers, ended up in hospitals with injuries. The following day, police and students clashed in a free-for-all on campus; dozens more were injured, including an officer who was permanently disabled when a student jumped on him from a second-story window. Radical students sustained a boycott of classes through the end of the semester. The university expelled over 70 sit-in participants but never built the planned gym and cut its ties with IDA that summer.[54]

A new, angrier student movement emerged from the Columbia confrontation, both locally and nationally. "We are out for social and political revolution, nothing less," declared sit-in leader Mark Rudd, who was expelled and became a traveling speaker and organizer for SDS. His SDS colleague Tom Hayden called for "two, three, many Columbias," and for "bringing the war home." In 1969, campus takeovers sparked by the war, demands for increased minority enrollment, and calls for Afro-American Studies programs erupted at City College, Queens College, and Brooklyn College, and again at Columbia. At the Bronx High School of Science, Stuyvesant High School, and other secondary schools, teenaged radicals linked up with SDS and organized their own underground newspapers (the "Revolutionaries Who Have to be Home by 7:30," Nicholas Pileggi labeled them in the *Times*).[55]

While radicals contemplated violent revolution, the mainstream of the city's antiwar movement, including liberals ensconced in the city's political establishment, continued to embrace more limited goals. Mayor Lindsay, a liberal Republican who, as a representative from Manhattan, had been the third member of Congress to go on record against the war, became an outspoken critic of Lyndon Johnson's and then Richard Nixon's continuation of the conflict. Lindsay underscored how the financial cost of the war was diverting money away from social spending in cities that desperately needed it, helping to kill LBJ's own dream of a "Great Society," which, once and for all, was supposed to banish poverty from American life. New York City itself was a "prisoner of war," Lindsay contended, with tax revenues that could pay for hospitals, teachers, police, and other municipal services drained off by the Pentagon; the mayor estimated in 1970 that New Yorkers were paying $3 billion a year in federal taxes for the war and another $6 billion for other defense expenditures. Lindsay narrowly won reelection in a three-way race in 1969, in which his opposition to the war helped cement a winning coalition of voters. Yet Lindsay also derided draft card burning and other provocative tactics as "negative, bizarre, and often self-indulgent." Rather than flying the Vietcong flag and rampaging on campuses, the young should copy those who "got haircuts, shaved, put on ties, and went into politics." Many had already anticipated Lindsay's advice, campaigning for the antiwar Democrats Eugene McCarthy and Robert Kennedy in 1968.[56]

But the more radical wing of the movement was moving in its own direction. By mid-1968, many in the New Left were turning their backs completely on the notion that peace, or any meaningful social progress, could come out of the existing political system. "Our goal was a much more fundamental change," Mark Rudd later wrote, "not just ending the war but ending the capitalist system that had caused the war. . . . Electoral politics were beneath our concern." The split in temperaments, styles, and goals was not overcome, dividing the city's and nation's left-of-center constituency against itself. Seventeen years later, Rudd met a man who had walked out of a Hiroshima Day rally in Central Park in August 1969, never to return to the antiwar movement. "A bunch of crazies took over the speakers' platform and began screaming about violent revolution," the man told him, not realizing that Rudd had been one of the "crazies." "It seemed like most of their hate was aimed at the other people in the movement. . . . I guess I didn't want any part of a movement which had so much hatred and violence." In New York as elsewhere, the antiwar movement that had initially united liberals and leftists, pacifists and revolutionaries, ultimately sharpened the divisions between them.[57]

The Vietnam War looked different in the sprawling working-class and middle-class Irish, German, Polish, and Italian American neighborhoods of Brooklyn, Queens, the Bronx, and Staten Island, populated by the families of construction workers, unionized technicians, clerical workers, shopkeepers, drivers, police officers, and firefighters. When criticism or doubts about this war surfaced, as they certainly did, they collided with strongly held values: a heartfelt patriotism, a devotion to the flag, pride in family legacies of military service, membership in unions and Democratic Party clubhouses with ties to Lyndon Johnson, and, in some cases, allegiance to the fledgling Conservative Party or the right wing of the Republican Party. (While LBJ had garnered over two million city votes in 1964, eight hundred thousand New Yorkers had voted for the ultraconservative Barry Goldwater.) Their newspaper of choice, the *Daily News*—the nation's highest-circulating daily paper—belittled protesters as "Peaceniks" and "Vietniks," and celebrated when GIs placed "Old Glory" atop captured Communist positions. Many shared the Catholic conviction that Communism was the enemy of everything right and true. Growing up in a family of Puerto Rican and Cuban émigrés, Mickey Melendez had been taught that "Communists were atheists who would destroy our way of life and would not hesitate to brainwash all of us and submit our whole society to misery forever."[58]

No community in the city or nation was more divided by the war than Roman Catholics. Time and again, it was militantly pacifist Catholics—Dorothy Day's Catholic Workers, radical priests and nuns, concerned laypeople—who undertook some of the movement's most daring actions, inviting jail sentences by burning draft cards and raiding government offices to destroy or steal military records. But the institutional church, personified by New York archbishop and cardinal Francis Spellman, who was also Catholic military vicar for the US Armed Forces, consistently backed the war; on a visit to South Vietnam, he pronounced it "a war for civilization." Many devout Catholics shared Spellman's sentiments.[59]

Many blue-collar New Yorkers also resented the privilege of draft exemption enjoyed by college protesters and harbored the bitter conviction that student radicals and antiwar liberals looked down their noses with arrogant disdain at the working stiffs of the "outer boroughs." Mayor Lindsay and his liberal supporters symbolized another New York, one that seemed to blend Manhattan-based snobbery, appeasement of poor blacks and student radicals, and a lack of patriotism, all in one distasteful bundle. "The rich liberals, they look down on my little piece of the American dream, my little backyard with the barbeque here," a Brooklyn construction worker remarked in 1969. Many whites reacted with anger, frustration, and a sharpened conservatism to rising crime, what they saw as the encroachment of blacks and Latinos into their neighborhoods, the civil rights movement, hippies, and the emerging women's and gay rights movements. "Two, four, six, eight, we don't want to integrate," young whites shouted at blacks in Brooklyn's East New York in 1966. "Go back to Africa, Niggers!" some of them also yelled.[60]

As the antiwar movement accelerated, war supporters countered with their own Loyalty Day parades, drawing thousands of marchers and applauding spectators. On May 13, 1967, seventy thousand marched down Fifth Avenue in the Support Our Boys in Vietnam parade. Wives of servicemen carried signs reading, "I'm Proud of My Guy in Vietnam," while other marchers held placards declaring "Escalate, Don't Capitulate" and "Down with the Reds." Two dozen nuns and about one hundred laywomen walked, reciting "Hail Mary" while telling their rosary beads. Contingents of off-duty police officers strode proudly, along with American Legion units from the city and suburbs; union locals of teamsters, longshoremen, merchant seamen, and carpenters smiled and waved as they carried banners and flags. But at Ninety-Third Street and Park Avenue, Abbie Hoffman, bedecked in a multicolored cape adorned with the word "Freedom," was waiting to join the parade with a "flower brigade" of twenty East Villagers. "Support Our Boys—Bring Them Home," their banners read. The provocation was too much for some of the spectators. "They came at us with fists, feet, beer, spit, red paint," Hoffman recalled later. "They even ripped up our American flags. Then a flying wedge of cops appeared out of nowhere and escorted us, bleeding and limping, all the way back to St. Mark's Place." Hecklers had already sought to disrupt earlier antiwar parades down the same avenue, hurling eggs and curses at the marchers.[61]

At Columbia, too, the two cities confronted each other. There, an ad hoc conservative student group calling itself the Majority Coalition sought to hinder the radicals during the April 1968 crisis. Among the counterprotesters were law student George Pataki, future Republican governor of New York, and William Barr, later to become George H. W. Bush's attorney general; other members of the coalition were athletes on Columbia's sports teams. By the spring of 1968, the two sides were in a state of barely contained warfare on campus; the previous year SDS members and conservative students traded punches at an antiwar rally after exchanging their favorite epithets. "Fucking jock," the radicals had taunted; "Commie puke," the "jocks" had returned. "Just looking at these dirty, bearded twerps with their sneers and their sloppy girlfriends is enough to make a guy vomit," one conservative student commented. Conservatives were further enraged when radical female students taunted police by shouting, "Go fuck yourself, you pig," and other obscenities.[62]

Beneath the mutual animosity lay a set of class and cultural differences that placed young conservatives and police on one side of the divide and radical students on the other. After the Columbia sit-in, one policeman commented, "Everything I got in life I worked for. It gets me sore when I see these kids, who been handed everything, pissing it away, talking like bums, dressing like pigs." "We're Staten Island.

Majority Coalition members (left) and student radicals fight at Columbia University, April 29, 1968. © BETTMANN / CORBIS.

They're Scarsdale," one young conservative explained. The "jocks" felt looked down upon by those they considered spoiled, arrogant subversives. The "pukes," frustrated at their failure to arouse working-class whites against the war and the system, resented their adversaries' quick resort to the fist. Given the intensity of their skirmishes, it seemed only a matter of time before these two New Yorks would collide in full force.[63]

On May 8, 1970, several hundred antiwar protesters, many of them students from New York University, Hunter College, and city high schools, marched down Broadway in protest against Nixon's invasion of Cambodia a week earlier and the killing of four demonstrators by National Guardsmen at Kent State University in Ohio on May 4. Their placards demanded the immediate withdrawal of American troops from Vietnam and Cambodia, and the termination of military research by local universities. Their destination was the intersection of Broad and Wall Streets, between the Federal Hall National Monument, the site of George Washington's presidential inauguration in 1789, and the New York

Stock Exchange—fitting symbols of the connections between the government's war and American capitalism. Many sat on the steps of Federal Hall, around Washington's statue, listening as speakers denounced the war.

Shortly before noon, the demonstrators heard chants—"All the way, U.S.A." and "Love it or leave it"—and saw American flags approaching above a sea of yellow hard hats. Two hundred construction workers from nearby worksites, including the World Trade Center project, converged around them. Some Wall Street workers out on their lunch break joined the counterdemonstrators. Within minutes, the hard hats had charged the steps of Federal Hall, sweeping away a thin line of police. "Kill the Commie bastards," some shouted. As students tried to dart away, the construction workers swatted at them with their helmets and pummeled them with their fists. At Exchange Place, Robert Bernhard, a Lehman Brothers partner, tried to shield a young man from attack, only to be slammed against a telephone pole himself. When another man tried to help Bernhard, a construction worker gashed the man's head with a pair of pliers. "These people are rampaging but the police are not arresting them," Michael Berknap, a lawyer and Democratic candidate for the state senate, told a reporter after he had been beaten and kicked. The hard hats next turned to Trinity Church at the head of Wall Street, which had become a makeshift hospital for injured students. Workers ripped down a Red Cross banner and tried to do the same to the flag of the Episcopal Church. "I suppose they thought it was a Vietcong flag," deadpanned Trinity's rector, the Reverend John Vernon Butler.[64]

The hard hats' final target was City Hall, ten blocks up Broadway. There, Mayor Lindsay had ordered the American flag flown at half mast in memory of the four Kent State martyrs. One group veered off to smash windows at Pace University on Park Row, where students on a rooftop were taunting them and throwing debris down on them. But the main body crowded the front steps of City Hall, demanding that the flag be raised to full staff. A mailman got to the roof and raised the flag, to cheers from below. Lindsay was uptown at Gracie Mansion, but his aide Sid Davidoff went out on the roof and lowered the flag again. A furious roar and chants of "Lindsay's a Red" erupted from City Hall

Park as hard hats tried to push past fifteen police officers into the building. Fearing total chaos, the police persuaded Deputy Mayor Richard Aurelio to have the flag raised again. The workers sang "The Star Spangled Banner," burned a peace banner seized from Pace students, and went back to their construction sites.[65]

The so-called hard hat riot of Bloody Friday left at least seventy people, mostly peace demonstrators, injured. Three days later, two thousand pro-war marchers rallied again in lower Manhattan. Most were construction workers and longshoremen. They carried flags and placards reading "Impeach the Red Mayor" and "We Support Nixon and Agnew." At Pace University, they yelled up to watching students, "Don't worry, they don't draft faggots." Once more, several peace demonstrators, including a student who flashed the two-fingered peace sign, were beaten. But this time, with the police out in force, fewer were injured; four marchers were arrested, and police acted quickly to get between the flag carriers and students on Centre Street, whom Homer Bigart of the *New York Times* watched as they shouted "obscene antiwar chants." The hard hats, however, were not done. On May 20, some hundred thousand "hawks," organized by Peter Brennan of the Building and Construction Trades Council of Greater New York, converged peacefully on City Hall Park to "show love of country and love and respect for our country's flag." Sympathizers rained ticker tape down on them from office windows. Some marchers briefly hung an effigy of Lindsay from a Murray Street lamppost.[66]

President Nixon rewarded Brennan for his support by making him secretary of labor in 1973. The war had already divided New York's labor movement. In a fiery speech, Victor Gotbaum of the American Federation of State, County and Municipal Employees denounced "a godforsaken war . . . that has turned brother against brother," and blasted American backing for the corrupt Thieu regime in South Vietnam, which "has turned Saigon into a vast whorehouse," just as fervently as Brennan declaimed that "we are supporting the boys in Vietnam and President Nixon." Far from the street rallies, Vietnam had become an issue in the city's worksites and union halls.[67]

The broader meaning of the hard hat riot and its aftermath was to make visible the anger, power, and numbers of the conservative

"Silent Majority" in the most liberal city in the country. The hundred thousand marchers—harbingers of the blue-collar "Reagan Democrats," who a decade later would transform American politics—were a warning omen both to urban liberals in Lindsay's camp and to student radicals who viewed the war as a lever for revolution. Watching the flag-waving workers parade by on May 20, Cliff Sloane, a University of Michigan freshman from Brooklyn, pondered the implications. "If this is what the class struggle is all about," he told a *New York Times* reporter, "there's something wrong somewhere."[68]

The war, and the movement against it, slogged on into the early 1970s. The stalwarts continued their marches, but Nixon's mixed strategy of bombing, negotiating with the North Vietnamese leadership in Hanoi, covert operations against domestic militants, and "Vietnamization" (gradually bringing American troops home and leaving the South Vietnamese to fight their own war) had its intended effect of blunting the interest of millions of moderates in the antiwar movement. Yet the activists' achievements were significant. The nationwide antiwar moratorium demonstration of October 15, 1969, followed by the November 15 march of half a million on Washington, which New York organizer Norma Becker helped to orchestrate, had given the president pause. Nixon and his national security advisor, Henry Kissinger, had planned a major escalation of the war, with massive bombing, mining, and a ground invasion of North Vietnam, and had even discussed the use of tactical nuclear weapons. But "after all the protests and the Moratorium," Nixon himself later wrote, "American public opinion would be seriously divided by any military escalation of the war," and the plan was shelved.[69]

Between 1964 and 1973, protesters numbering several dozen to over one hundred thousand had taken to New York's streets and parks in at least forty-three major antiwar demonstrations; they had also engaged in scores of smaller rallies, meetings, teach-ins, sit-ins, and acts of civil disobedience. Tens of thousands had repeatedly journeyed to Washington and points all over the country to bear witness against a war they felt to be unwise and immoral. Members of the city's congressional delegation, including Bella Abzug, Ed Koch, Elizabeth Holtzman, and Herman

Badillo had become recognized national figures in opposition to the war. When Saigon finally fell to North Vietnamese forces, fifty thousand people gathered in Central Park's Sheep Meadow on May 11, 1975, to listen to Joan Baez, Odetta, Phil Ochs, Harry Belafonte, Richie Havens, Paul Simon, and others celebrate the coming of peace. Despite the disagreements that had divided their efforts, and the continuing murderous turmoil that the conflict had brought to Cambodia, they could find momentary unity under the event's banner and balloons, which read, "THE WAR IS OVER!"[70]

The post-Vietnam era brought new commitments for the New Yorkers who had marched, rallied, and protested throughout the war. Former students settled into careers; many moved on from political activism altogether. But others found meaning in a new—or rather an old— cause: the antinuclear fight. This took the form of opposition to the dangers of nuclear power plants but also to the international proliferation of atomic weapons. True, the immediate local threat seemed to subside. The Nike missile bases around cities had been stepped down; the New York area's last installations, six in New York and four in New Jersey, were deactivated in 1974. Helicopters carried the nuclear warheads away; a few disarmed missiles remained at Fort Hancock on Sandy Hook, eventually becoming a National Parks Service exhibit on the history of the Cold War.

What had not subsided was Washington's commitment to a nuclear arsenal as a presumed deterrent against Communist aggression. Rather than Nike missile sites scattered around major cities, silos armed with offensive and defensive nuclear intercontinental missiles had sprouted across the Great Plains states starting in 1959. Out of sight, out of mind; to antinuclear activists, the remoteness of these warheads lulled Americans into thinking their cities and suburbs were safe from annihilation.

The Reagan administration's reescalation of Cold War tensions in the early 1980s brought old issues full-circle. FEMA (the Federal Emergency Management Agency), the successor to Eisenhower's and Kennedy's FCDA, followed Reagan's directive to "provide for the survival of a substantial portion of the U.S. population" in the event of nuclear war with the Soviet Union. Suburbanites once more were encouraged to dig up their backyards for protection. "Dig a hole, cover it with a couple of doors and then throw three feet of dirt on top," T. K. Jones of the Defense Department advised Americans. "It's the dirt that does it."[71]

For the cities, FEMA drafted "crisis relocation" plans: 150 million Americans would be expected to move to "low-risk rural areas" fifty to three hundred miles from their homes. "Sure, it'll be a hell of a mess . . . ," FEMA official Louis Guiffrida admitted in 1982. "It boggles the mind. But do we just throw up our hands and say, 'Forget it, the job's too big?'" Other government agencies toed the line. "Victory in a nuclear war will belong to the country that recovers first," a Federal Reserve System booklet intoned. To help maintain the postattack economy, Federal Reserve banks would still try to clear all checks, "including those drawn on destroyed banks." The nightmarish prognostications of the 1950s had returned, only with far more powerful warheads.[72]

Reagan's initiatives energized the antinuclear movement. For Norma Becker, Cora Weiss, David Dellinger, Abbie Hoffman, and thousands of others now engaged in that movement, the imperative to forestall World War III had always been a key aim of their opposition to the Vietnam War. Jonathan Schell's best-selling 1982 book, *The Fate of the Earth*, measured the dire realities of nuclear brinkmanship by describing the imagined results of a twenty-megaton Soviet bomb, 1,600 times more powerful than the Hiroshima bomb, exploding six miles above the Empire State Building: "people caught in the open twenty-three miles away from ground zero, in Long Island, New Jersey, and southern New York State, would be burned to death. . . . The mushroom cloud would be seventy miles in diameter. New York City and its suburbs would be transformed into a lifeless, flat, scorched desert in a few seconds."[73]

On July 12, 1982, some seven hundred thousand people flooded through midtown, marching from the United Nations to the Great Lawn in Central Park in support of the Second UN Special Session on Disarmament and the idea of a nuclear arms freeze. It was the largest political demonstration in American history and perhaps the most diverse. One reporter noticed "pacifists and anarchists, children and Buddhist monks, Roman Catholic bishops and Communist Party leaders" streaming by. Their ranks also included Vietnam veterans, Australian trade unionists, Japanese survivors of Nagasaki, and Montana Cowboys

Against Nuclear War. Present on the speaker's podium at Dag Hammarskjold Plaza, on stages in Central Park, and in the march itself were seasoned veterans of New York's tradition of activism, including Peter, Paul and Mary, the Bread and Puppet Theater, union leader Victor Gotbaum, Mayor Ed Koch, and Norma Becker, who once more had played a key organizational role in the day's events. But they were also joined by Bruce Springsteen, "a punk contingent with Mohawk hair tinted fuchsia," according to the *Times*' Anna Quindlen, and New Yorkers who had been children during the Vietnam years.[74]

As always in New York, unanimity was elusive. "I think they're oversimplifying the issue," said a young lawyer watching the procession. "To say let's disarm is simply naïve." "I don't need to be reminded that we're all going to die," a female passerby told a reporter. But Edwin Hernandez, a twenty-year-old City College student, felt differently. "I have a future to take care of. That's the most basic issue there is." Addressing the multitude, City Council president Carol Bellamy affirmed that "we shall not suffer silently the threat of nuclear holocaust." Without realizing it, the demonstrators were embracing one of New York's oldest traditions, that of understanding their home as a place whose vulnerability demanded action to ensure self-preservation and now, perhaps, the very survival of their city.[75]

CHAPTER 10

Declarations of War
Urban Terrorism, 1908–2001

In late 1948, an Egyptian teacher named Sayyid Qutb stepped off an Alexandria-to-New York ocean liner and into an enticing and threatening world. Qutb was a refugee; his political and religious writings had prompted Egypt's King Farouk to order his arrest, and he was fleeing his native land, at least temporarily, for sanctuary in the United States. Qutb remained in New York for only a few weeks, before moving on to Washington, DC, and then to Greeley, Colorado, where he enrolled in classes at the Colorado State College of Education.

But New York left an indelible first impression of America on the Egyptian. He craved meaningful conversation beyond what seemed the prevailing topics of "dollars, movie stars, brands of cars." American women, and their sexual openness, both excited and repelled him, as he had learned en route to New York. "A girl looks at you, appearing as if she were an enchanting nymph or an escaped mermaid. . . . Tasty flesh, truly, but flesh nonetheless." After a conversation with his hotel's elevator operator, he concluded that perversion was a New York City commonplace, with "pairs of boys or girls" enjoying the privacy and freedom the city offered to indulge in sinful homosexual practices. Qutb returned to Egypt in 1950 convinced that most Americans were "a reckless, deluded herd that only knows lust and money." Their culture was blighted by adultery, alcohol, and jazz, and undermined by racism, irreligion, a soulless materialism, and a "primitive" self-indulgence.[1]

Back in Cairo, with his devotion to a fundamentalist Islam sharp-ened by his American experiences, Qutb immersed himself in the Muslim Brotherhood, a militant group often at violent odds with the secular nationalist government of President Gamal Abdul Nasser. Qutb became the Brotherhood's intellectual voice; his writings spread widely through Islamist circles in Egypt and throughout the Middle East. In 1966, Nasser's government tried and hanged Qutb for treason. His mar-tyrdom, however, only confirmed Qutb's status as a thinker who had come to understand the need for an absolutist Islam at war with *jahil-iyyah*, the "barbarity" of the modern state, and with the "corruption" of Western secularism—a corruption he had experienced at close quarters in New York, Washington, Colorado, and California. Qutb's writings, and his personal example, would exert a lasting influence on radical fundamentalist groups in the Muslim world, including al Qaeda. On September 11, 2001, ten men influenced by Qutb's manifestos would fly two jet liners into the Twin Towers of the World Trade Center on the island where their spiritual guide had disembarked almost forty-two years earlier.[2]

Well before September 11, terrorism had become a threat to New York City, as it had to other cities around the world. Terror has always played a role in war, long before the English coined the term "terrorism" to describe the mass executions carried out by the French revolutionary government. ("Thousands of those Hell-hounds called Terrorists . . . are let loose on the people," Edmund Burke wrote in 1795.) For millennia, generals, admirals, and common soldiers had used pillage, arson, rape, and mass murder against the noncombatant populations so essential to supporting armies in the field. If the September 1776 fire in lower Man-hattan was augmented by revolutionary arsonists to deprive the British army and its Tory supporters of their base, as is likely, then it was an act of terrorism.[3]

Starting in the late nineteenth century, however, terrorism took on recognizably modern forms and aims. Radicals driven by new ideologies—anarchists outraged by the inequities of the existing social order, nationalists seeking independence for their homelands—resorted to assassinations and bombings to advance their causes. Their goals were to maximize their political leverage by sparking widespread fear, to gain optimal publicity in an era when public opinion was shaped by the newspaper and the telegraph (and eventually by radio, newsreels, and television), and sometimes to provoke a government backlash to drive the masses into full-fledged revolution. New York would become only one theater in the shifting international drama of twentieth-century terrorism.

But the link between Qutb's alienation and September 11 also suggests something about New York's persistent provocation, its recurring role as a challenge to those bent on violating it. Time and again in New York's modern history, militants have sought to attack and prevail over the city, leaving behind a litany of obscure dates and tragedies forgotten by all but a few. The history of terrorism in New York has its own trajectory, its own declarations of war, and its own cycles of shock, grief, fear, and forgetting. Only with the mass casualties and destruction of 9/11 has that history regained relevance as prelude and background.

The explosion tore through the red brick façade and scattered debris out onto the tree-lined Greenwich Village street. The shock wave shattered windows up and down the block. As smoke billowed from the wreckage, police officers pulled two dazed and bleeding women out of what had been the building's first floor. Within minutes, as firefighters arrived, two smaller blasts sent flames rolling up through the four stories of the building as the front wall collapsed into a pile of burning rubble. The actor Dustin Hoffman carried paintings and a Tiffany lampshade out of his damaged house next door before police barred him from re-entering. As firefighters' hoses poured water into the site and police pushed spectators away, the two unidentified women, who had taken shelter in the apartment of a neighbor, fled the scene, disappearing into thin air. It was the afternoon of March 6, 1970, and the townhouse that had stood for 125 years at 18 West Eleventh Street was no more, the evident casualty of a gas main leak and explosion.[4]

But, as the police soon discovered, the explosion was no ordinary accident. Sifting through the Eleventh Street rubble, investigators found fifty-seven sticks of dynamite and four homemade pipe bombs. Buried under the wreckage were also the remains of one woman and two men—twenty-eight-year-old Diana Oughton, twenty-three-year-old Ted Gold, and another man eventually identified as twenty-one-year-old Terry Robbins. All had been members of the antiwar group

Students for a Democratic Society and of its offshoot, the Weathermen. The two fleeing women, Cathy Wilkerson and Kathy Boudin,
were also identified as members of the Weathermen; the townhouse belonged to Wilkerson's father, a retired advertising executive who was
abroad at the time. The truth was soon clear: the townhouse's basement had been a clandestine bomb factory. Somehow, something had
gone wrong, and a bomb in the making had exploded, rupturing and ig-
niting the building's gas line and killing Gold, Oughton, and Robbins.[5]

The townhouse explosion happened at a time of great turbulence
in New York and around the country. Rallies against the Vietnam War,

A charred void marks the former location of 18 West
Eleventh Street, March 1970. PHOTO BY CO RENTMEESTER /
TIME LIFE PICTURES / GETTY IMAGES.

campus takeovers, marches by Black Panthers, protests by feminists and gay activists: New York in 1970 was a city at war with itself. Nationally, the 1969–1970 school year witnessed 247 arson cases and nearly 250 bombings on college campuses, most tied to racial or war-related policies. On the Lower East Side, Abbie Hoffman later claimed, "I was approached by several arms dealers during this period with offers of hand weapons, machine guns, plastiques, bazookas, mortars. 'You name it,' one dealer said, 'I can get you a tank, even a jet!'" But for the majority of the city's blue-collar, middle-class, and affluent white residents, New York was a place of longed-for privacy and security, a domain of apartments and houses where, its denizens hoped, violence would remain a distant reality consigned to news reports from Vietnam, Chicago, Berkeley, or still-segregated Harlem, watched in the safety of the family living room.[6]

Ted Gold, himself the product of a middle-class upbringing on the Upper West Side, saw things differently. He had been a leader of the 1968 student sit-in at Columbia and was a seasoned veteran of militant antiwar activism. "We've got to turn New York into Saigon," he told an old college friend over a drink in the West End Bar on Broadway shortly before his death. The Saigon he envisioned was the Saigon of the Tet offensive, when Vietcong guerillas brought war into the sanctum of that city's US embassy compound. In 1969, Gold, his Columbia comrade Mark Rudd, and a network of other former SDS members formed the Weathermen (later renamed the Weather Underground) to bring armed revolution to the streets of America.[7]

The roots of the Weathermen lay deep in the idealism of the student civil rights, antiwar, and community organizing movements. But as the Vietnam War dragged on, as the student left became more defiant, and as the government's reactive crackdown intensified, a select few young radicals turned, partly in desperation, to destruction as a tool for change. "After a certain amount of frustration you decide that at least you can make yourself into a brick and hurl yourself," one SDS member commented in 1969.[8]

"A mass revolutionary movement" was needed, the Weathermen's founding manifesto declared, something "akin to the Red Guard in China . . . a movement with a full willingness to participate in the violent and illegal struggle." That manifesto and others amounted to declarations of war against the entire American military-industrial complex. Along with Robbins, Oughton, Wilkerson, Boudin, and John Jacobs, Gold formed a New York collective of the Weathermen dedicated to the idea that only a violent response could end the violence manifested by the United States in Southeast Asia, in the domestic persecution of black activists, and in the malign neglect that left the poor to languish in their poverty. "We were going to bring the war home," Jacobs later recalled. "'Turn the imperialists' war into a civil war,' in Lenin's words. And we were going to kick ass."[9]

Behind the elegant nineteenth-century façade on quiet West Eleventh Street, the homegrown militants had found the perfect safe house. Already, in the early morning of February 21, 1970, two weeks before the deadly explosion in Greenwich Village, members of the collective had planted three gasoline bombs in front of the house of Judge John Murtagh in the Inwood section of northern Manhattan. They scrawled "Vietcong Have Won" and "Free the Panther 21" in red letters on the sidewalk but left no mark identifying themselves. Murtagh was presiding over pretrial hearings in the case of twenty-one members of the Black Panther Party arrested for allegedly planning to bomb Macy's, Bloomingdale's, and three other midtown department stores at the height of the Easter 1969 shopping season. Nobody was hurt when the Inwood gas bombs exploded, nor were there injuries when small bombs exploded that same morning in front of the Charles Street police precinct in Greenwich Village and at army and navy recruiting booths on the edge of the Brooklyn College campus.[10]

By March, the New York collective's immediate goal was to turn Fort Dix, New Jersey, seventy miles away, into Saigon. There, a dance for noncommissioned army officers and their wives and dates would provide a setting for bringing the horrors of Vietnam home to America. As they planned the bombing, Cathy Wilkerson later claimed, "we still didn't talk about the physical impact of the actions, either on buildings or people . . . 'You cannot act with such greed and recklessness without consequences!' I wanted our message to be, and I wanted to say it as loud as we could." It was the bomb they planned to plant in the Fort Dix dance hall, a dynamite pipe bomb studded with roofing nails to shred the dancers, that exploded accidentally in the town-house basement around noon on March 6.[11]

The Weather Underground was not the only activist group that turned to terrorism to achieve its ends. In March 1970, the same month as the accidental explosion at the group's safe house, thirteen other bombs exploded in New York City. On March 12, bombs caused damage but no injuries at Mobil Oil's corporate office on East Forty-Second Street, the IBM Building on Park Avenue, and the General Telephone and Electronics Building on Third Avenue. A letter sent to the offices of United Press International and signed "Revolutionary Force 9" accused the three corporations of profiting from the Vietnam War, "Amerikan imperialism," and "racist oppression." On March 22, a lead pipe bomb attached to a clock detonator wounded seventeen people at the Electric Circus discotheque on St. Mark's Place, and another pipe bomb damaged a stock brokerage on East Tremont Avenue in the Bronx. The incidents continued a trend. New York bombings between June 1969 and the end of March 1970 cost thousands of dollars in property damage and left forty-three New Yorkers injured and four radicals dead. "To hurt innocent people seems to be the fad these days," a police deputy inspector commented after the Electric Circus blast.[12]

A new era in international terrorism had begun in the mid and late 1960s. In Northern Ireland and Israel, guerillas launched surprise attacks that killed civilians. Hijackers commandeered planes (including one from Newark and two from Kennedy Airport) to Castro's Cuba. In New York and elsewhere, anti-Castro émigrés attacked those who countenanced the Communist government in Havana. Three Cuban émigrés were arrested in December 1964 for firing a bazooka at the United Nations headquarters as Castro's Minister of Industry, Che Guevara, addressed the General Assembly. (The shell, fired from the Long Island City waterfront, fell short, "sending up a 15-foot geyser of water" in the East River, according to a newspaper report.) In 1968, anti-Castro militants bombed fifteen New York City foreign consulates, tourist bureaus, and bookstores; two of the nine New York men later apprehended for the crimes were veterans of the 1961 Bay of Pigs invasion force. Black Panthers exchanged gunfire with police in New York and several other cities; incidents accelerated after Chicago police killed Panthers Fred Hampton and Mark Moore in December 1969. In 1970–1971, four New York patrolmen would be killed and two injured by black militants. ("The armed goons of this racist government will again meet the guns of oppressed Third World Peoples," warned a letter sent to the *New York Times* after one shooting.)[13]

Yet as New Yorkers pondered their city's sporadic explosions, and as FBI agents and bomb squads worked overtime to meet the threats, they rarely remembered the city's long history of radical bomb blasts. In the early twentieth century, New York had experienced its first wave of militant violence, one rooted in the era's tensions over industry, labor, and class. Firebrands like the German refugee Johann Most had brought the idea of "propaganda by the deed" from Europe, where some of his fellow anarchists, abetted by the increasing availability of concealable handguns and the invention of dynamite in 1866, assassinated monarchs and heads of state. Violence, anarchists argued, was the only fitting response to the daily violence of factory exploitation, strike-busting police, slum housing, and the other outrages of proletarian life. Their perception of New York, the great financial dynamo and hub of immigrant labor, was shared broadly in leftist circles. "If there is one place in America where the workers have reason to revolt against capitalism and this thing called 'civilization' and to overthrow it," Socialist Louis Duchez wrote in 1910, "it is New York City."[14]

New York's first explosion came in March 1908, when a Russian-born anarchist, Selig Silverstein, threw a bomb as police drove Socialist demonstrators from Union Square. The bomb exploded prematurely, mortally wounding Silverstein and injuring several policemen; the dying man proudly proclaimed that "I came to the park to kill the police. . . . I hate them." A flurry of unsolved explosions followed in 1914 and 1915: bombs went off at St. Patrick's Cathedral, St. Alphonsus Catholic Church on West Broadway, the Bronx Court House, the Tombs Police Court, and police headquarters on Centre Street. In February 1915, an undercover policeman helped to entrap two Harlem-based Italian-born anarchists, Frank Abarno and Carmine Carbone, in another bomb plot against St. Patrick's. Their aim, police alleged, was to attack "the ruling classes, law, order, and the churches." The class war was arriving on the doorsteps of the comfortable denizens of the capitalist metropolis, even if wounds were few and no lives were lost. Mabel Dodge Luhan, the Fifth Avenue socialite and patroness of Greenwich Village radicals, later remembered the era as one in which her anarchist friends frequently "referred to the day when blood would flow in the streets of New York."[15]

In 1919—a postwar year of nationwide economic stress, bitter industrial strikes, and the founding of two American Communist parties in the wake of the Bolshevik Revolution in Russia—leftist bombings resumed after a four-year hiatus. In late April, thirty-six packages containing "infernal machines," some with the false return address of Gimbel's department store on West Thirty-Third Street, were mailed from New York City to dignitaries and industrialists around the country, including J. P. Morgan Jr., Mayor John Hylan, and Police Commissioner Richard Enright in New York. All but one of the parcel bombs were intercepted and defused; the exception blew the hands off the maid of former Georgia senator Thomas Hardwick in Atlanta. On June 2, a month after this "May Day plot," dynamite bombs ripped apart a Philadelphia church rectory and the homes of eight officials and manufacturers across the country, including that of Attorney General A. Mitchell Palmer in Washington. The only fatality was a night watchman on the East Sixty-First Street premises of the New York target, Judge Charles Nott, who had sentenced Abarno and Carbone to prison in 1915. The other targets were linked by their public opposition to radicalism or their advocacy of immigration restriction.[16]

But it was on September 16, 1920, that full-blown terrorism, aimed indiscriminately at the largest possible number of victims, arrived in New York. A bomb on a horse-drawn wagon sitting at the Wall Street curb exploded, killing 38, mostly clerks, messenger boys, stenographers, and drivers in the thick noontime lunch crowd; 143 were seriously wounded. "Free the political prisoner or it will be sure death [for] all of you," demanded crudely printed flyers, signed "American Anarchist fighters," found in mailboxes nearby. (Five days earlier, on September 11, two Italian immigrant anarchists, Nicola Sacco and Bartolomeo Vanzetti, had been indicted for a Massachusetts payroll robbery in which two guards were killed; the flyer probably referred to them.) The site of the blast, next to the US Sub-Treasury, and across the street from the headquarters of J. P. Morgan and Company and the New York Stock Exchange, had profound symbolic value for radicals: no intersection better represented the beating heart of American financial and corporate capitalism. (Fifty years later, a few weeks after the West Eleventh Street bomb blast, the same crossroads would be the site of the hard hat riot against antiwar demonstrators.)[17]

Yet the September 16 bombing also represented something new: an indiscriminate attack on the mass of random passing pedestrians, an assault aimed at terrorizing the entire population, not just selected officials, businessmen, or landmarks. The wagon, packed with fifty pounds of blasting gelatin and five hundred pounds of iron window sash weights to cause maximum shrapnel damage, was the first major vehicle bomb in modern world history. The death count remains the third worst from a terrorist attack in America, following 9/11 and the 1995 Oklahoma City bombing. After tracking and interrogating numerous anarchists, alleged Soviet agents, and cranks, the New York police and federal investigators came up empty, as they also did with the 1919 attacks. To this day, the Wall Street bomber or bombers have never been conclusively identified. (Recent research points to Mario Buda or Boda, an Italian-born anarchist who left for Naples shortly after the event.)[18]

The 1920 Wall Street blast was the last major episode in the postwar wave of radical attacks, in New York and across the country. Anarchists may have been sobered by the horror of the severed body parts and mangled corpses, many belonging to working-class New Yorkers, which littered Wall Street that day. Fifty years later, other radicals also recoiled from bloodshed. A Weatherman bomb injured seven police officers at the NYPD's Centre Street headquarters on June 10, 1970, just over three months after the accidental explosion on West Eleventh Street. But these officers would be the last casualties taken by the Weathermen in New York, for following the deaths of Gold, Oughton, and Robbins, the Weather Underground had shifted its tactics. Henceforth, bombs would only be planted in secluded corners of "Amerikan" targets, with warning given to authorities to clear the area before detonation. "Targeting only buildings, not people, we switched over to 'bombing lite,'" Rudd later noted. Over the next seven years, the Weathermen planted bombs that damaged government and corporate property but avoided human casualties. By the mid-1970s, the Weathermen claimed credit for over twenty-four bombings around the country. But weary of living on the run, most members emerged from hiding in the late 1970s and early 1980s, cutting deals with prosecutors and judges to reduce their sentences.[19]

A few Weathermen, unable to give up a desperate vision of the coming revolution, persisted in violence. In October 1981, Kathy Boudin, David Gilbert, and several other Weather veterans, along with members of the militant Black Liberation Army, robbed a Brinks armored car at a mall in Nanuet, New York, killing two policemen and a guard in the process. Gilbert was sentenced to seventy-five years in prison; Boudin and some of the others were released after serving long terms. From 1983 to 1985, the Armed Resistance Unit, a Weather offshoot, bombed eight sites, including an FBI office on Staten Island, the South African consulate, and the Israeli Aircraft Industries building in Manhattan.

With the exception of these isolated incidents, the era of the Weathermen had passed. Looking back on the era, Abbie Hoffman distilled his own lesson: "'One cannot make an omelet without breaking some eggs,' remarked Lenin. This attitude, however, is a far cry from the terrorism of deliberately taking innocent lives, be they in a classroom, an airplane, or an apartment building." Several of the surviving Weather Underground bombers, continuing as activists, abandoned violence for other, more peaceful forms of political engagement.[20]

While the events of the early twentieth century and the Vietnam War era were hardly identical, some striking patterns linked the two. Anarchists and Weathermen both brought the war home to comfortable, complacent, powerful New York—whether the war in question was the "class war" of the Colorado coal mines or the "imperialist war" in Southeast Asia. New York City, thousands of miles from the brutal bloodshed Weathermen viewed as enriching its Wall Street banks and midtown corporate headquarters, had to become a battlefield, a place of vengeance, and a school of revolution whose lessons the city's own terrified media organs would trumpet around the country and the world.

Narrowly symbolic acts—bombs planted at famous landmarks of business power or government authority—would be strategic shortcuts to insurrection. The invulnerable, arrogant metropolis of the ruling class, its true capital city, would be made vulnerable. Indeed, in the eyes of these militants, the very violence, racism, and greed of the Establishment proved an underlying decay that already made the system vulnerable. Surely, a few well-placed bombs *had* to help precipitate the coming revolution.

But the revolution did not come, either in 1920 or in 1970—quite the opposite, in fact. Although most leftist organizations and spokesmen clearly distanced themselves from violence, the main outcome in both cases was redoubled government hostility and popular discredit for the broader Left in New York and throughout America. To no avail did radicals during the 1910s point out that the terror casualties were dwarfed by the scores of American workers killed each day in industrial accidents, or by the 25 percent of poor American children who died before adulthood, or by the one in twelve New York City corpses that had to be buried in pauper's graves. Instead, the events of 1908 and 1914–1915 earned new accolades for the city's twenty-odd National Guard armories, the Establishment's first line of defense in the class war.[21]

The June 1919 bombings prompted Attorney General Palmer to declare war on those who "seek to terrorize the country" and, using dubious legal maneuvers, to deport hundreds of foreign-born aliens, most of them having no provable connection to radical violence. The ensuing "Red Scare" helped build the career of a young Justice Department lawyer named J. Edgar Hoover, who stood on a Staten Island pier to watch the SS *Buford* carry 249 deported alien anarchists to the Soviet Union in 1919. Across the country, moreover, the bombings only confirmed anti-immigrant feeling and antipathy toward New York. It was natural for the "bomb massacre" to have occurred in New York, the *Washington Post* asserted in 1920; "rather it would have been surprising if this festering sore had not come to its horrid head."[22]

A half century later, the Weather Underground, the Black Panthers, and other militant groups existed in a strange symbiotic relationship with Hoover's FBI and Richard Nixon's Justice Department, which infiltrated radical groups. Undercover federal agents incited militants to violent, self-destructive deeds in order to discredit their movements. Sure enough, bombings and strident manifestos did not win over the hearts and minds of the American masses. An April 1970 Gallup Poll found that a clear majority of Americans wanted stiff prison sentences for bombers and hijackers.[23]

Perhaps the most damning verdict on terrorist bombings was that New Yorkers, and other Americans, simply forgot. Five years after the 1920 bombing, in an era of financial prosperity and a deflated left, a *Wall Street Journal* reporter found that young stenographers strolling through the fateful intersection of Wall and Broad Streets didn't know about the blast. "How quickly time effaces the memory of startling events," the paper commented. In a city bent on the future, new blood arrived, and tragedies faded. And, after all, in a city of 5.6 million, there had been fewer than 300 casualties; a New Yorker had highly favorable odds for surviving an unpredictable attack. The only "plaque" to the Wall Street explosion and its victims is the series of shrapnel pockmarks that still mottles the marble façade of the Morgan and Company edifice at 23 Wall Street. Similarly, rather than fearing another bomb after the West Eleventh Street explosion, a Greenwich Villager focused on the real estate: "In a couple of days they'll turn it into a parking lot." New Yorkers' short memories consigned the terrorists of 1970, like those of 1920, to the dustbin of history. Today, few passersby know why the townhouse rebuilt on the site of 18 West Eleventh Street in 1978 differs architecturally from its stately neighbors.[24]

Although largely discredited as a form of protest, bombings continued in the post-Vietnam years. Most deadly was the bomb planted in a locker near the TWA baggage claim terminal at LaGuardia Airport on December 29, 1975, which took eleven lives, probably the work of Croatian nationalists seeking their homeland's independence from Yugoslavia. But the city's history provided a backdrop for another blast, one that tore through the lunchtime dining room in Fraunces Tavern at Pearl and Broad Streets on January 24, 1975, killing four and injuring fifty-three. Notes left in nearby telephone booths, mimeographed on the letter head of FALN (Fuerzas Armadas de Liberacion Nacional

Puertorriquena, or Armed Forces of the Puerto Rican Nation) took credit for the attack.[25]

The notes denounced "the Yanki government" for resisting Puerto Rican independence and accused the CIA of murdering Puerto Rican activists; they also called for the release of five "political prisoners" held in US penitentiaries. FALN's stated target was the "reactionary corporate executives" lunching in the tavern, but the group had also picked a target of historical resonance. The original tavern building that stood on the site had hosted George Washington's farewell to his Continental army officers on December 4, 1783; FALN was declaring that, because the United States was a nation born in revolution, hypocrisy could be the only meaning of its withholding Puerto Rican independence.[26]

New York had long played a special role, both real and symbolic, for Puerto Ricans. More than any other North American city, New York had developed early trade links with the Spanish Caribbean. By the late nineteenth century, a community of émigré Cuban and Puerto Rican merchants and workers existed in the city. So did a small but active circle of Spanish-speaking revolutionaries. The most important was José Martí, who found work in lower Manhattan as a journalist and as consul for Uruguay, Paraguay, and Argentina after leaving his native Cuba in 1880. Like other revolutionaries—among them Giuseppe Garibaldi (an exile on Staten Island) and Leon Trotsky (a Bronx resident before the Bolshevik Revolution)—Martí embraced New York as a temporary haven. The city, with its Cubans and Puerto Ricans yearning for independence from Spain, was for Martí an incubator for Caribbean liberation. Yet before he returned to Cuba in 1895 to die in an abortive uprising, Martí also expressed his misgivings about America, felt most poignantly in the city he called home for fifteen years. With its banks, corporations, and shipping firms controlling much of the Latin Caribbean's sugar, coffee, and fruit crops, New York loomed as the leading edge of a North American imperialism that might well succeed Spain's. "I have lived inside the belly of the monster and know him from within," he wrote in 1892. New York, in the end, was simultaneously a safe haven and a menace to progress and justice.[27]

Much as Martí had warned, the Spanish-American War of 1898 gave New York businessmen a new role to play in the former Spanish colonies. New York sugar magnates and others made sure Cuba's and Puerto Rico's economies remained captive markets for American manufactures and Wall Street credit; a fundamentally colonial economic relationship dictated low wages and displacement from the land for many islanders. In 1917, Congress granted Puerto Ricans US citizenship but not statehood. Following World War II, thousands took advantage of cheap fares as airlines sought to create a market for passengers between the Caribbean and North America; most settled in New York City. By 1960, New York had more than six hundred thousand Puerto Rican residents and was the cultural capital of the Puerto Rican diaspora.[28]

As the city's Puerto Rican population grew, one of the Caribbean island's most important leaders, Pedro Albizu Campos, lived as a semi-prisoner in a New York hospital. A Harvard-educated lawyer and World War I US Army veteran, the dark-skinned Campos had been enraged by the racism he repeatedly experienced at the hands of Americans, both in Puerto Rico and on the mainland. His Puerto Rican Nationalist Party, founded in 1922, called for independence and resistance to "Yanqui" imperialism. In 1937, he was convicted of "seditious conspiracy to overthrow the U.S. government in Puerto Rico"; released from the Atlanta federal penitentiary in 1943, he spent the final four years of a suspended sentence ill in Columbus Hospital on East Thirty-Fourth Street.[29]

As some Puerto Rican New Yorkers became radicalized in the years following World War II, they began exporting their resistance beyond the city. In November 1950, two New York followers of Campos, Oscar Collazo and Griselio Torresola, journeyed to Washington and failed in an attempt to shoot President Truman at Blair House; Torresola was killed by a mortally wounded guard. On March 1, 1954, four other New Yorkers—Lolita Lebron, Irving Flores Rodriguez, Rafael Cancel Mirada, and Andres Figueroa Cordero—opened fire from the US House of Representatives gallery, injuring five Congressmen on the floor below. "The United States of America are betraying the sacred principles of mankind in their continuous subjugation of my country," read a note found in Lebron's purse after the shooters were restrained by police. The five revolutionaries captured in these two events—still held in

federal prisons in 1975, the year of the Fraunces Tavern explosion—
were the "political prisoners" FALN wanted released.[30]

Formed in the late 1960s, with roots in Puerto Rican nationalism
and pro-Cuban Marxism, FALN had planted ten bombs in New York
and Newark in late 1974 and early 1975. Prior to Fraunces Tavern, an
FALN booby-trap device had exploded in an abandoned East Harlem
tenement; a policeman, lured to the site, had been blinded in one eye.
(As it happened, the officer, Angel Poggi, was Puerto Rican himself.)
Between 1974 and 1982, the group set off at least 110 bombs in Chicago, Philadelphia, San Francisco, and Newark, as well as New York. Incendiary cigarette packs, designed to ignite after closing hours, were put
in the pockets of garments on the racks in eight New York department
stores; pipe bombs exploded in or near Lincoln Center, the Defense Department's Manhattan offices, and several corporate headquarters.[31]

Identifying and tracking the FALN bombers proved difficult. In July
1978, investigators received a break when an explosion in an Elmhurst
apartment led police to the bleeding body of Willie Morales, who had
been building a bomb when it accidentally exploded. Morales lost his
fingers and part of his face in the blast; his arrest took him out of circu-
lation as an FALN terrorist. Yet dramatic gestures continued. In March
1980, armed FALN members raided the New York offices of George
H. W. Bush's presidential campaign on East Fifty-Ninth Street, bound
ten campaign workers, and also threatened to target nuclear reactors
with bombs; the masked gunmen then fled after spraying pro–Puerto Rican independence slogans on the walls. (FALN simultaneously carried
out a similar raid on Jimmy Carter's Chicago campaign headquarters.)[32]

Unlike the Weather Underground, FALN never renounced taking
the blood of incidental victims; bringing war to America, in their
opinion, required it. On New Year's Eve 1982, in their last major attack, the group planted five dynamite devices, wired to pocket watches
and nine-volt batteries, in Kentucky Fried Chicken boxes outside police headquarters and the Federal Building in lower Manhattan, the
Foley Square Federal Courthouse, and the Federal Courthouse in
downtown Brooklyn. The Federal Building bomb blew out several
floors of windows into the street below. The police headquarters bomb
tore the leg off patrolman Rocco Pascarella, who, despite his agony,
was able to describe the KFC box he had seen. Trying to defuse two

bombs at Foley Square, bomb squad detectives Tony Senft and Richie Pastorella were blown into the air when one of the KFC boxes exploded. Both men were severely injured.[33]

A series of arrests finally helped to quell the FALN campaign. The group's terrorism had not brought independence for Puerto Rico, but it had divided New York's Puerto Rican community against itself. "Because of the horror of what they've done, I don't think these killers are going to get much support from Puerto Ricans," the head of a police anti-FALN task force commented after Fraunces Tavern. Indeed, dozens of tips were offered by Puerto Rican New Yorkers trying to help the police run down the culprits.[34]

An old paradox resurfaced: newcomers to the city found in New York a home, but also a political and economic order some blamed for their homeland's troubles. The largest Puerto Rican metropolis in the world was also a target for the island's angry nationalists. Nothing indicated to New Yorkers that in the future, religion, not nationalism or Marxism, would elicit declarations of war against their city.

At 12:18 PM on February 26, 1993, a 1,200-pound urea nitrate bomb, planted in a rental van parked in a subbasement garage beneath the World Trade Center's North Tower, erupted through four floors of reinforced concrete, instantly killing a female office worker, a male hotel worker, and three men lunching nearby. A fifth man, thrown by the blast, died of a heart attack induced by internal injuries. Dozens of cars in the garage burst into flame. People elsewhere in the complex, feeling the floor shudder under them, thought a plane might have hit the building. As police vehicles, ambulances, and fire trucks rushed to the scene, a chaotic evacuation began from the upper floors down the staircases of both towers of the World Trade Center. Fifty thousand people fled the building complex. Over one thousand, many covered in the soot that poured out of wall ducts and up elevator shafts, suffered from smoke inhalation. Dozens spent hours in elevators stuck between floors. Against a backdrop of light snow flurries, gray smoke wafted into the afternoon sky over lower Manhattan.[35]

Watching from the window of the J & R Music World store two blocks away on Park Row, an Egyptian named Mahmud Abouhalima was disappointed that the visible damage from the blast seemed so

Police help a woman flee the first terrorist bombing of the World Trade Center, February 26, 1993. PHOTO BY KEN MURRAY / NEW YORK DAILY NEWS ARCHIVE VIA GETTY IMAGES.

minimal. His comrade Ramzi Yousef, who was across the Hudson River on the Jersey City waterfront, was also chagrined; he had anticipated that the explosion would topple the North Tower sideways into the South Tower, with both buildings collapsing to kill a quarter of a million people in crowded downtown Manhattan.[36]

It was not long before Americans received an explanation for this latest deadly bombing. "The terrorism that Israel practices (Which is supported by America) must be faced with a similar one," lectured a letter, signed "the Liberation Army," that arrived at the New York Times several days later. "The dictatorship and terrorism (also supported by America) that some countries are practicing against their own people must also be faced with terrorism." Americans needed to know that their civilian deaths were no more tragic "than those who are getting killed by the American weapons and support." The letter demanded discontinuation of all American aid to Israel; otherwise other targets, including nuclear ones, would be attacked.[37]

Authorities had worried since the mid-1980s that Muslim extremists might plan to target the Twin Towers, but the actual attack, launched by other assailants, caught the city totally off guard. The contained nature of the mayhem allowed many to react calmly, even with bravado. "It's just another day at the park," a New York Stock Exchange trader told a reporter. But the confusion and shock of the first day, when the cause of the explosion was unknown, also left many feeling edgy and bewildered. "People were saying, 'Is it Bosnia? Somalia? Saddam Hussein?'" a tourist from California commented. "Then it was, like, 'What's next? The Chrysler Building?'" On a Tribeca street corner, Joan Weiss felt overwhelmed. "No one feels safe anymore. . . . You never know if you're going to come home alive."[38]

The identification number on the van's twisted chassis, recovered by investigators in the deep pit, led them to a rental outlet in Jersey City. There, workers reported that Muhammed Salameh, the man who had leased the van, had returned late on February 26, the day of the explosion, and tried to recover his $400 deposit, claiming that the van had been stolen. The arrest of the illegal Palestinian emigrant Salameh on March 4 led to the apprehension of three other suspects, all foreign-born Muslims. While three of the four men, Salameh, Abouhalima, and Ahmad Ajaj, circulated primarily in the metropolitan region's Arabic-speaking communities, Nidal Ayyad, a Kuwaiti-born Palestinian, was a Rutgers-trained engineer working for a Morristown chemical company and living in suburban Maplewood, New Jersey.[39]

A common link between the men was their devotion to a blind émigré Egyptian cleric named Sheikh Omar Abdel Rahman, who preached frequently at the Al-Farook Mosque on Atlantic Avenue in Brooklyn and at the Salaam Mosque in Jersey City, where he now lived. Rahman was an exile from Egypt, where he had played a background role in the 1981 assassination of President Anwar El Sadat. "We must terrorize the enemies of Islam . . . and shake the earth under their feet," he contended during a Brooklyn sermon in early 1993. "The enemies at the forefront of the work against Islam are America and the allies."[40]

In August 1993, the work of an informant named Emad Salem enabled the FBI to indict Rahman and fourteen other Muslim men for complicity in the World Trade Center attack and also for a plot to blow up the Holland and Lincoln tunnels and the United Nations (which

was considered a front for a "new government which rules the world"
on behalf of America, according to one conspirator). A new era in New
York's and the world's terrorist history, one driven by religious fervor,
had begun.[41]

New York's first Arab community, largely Christian, found a home in
lower Manhattan in the late nineteenth century. Not until the Immigration Act of 1965, which opened America's gates wide for the first time
since 1924, did New York and other cities acquire a sizeable population
of Muslim emigrants. By the 1990s, the city was home to some 120,000
New Yorkers of Arab origin, most of them Muslims. Like other newcomers, most of the Yemenis, Egyptians, Jordanians, Palestinians, and
Kuwaitis who formed enclaves in the Brooklyn neighborhoods of
Cobble Hill, Sunset Park, and Bay Ridge were law-abiding, hard-
working people dedicated to gaining a foothold in America and making
a living. By the 1980s, their stores, coffeehouses, and mosques had
brought a distinctive flavor to Atlantic Avenue, a corridor running between the gentrified brownstone districts of Brooklyn Heights, Cobble
Hill, and Boerum Hill. Beneath a surface unity provided by Islam and
the Arabic language, the Muslim community encompassed a variety of
national and ethnic traditions, as well as religious and political opinions
reflecting the diversity of the Arab world.

Despite this variety, for many Muslim immigrants it was hard during
the 1980s to ignore the call of jihad in Afghanistan, where Afghans and
other devout fighters were resisting a Soviet incursion that had begun in
1979. Recast by the Carter and Reagan administrations and the CIA as
a Cold War sideshow, the anti-Soviet war there could also be viewed as
a crusade joining the United States and the Muslim world in common
cause. But in the mid and late 1980s, as the war became a driving force
for Islamic fundamentalism, a more strident note sounded in the exhor-
tations of some clerics and activists. A charismatic Palestinian named
Abdullah Azzam crisscrossed America, urging mosque congregations in
over fifty cities to provide funds and recruits for the holy war against the
Russians. In Peshawar, Pakistan, Azzam had founded the Bureau of Services (Metkab al Khidmat, or MAK) as a recruiting center. Now he
established branch offices throughout Europe and the United States—

in Atlanta, Boston, Pittsburgh, Chicago, Tucson, Jersey City, and elsewhere. Arguably the most important of these American MAK offices, named the Al-Kifah Refugee Center and incorporated in 1987, was located at the Al-Farook mosque in Brooklyn, the same mosque where Omar Rahman would eventually preach.[42]

Some congregants at Al-Farook, including cabdriver Mahmud Abouhalima and Clement Hampton-el, a messenger for Long Island College Hospital, went forth from Brooklyn to wage jihad in Afghanistan. Meanwhile, Azzam continued to spread his message, usually in Arabic. "The jihad is not limited to Afghanistan. . . . You must fight in any place you can get," he told an audience at Al-Farook in 1988. Azzam was, in fact, a disciple of Sayyid Qutb, and he embraced a Manichean vision of a world divided between oppressive infidels and holy warriors. "Today humanity is ruled by Jews and Christians—the Americans, the British and others," he told Kansas Muslims that same year. "Behind them [are] the fingers of world Jewry, with their wealth, their women and their media." In 1989, however, Azzam was assassinated in Peshawar in the midst of factional power struggles. In the wake of his death, the movement Azzam had fostered passed largely into the hands of his disciple and colleague, Osama bin Laden.[43]

Prior to the 1993 World Trade Center bombing, American authorities had been aware of the radicalism of conspicuous Muslim immigrants. But a combination of bureaucratic inertia, lack of coordination and cooperation between different agencies, ignorance, other priorities, and sheer lack of urgency let these individuals enter the country and remain. For example, the US embassy in Sudan and its CIA attaché allowed Sheikh Rahman to obtain a visa to the United States in 1990, unaware that the blind sheikh was on the State Department's watch list for terrorists. A year later, while the New York office of INS was working to revoke his visa, Rahman obtained permanent residency status from the Newark INS office; he had moved from Bay Ridge, Brooklyn, to a new home in Jersey City and into Newark's jurisdiction. In the summer of 1989, the FBI watched the comings and goings of men from Al-Farook, including Salameh, Abouhalima, and Ayyad, who took AK-47s and semiautomatic pistols to a firing range at Calverton, Long

Island, for target practice. But the shooters discovered the surveillance, and without proof of illegal activities, the monitoring ended.[44]

Other clues eluded investigators. In November 1990, El Sayyid Nosair, an Egyptian emigrant, shot and killed the militant rabbi and former Knesset member Meir Kahane after a speech at the Marriott Hotel in midtown. Kahane, whose Jewish Defense League had itself been responsible for several bombings and a death in New York during the 1970s and 1980s, had become an outspoken advocate for driving all Palestinians out of the Israeli-occupied West Bank and Gaza. Nosair was tried and convicted as an angry "lone gunman." Police confiscated boxes of Arabic notebooks and cassette tapes from Nosair's Cliffside Park, New Jersey, apartment. The material included Nosair's musings on the need to "demoralize the enemies of God" by destroying "the pillars of their civilization such as the tourist attractions they are so proud of and the high buildings they are so proud of." But the notes and tapes were not rediscovered and translated until after the bombing of February 26, 1993.[45]

By 1997, five men responsible for the 1993 bombing were serving life terms in American prisons. The blind sheikh, Nosair, and eight others were also behind bars for the plot against the United Nations and tunnels, a plan to assassinate Egyptian president Hosni Mubarak at the Waldorf-Astoria Hotel, and charges linked to the WTC bombing and Kahane killing. Yet jihadist attacks on American targets—the Kobar Towers in Saudi Arabia, the American embassies in Kenya and Tanzania, the USS *Cole*—continued in the late 1990s, as did New York's prominence in the schemes of terrorists.

In July 1997, two illegal Palestinian emigrants living in an apartment on Fourth Avenue in Brooklyn, Gazi Abu Mezer and Lafi Khalil, planned to kill Hasidic Jews (and any others present) by committing suicide with five nail-studded pipe bombs on a B train speeding under the East River during the morning rush hour. Only the quick action of their terrified roommate, an Egyptian named Abdel Mosabbah, led police to the flat where, after a struggle and gunfire, the two were arrested. Four months later, six members of Islamic Jihad, demanding that the United States free Sheikh Omar Abdel Rahman, massacred fifty-eight tourists and four police officers at Luxor, Egypt. Like other

Americans, most New Yorkers saw these episodes as horrific but remote, or if too close for geographical comfort, then as forgettable in
the onrush of daily life. Few heeded the warning of a draft letter confiscated from Nidal Ayyad's computer in March 1993: "We promise
you that the next time it will be very precise and WTC will continue
to be one of our targets."[46]

September 11, 2001, of course, changed everything. The most deadly
terrorist attack in American history, it dwarfed all previous incidents,
propelling the United States into war against worldwide jihadism. The
assault—which saw jihadists using hijacked airliners to launch two
successful attacks on New York and one on the Pentagon—also once
more highlighted New York City's primacy in the terrorist imagination. In the vision shared by al Qaeda and other jihadists, the West
represented an affront to a militant Islam, which would ultimately
triumph and convert the world. American support for Israel, U.S. al-
liances with "apostate" leaders in Egypt and Saudi Arabia, and the
American military presence near Arabia's holiest shrines were outrages
to be ended. The jihad against the Russians in Afghanistan, bin Laden
believed, had led to the collapse of the godless Soviet Union. To provoke the United States into attacking Muslim Afghanistan, the grave-
yard of the Soviet empire, would be the key to the final downfall of the
"far enemy." Striking the American homeland on September 11 would
accomplish these goals.[47]

In bin Laden's scenario, New York played a distinctive role. A blow
against the Wall Street exchanges tantalized jihadists with the promise
of paralyzing the nation's economy. New York also became the target of
a jihadist anti-Semitism, rooted in the writings of Qutb and others, that
went beyond anti-Zionism to attack all Jews without distinction. Qutb,
for example, had taught that Jewish "machinations and evilness" concentrated "the proceeds of all human toil into the hands of the great
usurious Jewish financial institutions." A popular apocalyptic literature
circulating in the Arab world during the 1990s primed jihadists to believe that, since in New York "there are more Jews than in other places,
and in it is their wealth, their banks, their political foundations which
control the entire world . . . for this reason their portion will be a total

The World Trade Center site, September 12, 2001, as photographed from a satellite. Smoke billows over a landscape once occupied by Fort Amsterdam, Pavonia, Black Tom, and other landmarks of earlier conflicts. USGS Landsat 7 Team, at the EROS Data Center.

uprooting." While living in Hamburg, Germany, two of the future 9/11 hijackers, Mohammed Atta and Ramzi Binalshibh, denounced the "Jewish world conspiracy," based in New York City, which controlled international finance and media. New York was also a prime source and symbol of the material self-indulgence and sexual perversions favored, according to one Islamist tract, by "the children of fornication which are numerous today in the immoral prostrate West." Driven by such arguments, federal prosecutors later alleged, Kahane's assassin El Sayyid Nosair had probably planted a 1990 bomb that destroyed a Greenwich Village gay bar and injured three patrons.[48]

For all these reasons, New York's skyline, with its arrogant skyscrapers broadcasting the power of money and secular values, needed to be humbled and leveled. The collapse of the Twin Towers and the successful attack on the Pentagon on 9/11 seemed to confirm the beginning of a new epoch for holy warriors, one fulfilling the vision of an ignorant America drawn into the death trap of Afghanistan and the eventual conversion of the world to Islam and the vanquishing of all "Jews and Crusaders."[49]

For all its lurid novelty, the new vision offered by jihadists like bin Laden recalled older fantasies. Bringing the miseries of war home to a smug, comfortable enemy population had been a goal of the city's assailants from Robert Cobb Kennedy in 1864 to German propagandists in 1918 to Ted Gold in 1969 to al Qaeda hijackers in 2001. New York, seemingly invulnerable symbol of America in all its power and conceit, was supposedly rendered vulnerable to apocalypse by the very values and forces that made and sustained it. For the Virginian Edmund Ruffin in 1860, that force was the free labor system that had created the North's insupportable inequities of wealth and power; his fictional vision presented a New York consuming itself in a cataclysmic class war. For Adolf Hitler, Jewish capitalism and American decadence would collapse in a sea of flames on Manhattan, courtesy of the Luftwaffe.

September 11 was not the first time, moreover, that the city had been targeted in order to eradicate its threatening fascinations— whether in the form of "tasty flesh," financial power, cosmopolitan sophistication, or unfettered expression. In their plans to annihilate (or at least chasten) New York, militants seeking purity in their own lives attempted to exorcize the seductive demons of capitalism, pluralism, permissiveness, and/or imperialism.

None of these visions of the humbling of New York are interchangeable, and only a few of them have actually cost lives. The cataclysm of September 11, 2001, was an event unique in its tragedy, horror, and magnitude. Yet the recurring echo is there, a byproduct of New York's role as the signature city not only of America but also of nineteenth- and twentieth-century modernity.

Epilogue

New York City and its people are resilient. They have adjusted incrementally to an urban culture reshaped by war in the twenty-first century as well as in earlier centuries. Bomb-sniffing dogs and gun-toting officers wending through train terminals, metal detectors and ID checks in office lobbies, long lines at airport check-ins: all have become part of the accepted background static of our daily urban lives. One has to live in and with the city, after all.

This persistence is healthy and life-affirming, but it is also a form of sanity-saving denial. For if the shock, numbness, and urgent grief that New Yorkers felt after 9/11 have largely faded, a lingering vulnerability has not. If history is a guide, New York City will be attacked again in the future as it has been in the past; the difference is that future attacks hold the prospect of being indiscriminate, and perhaps more deadly. Only bad luck and blunders kept Najibullah Zazi and four other al Qaeda operatives from bombing the New York subway in September 2009 and Faisal Shahzad from setting off a car bomb in Times Square in May 2010. Nor has al Qaeda rescinded its post–9/11 threat to use "nuclear and biological equipment" to kill "hundreds of thousands" of Americans. Navigating on foot through a dense rush-hour crowd in Penn Station or Grand Central, one finds it hard not to have fleeting visions, quickly pushed away, of what another attack might bring. Anxieties lie just below the surface, even as most New Yorkers ignore the suggestion of the city's Office of Emergency Management that they compile a "Disaster Plan Checklist" and contemplate the possibility of evacuation or "sheltering" in the event of terrorism or natural catastrophe. The demise of Osama bin Laden and other al Qaeda leaders may bury the fears deeper, but they still exist.[1]

New York's experience of war affords another lesson. The recurrent challenge to New Yorkers has been how to tell enemies from friends in a city of varied, often insular micro-communities. The challenge has been to distinguish spies, saboteurs, and terrorists from their seemingly identical but innocent neighbors. But it has also been about how to balance freedom and diversity against the need for security and survival.

The lessons of the city's legacy in this regard are not especially cheery. Repeatedly, New York communities—black, Catholic, loyalist, German, Jewish, leftist—suffered for the sins of a few; ethnic and political antagonisms fueled sweeping accusations of disloyalty that tainted the innocent majority as well as the guilty minority. This legacy has echoed through the city's recent history and its ongoing public concerns. In the wake of the 9/11 attacks, for instance, many New Yorkers and other Americans opposed the plan to build an Islamic community center two blocks from Ground Zero, arguing that the center's location represented an affront to those lost on 9/11. Given the horrors of 9/11, and the still unhealed wounds of that day, anger and aversion were not surprising reactions to the proposal. But too often in the ensuing debate, fear, ignorance, wholesale stereotyping, and bigotry—embodied in allegations that the center would become an "Islamic Supremacist Mega-Mosque" for terrorist sympathizers or even a base for nefarious anti-American plots—stood in for temperate, discriminating scrutiny. The fact that telling friend from enemy can be a murky business does not exempt New Yorkers or other Americans from the ongoing need to try.[2]

The inevitable paradox of New York, and of America, has been that the very thing that makes them vulnerable—their heritage of taking in the peoples of the world—has always been their strength as well. Robert W. Snyder, a historian who was engulfed in the dust cloud near the collapsing South Tower on September 11, managed to duck into a nearby food court with two other men. There, "we were helped by one man who probably came from the Middle East, another who might trace his family to Ireland, and women with roots in Africa and Latin

America. . . . There might have been a Muslim among us, but we never got around to asking each other's religion. All we did was recognize each other as human beings who needed help."[3]

As during other moments of passion and stress in the city's history, the backlash against Islamic Americans in the wake of 9/11 implicitly denies the important contributions to the city's history of some New Yorkers: people like Abdel Rahman Mosabbah, who foiled the bomb plot against the B train; Emad Salem, who helped the FBI catch the 1993 bombers; the Muslim vendor Aliou Niasse, who alerted police to Shahzad's bomb-laden SUV in Times Square; and the Muslim first responders who sought to rescue New Yorkers at the World Trade Center on September 11, 2001. These men and women were no more "typical" of Muslims than were Ramzi Yousef or Omar Abdel-Rahman, but their stories suggest another legacy in New York, one just as validly part of the city's history. That is the legacy of Paddy M'Caffrey and other Irish New Yorkers who sheltered black children during the Draft Riot; it is the legacy of an unnamed Jew who helped William Powell's family escape a racist mob; it is the legacy of businessman Robert Bernhard, who tried to shield a student demonstrator from the blows of another mob on Wall Street in 1970. New York's wars have pitted New Yorkers against each other, testing and straining the limits of their tolerance and common humanity. It is a test whose challenges will recur.[4]

In the early morning hours of September 16, 2001, four New Yorkers— two white and two Latino—entered the café of Labib Salama, an Egyptian emigrant, on Steinway Street in Astoria, Queens. They began to overturn tables, smashing dishes and a mirrored wall—retribution for the attack on America perpetrated five days earlier. Salama had no link to either the 9/11 attack or to jihadism; his crime was to be an Arab New Yorker with an identifiably Arab business. Police quickly arrested the four, but Salama refused to press charges. "There's enough hatred already. We don't want to make more. Let them go," he told the patrolmen. An hour later, the four assailants returned, thanked Salama, and helped the café owner and his friends clean up the debris they had left behind. Salama, his Egyptian friends, and the four sat drinking coffee and chatting until well after sunrise, sharing their thoughts and emotions about the terrorist violation of their city. As the four men departed, Salama told them, "Next time you want to come and be friendly with us, you don't have to hit us and then say you're sorry. Just come and be friendly in the first place."[5]

In those few hours, Labib Salama and his four new friends experienced the worst and best of New York's long legacy of war.

Acknowledgments

Iwould like to thank the friends and colleagues who, in various ways, helped me to write this book. Marc Aronson provided encouragement and lively conversation throughout the planning and writing stages; our lunches often helped me to bring my evidence and arguments into sharper focus. Jan S. Ramirez, Amy Weinstein, and Katherine Edgerton of the National September 11 Memorial & Museum adroitly and graciously answered my research questions. So did Daniella Romano of the Brooklyn Navy Yard Development Corporation; Ken Yellis, content developer for the project The Brooklyn Navy Yard: Past, Present, and Future; and Robin Parkinson of Exhibition Art & Technology. The libraries and librarians of Summit, Millburn, Westfield, and Chatham, New Jersey, and of Princeton University and the New-York Historical Society provided congenial environments in which to read, think, and write.

Presentations by Mike Wallace at the Gotham Center for New York City History and at Columbia University helped to illuminate the city before and during World War II. Mark Levine shared with me his public school dog tag from his 1950s Brooklyn childhood—a type of artifact I was half-ready to consign to the realm of urban myth until he showed me one. Joshua Brown and Wendy Fisher helped me to understand New York's anti–Vietnam War movement, in which both were active participants.

I benefited from an insightful reading of the book proposal by Robert W. Snyder and from a similarly thoughtful scrutiny of a portion of the manuscript by Benjamin J. Kaplan. The book profited when Luke Dempsey employed his eagle eye to help me cut a bulky manuscript down to a more manageable length. Special thanks go to Robert Frankel, who served above and beyond the call of duty, reading every draft chapter of the manuscript and offering suggestions that saved me from numerous infelicities and errors.

My agent, Sam Stoloff of the Frances Goldin Literary Agency, supported what I was trying to do with enthusiasm and good humor. Lara Heimert, my editor at Basic Books, has strengthened the book with her keen understanding of the big picture and skill at separating the wheat from the chaff. I am indebted to both of them, and to associate editor Alexander Littlefield, senior project editor Sandra Beris, art director Nicole Caputo, Mike Morgenfeld and his mapmaking team, and editorial assistant Katy O'Donnell. Copyeditor Beth Wright added important finishing touches to the manuscript.

The enthusiasm of family members and friends helped to sustain me through the long process of researching and writing New York at War. In particular I would like to thank Deborah Jaffe and David Drake, Amy Worth and Joe Mayer, Roses Katz, Al Katz, Janice Katz, David Hines, Norman Worth and Charlotte Leigh, Kenneth Hechter, and Shirley Berger and Charles Cartwright for their support. Norman Worth generously shared with me his memories of being an air raid messenger in Borough Park, Brooklyn, during World War II, and his experiences as a soldier in the Korean War. His daughter Wendy, my first wife, would have been proud of his contribution to this book.

Finally, and most importantly, I would like to thank Jill, Toby, and Matt, who have ridden the author's roller coaster with me since the project's inception. Their collective love, support, sense of humor, and patience truly made the writing of this book possible. I hope they like the finished product.

Notes

Introduction

1. Edward Robb Ellis, *The Epic of New York City: A Narrative History* (New York: Coward-McCann, 1966), 596; Allan Nevins, editor, *The Diary of Philip Hone, 1828–1851* (New York: Dodd, Mead and Company, 1927), 2:730.

Chapter 1

1. Samuel Purchas, *Henry Hudson's Voyages from Purchas His Pilgrimes* (Chester, VT: Readex Microprint, 1966), 592. As with several of the quotations included in this book, for the sake of the modern-day reader I have modernized the spelling, capitalization, and punctuation of the original text here, which is excerpted from Robert Juet's logbook published in London by Samuel Purchas in 1625.

2. Ibid., 592. The name "Lenape" can be used interchangeably with "Munsee" and "Delaware." All refer to the native people of the New York City area and their kin in the mid-Atlantic region. For recent reassessments of their history, see Robert S. Grumet, *The Munsee Indians: A History* (Norman: University of Oklahoma Press, 2009); Amy C. Schutt, *People of the River Valleys: The Odyssey of the Delaware Indians* (Philadelphia: University of Pennsylvania Press, 2007); and Eric W. Sanderson, *Mannahatta: A Natural History of New York City* (New York: Harry N. Abrams, 2009).

3. Purchas, *Henry Hudson's Voyages*, 592.

4. Ibid.

5. Ibid., 586, 592.

6. Ibid., 592.

7. Ibid., 592–595.

8. Henri and Barbara van der Zee, *A Sweet and Alien Land: The Story of Dutch New York* (New York: Viking Press, 1978), 14; Edwin G. Burrows and

Mike Wallace, *Gotham: A History of New York City to 1898* (Oxford: Oxford University Press, 1999), 21.

9. Robert G. Albion, *The Rise of New York Port: 1815–1860* (New York: Charles Scribner's Sons, 1939), 19–20, 23–25, 28–35.

10. Charles McKew Parr, *The Voyages of David de Vries, Navigator and Adventurer* (New York: Thomas Y. Crowell, 1969), 46. For the Dutch-Spanish war and Dutch trade generally, see Jonathan I. Israel, *The Dutch Republic: Its Rise, Greatness, and Fall, 1477–1806* (Oxford: Clarendon Press, 1995).

11. Simon Schama, *The Embarrassment of Riches: An Interpretation of Dutch Culture in the Golden Age* (New York: Alfred A. Knopf, 1987), 240.

12. Jaap Jacobs, *New Netherland: A Dutch Colony in Seventeenth-Century America* (Leiden: Brill, 2005), 101.

13. Willem Frijhoff, "New Views of the Dutch Period of New York," *de Halve Maen: Magazine of the Dutch Colonial Period in America* 71, no. 2 (Summer 1998): 26; Ron van Oers, *Dutch Town Planning Overseas During VOC and WIC Rule (1600–1800)* (Zutphen, Netherlands: Walburg Pers, 2000), 9–16.

14. "Special Instructions for the Engineer and Surveyor," in Isaac Newton Phelps Stokes, *The Iconography of Manhattan Island* (New York: R. H. Dodd, 1915–1928), 6:10–11; "Special Instructions for Cryn Fredericksz," in *Documents Relating to New Netherland, 1624–1626, in the Henry E. Huntington Library*, trans. and ed. A. J. F. van Laer (San Marino, CA: The Henry E. Huntington Library and Art Gallery, 1924), 132, 135–136, 139–140; Frans Westra, "Lost and Found: Crijn Fredericx—A New York Founder," *de Haeve Maen* 71, no. 1 (Spring 1998): 7–12.

15. "From the 'Historisch Verhael,' by Nicholas van Wassenaer, 1624–1630," in *Narratives of New Netherland 1609–1664*, ed. J. Franklin Jameson (New York: Charles Scribner's Sons, 1909), 88–89.

16. Ibid., 89.

17. "Novum Belgium, by Father Isaac Jogues, 1646," in Jameson, ed., *Narratives*, 259; Edward Robb Ellis, *The Epic of New York City: A Narrative History* (New York: Coward-McCann, 1966), 31; Russell Shorto, *The Island at the Center of the World: The Epic Story of Dutch Manhattan and the Forgotten Colony That Shaped America* (New York: Doubleday, 2004), 187, 207.

18. Elizabeth Donnan, *Documents Illustrative of the History of the Slave Trade to America*, vol. 3, *New England and the Middle Colonies*, Carnegie Institution of Washington Publication 409 (Washington, DC: Carnegie Institution of Washington, 1932), 405, 410, 426; Edgar J. McManus, *A History of Negro Slavery in New York* (Syracuse, NY: Syracuse University Press, 1966), 3–4, 7–8, 11.

19. A. J. F. van Laer, *New York Historical Manuscripts: Dutch*, vol. 4, *Council Minutes, 1638–1649* (Baltimore: Genealogical Publishing, 1974), 269, quoted in Shorto, *Island*, 84–85; Burrows and Wallace, *Gotham*, 34.

20. Anne-Marie Cantwell and Diana diZerega Wall, *Unearthing Gotham: The Archaeology of New York City* (New Haven, CT: Yale University Press, 2001), 144.

21. Michael Kammen, *Colonial New York: A History* (New York: Scribner, 1975), 46; Burrows and Wallace, *Gotham*, 10; "The Representation of New Netherland, 1650," in Jameson, ed., *Narratives*, 300; Donna Merwick, *The Shame and the Sorrow: Dutch-Amerindian Encounters in New Netherland* (Philadelphia: University of Pennsylvania Press, 2006), 19; Paul Otto, *The Dutch-Munsee Encounter in America* (New York: Berghahn Books, 2006), 64.

22. "Letter of Reverend Jonas Michaelius, 1628," in Jameson, ed., *Narratives*, 126–127; Anonymous, "Journal of New Netherland, 1647," in Jameson, ed., *Narratives*, 274.

23. Jacobs, *New Netherland*, 36, 116; "'Historisch Verhael,'" in Jameson, ed., *Narratives*, 84–85; Evan Haefeli, "Kieft's War and the Cultures of Violence in Colonial America," in *Lethal Imagination: Violence and Brutality in American History*, ed. Michael A. Bellesiles (New York: New York University Press, 1999), 33.

24. Van der Zee, *A Sweet and Alien Land*, 106–108, 109–110.

25. Stokes, *Iconography*, 4:148–149.

26. Jacobs, *New Netherland*, 133.

27. Van der Zee, *A Sweet and Alien Land*, 110.

28. Merwick, *The Shame*, 95–101, 109, 114, 172.

29. Jacobs, *New Netherland*, 51–54, 57, 388, 438–439; Burrows and Wallace, *Gotham*, 34.

30. "From the 'Korte Historiael Ende Journals Aenteyckeninge,' by David Pietersz. De Vries, 1633–1643 (1655)," in Jameson, ed., *Narratives*, 208–209; van der Zee, *A Sweet and Alien Land*, 110–112.

31. Van der Zee, *A Sweet and Alien Land*, 112–113; Merwick, *The Shame*, 123–124; Allen W. Trelease, *Indian Affairs in Colonial New York: The Seventeenth Century* (Ithaca, NY: Cornell University Press, 1960), 66–67.

32. Van der Zee, *A Sweet and Alien Land*, 112–113.

33. Parr, *Voyages*, 60–63.

34. "From the 'Korte Historiael' . . . by de Vries," in Jameson, ed., *Narratives*, 191.

35. Ibid., 234; van der Zee, *A Sweet and Alien Land*, 116; Parr, *Voyages*, 212.

36. "From the 'Korte Historiael' . . . by de Vries," in Jameson, ed., *Narratives*, 225–226; van der Zee, *A Sweet and Alien Land*, 117–118.

37. "From the 'Korte Historiael' . . . by de Vries," in Jameson, ed., *Narratives*, 227–228; van der Zee, *A Sweet and Alien Land*, 118–119.

38. "From the 'Korte Historiael' . . . by de Vries," in Jameson, ed., *Narratives*, 228.

39. Van der Zee, *A Sweet and Alien Land*, 109.

40. "From the 'Korte Historiael' . . . by de Vries," in Jameson, ed., *Narratives*, 229.

41. Ibid., 229–232.

42. Van der Zee, *A Sweet and Alien Land*, 137; Merwick, *The Shame*, 135–136, 157–158.

43. Jacobs, *New Netherland*, 139; Merwick, *The Shame*, 175.

44. "From the 'Korte Historiael' . . . by de Vries," in Jameson, ed., *Narratives*, 234.

45. Merwick, *The Shame*, 220–222; Ellis, *Epic*, 67–69.

46. Ellis, *Epic*, 67–69; Burrows and Wallace, *Gotham*, 68–70.

47. This, however, is not to suggest that the Lenape ceased to be a military presence, albeit a diminished one. As late as the 1760s, British colonial authorities had to take into account the belligerence of Lenape groups in Pennsylvania, in New Jersey, and on the New York frontier. See Grumet, *Munsee Indians*, 75–79, 140–141, 190–191, 197–198, 224, 226, 227, 239–240, 261–267.

Chapter 2

1. Isaac Newton Phelps Stokes, *The Iconography of Manhattan Island* (New York: R. H. Dodd, 1915–1928), 4:128, 137–138; "From the 'Korte Historiael Ende Journals Aenteyckeninge,' by David Pietersz. De Vries, 1633–1643 (1655)," in *Narratives of New Netherland 1609–1664*, ed. J. Franklin Jameson (New York: Charles Scribner's Sons, 1909), 196. The English statesman was Sir William Batten, surveyor of the navy, whose anti-Dutch comment was recorded by Samuel Pepys in his famous diary; see Simon Schama, *The Embarrassment of Riches: An Interpretation of Dutch Culture in the Golden Age* (New York: Alfred A. Knopf, 1987), 234.

2. Stokes, *Iconography*, 4:133.

3. Ibid., 4:138–139; Henri and Barbara van der Zee, *A Sweet and Alien Land: The Story of Dutch New York* (New York: Viking Press, 1978), 232.

4. Stokes, *Iconography*, 4:146.

5. Ibid., 4:149.

6. Ibid., 4:133–135; "Report on the Surrender of New Netherland, by Peter Stuyvesant, 1665," in Jameson, ed., *Narratives*, 460.

7. Van der Zee, *A Sweet and Alien Land*, 150–157; Edwin G. Burrows and Mike Wallace, *Gotham: A History of New York City to 1898* (Oxford: Oxford University Press, 1999), 41–42.

8. Edward Robb Ellis, *The Epic of New York City: A Narrative History* (New York: Coward-McCann, 1966), 41; van der Zee, *A Sweet and Alien Land*, 159; Stokes, *Iconography*, 4:118–119; "The Representation of New Netherland, 1650," in Jameson, ed., *Narratives*, 331, 342–343, 347, 352.

9. Van der Zee, *A Sweet and Alien Land*, 28.

10. Ibid., 139, 213, 219–222.

11. Stokes, *Iconography*, 4:212; ibid., 314.

12. Burrows and Wallace, *Gotham*, 40; van der Zee, *A Sweet and Alien Land*, 89–93.

13. Jaap Jacobs, *New Netherland: A Dutch Colony in Seventeenth-Century America* (Leiden: Brill, 2005), 305–312; Stokes, *Iconography*, 4:142; Burrows and Wallace, *Gotham*, 59–61.

14. Michael Kammen, *Colonial New York: A History* (New York: Scribner, 1975), 60–63.

15. Van der Zee, *A Sweet and Alien Land*, 239–242, 249; Stokes, *Iconography*, 4:147.

16. Van der Zee, *A Sweet and Alien Land*, 383, 445.

17. Ibid., 242–243.

18. Ibid., 383–384.

19. Ibid., 381–383; Russell Shorto, *The Island at the Center of the World: The Epic Story of Dutch Manhattan and the Forgotten Colony That Shaped America* (New York: Doubleday, 2004), 285–288.

20. Introduction, "Letter of the Town Council of New Amsterdam, 1664," in Jameson, ed., *Narratives*, 449–450; van der Zee, *A Sweet and Alien Land*, 447–450.

21. "Letters of the Dutch Ministers to the Classis of Amsterdam, 1655–1664," in Jameson, ed., *Narratives*, 414; Kammen, *Colonial New York*, 72.

22. Van der Zee, *A Sweet and Alien Land*, 450–458.

23. Stokes, *Iconography*, Volume 4, 201.

24. Van der Zee, *A Sweet and Alien Land*, 274–275, 431.

25. Ibid., 455, 457; "Report by Stuyvesant, 1665," in Jameson, ed., *Narratives*, 460; Stokes, *Iconography*, 4:239.

26. Stokes, *Iconography*, 4:240; van der Zee, *A Sweet and Alien Land*, 459.

27. Van der Zee, *A Sweet and Alien Land*, 459–460; Stokes, *Iconography*, 4:240; Kammen, *Colonial New York*, 71–72; Burrows and Wallace, *Gotham*, 73.

28. Stokes, *Iconography*, 4:243–244; Kammen, *Colonial New York*, 71–73; van der Zee, *A Sweet and Alien Land*, 460–461; Burrows and Wallace, *Gotham*, 73.

29. Stokes, *Iconography*, 4:244; "Report by Stuyvesant, 1665," in Jameson, ed., *Narratives*, 465.

30. Van der Zee, *A Sweet and Alien Land*, 461–462.

31. Stokes, *Iconography*, 4:244; Kammen, *Colonial New York*, 71–72; van der Zee, *A Sweet and Alien Land*, 463, 473–474.

32. Jacobs, *New Netherland*, 185–186; Burrows and Wallace, *Gotham*, 82; Donald G. Shomette and Robert D. Haslach, *Raid on America: The Dutch Naval Campaign of 1672–1674* (Columbia: University of South Carolina Press, 1988), 165–169, 172–175.

33. Shomette and Haslach, *Raid*, 311–313.

Chapter 3

1. Robert C. Ritchie, *Captain Kidd and the War Against the Pirates* (Cambridge, MA: Harvard University Press, 1986), 87–88, 96–98.

2. Ibid., 50–55, 64–65.

3. Ibid., 113–116, 282; Jacob Judd, "Frederick Philipse and the Madagascar Trade," *New-York Historical Society Quarterly* 55, no. 4 (October 1971): 354–374;

James G. Lydon, *Pirates, Privateers, and Profits* (Upper Saddle River, NJ: Gregg Press, 1970), 49.

4. Lydon, *Pirates, Privateers*, 39–47; Ritchie, *Captain Kidd*, 132–135.

5. Ritchie, *Captain Kidd*, 39, 78, 251 n28.

6. Ibid., 210–211, 222–227.

7. Cathy Matson, *Merchants and Empire: Trading in Colonial New York* (Baltimore: Johns Hopkins University Press, 1998), 63.

8. Ibid., 99, 135, 159, 184–187, 275; Isaac Newton Phelps Stokes, *The Iconography of Manhattan Island* (New York: R. H. Dodd, 1915–1928), 4:453.

9. Wayne Andrews, editor, "A Glance at New York in 1697: The Travel Diary of Dr. Benjamin Bullivant," *New-York Historical Society Quarterly* 40, no. 1 (January 1956): 61–62; Lawrence H. Leder, "'Dam'me Don't Stir a Man': Trial of New York Mutineers in 1700," *New-York Historical Society Quarterly* 42 (July 1958): 280.

10. Stanley McCrory Pargellis, "The Four Independent Companies of New York," in *Essays in Colonial History Presented to Charles McLean Andrews by His Students* (New Haven, CT: Yale University Press, 1931), 104; Michael Kammen, *Colonial New York: A History* (New York: Scribner, 1975), 307.

11. Thomas J. Archdeacon, *New York City, 1664–1710: Conquest and Change* (Ithaca, NY: Cornell University Press, 1976), 107–121; Robert C. Ritchie, *The Duke's Province: A Study of New York Politics and Society, 1664–1691* (Chapel Hill: University of North Carolina Press, 1977), 198–231; David William Voorhees, "The 'Fervent Zeale' of Jacob Leisler," *William and Mary Quarterly*, 3rd ser., 51, no. 3 (July 1994): 447–472; Randall Balmer, "Traitors and Papists: The Religious Dimensions of Leisler's Rebellion," *New York History* (October 1989): 341–372.

12. Kammen, *Colonial New York*, 113–117; Allen W. Trelease, *Indian Affairs in Colonial New York: The Seventeenth Century* (Ithaca, NY: Cornell University Press, 1960), 228–253, 332–336, 340–348.

13. Francis Parkman, *France and England in North America: A Series of Historical Narratives, Part Fifth*, 4th ed. (Boston: Little, Brown, 1877), 187–191; Trelease, *Indian Affairs*, 296–301.

14. Stokes, *Iconography*, 4:639, 666–667, 671.

15. Ibid., 4:451, 702.

16. Carl E. Swanson, *Predators and Prizes: American Privateering and Imperial Warfare, 1739–1748* (Columbia: University of South Carolina Press, 1991), 14, 51; Lydon, *Pirates, Privateers*, 217–218.

17. Stokes, *Iconography*, 4:424–425, 637; Paul A. Gilje, *The Road to Mobocracy: Popular Disorder in New York City, 1763–1834* (Chapel Hill: University of North Carolina Press, 1987), 25–30; Jill Lepore, *New York Burning: Liberty, Slavery, and Conspiracy in Eighteenth-Century Manhattan* (New York: Alfred A. Knopf, 2005), 182–183.

18. Stokes, *Iconography*, 4:450, 625; Carl Bridenbaugh, editor, *Gentleman's Progress: The Itinerarium of Dr. Alexander Hamilton, 1744* (Chapel Hill: University of North Carolina Press, 1948), 50.

19. Pargellis, "Four Independent Companies," 96, 100–123.

20. Leder, "'Dam'me . . . ,'" 261–283.

21. Stokes, *Iconography* 4:429, 674; Ritchie, *Captain Kidd*, 69, 159.

22. Stokes, *Iconography* 4:572.

23. Ibid., 4:444, 445, 456, 684.

24. Ibid., 4:472, 568–569, 572, 590–591, 664–665, 667, 669, 685–686, 692.

25. Ibid., 4:683.

26. Ibid., 4:594, 596, 599, 689, 694, 706, 708, 721; Lydon, *Pirates, Privateers*, 147–148, 226; Gary B. Nash, *The Urban Crucible: Social Change, Political Consciousness, and the Origins of the American Revolution* (Cambridge, MA: Harvard University Press, 1979), 467 n66; Bridenbaugh, *Gentleman's Progress*, 46.

27. Nash, *Urban Crucible*, 177, 235–236, 257; Matson, *Merchants*, 156, 157–158, 266–270.

28. Thomas M. Truxes, *Defying Empire: Trading with the Enemy in Colonial New York* (New Haven, CT: Yale University Press, 2008), 37–48, 50, 145; Matson, *Merchants*, 277, 279–280; Stokes, *Iconography*, 4:475, 583, 586, 589, 609, 673, 690; Lydon, *Pirates, Privateers*, 103–105, 119–121.

29. Truxes, *Defying Empire*, 87–104, 149–151.

30. Lydon, *Pirates, Privateers*, 147–148; Nash, *Urban Crucible*, 236–239; Matson, *Merchants*, 158, 219–220, 232, 273–274; Swanson, *Predators and Prizes*, 106, 187; Stokes, *Iconography*, 4:456, 471, 472, 564, 565, 580, 597, 668, 671, 680, 694, 697, 706.

31. "Muster Rolls of the New York Provincial Troops," *Collections of the New-York Historical Society, 1881* (New York, 1882), 162–167, 170–175, 206–213, 292–309, 374–379.

32. Lydon, *Pirates, Privateers*, 35, 153, 221, 233, 274–279; Swanson, *Predators and Prizes*, 76, 77, 89, 93, 95, 120, 124, 216; Stokes, *Iconography*, 4:576, 697; Stuyvesant Fish, *The New York Privateers, 1756–1763* (New York: George Grady Press, 1945), 12–15.

33. Lydon, *Pirates, Privateers*, 131–132, 173, 178.

34. Ibid., 151–152, 171; Stokes, *Iconography*, 4:583; James G. Lydon, "The Great Capture of 1744," *New-York Historical Society Quarterly* 52, no. 3 (July 1968): 255–269.

35. Swanson, *Predators and Prizes*, 15, 40–41, 47; Lydon, *Pirates, Privateers*, 110–125.

36. Swanson, *Predators and Prizes*, 59; Lydon, *Pirates, Privateers*, 87–88, 103, 113–114, 200; Lepore, *New York Burning*, 161.

37. Lepore, *New York Burning*, 49–50, 78–79; Serena R. Zabin, editor, *The New York Conspiracy Trials of 1741: Daniel Horsmanden's Journal of the Proceedings with Related Documents* (Boston: Bedford/St. Martin's Press, 2004), 56–57, 99.

38. Lepore, *New York Burning*, xi; Zabin, *Conspiracy Trials*, 16; Kenneth Scott, "The Slave Insurrection in New York in 1712," *New-York Historical Society Quarterly* 45, no. 1 (January 1961): 43–74.

39. Lepore, *New York Burning*, xvi; Zabin, *Conspiracy Trials*, 45, 60, 85, 91–92, 112, 117.

40. Lepore, *New York Burning*, 126, 176–178; Zabin, *Conspiracy Trials*, 159, 174.

41. Edwin G. Burrows and Mike Wallace, *Gotham: A History of New York City to 1898* (Oxford: Oxford University Press, 1999), 163–165; Peter Linebaugh and Marcus Rediker, *The Many-Headed Hydra: Sailors, Slaves, Commoners, and the Hidden History of the Revolutionary Atlantic* (Boston: Beacon Press, 2000), 174–210; Zabin, *Conspiracy Trials*, 46.

42. Nash, *Urban Crucible*, 236, 248; Pargellis, "Four Independent Companies," 121.

43. Nash, *Urban Crucible*, 248.

44. Matson, *Merchants & Empire*, 83; Lydon, *Pirates, Privateers*, 18, 193–195; Pauline Maier, *The Old Revolutionaries: Political Lives in the Age of Samuel Adams* (New York: Alfred A. Knopf, 1980), 59–61; "George Clinton's Cruise on the Privateer *Defiance*," *New York History* 16, no. 1 (January 1935): 89–95.

Chapter 4

1. Isaac Newton Phelps Stokes, *The Iconography of Manhattan Island* (New York: R. H. Dodd, 1915–1928), 4:916, 919, 923–924; Barnet Schecter, *The Battle for New York: The City at the Heart of the American Revolution* (New York: Penguin Books, 2002), 84.

2. Schecter, *Battle for New York*, 59–60.

3. Stokes, *Iconography*, 4:928; David McCullough, *1776* (New York: Simon & Schuster, 2005), 125; John J. Gallagher, *The Battle of Brooklyn, 1776* (Edison, NJ: Castle Books, 1995), 69; Thomas Jefferson Wertenbaker, *Father Knickerbocker Rebels: New York City During the Revolution* (New York: Charles Scribner's Sons, 1948), 79.

4. Bayrd Still, *Mirror for Gotham: New York as Seen by Contemporaries from Dutch Days to the Present* (1956; repr., New York: Fordham University Press, 1994), 16; Richard M. Ketchum, *Divided Loyalties: How the American Revolution Came to New York* (New York: Henry Holt, 2002), 278.

5. Ketchum, *Divided Loyalties*, 208, 240–241.

6. Pauline Maier, *The Old Revolutionaries: Political Lives in the Age of Samuel Adams* (New York: Alfred A. Knopf, 1980), 59–60, 63–73, 74–76, 80, 91–92, 99–100; Peter Linebaugh and Marcus Rediker, *The Many-Headed Hydra: Sailors, Slaves, Commoners, and the Hidden History of the Revolutionary Atlantic* (Boston: Beacon Press, 2000), 40–42, 48; Ketchum, *Divided Loyalties*, 218–220.

7. Stokes, *Iconography*, 4:854, 882; Ketchum, *Divided Loyalties*, 266–267, 276.

8. Ketchum, *Divided Loyalties*, 150; Stokes, *Iconography*, 4:866.

9. Wertenbaker, *Father Knickerbocker*, 57; Ketchum, *Divided Loyalties*, 353–354; Bruce Bliven Jr., *Under the Guns: New York: 1775–1776* (New York: Harper & Row, 1972), 35–39; Schecter, *Battle for New York*, 63–64.

10. Maier, *Old Revolutionaries*, 89; Wertenbaker, *Father Knickerbocker*, 55, 80–81; Stokes, *Iconography*, 4:901; Alexander Rose, *Washington's Spies: The Story of America's First Spy Ring* (New York: Bantam Books, 2006), 256; Ketchum, *Divided Loyalties*, 342–343.

11. Bliven, *Under the Guns*, 185–186, 281.

12. Schecter, *Battle for New York*, 96–97; Bliven, *Under the Guns*, 301–312, 315–316.

13. Gallagher, *Battle of Brooklyn*, 50, 53; McCullough, *1776*, 210.

14. McCullough, *1776*, 193.

15. Schecter, *Battle for New York*, 96, 99; Bliven, *Under the Guns*, 319; Gallagher, *Battle of Brooklyn*, 66–67; Stokes, *Iconography*, 4:935; Ketchum, *Divided Loyalties*, 336.

16. Rose, *Washington's Spies*, 11; Stokes, *Iconography*, 5:992.

17. Stokes, *Iconography*, 4:937.

18. Gallagher, *Battle of Brooklyn*, 93–94.

19. Edwin G. Burrows, "Kings County," in *The Other New York: The American Revolution Beyond New York City, 1763–1787*, ed. Joseph S. Tiedemann and Eugene R. Fingerhut (Albany: State University of New York Press, 2005), 27; Schecter, *Battle for New York*, 131.

20. Schecter, *Battle for New York*, 123.

21. Ibid., 136–137.

22. Gallagher, *Battle of Brooklyn*, 107.

23. The Red Lion Tavern was located at the approximate site of Thirty-Ninth Street and Fifth Avenue in Brooklyn. Ibid., 102; Schecter, *Battle for New York*, 141.

24. Joseph Plumb Martin, *A Narrative of a Revolutionary Soldier* (New York: Signet Classic, 2001), 22.

25. McCullough, *1776*, 173–174.

26. Burrows, "Kings County," 24–30.

27. Gallagher, *Battle of Brooklyn*, 127.

28. Ibid., 54, 131–132; Martin, *Narrative*, 24; McCullough, *1776*, 177.

29. Gallagher, *Battle of Brooklyn*, 113, 135–136.

30. Martin, *Narrative*, 26–27.

31. Schecter, *Battle for New York*, 156–157; McCullough, *1776*, 120; Gallagher, *Battle of Brooklyn*, 147–148.

32. Gallagher, *Battle of Brooklyn*, 149, 152–153.

33. Schecter, *Battle for New York*, 149, 166, 175–177; Wertenbaker, *Father Knickerbocker*, 94.

34. Martin, *Narrative*, 30–31.

35. Schecter, *Battle for New York*, 185–186.

36. Ibid., 197–198; Stokes, *Iconography*, 5:1025.

37. Stokes, *Iconography*, 5:1017; Gallagher, *Battle of Brooklyn*, 163.

38. Stokes, *Iconography*, 5:1020–1024; Wertenbaker, *Father Knickerbocker*, 98–102.

39. Wertenbaker, *Father Knickerbocker*, 102; Stokes, *Iconography*, 5:1169.

40. Wertenbaker, *Father Knickerbocker*, 98–99; McCullough, *1776*, 223.

41. Schecter, *Battle for New York*, 254; Edwin G. Burrows, *Forgotten Patriots: The Untold Story of American Prisoners During the Revolutionary War* (New York: Basic Books, 2008), 44–46.

42. McCullough, *1776*, 179; Wertenbaker, *Father Knickerbocker*, 97, 113.

43. McCullough, *1776*, 283.

44. Stokes, *Iconography*, 5:1075;Wertenbaker, *Father Knickerbocker*, 104.

45. Wertenbaker, *Father Knickerbocker*, 209; Stokes, *Iconography*, 5:1047, 1081, 1083; Rose, *Washington's Spies*, 103–104.

46. Stokes, *Iconography*, 5:1027, 1058, 1083, 1096, 1123, 1143; Jacob Judd, "Westchester County," in Tiedemann and Fingerhut, eds., *The Other New York*, 119.

47. Schecter, *Battle for New York*, 113–114; Cassandra Pybus, *Epic Journeys of Freedom: Runaway Slaves of the American Revolution and Their Global Quest for Liberty* (Boston: Beacon Press, 2006), 24–27; Graham Russell Hodges, *Root & Branch: African Americans in New York & East Jersey, 1613–1863* (Chapel Hill: University of North Carolina Press, 1999), 139–140, 144–151.

48. Pybus, *Epic Journeys*, 26, 31, 33–34, 212, 218, 219; Hodges, *Root & Branch*, 151–152, 159.

49. Stokes, *Iconography*, 5:1021–1022, 1058, 1100–1101; Schecter, *Battle for New York*, 275.

50. Burrows, *Forgotten Patriots*, xi, 200–201, 209–210; Kenneth T. Jackson, "The Forgotten Saga of New York's Prison Ships," *Seaport: New York's History Magazine* 24, no. 1 (Summer 1990): 26–28; Stokes, *Iconography*, 5:1040, 1133, 1153; Wertenbaker, *Father Knickerbocker*, 161–164; Schecter, *Battle for New York*, 274–275; Philip Papas, "Richmond County, Staten Island," in Tiedemann and Fingerhut, eds., *The Other New York*, 94–95; Judith L. Van Buskirk, *Generous Enemies: Patriots and Loyalists in Revolutionary New York* (Philadelphia: University of Pennsylvania Press, 2002), 193.

51. Stokes, *Iconography*, 5:1009, 1108.

52. Ibid., 5:1069–1070, 1071, 1094, 1096, 1114; Rose, *Washington's Spies*, 178; Schecter, *Battle for New York*, 310–312, 315–317.

53. Rose, *Washington's Spies*, 15, 90, 101, 125. 132–133, 154.

54. Schecter, *Battle for New York*, 324; Stokes, *Iconography*, 5:1054, 1092, 1100, 1132.

55. Schecter, *Battle for New York*, 345.

56. Ibid., 347–348, 353–354; Stokes, *Iconography*, 5:1132.

57. Schecter, *Battle for New York*, 354–355; Stokes, *Iconography*, 5:1134–1135.

58. Stokes, *Iconography*, 5:1135.

59. Ibid., 5:1138–1139.

60. Ibid., 5:1169, 1172, 1173.

61. Wertenbaker, *Father Knickerbocker*, 250, 251, 257.

62. Ibid., 260–266; Stokes, *Iconography*, 5:1159, 1160–1161, 1168; Pybus, *Epic Journeys*, 67–68; Van Buskirk, *Generous Enemies*, 175–176; Hodges, *Root & Branch*, 158.

63. Stokes, *Iconography*, 5:1180.

Chapter 5

1. *Diary* (New York), July 30, 1793, 2, August 6, 1793, 3; *New-York Journal, & Patriotic Register*, July 31, 1793, 3, August 7, 1793, 3; Isaac Newton Phelps Stokes, *The Iconography of Manhattan Island* (New York: R. H. Dodd, 1915–1928), 5:1299.

2. New York *Diary*, August 2, 1793, 3, August 3, 1793, 3, August 6, 1793, 3; *New-York Journal, & Patriotic Register*, August 7, 1793, 3; New York *Weekly Museum*, August 3, 1793, 3.

3. Charles William Janson, *The Stranger in America, 1796–1806* (New York: The Press of the Pioneers, 1935), 439; New York *Weekly Museum*, August 3, 1793, 3; New York *Diary*, August 6, 1793, 3.

4. Janson, *Stranger*, 439.

5. Stokes, *Iconography*, 5:1296, 1297, 1300; ibid., 439–440.

6. Stokes, *Iconography*, 5:1476.

7. John P. Kaminski, *George Clinton: Yeoman Politician of the New Republic* (Madison, WI: Madison House Publishers, 1993), 240.

8. Ibid., 241; Stokes, *Iconography*, 5:1307–1309, 1353–1355.

9. Stokes, *Iconography*, 1354–1355, 1356.

10. James Fulton Zimmerman, *Impressment of American Seamen* (Port Washington, NY: Kennikat Press, 1966), 30, 33–35.

11. William M. P. Dunne and Frederick C. Leiner, "An 'Appearance of Menace': The Royal Navy's Incursion in New York Bay, September 1807," *The Log of Mystic Seaport* 44, no. 44 (Spring 1993): 90–91; Paul A. Gilje, *Liberty on the Waterfront: American Maritime Culture in the Age of Revolution* (Philadelphia: University of Pennsylvania Press, 2004), 158.

12. Alfred F. Young, *The Democratic Republicans of New York: The Origins, 1763–1797* (Chapel Hill: University of North Carolina Press, 1967), 478; Stokes, *Iconography*, 5:1445–1446; Edwin G. Burrows and Mike Wallace, *Gotham: A History of New York City to 1898* (Oxford: Oxford University Press, 1999), 409–410.

13. Stokes, *Iconography*, 5:1472; Dunne and Leiner, "'Appearance,'" 89–91.

14. John C. Fredriksen, "Williams, Jonathan," in *American National Biography*, ed. John A. Garraty and Mark C. Carnes (New York: Oxford University Press, 1999), 23:483–484; Stokes, *Iconography*, 5:1450.

15. Stokes, *Iconography*, 5:1464–1465.

16. Ibid., 5:1450–1451, 1464–1465, 1466–1468, 1469–1470, 1478–1479, 1496, 1538; R. S. Guernsey, *New York City and Vicinity During the War of 1812–15* (New York: Charles L. Woodward, 1889), 1:68, 69.

17. Stokes, *Iconography*, 5:1463, 1468–1470, 1478, 1491, 1496, 1499, 1515, 1526, 1538, 1559.

18. Ibid., 5:1549; William S. Dudley, editor, *The Naval War of 1812: A Documentary History* (Washington, DC: Naval Historical Center, 1985), 1:119.

19. Stokes, *Iconography*, 5:1475–1478, 1536, 1545, 1550; Guernsey, *New York City and Vicinity*, 1:9.

20. Guernsey, *New York City and Vicinity*, 1:17, 188–189.

21. Stokes, *Iconography*, 5:1550, 1564, 1570; Ibid., 1:123, 125–126, 317; R. S. Guernsey, *New York City and Vicinity During the War of 1812–15* (New York: Charles L. Woodward, 1895), 2:530, 532–534; Robert G. Albion, *The Rise of New York Port: 1815–1860* (New York: Charles Scribner's Sons, 1939), 287, 289; Dudley, ed., *Naval War*, 1: 296–298, 303, 315, 324, 370, 502.

22. Guernsey, *New York City and Vicinity*, 1:20–21, 345–353; Guernsey, *New York City and Vicinity*, 2:66–67, 270, 404–406; David S. Heidler and Jeanne T. Heidler, editors, *Encyclopedia of the War of 1812* (Santa Barbara: ABC-Clio, 1997), 36–37, 182–185.

23. Guernsey, *New York City and Vicinity*, 1:120–121.

24. Ibid., 1:275–276, 381, 383; Stokes, *Iconography*, 5:1541, 1561.

25. Guernsey, *New York City and Vicinity*, 1:217–218, 273.

26. Ibid., 1:120; Dudley, ed., *Naval War*, 1:202.

27. Guernsey, *New York City and Vicinity*, 1:218–219, 277.

28. Ibid., 1:86–87, 202.

29. Stokes, *Iconography*, 5:1543, 1555, 1557; Guernsey, *New York City and Vicinity*, 2:39–40; Guernsey, *New York City and Vicinity*, 1:116.

30. Guernsey, *New York City and Vicinity*, 2:142–144.

31. Guernsey, *New York City and Vicinity*, 1:12, 166–167, 173–175, 179, 301, 325–326, 344; ibid., 2:40–42, 87–88, 307; William S. Dudley, editor, *The Naval War of 1812: A Documentary History* (Washington, DC: Naval Historical Center, 1992), 2:39–41, 52, 106; Stokes, *Iconography*, 5:1561.

32. Dudley, ed., *Naval War*, 2:109; Guernsey, *New York City and Vicinity*, 1:216.

33. Guernsey, *New York City and Vicinity*, 1:266–267, 298–300; Stokes, *Iconography*, 5:1564.

34. Guernsey, *New York City and Vicinity*, 1:382–383.

35. Kirkpatrick Sale, *The Fire of His Genius: Robert Fulton and the American Dream* (New York: Touchstone, 2002), 6, 66–67, 81, 96, 105, 112–113, 141.

36. Barnet Schecter, *The Battle for New York: The City at the Heart of the American Revolution* (New York: Penguin Books, 2002), 171–174; Stokes, *Iconography*, 5:1463, 1467; Guernsey, *New York City and Vicinity*, 1:277–279; "Plans for Defending Our Harbour. By William Wizard, Esq.," *Salmagundi* No. XIII, Friday, August 14, 1807, in Washington Irving, *History, Tales and Sketches* (New York: The Library of America, 1983), 239–240.

37. Stokes, *Iconography*, 5:1559, 1560; Guernsey, *New York City and Vicinity*, 1:277–280.

38. Stokes, *Iconography*, 5:1567, 1568, 1571, 1572, 1577; Sale, *Fire*, 158–160.

39. Stokes, *Iconography*, 5:1576, 1577, 1582, 1582; Sale, *Fire*, 171, 179.

40. Sale, *Fire*, 169, 179–180.

41. Stokes, *Iconography*, 5:1565; Raymond A. Mohl, *Poverty in New York: 1783–1825* (New York: Oxford University Press, 1971), 113–114.

42. Guernsey, *New York City and Vicinity*, 1:5, 8, 216, 217, 236.

43. Stokes, *Iconography*, 5:1561, 1571; Guernsey, *New York City and Vicinity*, 2:90, 151, 213.

44. Stokes, *Iconography*, 5:1481, 1571, 1572, 1573, 1577; Guernsey, *New York City and Vicinity*, 2:45–46, 190–191, 389–400.

45. Stokes, *Iconography*, 5:1574; Guernsey, *New York City and Vicinity*, 2: 247.

46. Guernsey, *New York City and Vicinity*, 2: 196, 199, 230, 293, 331; Stokes, *Iconography*, 5:1573–1574, 1576.

47. New York *Columbian*, September 1, 1814, 3.

48. Stokes, *Iconography*, 5:1574; *New-York Evening Post*, August 22, 1814, 2.

49. Guernsey, *New York City and Vicinity*, 2: 232–233; Stokes, *Iconography*, 5:1575.

50. Michael J. Crawford, editor, *The Naval War of 1812: A Documentary History* (Washington, DC: Naval Historical Center, 2002), 3:129, 133.

51. Guernsey, *New York City and Vicinity*, 2:222.

52. Ibid., 2:456–457.

53. Ibid., 2:441.

54. Stokes, *Iconography*, 5:1558.

Chapter 6

1. Allan Nevins and Milton Halsey Thomas, editors, *The Diary of George Templeton Strong* (New York: Macmillan, 1952), 3:124, 127.

2. Ibid., 3:129, 236; Emory Holloway, editor, *The Uncollected Poetry and Prose of Walt Whitman* (New York: Doubleday, 1921), 142; George J. Lankevich, *New York City: A Short History* (New York: New York University Press, 2002), 68.

3. Mike Wallace, "Nueva York: The Back Story," in *Nueva York: 1613–1945*, ed. Edward J. Sullivan (New York: New-York Historical Society, 2010), 26–28,

38; Thomas P. Southwick, *A Duryee Zouave* (Brookneal, VA: Patrick A. Schroeder Publications, 1995), 36.

4. Maria Lydig Daly, *Diary of a Union Lady, 1861–1865* (Lincoln: University of Nebraska Press, 2000), 19–21; Edward K. Spann, *Gotham at War: New York City, 1860–1865* (Wilmington, DE: Scholarly Resources, 2002), 21, 23, 25; Ernest A. McKay, *The Civil War and New York City* (Syracuse, NY: Syracuse University Press, 1990), 63.

5. Nevins and Thomas, *Strong Diary*, 3:169; Daly, *Diary*, 41.

6. Robert G. Albion, *The Rise of New York Port, 1815–1860* (New York: Charles Scribner's Sons, 1939), 400.

7. McKay, *Civil War and New York*, 13, 18; Warren S. Howard, *American Slavers and the Federal Law, 1837–1862* (Berkeley: University of California Press, 1963), 49–53, 79, 81–83, 127–129, 223, 224–235, 249–252; Philip S. Foner, *Business and Slavery: The New York Merchants and the Irrepressible Conflict* (Chapel Hill: University of North Carolina Press, 1941), 164–168.

8. McKay, *Civil War and New York*, 19, 44, 45; Harold Holzer, "Housekeeping on Its Own Terms: Abraham Lincoln in New York," in *State of the Union: New York and the Civil War*, ed. Harold Holzer (New York: Fordham University Press, 2002), 4, 8.

9. Allan Nevins and Milton Halsey Thomas, editors, *The Diary of George Templeton Strong* (New York: Macmillan, 1952), 2:240, 273–274, 480.

10. Ibid., 2:182; McKay, *Civil War and New York*, 231.

11. Hasia R. Diner, "'The Most Irish City in the Union': The Era of the Great Migration, 1844–1877," in *The New York Irish*, ed. Ronald H. Bayor and Timothy J. Meagher (Baltimore: Johns Hopkins University Press, 1996), 92; McKay, *Civil War and New York*, 296; Adrian Cook, *The Armies of the Streets: The New York City Draft Riots of 1863* (Lexington: University Press of Kentucky, 1974), 14.

12. Barnet Schecter, *The Devil's Own Work: The Civil War Draft Riots and the Fight to Reconstruct America* (New York: Walker, 2006), 70; Iver Bernstein, *The New York City Draft Riots: Their Significance for American Society and Politics in the Age of the Civil War* (New York: Oxford University Press, 1990), 146.

13. Daly, *Diary*, 43; Schecter, *Devil's Own Work*, 44.

14. Schecter, *Devil's Own Work*, 143; Edwin G. Burrows and Mike Wallace, *Gotham: A History of New York City to 1898* (Oxford: Oxford University Press, 1999), 856–857.

15. Schecter, *Devil's Own Work*, 40–41.

16. Spann, *Gotham at War*, 23–25, 32–42, 45–46, 137; McKay, *Civil War and New York*, 94–96, 101–102, 140–141, 289; Nevins and Thomas, *Strong Diary*, 3:137–138, 144, 244; Burrows and Wallace, *Gotham*, 875.

17. Spann, *Gotham at War*, 149–153.

18. Schecter, *Devil's Own Work*, 91.

19. Thomas Kessner, *Capital City: New York City and the Men Behind America's Rise to Economic Dominance, 1860–1900* (New York: Simon & Schuster, 2003), 39; McKay, *Civil War and New York*, 216; Spann, *Gotham at War*, 145; Daly, *Diary*, 192–193.

20. Southwick, *Duryee Zouave*, 63; McKay, *Civil War and New York*, 130, 171.

21. Southwick, *Duryee Zouave*, 67; Schecter, *Devil's Own Work*, 18.

22. McKay, *Civil War and New York*, 31; Schecter, *Devil's Own Work*, 1–2, 11; Cook, *Armies of the Streets*, xi.

23. Raimondo Luraghi, *A History of the Confederate Navy* (London: Chatham Publishing, 1996), 146. Ironically, Mallory's interest in ironclad warships had been sparked by the work of the Hoboken inventor Robert L. Stevens, who in the wake of Robert Fulton's *Demologos* sought to perfect an armored, steam-powered warship.

24. Ibid., 146–147.

25. Nevins and Thomas, *Strong Diary*, 3:196; Spann, *Gotham at War*, 157.

26. McKay, *Civil War and New York*, 137; "The Rebel Pirate '290,'" *New York Times*, November 3, 1862, 1; Stephen Fox, *Wolf of the Deep: Raphael Semmes and the Notorious Confederate Raider* CSS Alabama (New York: Alfred A. Knopf, 2007), 17, 71–75.

27. Fox, *Wolf*, 75, 90; Raphael Semmes, *My Adventures Afloat: A Personal Memoir of My Cruises and Services in 'The Sumter' and 'Alabama'* (London: Richard Bentley, 1869), 489–490, 492.

28. "Highly Important: A Rebel Pirate Off the Coast," *New York Times*, August 13, 1864, 1; "The Pirate Tallahassee," *New York Times*, August 14, 1864, 1; "Marine Intelligence," *New York Times*, August 14, 1864, 8; "The Pirate," *New York Times*, August 15, 1864, 1; "The Pirate Tallahassee," *New York Times*, August 16, 1864, 1; "The Tallahassee," *New York Times*, August 17, 1864, 1.

29. McKay, *Civil War and New York*, 272–273; Spann, *Gotham at War*, 158.

30. Russell S. Gilmore, *Guarding America's Front Door: Harbor Forts in the Defense of New York City* (New York: The Fort Hamilton Historical Society, 1983), 3–4, 7–8; Norman Brouwer, "Fortress New York," *Seaport: New York's History Magazine* 24, no. 1 (Summer 1990): 37; Nevins and Thomas, *Strong Diary*, 1:276.

31. Spann, *Gotham at War*, 156–157; McKay, *Civil War and New York*, 134–136; "Delafield, Richard," in *Dictionary of American Biography* (New York: Charles Scribner's Sons, 1996), 5:210; Q. A. Gillmore, *A Memorial Sketch of the Character and Public Services of the Late Brig.-Gen. Richard Delafield, Chief of Engineers and Brevet Maj.-Gen. U.S. Army* (New York, 1874), 5–22.

32. Richard Delafield, Letter Press Book, 1862–1864, New-York Historical Society Library, Manuscript Collection, 433–451, 493.

33. McKay, *Civil War and New York*, 134; Spann, *Gotham at War*, 158.

34. Delafield, Letter Press Book, 376–379.

35. McKay, *Civil War and New York*, 191.

36. Spann, *Gotham at War*, 4; Daly, 183.

37. McKay, *Civil War and New York*, 197; Cook, *Armies of the Streets*, 51–52.

38. Spann, *Gotham at War*, 98; Schecter, *Devil's Own Work*, 131.

39. Nevins and Thomas, *Strong Diary*, 3:335–336.

40. Joel Tyler Headley, *The Great Riots of New York, 1712 to 1873* (New York: E. B. Treat, 1873), 211; Schecter, *Devil's Own Work*, 135, 137, 200.

41. Schecter, *Devil's Own Work*, 193–194.

42. Cook, *Armies of the Streets*, 58–59, 119, 125–126.

43. Ibid., 77; Schecter, *Devil's Own Work*, 146–149.

44. Iver Bernstein, *Draft Riots*, 28–30; Schecter, *Devil's Own Work*, 157, 203–206; Cook, *Armies of the Streets*, 83, 143.

45. Schecter, *Devil's Own Work*, 143–145, 160–161, 171.

46. Nevins and Thomas, *Strong Diary*, 3:335–336.

47. Schecter, *Devil's Own Work*, 203; Headley, *Riots*, 180.

48. Schecter, *Devil's Own Work*, 191.

49. Ibid., 250–252; Cook, *Armies of the Streets*, 193–195.

50. Cook, *Armies of the Streets*, 233–255.

51. Spann, *Gotham at War*, 178–185; Schecter, *Devil's Own Work*, 256–257, 338.

52. Schecter, *Devil's Own Work*, 253–254.

53. Ibid., 265–266.

54. Nevins and Thomas, *Strong Diary*, 3:411–412; Daly, *Diary*, 278.

55. McKay, *Civil War and New York*, 240–244, 298; Spann, *Gotham at War*, 73–78, 81–82, 188–89; Daly, *Diary*, 129–132, 139.

56. Schecter, *Devil's Own Work*, 212; McKay, *Civil War and New York*, 224, 252; Nat Brandt, *The Man Who Tried to Burn New York* (Syracuse, NY: Syracuse University Press, 1986), 85, 94.

57. Brandt, *Man*, 68–69, 71; Spann, *Gotham at War*, 164.

58. Brandt, *Man*, 88–91; McKay, *Civil War and New York City*, 279–284; Schecter, *Devil's Own Work*, 294–295.

59. Brandt, *Man*, 249 n2.

60. Ibid., 85, 128, 129.

61. Ibid., 151.

62. Ibid., 222, 273.

63. Ibid., 100; "The Reign of the Rabble," *New York Times*, July 15, 1863, 1.

64. Nevins and Thomas, *Strong Diary*, 3:483, 574–575, 582–583; Daly, *Diary*, 305.

65. Nevins and Thomas, *Strong Diary*, 3:490, 600.

66. Spann, *Gotham at War*, 132–133; Burrows and Wallace, *Gotham*, 904–905; David Quigley, *Second Founding: New York City, Reconstruction, and the Making of American Democracy* (New York: Hill and Wang, 2004), 63; Nevins and Thomas, *Strong Diary*, 4:538.

67. Bernstein, *Draft Riots*, 235.

Chapter 7

1. "Prince Henry to the German Society," *New York Times*, March 9, 1902, 1.

2. "Prince Henry Incidents," *New York Times*, March 2, 1902, SM3.

3. "Popular Souvenirs of Prince Henry," *New York Times*, March 2, 1902, SM5.

4. Holger H. Herwig, *Politics of Frustration: The United States in German Naval Planning, 1889–1941* (Boston: Little, Brown, 1976), 20.

5. Ibid., 42–66.

6. Ibid., 56, 62–63, 85–87, 90–92. In 1901, an indiscreet book by a German general staff attaché, Baron Franz von Edelsheim, argued that Germany could easily invade and conquer the American eastern seaboard. After Prince Heinrich's visit, the book was largely forgotten by the American public.

7. John Steele Gordon, *The Great Game: The Emergence of Wall Street as a World Power, 1653–2000* (New York: Touchstone, 1999), 200–201; H. W. Brands, *Woodrow Wilson* (New York: Times Books/Henry Holt, 2003), 52.

8. Ronald Schaffer, *America in the Great War: The Rise of the War Welfare State* (New York: Oxford University Press, 1991), 28.

9. H. C. Peterson, *Propaganda for War: The Campaign Against American Neutrality, 1914–1917* (Norman: University of Oklahoma Press, 1939), 16–17, 23–25, 48–49, 69; Schaffer, *America in the Great War*, 11.

10. "For Liberty and Democracy," *New York Times*, May 27, 1915, 10.

11. "Italians Here Talk Nothing but War," *New York Times*, May 24, 1915, 2.

12. Jules Witcover, *Sabotage at Black Tom: Imperial Germany's Secret War in America, 1914–1917* (Chapel Hill, NC: Algonquin Books of Chapel Hill, 1989), 56; Frederick C. Luebke, *Bonds of Loyalty: German Americans and World War I* (DeKalb: Northern Illinois University Press, 1974), 92, 97; Phyllis Keller, *States of Belonging: German-American Intellectuals and the First World War* (Cambridge, MA: Harvard University Press, 1979), 146.

13. Keller, *States*, 222–223, 232.

14. Edward Robb Ellis, *The Epic of New York City: A Narrative History* (New York: Coward-McCann, 1966), 501; "Reservists Flock to the Consulates," *New York Times*, August 5, 1914, 6; Luebke, *Bonds*, 96; Ibid., 149–150; Richard O'Connor, *The German-Americans: An Informal History* (Boston: Little, Brown, 1968), 389–390.

15. Luebke, *Bonds*, 48; Keller, *States*, 146.

16. David Brundage, "'In Time of Peace, Prepare for War': Key Themes in the Social Thought of New York's Irish Nationalists, 1890–1916," in *The New York Irish*, ed. Ronald H. Bayor and Timothy J. Meagher (Baltimore: Johns Hopkins University, 1996), 322, 327, 331.

17. O'Connor, *German-Americans*, 395–396.

18. Luebke, *Bonds*, 144, 159, 174, 215–217; David M. Kennedy, *Over Here: The First World War and American Society* (New York: Oxford University Press, 1980), 31.

19. Max Page, *The City's End: Two Centuries of Fantasies, Fears, and Premonitions of New York's Destruction* (New Haven, CT: Yale University Press, 2008), 52–54; David Nasaw, *Going Out: The Rise and Fall of Public Amusements* (New York: Basic Books, 1993), 207–208; Russell S. Gilmore, *Guarding America's Front Door: Harbor Forts in the Defense of New York City* (New York: The Fort Hamilton Historical Society, 1983); Edwin G. Burrows and Mike Wallace, *Gotham: A History of New York City to 1898* (Oxford: Oxford University Press, 1999), 1211, 1215; Leo Polaski and Glen Williford, *New York City's Harbor Defenses* (Charleston, SC: Arcadia Publishing, 2003), 35. The new long-range guns, the result of a modernization plan advanced by Secretary of War William Endicott during the late 1880s, were known to the American public as "Endicott guns."

20. Robert M. Fogelson, *America's Armories: Architecture, Society, and Public Order* (Cambridge, MA: Harvard University Press, 1989), 2, 13, 24, 30.

21. Ibid., 30, 32, 50–51, 64, 66, 71–73, 78, 149, 160–164, 182.

22. John Higham, *Strangers in the Land: Patterns of American Nativism, 1860–1925* (New Brunswick, NJ: Rutgers University Press, 1955), 155–157; Schaffer, *America in the Great War*, 81.

23. Chad Millman, *The Detonators: The Secret Plot to Destroy America and an Epic Hunt for Justice* (New York: Little, Brown, 2006), 41; Theodore Roosevelt, *The Foes of Our Own Household* (New York: George H. Doran, 1917), 293.

24. Luebke, *Bonds*, 169; Higham, *Strangers*, 200.

25. Ron Chernow, *The House of Morgan: An American Banking Dynasty and the Rise of Modern Finance* (New York: Grove Press, 1990), 186–188, 195–198, 200–201.

26. Ibid., 197–198.

27. Ibid., 188–189; Gordon, *Great Game*, 205; George Wellington Porter, "How U.S. Supplies War Munitions," *New York Times*, July 18, 1915, SM18.

28. "398,000 Unemployed Here in February," *New York Times*, May 1, 1915, 8; "Railroads Begin to Buy Equipment," *New York Times*, October 10, 1915, 42; Witcover, *Sabotage*, 23–24; "Railroad Heads to be Arrested for Explosion," *New York Times*, August 1, 1916, 1. The influx of war exports into New York harbor—and the huge traffic bottleneck it caused on the rail network across the Northeast and Midwest—played a key role in reshaping the region's transportation planning and infrastructure by helping to prompt the formation of the Port of New York Authority in 1921.

29. William Frieburger, "War Prosperity and Hunger: The New York Food Riots of 1917," *Labor History* 25, no. 2 (Spring 1984): 217–239; Dana Frank, "Housewives, Socialists, and the Politics of Food: The 1917 New York Cost-of-Living Protests," *Feminist Studies* 11, no. 2 (Summer 1985): 255–285.

30. Witcover, *Sabotage*, 11–14, 19–20; Millman, *Detonators*, 91–94, 296; "Barge Cargoes Blow Up," *New York Times*, July 30, 1916, 1; "Ellis Island Like War-Swept Town; Damage Estimated at $75,000," *New York Times*, July 31, 1916, 1.

31. "Millions of Persons Heard and Felt Shock," *New York Times*, July 31, 1916, 2; Witcover, *Sabotage*, 20–22; Millman, *Detonators*, 94–96.

32. Witcover, *Sabotage*, 56, 58–59; O'Connor, *German-Americans*, 400.

33. Witcover, *Sabotage*, 62–63, 68–69,120–121; Herwig, *Politics*, 153–155; Luebke, *Bonds*, 138–140; Millman, *Detonators*, 32.

34. Witcover, *Sabotage*, 116–117, 126–127, 136–137, 270; O'Connor, *German-Americans*, 402–403; Luebke, *Bonds*,126, 128.

35. Witcover, *Sabotage*, 88–99.

36. Witcover, *Sabotage*, 23; Millman, *Detonators*, 97; "Railroad Heads to Be Arrested for Explosion," *New York Times*, August 1, 1916, 1; "Three Held in Bail for Manslaughter," *New York Times*, August 1, 1916, 3; "Lehigh Road Earns $7,666,439 in a Year," *New York Times*, August 5, 1916, 13.

37. Witcover, *Sabotage*, 138–139, 160, 186–190, 43; Millman, *Detonators*, 88–90.

38. Witcover, *Sabotage*, 306–310.

39. Ibid., 129; Luebke, *Bonds*,146.

40. Luebke, *Bonds*, 207–208; Kathleen Hall Jamieson, *Eloquence in an Electronic Age: The Transformation of Political Speechmaking* (New York: Oxford University Press, 1988), 99–100.

41. Christopher M. Sterba, *Good Americans: Italian and Jewish Immigrants During the First World War* (New York: Oxford University Press, 2003), 53, 57; "The Weather," *New York Times*, June 5, 1917, 19; "The Weather," *New York Times*, June 6, 1917, 17; "No Trouble at the Polls," *New York Times*, June 6, 1917, p.1.

42. Sterba, *Good Americans*, 53–54.

43. Ibid., 4, 79–80, 108–109, 114–115, 119.

44. Ibid., 70, 110, 177.

45. Ellen Snyder-Grenier, *Brooklyn! An Illustrated History* (Philadelphia: Temple University Press, 1996), 126; Kennedy, *Over Here*, 135.

46. Nasaw, *Going Out*, 215; Kennedy, *Over Here*, 61–62; Schaffer, *America in the Great War*, 5; James R. Mock and Cedric Larson, *Words That Won the War: The Story of the Committee on Public Information, 1917–1919* (Princeton, NJ: Princeton University Press, 1939), 64–65.

47. Kennedy, *Over Here*, 39, 51.

48. Ibid., 279; Schaffer, *America in the Great War*, 77–78, 91–92, 94; Jervis Anderson, *This Was Harlem: A Cultural Portrait, 1900–1950* (New York: Farrar Straus Giroux, 1982), 104–105; Jervis Anderson, *A. Philip Randolph: A Biographical Portrait* (New York: Harcourt Brace Jovanovich, 1973), 98–99, 104.

49. David A. Shannon, *The Socialist Party of America: A History* (Chicago: Quadrangle Books, Inc., 1967), 85; Julian F. Jaffe, *Crusade Against Radicalism: New York During the Red Scare, 1914–1924* (Port Washington, NY: Kennikat Press, 1972), 70–72; Sterba, *Good Americans*, 156–159, 162–163.

50. Jaffe, *Crusade*, 24; Shannon, *Socialist Party*, 104; Luebke, *Bonds*, 253, 268.

51. Witcover, *Sabotage*, 233.

52. Kennedy, *Over Here*, 75–77; Schaffer, *America in the Great War*, 218–221; Jaffe, *Crusade*, 55; "The Sedition Bill," *New York Times*, April 10, 1918, 12.

53. Joe Doyle, "Striking for Ireland on the New York Docks," in Bayor and Meagher, eds., *The New York Irish*, 359; Jaffe, *Crusade*, 59–60, 62–64; Shannon, *Socialist Party*, 103–105.

54. "Start Drive Today for Draft Slackers, *New York Times*, September 3, 1918, 8; "Seize 20,000 Here in Slacker Search," *New York Times*, September 4, 1918, 1; "Second Day Nets Few Slackers Here," *New York Times*, September 5, 1918, 3; "Hunting the Slacker," *New York Times*, September 6, 1918, 12; "Get 1,500 Slackers in 3-Day Roundup," *New York Times*, September 6, 1918, 24; "60,187 Men Taken in Slacker Raids," *New York Times*, September 8, 1918, 9.

55. Sterba, *Good Americans*, 56; Kennedy, *Over Here*, 81–82, 165–166; Schaffer, *America in the Great War*, 17; Higham, *Strangers*, 211–212.

56. Schaffer, *America in the Great War*, 147–148; Geoffrey R. Stone, *Perilous Times: Free Speech in Wartime From the Sedition Act of 1798 to the War on Terrorism* (New York: W. W. Norton, 2004), 183; Christopher M. Finan, *From the Palmer Raids to the Patriot Act: A History of the Fight for Free Speech in America* (Boston: Beacon Press, 2007), 21, 4–25; "Hunting the Slacker," *New York Times*, September 6, 1918, 12; Kennedy, *Over Here*, 89.

57. Luebke, *Bonds*, 237, 276.

58. Ibid., 216, 249; Erik Kirschbaum, *The Eradication of German Culture in the United States: 1917–1918* (Stuttgart: Hans-Dieter Heinz Akademischer Verlag, 1986), 99, 101–102, 105–106, 135, 140.

59. Luebke, *Bonds*, 10, 14–15, 227–228, 243; Jeff Kisseloff, *You Must Remember This: An Oral History of Manhattan from the 1890s to World War II* (San Diego: Harcourt Brace Jovanovich, 1989), 118.

60. William Bell Clark, *When the U-Boats Came to America* (Boston: Little, Brown, 1929), 49–56, 73–74; "29 Survivors Reach Atlantic City Beach," *New York Times*, June 5, 1918, 2.

61. Clark, *U-Boats*, 42–50.

62. Ibid., 32, 34–35, 42, 49–50, 72.

63. Kennedy, *Over Here*, 169, 189; John Maxtone-Graham, *Dazzle & Drab: Ocean Liners at War* (New York: The Ocean Liner Museum, 2001), 15–17, 20; Ellis, *Epic*, 505.

64. Clark, *U-Boats*, 64–65, 93–95, 131; Ellis, *Epic*, 505; Douglas Botting and the Editors of Time-Life Books, *The U-Boats* (Alexandria, VA: Time-Life Books, 1979), 64.

65. Page, *City's End*, frontispiece; Clark, *U-Boats*, 78–79; "City Lights Out in Air Raid Test," *New York Times*, June 5, 1918, 1; "Police Rules for Citizens Should Air Raid Be Made," *New York Times*, June 5, 1918, 1; "Dim Some Streets to Foil Air Raids," *New York Times*, June 6, 1918, 1; "To Cope with Air Raids," *New York Times*, June 15, 1918, 6; "Huge Air-Raid Siren Tested by the Police," *New York*

Times, June 26, 1918, 8; "Air Raid Scare in Bronx," *New York Times*, July 2, 1918, 14; "Siren Test Stirs Many," *New York Times*, July 10, 1918, 10.

66. Clark, *U-Boats*, 144, 159–163, 214–216, 309–311.

67. Ibid., 107, 108.

68. Ibid., 165, 255, 256; "Take Enemy Aliens in Barred Zone," *New York Times*, July 20, 1918, 18.

69. Sterba, *Good Americans*, 172–173; Schaffer, *America in the Great War*, 115.

70. Kennedy, *Over Here*, 207; Kisseloff, *You Must Remember*, 551; Sterba, *Good Americans*, 3, 8, 80, 181; Schaffer, *America in the Great War*, 88, 89; Anderson, *This Was Harlem*, 107–108.

71. Kennedy, *Over Here*, 291; Jaffe, *Crusade*, 231.

72. Jaffe, *Crusade*, 85–91, 183–189; Kate Holladay Claghorn, *The Immigrant's Day in Court* (New York: Harper & Brothers, 1923), 418–421, 426–429, 447–448, 455.

73. Joseph W. Bendersky, *The "Jewish Threat": Anti-Semitic Politics of the U.S. Army* (New York: Basic Books, 2000), 69, 126–132.

74. Ibid., 158–163, 166.

Chapter 8

1. The previous paragraphs are based on the following: "City to Ward Off 'Invasion' by Air," *New York Times*, January 19, 1941, 19; "'Air Raids' in East Start 4-Day Test," *New York Times*, January 22, 1941, 12; "'Foe's' Planes Rain 'Bombs' onto City," *New York Times*, January 23, 1941, 13; "Coast Vulnerable, War Games Show," *New York Times*, January 24, 1941, 11; Hanson W. Baldwin, "Types of Aerial Missiles," *New York Times*, January 24, 1941, 11; "The Nation," *New York Times*, January 26, 1941, E2; "Air Raid Spotters to Be Permanent," *New York Times*, January 25, 1941, 8.

2. Brehon Somervell, "City Unemployment Figures," *New York Times*, March 23, 1940, 10.

3. Leo Polaski and Glen Williford, *New York City's Harbor Defenses* (Charleston, SC: Arcadia Publishing, 2003), 63–68, 71–73, 97, 104, 107, 109–111; Russell S. Gilmore, "fortifications," in *The Encyclopedia of New York City*, ed. Kenneth T. Jackson (New Haven, CT: Yale University Press, 1995), 431–432.

4. Baldwin, "Types of Aerial Missiles," *New York Times*, January 24, 1941, 11.

5. Richard M. Ketchum, *The Borrowed Years 1938–1941: America on the Way to War* (New York: Random House, 1989), 87–92.

6. "Mayor Tells City He Will Run Again If Voters Call Him," *New York Times*, May 22, 1941, 1; "City Defense Group Plans for Air Raids," *New York Times*, January 16, 1941, 1; "Mayor Emphasizes Need of Discipline," *New York Times*, June 14, 1941, 9; "Mayors Hear Poletti Warn of Invasion," *New York Times*, June 12, 1941, 11; August Heckscher with Phyllis Robinson, *When LaGuardia Was Mayor:*

New York's Legendary Years (New York: W. W. Norton, 1978), 280, 297–298, Thomas Kessner, *Fiorello H. La Guardia and the Making of Modern New York* (New York: McGraw-Hill, 1989), 491–493.

7. "Slums and Penthouses Send Forth Volunteers Eager to 'Do Our Bit,'" *New York Times*, June 21, 1941, 8; "Post Wardens in Training," *New York Times*, September 16, 1941, 7.

8. "Mayor Emphasizes Need of Discipline," *New York Times*, June 14, 1941, 9; "Urges Permanency in Defense Housing," *New York Times*, April 25, 1941, 35; "Air Raid Drills Held in Schools," *New York Times*, June 7, 1941, 19; "Tests Evacuation Plan," *New York Times*, March 13, 1941, p.23; "Defense Exhibit Begins Saturday," *New York Times*, September 14, 1941, 39; "Newest Weapons to Be on Exhibit," *New York Times*, September 20, 1941, 34.

9. Norman Brouwer, "Fortress New York," *Seaport: New York's History Magazine* 24, no. 1 (Summer 1990): 40.

10. Sander A. Diamond, *The Nazi Movement in the United States, 1924–1941* (Ithaca, NY: Cornell University Press, 1974), 92, 101–102, 206, 224, 228, 229, 245; Ronald H. Bayor, *Neighbors in Conflict: The Irish, Germans, Jews, and Italians of New York City, 1929–1941* (Baltimore: Johns Hopkins University Press, 1978), 61.

11. Diamond, *Nazi Movement*, 144–145, 317; Stan Cohen and Don DeNevi with Richard Gay, *They Came to Destroy America: The FBI Goes to War Against Nazi Spies & Saboteurs Before and During World War II* (Missoula, MT: Pictorial Histories, 2003), 3.

12. Diamond, *Nazi Movement*, 8, 150, 151, 156, 203, 209, 225, 277; Cohen and DeNevi, *They Came*, 17–18; Bayor, *Neighbors*, 63, 66–67, 73–74, 76; Mike Wallace, "New York and the World: The Global Context," in *Facing Fascism: New York and the Spanish Civil War*, ed. Peter N. Carroll and James D. Fernandez (New York: Museum of the City of New York/New York University Press, 2007), 22.

13. "100,000 March Here in 6-Hour Protest over Nazi Policies," *New York Times*, May 11, 1933, 1; Diamond, *Nazi Movement*, 107; Bayor, *Neighbors*, 68–70; Wallace, "New York and the World," 21–22.

14. Diamond, *Nazi Movement*, 230; Cohen and DeNevi, *They Came*, 4.

15. "La Guardia Scores Nazi Racial Bias," *New York Times*, January 20, 1935, 31; Kessner, *La Guardia*, 400–403.

16. Kessner, *La Guardia*, 403, Heckscher, *When LaGuardia*, 163; William Manners, *Patience and Fortitude: Fiorello La Guardia* (New York: Harcourt Brace Jovanovich, 1976), 245.

17. Heckscher, *When LaGuardia*, 163–164.

18. Diamond, *Nazi Movement*, 324–329; Cohen and DeNevi, *They Came*, 9–10.

19. Diamond, *Nazi Movement*, 324–329; "Mayor to Permit Big Bund Meeting," *New York Times*, February 18, 1939, 30; "22,000 Nazis Hold Rally in Garden; Police Check Foes," *New York Times*, February 21, 1939, 1; "Bund Foes

Protest Policing of Rally," *New York Times*, February 22, 1939, 6; "New York: Nazi Garden Party," *New York Times*, February 26, 1939, 66.

20. Bayor, *Neighbors*, 24–29, 93; Wallace, "New York and the World," 28–9; Patrick J. McNamara, "Pro-Franco Sentiment and Activity in New York City," in Carroll and Fernandez, eds., *Facing Fascism*, 95–100.

21. Bayor, *Neighbors*, 88–90, 92–93, 105–107.

22. Ibid., 94–96, 97–104, 155–156, 160–163; Diamond, *Nazi Movement*, 319; Stephen H. Norwood, "Marauding Youth and the Christian Front: Antisemitic Violence in Boston and New York During World War II," *American Jewish History* 91, no. 2 (June 2003): 241–242.

23. Bayor, *Neighbors*, 102–103, 113.

24. Ibid., 36, 78–79; Kessner, *La Guardia*, 136; John P. Diggins, *Mussolini and Fascism: The View from America* (Princeton, NJ: Princeton University Press, 1972), 32, 79; Wallace, "New York and the World," 23–24, 26–27.

25. Diggins, *Mussolini and Fascism*, 43; Kessner, *La Guardia*, 136.

26. Diggins, *Mussolini and Fascism*, 125–138; Nunzio Pernicone, "Italian Immigrant Radicalism in New York," in *The Italians of New York: Five Centuries of Struggle and Achievement*, ed. Philip V. Cannistraro (New York: The New-York Historical Society, 1999), 85–88; "100 Police Break Up Anti-Fascist Riot," *New York Times*, July 5, 1932, 1; "In Court as Slayer in Anti-Fascist Riot," *New York Times*, July 6, 1932, 42; "Envoy at Service for Slain Fascist," *New York Times*, July 8, 1932, 36.

27. Diggins, *Mussolini and Fascism*, 306–308; "Harlem Ponders Ethiopia's Fate," *New York Times*, July 14, 1935, E10.

28. "Italians Execute Many in Ethiopia; Oust 4 Journalists," *New York Times*, May 18, 1936, 1; "Plans Take Form to Rule Ethiopia," *New York Times*, May 18, 1936, 11; "Mob of 400 Battles the Police in Harlem; Italian Stores Raided, Man Shot in Crowd," *New York Times*, May 19, 1936, 6; Diggins, *Mussolini and Fascism*, 306–307.

29. Diggins, *Mussolini and Fascism*, 306; Jervis Anderson, *This Was Harlem: A Cultural Portrait, 1900–1950* (New York: Farrar Straus Giroux, 1982), 286–88; Langston Hughes, *The Collected Works of Langston Hughes* (Columbia, MO: University of Missouri Press, 2003), 14:307–308; Richard Wright, "High Tide in Harlem: Joe Louis as a Symbol of Freedom," in *The Unlevel Playing Field: A Documentary History of the African American Experience in Sports*, ed. David K. Wiggins and Patrick B. Miller (Urbana: University of Illinois Press, 2003), 172.

30. Peter Kwong, *Chinatown, N.Y.: Labor and Politics, 1930–1950*, rev. ed. (New York: New Press, 1979), 38, 47, 52, 77, 97–107.

31. Ibid., 112, 130; Wallace, "New York and the World," 27–28.

32. Studs Terkel, *"The Good War": An Oral History of World War Two* (New York: Ballantine Books, 1985), 96–98; Peter N. Carroll, *The Odyssey of the Abraham Lincoln Brigade: Americans in the Spanish Civil War* (Stanford, CA: Stanford University Press, 1994), 51–53.

33. Letter from Volunteer Hyman Katz to his mother, November 5, 1937, in Carroll and Fernandez, eds., *Facing Fascism*, 24–25.

34. Eric R. Smith, "New York's Aid to the Spanish Republic," in Carroll and Fernandez, eds., *Facing Fascism*, 43.

35. Maurice Isserman, *Which Side Were You On? The American Communist Party During the Second World War* (Urbana: University of Illinois Press, 1993), 35; James P. Duffy, *Target: America: Hitler's Plan to Attack the United States* (Westport, CT: Praeger Publishers, 2004), 15; Hyman Katz to his mother, in Carroll and Fernandez, eds. *Facing Fascism*, 25.

36. Manfred Griehl, *Luftwaffe Over America: The Secret Plans to Bomb the United States in World War II* (London: Greenhill Books, 2004), 20–21, 28–29, 35; Duffy, *Target: America*, 46–47.

37. Griehl, *Luftwaffe*, 33–34, 37; Major Gerhard Engel, *At the Heart of the Reich: The Secret Diary of Hitler's Army Adjutant* (London: Greenhill Books, 2005), 107.

38. Barry Rubin and Judith Colp Rubin, *Hating America: A History* (New York: Oxford University Press, 2004), 95–98; H. Paul Jeffers, *The Napoleon of New York: Mayor Fiorello La Guardia* (New York: John Wiley & Sons, 2002), 278.

39. Rubin and Rubin, *Hating America*, 97–98; Ketchum, *Borrowed Years*, 179; Griehl, *Luftwaffe*, 34; Albert Speer, *Inside the Third Reich* (New York: Macmillan, 1970), 540.

40. Cohen and DeNevi, *They Came*, 21–23, 28; Ladislas Farago, *The Game of the Foxes* (New York: David McKay, 1971), 25–27, 39, 45, 47, 54, 496–500, 506.

41. Farago, *Foxes*, 63–64, 71–73, 532–533, 575.

42. Cohen and DeNevi, *They Came*, vi–vii, 22–23; ibid., 373–377, 533–541; "U.S. Bomb Site Sold to Germany, Spy Jury Is Told," *New York Times*, September 9, 1941, 1.

43. Otto D. Tolischus, "Nipponese Face War They Thought Impossible," *New York Times*, December 7, 1941, E3; "On the Radio This Week," *New York Times*, December 7, 1941, X15; Ketchum, *Borrowed Years*, 776–778.

44. Heckscher, *When LaGuardia*, 313–314; Jeffers, *Napoleon of New York*, 311–312; Kessner, *La Guardia*, 501–502; Ketchum, *Borrowed Years*, 777–778; "Entire City Put on War Footing," *New York Times*, December 8, 1941, 1; "Planes Guard City from Air Attacks," *New York Times*, December 9, 1941, 1; Lorraine B. Diehl, *Over Here! New York City During World War II* (New York: HarperCollins, 2010), 63–64. Consul General Morishima was allowed to return home to Japan and soon was reassigned as Japan's minister in the embassy to the Soviet Union.

45. Michael Gammon, *Operation Drumbeat: The Dramatic True Story of Germany's First U-Boat Attacks Along the American Coast in World War II* (New York: Harper & Row, 1990), xv–xvii.

46. Ibid., 208–213, 216–223, 225. For a useful summary of U-123's voyage and "kills," see the website www.uboat.net.

47. Ibid., 137–138; Andrew Williams, *The Battle of the Atlantic* (London: BBC Worldwide, 2002), 166.

48. Gammon, *Drumbeat*, 19–21.

49. Ibid., 224–225, 230–232; Williams, *Battle*, 166–167.

50. Williams, *Battle*, 176.

51. Ibid., 166–167.

52. "Ship Found Awash," *New York Times*, January 15, 1942, 1.

53. Gammon, *Drumbeat*, 84–92.

54. Ibid., 181–185; Polaski and Williford, *Harbor Defenses*, 109.

55. Williams, *Battle*, 174–175; Gammon, *Drumbeat*, 352–355.

56. John McPhee, *Looking for a Ship* (New York: Farrar Straus Giroux, 1990), 155; Gammon, *Drumbeat*, 271, 344; Arnold S. Lott, *Most Dangerous Sea: A History of Mine Warfare, and an Account of U. S. Navy Mine Warfare Operations in World War II and Korea* (Annapolis: US Naval Institute, 1959), 48–49.

57. Gammon, *Drumbeat*, xviii, 388–389.

58. Ibid., 231.

59. W.A. Haskell, *Shadows on the Horizon: The Battle of Convoy HX-233* (London: Chatham Publishing, 1998), 22, 25.

60. Joseph F. Meany Jr., "New York: Sally Port to Victory," *Sea History* 65 (Spring 1993): 13; Joseph F. Meany Jr., "Port in a Storm: The Port of New York in World War II," in *To Die Gallantly: The Battle of the Atlantic*, ed. Timothy J. Runyan and Jan M. Copes (Boulder: Westview Press, 1994), 284, 289.

61. Meany, "Sally Port," 14; Roy Hoopes, *Americans Remember the Home Front: An Oral Narrative* (New York: Berkley Books, 2002), 160–161.

62. Moray Epstein, *Ports in a Storm: The Voyage of a Merchant Seaman Through World War II* (San Diego: Moray Epstein, 1995), 56.

63. George Sandiford in *Eyewitness Accounts of the World War II Murmansk Run*, ed. Mark Scott (Lewiston, NY: Edwin Mellen Press, 2006), 71.

64. Sam Hakam in Scott, *Eyewitness Accounts*, 39, 41; Epstein, *Ports*, 96.

65. Gammon, *Drumbeat*, xx; Meany, "New York: Sally Port to Victory," 15. For wartime casualty rates, see www.usmm.org/casualty.html.

66. Meany, "Sally Port," 14; Meany, "Port in a Storm," 289–290; William H. Miller and David F. Hutchings, *Transatlantic Liners at War: The Story of the Queens* (New York: Arco, 1985), 76, 82; Richard Goldstein, *Helluva Town: The Story of New York City During World War II* (New York: Free Press, 2010), 56. San Francisco, the second busiest of the nation's nine wartime embarkation ports, sent abroad only a bit more than half the number of troops dispatched by New York.

67. Gammon, *Drumbeat*, 274; Joseph F. Meany Jr., "Port in a Storm: The Port of New York in World War II," typescript, South Street Seaport Museum Library, 62–63.

68. Meany, "Sally Port," 16; "Division of Work for Defense Urged," *New York Times*, August 15, 1941, 10; Geoffrey Rossano, "Suburbia Armed: Nassau County

Development and the Rise of the Aerospace Industry, 1909–60," in *The Martial Metropolis: U.S. Cities in War and Peace*, ed. Roger W. Lotchin (New York: Praeger Publishers, 1984), 73; "Knudsen Pledges 30 Billion Output," *New York Times*, August 14, 1941, 1; Karl Drew Hartzell, *The Empire State at War: World War II* (Albany: The State of New York, 1949), 54–55; Dominic J. Capeci Jr., *The Harlem Riot of 1943* (Philadelphia: Temple University Press, 1977), 61–63.

69. Ellen Snyder-Grenier, *Brooklyn! An Illustrated History* (Philadelphia: Temple University Press, 1996), 134–135; Debra E. Bernhardt and Rachel Bernstein, *Ordinary People, Extraordinary Lives: A Pictorial History of Working People in New York City* (New York: New York University Press, 2000), 60.

70. Snyder-Grenier, *Brooklyn!*, 119, 126–127, 132–133; Thomas F. Berner, *The Brooklyn Navy Yard* (Charleston, SC: Arcadia Publishing, 1999), 83; Meany, "Sally Port," 16; Lucille Kolkin, remarks at Veteran's Day event, South Street Seaport Museum, November 1993, transcript, Seaport Museum.

71. Edward Robb Ellis, *The Epic of New York City* (New York: Coward-McCann, 1966), 561–564.

72. Ric Burns and James Sanders, with Lisa Ades, *New York: An Illustrated History* (New York: Alfred A. Knopf, 1999), 471; Ronald H. Bailey and the Editors of Time-Life Books, *Home Front: U.S.A.* (Alexandria, VA: Time-Life Books, 1978), 168–179; Scott DeVeaux, *The Birth of Bebop: A Social and Musical History* (Berkeley: University of California Press, 1997), 284–290, 291, 367.

73. "Drastic Dimout of All City Lights Effective Tonight," *New York Times*, May 18, 1942, 1; "Dimout Gives Way to New 'Brownout,' Effective Monday," *New York Times*, October 28, 1943, 1.

74. Meany, "Port in a Storm," 294; George Goldman, remarks at Veteran's Day event, South Street Seaport Museum, November 1993, transcript, Seaport Museum.

75. Jan Morris, *Manhattan '45* (New York: Oxford University Press, 1987), 37; Charles Kaiser, *The Gay Metropolis: 1940–1996* (Boston: Houghton Mifflin, 1997), 13, 19, 51, 64.

76. Kaiser, *Gay Metropolis*, 39.

77. Ellis, *Epic*, 564; Ida Pollack, remarks at Veteran's Day event, South Street Seaport Museum, November 1993, transcript, Seaport Museum.

78. Hoopes, *Americans Remember*, 178, 276–277.

79. Ibid., 276–277; author's interview with Norman Worth, January 7, 2007.

80. Michael Dobbs, *Saboteurs: The Nazi Raid on America* (New York: Alfred A. Knopf, 2004), 91–94, 101.

81. Ibid., 62, 127–128.

82. Louis Fisher, *Nazi Saboteurs on Trial: A Military Tribunal and American Law*, 2nd ed., abridged and updated (Lawrence: University Press of Kansas, 2005), 135–147.

83. Dobbs, *Saboteurs*, 221, 273; ibid., 116–120.

84. Griehl, *Luftwaffe*,130, 148; Duffy, *Target*, 95–99, 119–124.

85. Zenji Orita with Joseph D. Harrington, *I-Boat Captain* (Canoga Park, CA: Major Books, 1976), 276, 311, 317–318, 322; see also the documentary film *Secrets of the Dead: Japanese SuperSub*, directed by Eric Stange (Windfall Films and Spy Pond Productions for Thirteen, National Geographic Channel, WNET.org, PBS, 2010).

86. Duffy, *Target*, 135–148.

87. Ibid., 103–105; Clay Blair, *Hitler's U-Boat War: The Hunted, 1942–1945* (New York: Random House, 1998), 682–684; "Robot Bomb Attacks Here Held 'Probable' by Admiral, *New York Times*, January 9,1945, 1; "Bombs for New York?" *New York Times*, January 10, 1945, 22; "Officials Silent on Robot Threat," *New York Times*, January 10, 1945, 7; "Sirens to Sound Long Note If Robot Bombs Fall Here," *New York Times*, January 16, 1945, p . 21; "Topics of the Times: Bombs Help Planners," *New York Times*, January 18, 1945, 18; "Bombing the Atlantic Coast," *New York Times*, January 21,1945, 70.

88. Philip K. Lundeberg, "Operation *Teardrop* Revisited," in Runyan and Copes, eds., *To Die Gallantly*, 210–230.

89. Gary R. Mormino and George E. Pozzetta, "Italian Americans and the 1940s," in *The Italians of New York: Five Centuries of Struggle and Achievement*, ed. Philip V. Cannistraro (New York: The New-York Historical Society, 1999), 140. Also caught in the anti-Nazi dragnet was the World War I propagandist George Sylvester Viereck, imprisoned in 1942 for failing to register as an agent of Germany. Viereck's postwar memoir of his prison years, *Men into Beasts* (1952), is considered a founding work of American gay pulp fiction. His son, Peter Viereck, became a leading American conservative thinker.

90. Greg Robinson, "Japanese," in *The Encyclopedia of New York State*, ed. Peter Eisenstadt (Syracuse, NY: Syracuse University Press, 2005), 808; ibid., 138, 141–142; Kessner, *La Guardia*, 519.

91. Craig Steven Wilder, *A Covenant with Color: Race and Social Power in Brooklyn* (New York: Columbia University Press, 2000), 168–171; Martha Biondi, *To Stand and Fight: The Struggle for Civil Rights in Postwar New York City* (Cambridge, MA: Harvard University Press, 2003), 3, 7–8, 23; Jervis Anderson, *A. Philip Randolph: A Biographical Portrait* (New York: Harcourt Brace Jovanovich, 1973), 246–253, 255–265, 274; Kolkin, Veteran's Day remarks, transcript.

92. Anderson, *Harlem*, 290–291; Terkel, *"The Good War,"* 365–368.

93. Anderson, *Harlem*, 295–298; Nat Brandt, *Harlem at War: The Black Experience in WWII* (Syracuse, NY: Syracuse University Press, 1996), 184–206; Capeci, *Harlem Riot*, 99–105.

94. Ketchum, *Borrowed Years*, 267; Geoffrey Perrett, *Days of Sadness, Years of Triumph: The American People, 1939–1945* (New York: Coward, McCann & Geoghegan, 1973), 363.

95. Perrett, *Days*, 420.

96. "Rabbis Present Plea to Wallace," *New York Times*, October 7, 1943, 14.

97. Norwood, "Marauding Youth," 246; Bayor, *Neighbors*, 150, 155, 156.

98. Jeff Kisseloff, *You Must Remember This: An Oral History of Manhattan from the 1890s to World War II* (San Diego: Harcourt Brace Jovanovich, 1989), 250.

99. Allon Schoener, *New York: An Illustrated History of the People* (New York: W. W. Norton, 1998), 312–313.

Chapter 9

1. Kalman Seigel, "Biggest Raid Test Turns New York into a 'Ghost City'," *New York Times*, December 14, 1952, 1.

2. Ibid.; "'Operation Alert,'" *New York Times*, June 16, 1955, 30; Will Lissner, "Streets Cleared Swiftly," *New York Times*, July 13, 1957, 1.

3. "'Operation Alert,'" 30.

4. E.B. White, *Here Is New York* (1949; repr., New York: The Little Bookroom, 1999), 54–55.

5. Andrew D. Grossman, *Neither Dead Nor Red: Civilian Defense and American Political Development During the Early Cold War* (New York: Routledge, 2001), 19, 49–50; Laura McEnaney, *Civil Defense Begins at Home: Militarization Meets Everyday Life in the Fifties* (Princeton, NJ: Princeton University Press, 2000), 35; Elaine Tyler May, *Homeward Bound: American Families in the Cold War Era*, fully rev. and updated ed. (New York: Basic Books, 2008), 100.

6. Paul Boyer, *By the Bomb's Early Light: American Thought and Culture at the Dawn of the Atomic Age* (1985; repr., Chapel Hill: University of North Carolina Press, 1994), 20, 67. For apocalyptic imaginings by magazine illustrator Chesley Bonestell of Soviet nuclear attacks on New York in 1950–1951, see Max Page, *The City's End: Two Centuries of Fantasies, Fears, and Premonitions of New York's Destruction* (New Haven, CT: Yale University Press, 2008), 107–108.

7. Howard Fast, *Being Red: A Memoir* (Boston: Houghton Mifflin, 1990), 184–185.

8. Ibid., 184, 185–187.

9. Grossman, *Neither Dead Nor Red*, 113; John Cogley, *Report on Blacklisting II: Radio-Television* (n.p.: The Fund for the Republic, 1956), 1–22, 129–135. Author's note: as a child and young adult, I remember these books of my father's still covered with brown wrapping through the 1960s and 1970s.

10. H.P. Albarelli Jr., *A Terrible Mistake: The Murder of Frank Olson and the CIA's Secret Cold War Experiments* (Walterville, OR: Trine Day, 2009), 110, 632; Leonard A. Cole, *Clouds of Secrecy: The Army's Germ Warfare Tests over Populated Areas* (Lanham, MD: Rowman & Littlefield, 1988), 65–69; Philip Messing, "Long, Strange Trip: Did the CIA Test LSD in the New York City Subway System?" *New York Post*, March 13, 2010; Nicholas M. Horrock, "Senators Are Told of Test of a Gas Attack in Subway," *New York Times*, September 19, 1975, 14.

11. Robert C. Doty, "City's First Draftees Enter Army; 108 Honored by Review at Fort Jay," *New York Times*, August 31, 1950, 1; "2,000 Skilled Hands Needed at Navy Yard," *New York Times*, December 22, 1950, 7; "Shipyard Policy at Issue," *New York Times*, May 29, 1953, 41; Geoffrey Rossano, "Suburbia Armed: Nassau County Development and the Rise of the Aerospace Industry, 1909–60," in *The Martial Metropolis: U.S. Cities in War and Peace*, ed. Roger W. Lotchin (New York: Praeger Publishers, 1984), 76–77.

12. Sam Tanenhaus, *Whittaker Chambers: A Biography* (New York: Random House, 1997), 158–159, 168–169; "Gen. Krivitsky Found Dead; Suicide Finding Questioned," *New York Times*, February 11, 1941, 1; John P. Diggins, *Mussolini and Fascism: The View from America* (Princeton, NJ: Princeton University Press, 1972), 411; "Woman Communist Missing 7 Months," *New York Times*, December 18, 1937, 10.

13. Tanenhaus, *Chambers*, 75, 79, 80–82, 83–86.

14. Ibid., 83, 108, 110–115, 125, 363.

15. Richard Goldstein, *Helluva Town: The Story of New York City During World War II* (New York: Free Press, 2010), 45–48; Lorraine B. Diehl, *Over Here! New York City During World War II* (New York: HarperCollins, 2010), 52–53; Sam Roberts, *The Brother: The Untold Story of the Rosenberg Case* (New York: Random House, 2001), 127; Cynthia C. Kelly and Robert S. Norris, *A Guide to Manhattan Project Sites in Manhattan* (Washington, DC: The Atomic Heritage Foundation, 2008), 28–29.

16. Roberts, *The Brother*, 108–109, 243–244.

17. Ibid., 282, 419–420, 430, 494, 522–523; John Earl Haynes and Harvey Klehr, *Venona: Decoding Soviet Espionage in America* (New Haven, CT: Yale University Press, 1999), 10–11, 309–310, 363; "Spy Case a Story of Legal Battles," *New York Times*, June 20, 1953, 6.

18. Stefan Kanfer, *A Journal of the Plague Years* (New York: Atheneum, 1973), 73.

19. Roberts, *The Brother*, 386, 466, 490.

20. B. Bruce-Briggs, *The Shield of Faith: A Chronicle of Strategic Defense from Zeppelins to Star Wars* (New York: Simon & Schuster, 1988), 175; Allan M. Winkler, *Life Under a Cloud: American Anxiety About the Atom* (Urbana: University of Illinois Press, 1999), 122; Studs Terkel, *"The Good War": An Oral History of World War II* (New York: Ballantine Books, 1985), 521–522.

21. Guy Oakes, *The Imaginary War: Civil Defense and American Cold War Culture* (New York: Oxford University Press, 1994), 52–54.

22. Winkler, *Life Under a Cloud*, 115–116; Todd Gitlin, *The Sixties: Years of Hope, Days of Rage*, rev. ed. (New York: Bantam Books, 1993), 22–24; Miguel "Mickey" Melendez, *We Took the Streets: Fighting for Latino Rights with the Young Lords* (New York: St. Martin's Press, 2003), 33; Grossman, *Neither Dead Nor Red*, 84; "School Children Get Identification Tags," *New York Times*, October 19, 1951, 14.

23. Bruce-Briggs, *The Shield of Faith*, 117–119; Robert A. M. Stern, Thomas Mellins, and David Fishman, *New York 1960: Architecture and Urbanism Between the Second World War and the Bicentennial* (New York: Monacelli Press, 1995), 95–99.

24. Bernard Stengren, "City Lags on Civil Defense, With Plans in A-Bomb Era," *New York Times*, June 13, 1955, 1; Boyer, *By the Bomb's Early Light*, 282.

25. Bruce-Briggs, *The Shield of Faith*, 164, 169; Norimitsu Onishi, "Frozen in Time, Cold War Kitsch," *New York Times*, February 20, 1995, B1.

26. Nan Robertson, "Feeling of Futility Voiced," *New York Times*, September 2, 1961, 1.

27. Winkler, *Life Under a Cloud*, 117; May, *Homeward Bound*, 161.

28. Russell Porter, "City Evacuation Plan," *New York Times*, March 12, 1955, 1; Warren Weaver Jr., "State Discloses Evacuation Plan," *New York Times*, August 4, 1955, 10; Milton Bracker, "Atom Survival Plan Drawn Up by State," *New York Times*, September 1, 1958, 1.

29. Porter, "City Evacuation Plan," 1.

30. Stengren, "City Lags on Civil Defense," 1.

31. "Westchester Ban on Evacuees Kept," *New York Times*, April 21, 1955, 16.

32. "Evacuation Rule of City Clarified," *New York Times*, April 22, 1955, 12.

33. Bruce-Briggs, *The Shield of Faith*, 67, 92–94; Mark L. Morgan and Mark A. Berhow, *Rings of Supersonic Steel: Air Defenses of the United States Army 1950–1979*, 2nd ed. (Bodega Bay, CA: Fort MacArthur Military Press, 2002), 2, 8–16, 117–125.

34. "U.S. Confirms Atomic Defense Here," *New York Times*, April 23, 1957, 20.

35. Bruce-Briggs, *The Shield of Faith*, 139–141; Morgan and Berhow, *Rings*, 25; Bill Becker, "8 Nikes Explode at New Jersey Base; 10 Killed, 3 Hurt," *New York Times*, May 23, 1958, 1; "Civil Defense Alerted In City by Missile Fire," *New York Times*, June 8, 1960, 1; George Cable Wright, "General Regrets Explosion Scare," *New York Times*, June 9, 1960, 4.

36. Page, *The City's End*, 135–136; Dee Garrison, "'Our Skirts Gave Them Courage': The Civil Defense Protest Movement in New York City, 1955–1961," in *Not June Cleaver: Women and Gender in Postwar America, 1945–1960*, ed. Joanne Meyerowitz (Philadelphia: Temple University Press, 1994), 207.

37. Garrison, "'Our Skirts Gave Them Courage'," 210–211, 215.

38. Ibid., 212–216, 217–220.

39. Ibid., 216; Robert K. Musil, "Growing Up Nuclear," *Bulletin of the Atomic Scientists* 38, no 1 (January1982): 19.

40. John Cohen, in *No Direction Home: Bob Dylan*, directed by Martin Scorsese (Spitfire Pictures, Grey Water Park Productions, Thirteen/WNET New York/PBS, and Sikelia Productions, 2005).

41. Nancy Zaroulis and Gerald Sullivan, *Who Spoke Up? American Protest Against the War in Vietnam 1963–1975* (Garden City, NY: Doubleday, 1984), 24–25.

42. Joseph Lelyveld, "Police Break Up Antiwar Rally," *New York Times*, August 9, 1964, 1.

43. Zaroulis and Sullivan, *Who Spoke Up?* 12–13.

44. Ibid., 24, 26.

45. Melendez, *We Took the Streets*, 67.

46. Zaroulis and Sullivan, *Who Spoke Up?* 49; Abbie Hoffman, *The Autobiography of Abbie Hoffman* (New York: Four Walls Eight Windows, 2000), 82–83.

47. Gitlin, *The Sixties*, 90; Melendez, *We Took the Streets*, 68.

48. Hoffman, *Autobiography*, 107–108; Zaroulis and Sullivan, *Who Spoke Up?* 110–114; Douglas Robinson, "Throngs to Parade to the U.N. Today for Antiwar Rally," *New York Times*, April 15, 1967, 1; Douglas Robinson, "100,000 Rally at U.N. Against Vietnam War," *New York Times*, April 16, 1967, 1; Mark Rudd, *Underground: My Life with SDS and the Weathermen* (New York: HarperCollins, 2009), 30–31.

49. Zaroulis and Sullivan, *Who Spoke Up?* 51, 56–57, 81, 112–113. Another act of protest was the self-immolation by a young Catholic Worker, Roger LaPorte, who doused himself with gasoline and set himself on fire outside the United Nations on November 9, 1965, one week after a Quaker named Norman Morrison similarly burned himself to death outside the Pentagon. Both pacifists were emulating the suicides of Buddhist monks protesting the Diem regime in South Vietnam.

50. Kenneth T. Jackson, "The City Loses the Sword: The Decline of Major Military Activity in the New York Metropolitan Region," in Lotchin, ed., *The Martial Metropolis*, 151–162.

51. Vincent J. Cannato, *The Ungovernable City: John Lindsay and His Struggle to Save New York* (New York: Basic Books, 2001), 133.

52. Ibid., 400–401, 407; Jennifer S. Light, *From Warfare to Welfare: Defense Intellectuals and Urban Problems in Cold War America* (Baltimore: Johns Hopkins University Press, 2003), 62.

53. James Simon Kunen, *The Strawberry Statement: Notes of a College Revolutionary* (New York: Random House, 1969), 120.

54. Cannato, *Ungovernable City*, 239–243, 253–254, 257.

55. Ibid., 243; Rudd, *Underground*, 115; Zaroulis and Sullivan, *Who Spoke Up?* 167–168; Nicolas Pileggi, "Revolutionaries Who Have to be Home by 7:30," *New York Times*, March 16, 1969, SM26.

56. Richard Reeves, "Mayor Urges Youths to Aid War Resistance," *New York Times*, March 20, 1968, 1; John V. Lindsay, *The City* (New York: Norton, 1970), 39, 204.

57. Gitlin, *The Sixties*, 183; Rudd, *Underground*, 43, 168–169.

58. "State Presidential Vote," *New York Times*, November 4, 1964, 24; Daniel C. Hallin, *The "Uncensored War": The Media and Vietnam* (Berkeley: University of California Press, 1986), 11, 218; Melendez, *We Took the Streets*, 33.

59. Zaroulis and Sullivan, *Who Spoke Up?* 92, 101, 168.

60. Cannato, *Ungovernable City*, 122–124, 427.

61. Murray Schumach, "70,000 Turn Out to Back U.S. Men in Vietnam War," *New York Times*, May 14, 1967, 1; Hoffman, *Autobiography*, 108.

62. Rudd, *Underground*, 29; Cannato, *Ungovernable City*, 245–246, 258–260, 627 n39.

63. Cannato, *Ungovernable City*, 246, 260.

64. Homer Bigart, "War Foes Here Attacked by Construction Workers," *New York Times*, May 9, 1970, 1; Linda Charlton, "Some Protests Heckled; Fires Reported at Colleges," *New York Times*, May 9, 1970, 10; ibid., 448–449.

65. Cannato, *Ungovernable City*, 449–452.

66. Ibid., 452–453; Zaroulis and Sullivan, *Who Spoke Up?* 334–335; Homer Bigart, "Huge City Hall Rally Backs Nixon's Indochina Policies," *New York Times*, May 21, 1970, 1.

67. Victor Gotbaum, Anti–Vietnam War address (c. 1970), VHS 25—Can 2282, WNYC videotape collection, Municipal Archives of New York City; Bigart, "Huge City Hall Rally," 1.

68. Bigart, "Huge City Hall Rally," 1.

69. Zaroulis and Sullivan, *Who Spoke Up?* 387; Gitlin, *The Sixties*, 379.

70. Zaroulis and Sullivan, *Who Spoke Up?* 420; Paul L. Montgomery, "End-of-War Rally Brings Out 50,000," May 12, 1975, 1.

71. Jennifer Leaning and Langley Keyes, "Introduction," in *The Counterfeit Ark: Crisis Relocation for Nuclear War*, ed. Jennifer Leaning and Langley Keys (Cambridge, MA: Ballinger Publishing, 1984), xvii; Winkler, *Life Under a Cloud*, 133.

72. Leaning and Keyes, "Introduction," xviii; Winkler, *Life Under a Cloud*, 133–134.

73. Jonathan Schell, *The Fate of the Earth* (New York: Knopf, 1982), 47–54.

74. Paul L. Montgomery, "Throngs Fill Manhattan to Protest Nuclear Weapons," *New York Times*, June 13, 1982, 1; Anna Quindlen, "About New York: Earnestness as Whimsey in a Colorful Panorama," *New York Times*, June 13, 1982, 43.

75. Quindlen, "About New York," 43.

Chapter 10

1. Lawrence Wright, *The Looming Tower: Al-Qaeda and the Road to 9/11* (New York: Alfred A. Knopf, 2006), 9–10, 12, 14–15.

2. Ibid., 32, 36–37.

3. Randall D. Law, *Terrorism: A History* (Malden, MA: Polity Press, 2009), 65.

4. Douglas Robinson, "Townhouse Razed by Blast and Fire; Man's Body Found," *New York Times*, March 7, 1970, 1.

5. Linda Charlton, "'Village' Fire Victim Identified as Leader of '68 Columbia Strike," *New York Times*, March 9, 1970, 32; Robert D. McFadden, "More

Body Parts Discovered in Debris of Blast on 11th Street," *New York Times*, March 16, 1970, 49.

6. Nancy Zaroulis and Gerald Sullivan, *Who Spoke Up? American Protest Against the War in Vietnam 1963–1975* (Garden City, NY: Doubleday, 1984), 301; Abbie Hoffman, *The Autobiography of Abbie Hoffman* (New York: Four Walls Eight Windows, 2000), 248.

7. Todd Gitlin, *The Sixties: Years of Hope, Days of Rage*, rev. ed. (New York: Bantam Books, 1993), 402.

8. Mark Rudd, *Underground: My Life with SDS and the Weathermen* (New York: HarperCollins, 2009), 313; ibid., 377.

9. Vincent Burns and Kate Dempsey Peterson, *Terrorism: A Documentary and Reference Guide* (Westport, CT: Greenwood Press, 2005), 35, 36.

10. Rudd, *Underground*, 192–193; Cathy Wilkerson, *Flying Close to the Sun: My Life and Times as a Weatherman* (New York: Seven Stories Press, 2007), 324–325; Morris Kaplan, "Bomb Plot Is Laid to 21 Panthers," *New York Times*, April 3, 1969, 1; Emanuel Perlmutter, "Justice Murtagh's Home Target of 3 Fire Bombs," *New York Times*, February 22, 1970, 1.

11. Rudd, *Underground*, 194–195; Wilkerson, *Flying Close*, 340–341.

12. Homer Bigart, "Many Buildings Evacuated Here in Bomb Scares," *New York Times*, March 13, 1970, 1; "History of Bombings Before 'Village' Explosion," *New York Times*, March 13, 1970, 26; Michael Knight, "15 at the Electric Circus Injured in Bomb Explosion," *New York Times*, March 23, 1970, 1.

13. Peter Kihss, "Three Castro Foes Arrested in Firing of Bazooka at U.N.," *New York Times*, December 23, 1964, 1; Vincent J. Cannato, *The Ungovernable City: John Lindsay and His Struggle to Save New York* (New York: Basic Books, 2001), 478–481; Joseph P. Fried, "2 Policemen Slain by Shots in Back; 2 Men Are Sought," *New York Times*, May 22, 1971, 1.

14. Beverly Gage, *The Day Wall Street Exploded: A Story of America in Its First Age of Terror* (New York: Oxford University Press, 2009), 24.

15. "Bomb Kills One; Police Escape," *New York Times*, March 29, 1908, 1; "No 'Red' Plot, Say the Police," *New York Times*, March 30, 1908, 1; "Bomb Thrower Tells All," *New York Times*, April 7, 1908, 1; Ibid., 96, 99, 101, 104–106.

16. Julian F. Jaffe, *Crusade Against Radicalism: New York During the Red Scare, 1914–1924* (Port Washington, NY: Kennikat Press, 1972), 87–88, 93.

17. Gage, *The Day Wall Street*, 31–37, 171, 329–330.

18. Ibid., 325–326; Paul Avrich, *Sacco and Vanzetti: The Anarchist Background* (Princeton, NJ: Princeton University Press, 1991), 204–207, 245 n32. In a sense, the Wall Street bombing was anticipated by the similarly indiscriminate Preparedness Day bombing in San Francisco in July 1916, in which a suitcase bomb, allegedly planted by leftists, killed ten and wounded forty.

19. Rudd, *Underground*, 215.

20. Gitlin, *The Sixties*, 403; Hoffman, *Autobiography*, 249.

21. Gage, *The Day Wall Street*, 28, 95; Robert M. Fogelson, *America's Armories: Architecture, Society, and Public Order* (Cambridge: Harvard University Press, 1989), 163.

22. Gage, *The Day Wall Street*, 3; Richard Esposito and Ted Gerstein, *Bomb Squad: A Year Inside the Nation's Most Exclusive Police Unit* (New York: Hyperion, 2007), 68–69.

23. "Public Found to Take Hard View on Bombings, Hijackings, Riots," *New York Times*, April 23, 1970, 26.

24. Gage, *The Day Wall Street*, 313; Mel Gussow, "Tranquility Is Shaken On 11th Street," *New York Times*, March 10, 1970, 45.

25. Esposito and Gerstein, *Bomb Squad*, 78, 79, 255; Joseph T. McCann, *Terrorism on American Soil: A Concise History of Plots and Perpetrators from the Famous to the Forgotten* (Boulder, CO: Sentient Publications, 2006), 119, 120–121.

26. Esposito and Gerstein, *Bomb Squad*, 79.

27. Philip Foner, editor, *The Black Panthers Speak* (Cambridge, MA: Da Capo Press, 1995), 280.

28. Mike Wallace, "Nueva York: The Back Story," in *Nueva York: 1613–1945*, ed. Edward J. Sullivan (New York: The New-York Historical Society, 2010), 51–53, 64; Ira Rosenwaike, *Population History of New York City* (Syracuse, NY: Syracuse University Press, 1972), 197.

29. McCann, *Terrorism on American Soil*, 87–88.

30. Ibid., 88–89, 91, 93–95.

31. Esposito and Gerstein, *Bomb Squad*, 25, 45, 79–81.

32. Ibid., 82–85.

33. David A. Andelman, "Groups Claiming F.A.L.N. Ties Raid Offices of Bush and Carter," *New York Times*, March 16, 1980, 1.

34. Esposito and Gerstein, *Bomb Squad*, 87; Robert D. McFadden, "4 Killed, 44 Injured in Fraunces Tavern Blast," *New York Times*, January 25, 1975, 1; Selwyn Raab, "F.A.L.N. Terrorists Tied to 10 Bombings Here and in Newark," *New York Times*, February 7, 1975, 1.

35. Wright, *Looming Tower*, 201–203; McCann, *Terrorism on American Soil*, 187–188; Esposito and Gerstein, *Bomb Squad*, 96–104.

36. Steven Emerson, *American Jihad: The Terrorists Living Among Us* (New York: Free Press, 2002), 52; Mark Juergensmeyer, *Terror in the Mind of God: The Global Rise of Religious Violence*, 3rd ed. (Berkeley: University of California Press, 2003), 62–63.

37. Andrew C. McCarthy, *Willful Blindness: A Memoir of the Jihad* (New York: Encounter Books, 2009), 192–193.

38. Deborah Sontag, "Manhattan Is Held in the Grip of Traffic Snarls and Anxiety," *New York Times*, February 27, 1993, 1.

39. Esposito and Gerstein, *Bomb Squad*, 101; Emerson, *American Jihad*, 45–47.

40. McCarthy, *Willful Blindness*, 188.

41. Ibid., 231.

42. Ibid., 78–79; Emerson, *American Jihad*, 130–131; Wright, *Looming Tower*, 204.

43. Emerson, *American Jihad*, 51, 130, 251; Wright, *Looming Tower*, 164; The 9/11 Commission, *The 9/11 Commission Report: Final Report of the National Commission on Terrorist Attacks Upon the United States*, authorized ed. (New York: W. W. Norton, 2004), 55–56, 58–59, 466–467n22.

44. McCarthy, *Willful Blindness*, 89–90, 119–121, 127, 182.

45. Emerson, *American Jihad*, 43–44; ibid., 127–134.

46. McCann, *Terrorism on American Soil*, 191, 240–248; Samuel M. Katz, *Jihad in Brooklyn: The NYPD Raid That Stopped America's First Suicide Bombers* (New York: New American Library, 2005), 128–136.

47. Email communications to author from Katherine Edgerton, National September 11 Memorial & Museum, July 29 and September 16, 2010.

48. Daniel Benjamin and Steven Simon, *The Age of Sacred Terror: Radical Islam's War Against America* (New York: Random House, 2002), 66–68, 91–93; *9/11 Commission Report*, 161; James C. McKinley Jr., "Man Accused in Terror Plot Bombed Gay Bar, U.S. Says," *New York Times*, January 14, 1995, 26.

49. Benjamin and Simon, *Age of Sacred Terror*, 6, 92.

Epilogue

1. New York City Office of Emergency Management, *Ready New York: Preparing for Emergencies in New York City*, n.d., 4, 7.

2. Mark Jacobson, "Muhammad Comes to Manhattan," *New York*, August 30–September 6, 2010, 27–28; Fareed Zakaria, "The Real Ground Zero," *Newsweek*, August 16, 2010, 18.

3. Rob Snyder, "Losing the Best of 9/11," *Greater New York: A Blog About New York's Politics, Culture and History*, September 12, 2010.

4. Steve Benen, "Meet Aliou Niasse," *Washington Monthly*, May 5, 2010.

5. Warren Lehrer and Judith Sloan, *Crossing the BLVD: Strangers, Neighbors, Aliens in a New America* (New York: W. W. Norton, 2003), 321–329; Jack Canfield, Mark Victor Hansen, Candice C. Carter, Susanna Palomares, Linda K. Williams, and Bradley L. Winch, *Chicken Soup for the Soul: Stories for a Better World* (Deerfield Beach, FL: Health Communications, 2005), 158–159.

For Further Reading

General

Albion, Robert G. *The Rise of New York Port: 1815–1860*. New York: Charles Scribner's Sons, 1939.

Bayor, Ronald H., and Timothy J. Meagher, editors. *The New York Irish*. Baltimore: Johns Hopkins University Press, 1996.

Burns, Ric, and James Sanders, with Lisa Ades. *New York: An Illustrated History*. New York: Alfred A. Knopf, 1999.

Burrows, Edwin G., and Mike Wallace. *Gotham: A History of New York City to 1898*. Oxford: Oxford University Press, 1999.

Ellis, Edward Robb. *The Epic of New York City: A Narrative History*. New York: Coward-McCann, 1966.

Gilmore, Russell S. *Guarding America's Front Door: Harbor Forts in the Defense of New York City*. New York: The Fort Hamilton Historical Society, 1983.

Homberger, Eric. *The Historical Atlas of New York City: A Visual Celebration of 400 Years of New York City's History, Revised and Updated*. New York: Henry Holt, 2005.

Lehrer, Warren, and Judith Sloan. *Crossing the BLVD: Strangers, Neighbors, Aliens in a New America*. New York: W. W. Norton, 2003.

Lotchin, Roger W., editor. *The Martial Metropolis: U.S. Cities in War and Peace*. New York: Praeger Publishers, 1984.

Page, Max. *The City's End: Two Centuries of Fantasies, Fears, and Premonitions of New York's Destruction*. New Haven, CT: Yale University Press, 2008.

Polaski, Leo, and Glen Williford. *New York City's Harbor Defenses*. Charleston, SC: Arcadia Publishing, 2003.

Stokes, Isaac Newton Phelps. *The Iconography of Manhattan Island*. 6 volumes. New York: R. H. Dodd, 1915–1928.

Dutch Colonial Era

Haefeli, Evan. "Kieft's War and the Cultures of Violence in Colonial America." In *Lethal Imagination: Violence and Brutality in American History*. Edited by Michael A. Bellesiles. New York: New York University Press, 1999.

Jacobs, Jaap. *New Netherland: A Dutch Colony in Seventeenth-Century America*. Leiden: Brill, 2005.

Jameson, J. Franklin, editor. *Narratives of New Netherland 1609–1664*. New York: Charles Scribner's Sons, 1909.

Kammen, Michael. *Colonial New York: A History*. New York: Scribner, 1975.

Merwick, Donna. *The Shame and the Sorrow: Dutch-Amerindian Encounters in New Netherland*. Philadelphia: University of Pennsylvania Press, 2006.

Otto, Paul. *The Dutch-Munsee Encounter in America*. New York: Berghahn Books, 2006.

Shomette, Donald G., and Robert D. Haslach. *Raid on America: The Dutch Naval Campaign of 1672–1674*. Columbia: University of South Carolina Press, 1988.

Van der Zee, Henri and Barbara. *A Sweet and Alien Land: The Story of Dutch New York*. New York: Viking Press, 1978.

English Colonial Era

Davis, Thomas J. *A Rumor of Revolt: The "Great Negro Plot" in Colonial New York*. New York: Free Press, 1985.

Kammen, Michael. *Colonial New York: A History*. New York: Scribner, 1975.

Lepore, Jill. *New York Burning: Liberty, Slavery, and Conspiracy in Eighteenth-Century Manhattan*. New York: Alfred A. Knopf, 2005.

Linebaugh, Peter, and Marcus Rediker. *The Many-Headed Hydra: Sailors, Slaves, Commoners, and the Hidden History of the Revolutionary Atlantic*. Boston: Beacon Press, 2000.

Matson, Cathy. *Merchants and Empire: Trading in Colonial New York*. Baltimore: Johns Hopkins University Press, 1998.

Nash, Gary B. *The Urban Crucible: Social Change, Political Consciousness, and the Origins of the American Revolution*. Cambridge, MA: Harvard University Press, 1979.

Ritchie, Robert C. *Captain Kidd and the War Against the Pirates*. Cambridge, MA: Harvard University Press, 1986.

Swanson, Carl E. *Predators and Prizes: American Privateering and Imperial Warfare, 1739–1748*. Columbia: University of South Carolina Press, 1991.

Truxes, Thomas M. *Defying Empire: Trading with the Enemy in Colonial New York*. New Haven, CT: Yale University Press, 2008,

Zabin, Serena R., editor. *The New York Conspiracy Trials of 1741: Daniel Horsmanden's Journal of the Proceedings with Related Documents*. Boston: Bedford/St. Martin's, 2004.

American Revolution

Burrows, Edwin G. *Forgotten Patriots: The Untold Story of American Prisoners During the Revolutionary War*. New York: Basic Books, 2008.

Gallagher, John J. *The Battle of Brooklyn, 1776*. Edison, NJ: Castle Books, 1995.

Gilje, Paul A. *The Road to Mobocracy: Popular Disorder in New York City, 1763–1834*. Chapel Hill: University of North Carolina Press, 1987.

Hodges, Graham Russell. *Root & Branch: African Americans in New York & East Jersey, 1613–1863*. Chapel Hill: University of North Carolina Press, 1999.

Ketchum, Richard M. *Divided Loyalties: How the American Revolution Came to New York*. New York: Henry Holt, 2002.

Martin, Joseph Plumb. *A Narrative of a Revolutionary Soldier*. New York: Signet Classic, 2001.

McCullough, David. *1776*. New York: Simon & Schuster, 2005.

Rose, Alexander. *Washington's Spies: The Story of America's First Spy Ring*. New York: Bantam Books, 2006.

Schecter, Barnet. *The Battle for New York: The City at the Heart of the American Revolution*. New York: Penguin Books, 2002.

Tiedemann, Joseph S., and Eugene R. Fingerhut, editors. *The Other New York: The American Revolution Beyond New York City, 1763–1787*. Albany: State University of New York Press, 2005.

Van Buskirk, Judith L. *Generous Enemies: Patriots and Loyalists in Revolutionary New York*. Philadelphia: University of Pennsylvania Press, 2002.

French Revolutionary Era and War of 1812

Crawford, Michael J., editor. *The Naval War of 1812: A Documentary History*. Volume 3. Washington, DC: Naval Historical Center, 2002.

Dudley, William S., editor. *The Naval War of 1812: A Documentary History*. Volumes 1 and 2. Washington, DC: Naval Historical Center, 1985, 1992.

Gilje, Paul A. *Liberty on the Waterfront: American Maritime Culture in the Age of Revolution*. Philadelphia: University of Pennsylvania Press, 2004.

Guernsey, R. S. *New York City and Vicinity During the War of 1812–15* (2 volumes). New York: Charles L. Woodward, 1889, 1895.

Sale, Kirkpatrick. *The Fire of His Genius: Robert Fulton and the American Dream*. New York: Touchstone, 2002.

Young, Alfred F. *The Democratic Republicans of New York: The Origins, 1763–1797*. Chapel Hill: University of North Carolina Press, 1967.

Civil War

Bernstein, Iver. *The New York City Draft Riots: Their Significance for American Society and Politics in the Age of the Civil War*. New York: Oxford University Press, 1990.

Brandt, Nat. *The Man Who Tried to Burn New York*. Syracuse, NY: Syracuse University Press, 1986.

Cook, Adrian. *The Armies of the Streets: The New York City Draft Riots of 1863*. Lexington: University Press of Kentucky, 1974.

Daly, Maria Lydig. *Diary of a Union Lady, 1861–1865*. Lincoln: University of Nebraska Press, 2000.

Holzer, Harold, editor. *State of the Union: New York and the Civil War*. New York: Fordham University Press, 2002.

McKay, Ernest A. *The Civil War and New York City*. Syracuse, NY: Syracuse University Press, 1990.

Nevins, Allan, and Milton Halsey Thomas, editors. *The Diary of George Templeton Strong*. 4 volumes. New York: Macmillan, 1952.

Quigley, David. *Second Founding: New York City, Reconstruction, and the Making of American Democracy*. New York: Hill and Wang, 2004.

Quigley, David, and David N. Gelman, editors. *Jim Crow New York: A Documentary History of Race and Citizenship, 1777–1877*. New York: New York University Press, 2003.

Schecter, Barnet. *The Devil's Own Work: The Civil War Draft Riots and the Fight to Reconstruct America*. New York: Walker, 2006.

Seraile, William. *New York's Black Regiments During the Civil War*. New York: Routledge, 2001.

Southwick, Thomas P. *A Duryee Zouave*. Brookneal, VA: Patrick A. Schroeder Publications, 1995.

Spann, Edward K. *Gotham at War: New York City, 1860–1865*. Wilmington, DE: Scholarly Resources, 2002.

World War I

Bendersky, Joseph W. *The "Jewish Threat": Anti-Semitic Politics of the U.S. Army*. New York: Basic Books, 2000.

Chernow, Ron. *The House of Morgan: An American Banking Dynasty and the Rise of Modern Finance*. New York: Grove Press, 1990.

Clark, William Bell. *When the U-Boats Came to America*. Boston: Little, Brown, 1929.

Herwig, Holger H. *Politics of Frustration: The United States in German Naval Planning, 1889–1941*. Boston: Little, Brown, 1976.

Jaffe, Julian F. *Crusade Against Radicalism: New York During the Red Scare, 1914–1924*. Port Washington, NY: Kennikat Press, 1972.

Kennedy, David M. *Over Here: The First World War and American Society*. New York: Oxford University Press, 1980.

Luebke, Frederick C. *Bonds of Loyalty: German Americans and World War I*. DeKalb: Northern Illinois University Press, 1974.

Millman, Chad. *The Detonators: The Secret Plot to Destroy America and an Epic Hunt for Justice*. New York: Little, Brown, 2006.

Schaffer, Ronald. *America in the Great War: The Rise of the War Welfare State*. New York: Oxford University Press, 1991.

Sterba, Christopher M. *Good Americans: Italian and Jewish Immigrants During the First World War*. New York: Oxford University Press, 2003.

Stone, Geoffrey R. *Perilous Times: Free Speech in Wartime From the Sedition Act of 1798 to the War on Terrorism*. New York: W. W. Norton, 2004.

Witcover, Jules. *Sabotage at Black Tom: Imperial Germany's Secret War in America, 1914–1917*. Chapel Hill: Algonquin Books of Chapel Hill, 1989.

World War II

Anderson, Jervis. *This Was Harlem: A Cultural Portrait, 1900–1950*. New York: Farrar Straus Giroux, 1982.

Bayor, Ronald H. *Neighbors in Conflict: The Irish, Germans, Jews, and Italians of New York City, 1929–1941*. Baltimore: Johns Hopkins University Press, 1978.

Brandt, Nat. *Harlem at War: The Black Experience in WWII*. Syracuse, NY: Syracuse University Press, 1996.

Capeci, Dominic J., Jr. *The Harlem Riot of 1943*. Philadelphia: Temple University Press, 1977.

Diamond, Sander A. *The Nazi Movement in the United States, 1924–1941*. Ithaca, NY: Cornell University Press, 1974.

Diehl, Lorraine B. *Over Here! New York City During World War II*. New York: HarperCollins, 2010.

Diggins, John P. *Mussolini and Fascism: The View from America*. Princeton, NJ: Princeton University Press, 1972.

Dobbs, Michael. *Saboteurs: The Nazi Raid on America*. New York: Alfred A. Knopf, 2004.

Duffy, James P. *Target: America: Hitler's Plan to Attack the United States*. Westport, CT: Praeger Publishers 2004.

Farago, Ladislas. *The Game of the Foxes*. New York: David McKay, 1971.

Gammon, Michael. *Operation Drumbeat: The Dramatic True Story of Germany's First U-Boat Attacks Along the American Coast in World War II*. New York: Harper & Row, 1990.

Goldstein, Richard. *Helluva Town: The Story of New York City During World War II*. New York: Free Press, 2010.

Griehl, Manfred. *Luftwaffe Over America: The Secret Plans to Bomb the United States in World War II*. London: Greenhill Books, 2004.

Hartzell, Karl Drew. *The Empire State at War: World War II*. Albany: The State of New York, 1949.

Kessner, Thomas. *Fiorello H. La Guardia and the Making of Modern New York.* New York: McGraw-Hill, 1989.

Ketchum, Richard M. *The Borrowed Years 1938–1941: America on the Way to War.* New York: Random House, 1989.

Kwong, Peter. *Chinatown, N.Y.: Labor and Politics, 1930–1950.* Revised edition. New York: New Press, 1979.

Lingeman, Richard. *Don't You Know There's A War On? The American Home Front 1941–1945.* New York: G. P. Putnam's Sons, 1970.

Meany, Joseph F., Jr. "Port in a Storm: The Port of New York in World War II." In *To Die Gallantly: The Battle of the Atlantic.* Edited by Timothy J. Runyan and Jan M. Copes. Boulder: Westview Press, 1994.

Morris, Jan. *Manhattan '45.* New York: Oxford University Press, 1987.

Perrett, Geoffrey. *Days of Sadness, Years of Triumph: The American People, 1939–1945.* New York: Coward, McCann & Geoghegan, 1973.

Terkel, Studs. *"The Good War": An Oral History of World War Two.* New York: Ballantine Books, 1985.

Wallace, Mike. "New York and the World: The Global Context." In *Facing Fascism: New York and the Spanish Civil War.* Edited by Peter N. Carroll and James D. Fernandez. New York: Museum of the City of New York / New York University Press, 2007.

Wilder, Craig Steven. *A Covenant with Color: Race and Social Power in Brooklyn.* New York: Columbia University Press, 2000.

Cold War and Vietnam

Boyer, Paul. *By the Bomb's Early Light: American Thought and Culture at the Dawn of the Atomic Age.* 1985. Reprint, Chapel Hill: University of North Carolina Press, 1994.

Cannato, Vincent J. *The Ungovernable City: John Lindsay and His Struggle to Save New York.* New York: Basic Books, 2001.

Fast, Howard. *Being Red: A Memoir.* Boston: Houghton Mifflin, 1990.

Garrison, Dee. "'Our Skirts Gave Them Courage': The Civil Defense Protest Movement in New York City, 1955–1961." In *Not June Cleaver: Women and Gender in Postwar America, 1945–1960.* Edited by Joanne Meyerowitz. Philadelphia: Temple University Press, 1994.

Gitlin, Todd. *The Sixties: Years of Hope, Days of Rage.* Revised edition. New York: Bantam Books, 1993.

Grossman, Andrew D. *Neither Dead Nor Red: Civilian Defense and American Political Development During the Early Cold War.* New York: Routledge, 2001.

Haynes, John Earl, and Harvey Klehr. *Venona: Decoding Soviet Espionage in America.* New Haven, CT: Yale University Press, 1999.

Hoffman, Abbie. *The Autobiography of Abbie Hoffman.* New York: Four Walls Eight Windows, 2000.

Jackson, Kenneth T. "The City Loses the Sword: The Decline of Major Military Activity in the New York Metropolitan Region." In *The Martial Metropolis: U.S. Cities in War and Peace*. Edited by Roger W. Lotchin. New York: Praeger Publishers, 1984.

Kelly, Cynthia C., and Robert S. Norris. *A Guide to Manhattan Project Sites in Manhattan*. Washington, DC: The Atomic Heritage Foundation, 2008.

May, Elaine Tyler. *Homeward Bound: American Families in the Cold War Era*. Fully revised and updated edition. New York: Basic Books, 2008.

McEnaney, Laura. *Civil Defense Begins at Home: Militarization Meets Everyday Life in the Fifties*. Princeton, NJ: Princeton University Press, 2000.

Melendez, Miguel "Mickey." *We Took the Streets: Fighting for Latino Rights with the Young Lords*. New York, St. Martin's Press, 2003.

Oakes, Guy. *The Imaginary War: Civil Defense and American Cold War Culture*. New York: Oxford University Press, 1994.

Roberts, Sam. *The Brother: The Untold Story of the Rosenberg Case*. New York: Random House, 2001.

Rudd, Mark. *Underground: My Life with SDS and the Weathermen*. New York: HarperCollins, 2009.

Schell, Jonathan. *The Fate of the Earth*. New York: Alfred A. Knopf, 1982.

Tanenhaus, Sam. *Whittaker Chambers: A Biography*. New York: Random House, 1997.

Winkler, Allan M. *Life Under a Cloud: American Anxiety About the Atom*. Urbana: University of Illinois Press, 1999.

Zaroulis, Nancy, and Gerald Sullivan. *Who Spoke Up? American Protest Against the War in Vietnam 1963–1975*. Garden City, NY: Doubleday, 1984.

Terrorism

Benjamin, Daniel, and Steven Simon. *The Age of Sacred Terror: Radical Islam's War Against America*. New York: Random House, 2002.

Emerson, Steven. *American Jihad: The Terrorists Living Among Us*. New York: Free Press, 2002.

Esposito, Richard, and Ted Gerstein. *Bomb Squad: A Year Inside the Nation's Most Exclusive Police Unit*. New York: Hyperion, 2007.

Fogelson, Robert M. *America's Armories: Architecture, Society, and Public Order*. Cambridge, MA: Harvard University Press, 1989.

Gage, Beverly. *The Day Wall Street Exploded: A Story of America in Its First Age of Terror*. New York: Oxford University Press, 2009.

McCarthy, Andrew C. *Willful Blindness: A Memoir of the Jihad*. New York: Encounter Books, 2009.

The 9/11 Commission. *The 9/11 Commission Report: Final Report of the National Commission on Terrorist Attacks Upon the United States*. Authorized edition. New York: W. W. Norton, 2004.

Rudd, Mark. *Underground: My Life with SDS and the Weathermen*. New York: HarperCollins, 2009.

Wilkerson, Cathy. *Flying Close to the Sun: My Life and Times as a Weatherman*. New York: Seven Stories Press, 2007.

Wright, Lawrence. *The Looming Tower: Al-Qaeda and the Road to 9/11*. New York: Alfred A. Knopf, 2006.

Index